W9-BJJ-628

PRENTICE-HALL SERIES IN SPEECH COMMUNICATION
Larry L. Barker and Robert J. Kibler,
Consulting Editors

Argument: An Alternative to Violence
ABNE M. EISENBERG AND JOSEPH ILARDO

Argumentation: Inquiry and Advocacy
GEORGE W. ZIEGELMUELLER AND CHARLES A. DAUSE

*Beyond Words: An Introduction to
Nonverbal Communication*
RANDALL HARRISON

Communication: Concepts and Processes
JOSEPH A. DEVITO

Communication Vibrations
LARRY L. BARKER

Designs for Persuasive Communication
OTTO LERBINGER

The Great American Communication Catalogue
IRVING J. REIN

*Groups Communication: Discussion Processes
and Applications*
ALVIN A. GOLDBERG AND CARL E. LARSON

Language: Concepts and Processes
JOSEPH A. DEVITO

Living Communication
ABNE M. EISENBERG

(Cont.)

(Cont.)

LIVING
COMMUNICATION

Abne M. Eisenberg

Herbert H. Lehman College
City University of New York

Prentice-Hall, Inc., Englewood Cliffs, New Jersey

Library of Congress Cataloging in Publication Data

EISENBERG, ABNE M.
  Living communication.

  (Prentice-Hall series in speech communication)
  Bibliography: p.
  Includes index.
  1. Communication—Psychological aspects. I. Title.
BF637.C45E36   153   74-23718
ISBN 0-13-538900-3

Cover Design by Anna Gross
Cartoon Illustrations by Dennis Ougourlian

10 9 8 7 6 5 4 3 2 1

Prentice-Hall International, Inc., *London*
Prentice-Hall of Australia, Pty. Ltd., *Sydney*
Prentice-Hall of Canada, Ltd., *Toronto*
Prentice-Hall of India Private Limited, *New Delhi*
Prentice-Hall of Japan, Inc., *Tokyo*

To Beverly and Benjamin Eisenberg, my parents.

Contents

Read This First

As you shall soon learn, the most distinguished book, speech, film, article, or play invites failure if it neglects to accurately analyze its audience.

Many textbooks have the reputation of being a bore. Long aware of this phenomenon, I became curious to discover why so many students felt this way. I decided to spend some class time on the subject, "Why textbooks turn me off." After much discussion, the following reasons emerged in considerable force: Textbooks usually (1) are too impersonal, (2) lack a sense of humor, (3) use language that is excessively flowery and pompous, (4) use charts and diagrams which are not satisfactorily explained, (5) employ illustrations that are unimaginative and often irrelevant, (6) are not entertaining,* (7) give the students the feeling that whatever they read in them should be taken as gospel, (8) seem out of touch with the lifestyle and life experiences of the students.

While I could easily argue for or against each of these criticisms, I prefer instead to behave as though they all had the support of honest and sincere convictions. I reason this way. Assume that their criticisms could be exposed as irresponsible and totally unwarranted—what would have been

---

* From childhood, most of us were given the impression that reading can or should be fun. Textbooks seem to contradict such a notion.

accomplished? No matter how I turned the issues, my thoughts led me back to one conclusion: If this textbook were to succeed even modestly, my students' opinions dared not go unheeded.

As you have already noticed, the title, *Living Communication*, can be taken in two ways: one, that it will bring the reader various ways and means of improving his communication in everyday life; and two, that the very manner in which such material will be presented possesses an exciting or living quality.

Ahead of you lie ten chapters, each designed to provide a specific insight into the communication process. Although my bias persuades me that every chapter is of paramount importance, you and your teacher may differ, depending upon your biases. Be that as it may, here is a brief description (a menu if you like) of each chapter's focus.

Chapter 1, MESSAGES, MODELS, AND TYPES OF COMMU-NICATION, explains how the messages people exchange can seriously affect their lives, and how the nature of these messages undergoes change. You will be introduced into the world of communication models and how they are made. Rather than overwhelming you with an extremely cluttered diagram, however, this chapter will take you step-by-step through the construction of a model. Beginning with what students call a "Mickey Mouse" model, it is slowly compounded into a complex one. The chapter dissolves with the presentation of various types of communication encountered in everyday life.

Chapter 2, DIMENSIONS OF THE SELF, after explaining why it should be included as a vital part of any study of communication, proceeds to explore the manner in which the SELF you see in your mirror and the one others see can affect your life as a communicator. Of particular interest will be the mention of your prenatal, post-natal, and postmortem SELF and the different ways they can be altered psychologically, surgically, cosmetically, and chemically. In short, the communicator is a multidimensional unit.

Chapter 3, INTRAPERSONAL COMMUNICATION, is a new-comer to the field of speech-communication. Actually, it poaches on the borderline between communication and psychology because so much of its content is body-oriented (anatomical and physiological). It describes some of the biological mechanisms underlying such phenomena as talking to oneself, writing to oneself, and a variety of other nonverbal behavior in which the *sender* and *receiver* are residents of the same body. Tersely put, this chapter permits the reader to look inside himself and witness the basis for some of the noises and gestures he makes.

Chapter 4, EXTRAPERSONAL COMMUNICATION, is perhaps the most alien to communication literature, yet familiar to us all. It deals with how we communicate with animals, plants, and inanimate objects. Obviously, to those who are animal lovers, it will have a very special meaning and message; to those who have an exceptional affection for their car, a favorite painting, or a piece of jewelry, it will convey still another kind of message. But, no matter what the reader's personal reaction is to the chapter, it should be recognized as having a distinct place in communication theory and practice.

Chapter 5, NONVERBAL MESSAGES, deals with one of the faster-growing areas of human communication. Otherwise known by its alias, "body language," it promises to fascinate a great many college students. Championed by celebrities such as Marcel Marceau, Charlie Chaplin, and Cantinflas (masters of pantomime), nonverbal communication, in many instances, sidesteps the ofttimes ambiguous nature of spoken language by creating a sense of credibility. The treatment of this subject here will be found to be extensive as compared with that in other similar texts.

Chapter 6, VERBAL MESSAGES, endeavors to show how words are woven into meaningful (and sometimes meaningless) units of thought. It attempts to sneak the reader in through the side door of language and expose some of its magical properties. If properly digested, it should cause anyone who has not looked into our language system before, to experience a somewhat different impression of it.

Chapter 7, MESSAGES IN CONFLICT, could represent an invaluable multipurpose tool capable of either opening new avenues of communication, mending those in need of repair, or closing off those which are threatening. The theme is one of argumentation and its rationale: people should be able to disagree without becoming disagreeable. In effect, the stance taken in this chapter addresses itself to the contention that knowing how to deal with messages in conflict is equivalent to wielding an iron fist in a velvet glove.

Chapter 8, COPING WITH AN AUDIENCE, will appeal to the student of public address, particularly one who has known the ravages of stage fright. Unless such fears are dealt with constructively, anxiety and apprehension can spoil a performance. After a discussion of stage fright and its management, the chapter tells the speaker how to analyze his audience so as to provide himself with a maximum of speech insurance.

Chapter 9, SURVIVAL IN A SMALL GROUP, will probably have the widest appeal for the college student. Although few will be called upon now or in later life to deliver a formal speech, a far greater number will become involved in varying forms of group discussions—in the family circle, on the job, in community affairs, and so on. A surprising number of people are extremely uncomfortable and intimidated by being in a group. They appear to harbor an exaggerated sense of risk in speaking out. Mindful of their need to be able to survive under these circumstances, this chapter pays special attention to a description of the characters indigenous to most groups and offers some suggestions as to how they might best be dealt with.

Chapter 10, CLASSROOM EXERCISES, welcomes the reader to participate in a battery of uniquely constructed exercises. Each has built into it a variety of the principles talked about throughout the text. If the student has "done his homework," it will become evident both in his reaction to these exercises and in his behavior performing them. They do not have to be done in any particular order and freely invite being changed according to the whim of any teacher or student.

Acknowledgments

While some authors work well in seclusion and are disturbed by feedback, others require feedback both intensive and frequent. I fall into the latter category. Among those who have supplied me with the greatest support in this sense have been my wife Pearl Gwen, whose indefatigable patience and editorial giftedness were indispensable; my son Eric and daughter Danya, who kept me from straying too far afield from the generation for whom I was writing; and my dear friend and colleague Professor Robert Myers, who offered willing and valuable counsel on each chapter as it trickled through my brain and out of my typewriter. My heartfelt gratitude goes also to the many teenagers who visited our house while I was working on the manuscript and were kind enough to answer my endless questions and test-perform many of the exercises found in the last chapter.

To my editors and friends, Ted Arnold and Art Rittenberg, I offer my appreciation for their wise and always available consultation on the manuscript—and an affectionate hug to the world's best secretary, Shirley Chlopak, for her ready courtesy and assistance whenever I needed help. My personal applause to Dennis Ougourlian for his outstandingly creative job of illustrating the text; to Stuart Zionch and his father Philip Zionch for supplying me with a bottomless pit of marvelous manuscript paper (which they insisted that I ate), and finally to my beautiful students who patiently indulged my preoccupation with the birth and delivery of this book. In this context, you are all its godparents. Thanks.

A.M.E.

CHAPTER 1

MESSAGES, MODELS, AND TYPES OF COMMUNICATION

INSIGHTS

After reading this chapter you should have a clearer understanding of:

- *the role messages play in our lives.*
- *the difference between mini- and maxi-messages.*
- *how the hurry-hurry, rush-rush society in which we live has affected our communication with one another.*
- *the dynamic rather than static nature of the messages we send and receive.*
- *how a communication model is constructed.*
- *why communication models tend to turn most students off.*
- *the many types of communication that exist and how each has the capacity to shape meaning a little differently.*

Unless you realize the importance of knowing that messages involve more than simply stringing a bunch of words together, that understanding how these messages travel from individual to individual can make a significant difference in their effectiveness, and that selecting the wrong type of communication to carry out your intentions can have serious consequences, you run a high risk of having communication breakdowns at home, in school, or at work. The purpose of this chapter is to reduce such a risk.

We have always had, and continue to have, a compulsive need "to know." As incurable message hunters, we crave answers to questions ranging from the mundane to the metaphysical. Some of us are preoccupied with the present—the here and now—and couldn't care less about what used to be. Others bypass both past and present and dwell only on the future—on things to come. To service these needs, society has produced a historian to care for our past, a newscaster for our present, and a prophet for our future. Each in his fashion supplies us with a variety of messages.

For centuries we have exhibited a peculiar tendency to accept these messages with comparatively little verification. And, when information was not available, we invented whatever we wanted to hear. Myths, legends, fairy tales, and folklore are the forms these messages took, all devised to satisfy our compulsive need "to know." Mankind could be divided into two classes of people: those who would believe almost anything and those who, no matter how incontrovertible the proof, wouldn't. Chances are, more of us than we would like to believe fall into the first class; that is, we want to believe almost anything because of a deep-seated need to trust each other.

To facilitate effective communication, the following is a proposed working definition of the word MESSAGE as it will be used in this text:

> MESSAGE: Anything, real or imagined,
> capable of eliciting one or more responses
> directly or indirectly from a human,
> subhuman, or nonhuman receiver in a
> time-free context.

MESSAGES

Fully aware that the length of a message is but one basis for judging its meaning, let us, for the purposes of the following discussion, classify them as either *mini-* or *maxi-messages*.

Mini-messages will be used to describe those thousands of short-lived interpersonal transactions we all have had with friends, neighbors, and relatives. They are characterized by a volley of three to six words and rarely last more than a few seconds. For example:

Frank: Hi Mary, what's new?
Mary: Not much Frank, and you?
Frank: Seen Jim lately?
Mary: No. Well, gotta run to class. See ya!

Listening around these days, one gets the impression that people are actually saying less to each other; fewer words are being spoken. Perhaps one reason is the spread of a curious social disease called *communicatus interruptus*. When someone pleads, "Do you mind if I finish what I am saying?" or "Would you please hear me out first?" they are being exposed to *communicatus interruptus*. For reasons that will not be examined here (reasons, for example, psychological, sociological, and physiological) certain people seem unable to resist the temptation of preventing others from finishing what they are either saying or doing. In *verbal communicatus interruptus* an individual is blocked from finishing what he is saying; in *nonverbal communicatus interruptus* he is kept from completing a particular action he has begun.

Maxi-messages, in contrast to mini-messages, seem to be undergoing an atrophy of disuse, a wasting away. Although many people seem to hunger for a deep and meaningful communication, life in today's society often stands in its way. Further evidence of this need is the existence of such services as DIAL-A-SHOULDER and DIAL-A-FRIEND. If you want to talk and no one will listen, simply pick up your telephone and dial one of these services. For a fee, you can engage in paid maxi-message communication.

We live in an age of brevity. The more quickly something can be done, the better. This penchant for "hurry, hurry" behavior traces back to public school when certain teachers immediately passed to another child if the one called upon couldn't spit out an answer quickly enough. Even I.Q. tests require that a child "beat the clock," so to speak.

The general public is little more than a target for the mass media. Although an illusion of caring for what the public thinks and feels is often created in the form of a "number to call" or "an address to write to," genuine concern does not seem to run very high. This impression of the mass media should by no means be taken as gospel but rather as an observed symptom of its behavior.

Today, the "hurry, hurry" tradition is being carried on by the television industry. Commercials, rarely running more than a minute, are enormously expensive. In greatest demand are the services of mini-message specialists —men and women having a talent for condensing, consolidating, and concentrating information into the least amount of time and space. Exceptions not withstanding, our lives are frightfully routinized, abbreviated, and reduced to the bare essentials when it comes to interpersonal communication. Even hard-covered books are rapidly being displaced by the little, highly specialized, less expensive, and quickly read paperback. Newscasters on radio and television can, in minutes, capsulize all that has happened in the previous 24 hours throughout the United States (or the world for that matter). Mini-courses are providing young and old alike with the gist of practically any subject. The seven wonders of the world can be packed into a tiny vitamin pill; you name it and someone has probably designed a mini-version of it. We seem to have become a nation of bits and pieces, capable only of digesting information taken in small frequent feedings.

Not unlike little bullets, messages reach us daily. From sunup to sundown the average school-age child comes under the heavy influence of radio, television, records, and audio-visual equipment. In rapid fire, messages are disseminated by the mass media without any sign of relief. Where does one go to get immunized against its effects? Can shots be made available by which Mr. and Mrs. America and their two and one-half statistical children can protect themselves? The prognosis, at best, seems guarded.

Another aspect of the MESSAGE is its static or dynamic nature. A static message remains the same, while a dynamic message undergoes change. Words, like people, have a lifespan and in that sense are dynamic. On the other hand, the unchanging Great Sphinx of Egypt is a static message. Therefore, if we are to use communication meaningfully, both its static and dynamic characteristics must be taken into consideration.

To further our understanding of messages, it now becomes necessary to place them in a more specific context—a communication model. The function of the communication model in the study of communication is to show the student what happens when people interact. Like a blueprint, it allows us to see exactly what is going on at any given time, where it is going, and where it has been. Even more valuable, a model makes possible the detection of where a communication breakdown might have taken place. In short, a communication model enables us to know at a glance what could be, should be, or is going on either verbally, nonverbally, or vocally, plus the context or situation in which it is occurring.

MODELS

On first hearing, the word *model* conjures up several different images—fashion models, airplane models, model citizens, model homes, and so on. Synonyms for it include archetype, copy, pattern, sample, specimen, example, mold, or design. Simply, it refers to any situation in which one thing represents another for purposes of examination, description, or clarification. While each contains those principal elements necessary for its identification, each differentiates itself by including special terminology. It should also be mentioned that models, as learning tools, fail to enjoy the popularity serious writers in the field insist they rightly deserve. This writer includes himself among them.

At the risk of generalizing, model makers are made up of those who "overexplain" and those who "underexplain." Both appear to harbor a fear of either confusing or patronizing the reader. Shortly, you will see examples of each type and you may decide for yourself into which group they fall.

Designed to supplement one's understanding of communication theory and processes, many models miss their mark. One of the most compelling reasons for this seems to stem from some of the assumptions made by their designers. These include the belief that students (1) can handle the terminology, (2) have at least a casual interest in the subject, (3) are able to see the relationships illustrated by the model, and (4) are able to digest their meaning. Tabling a value judgment on these assumptions, one thing is evident: students, as a whole, find most models threatening and extremely unappetizing. Why? What is there about models that turns them off? Accusing students of being lazy and inept is too convenient a "cop out." Is it at all possible that because so many students have only a limited background in the field of communication, they, being confronted by a series of unfamiliar lines and symbols, are overwhelmed? As a result, it is only reasonable to expect that many of them have been known to resort to rote memorization for the sole purpose of passing examinations. Is it possible to make models more inviting, or must they continue as the stepchildren of communication theory?

While in search of a cure for this model phobia, it might be a good idea to relieve the students' pain and suffering. Let us begin with the cornerstones common to all communication models and gradually add to them. Keep in mind, however, that the perfect model is rarely ever achieved. At no time can all of the elements involved in a communicative act be captured—only a reasonable approximation.

Models are tools for the student of communication and must be selected in accordance with the task in question. Our task here, then, is to dispel some of the negative feelings many students have toward communication models. And to be of further assistance, each stage is supplied with a hypothetical situation involving Mary and John which will reflect whatever is going on in the model. One way of beginning is to use what some students call a "Mickey Mouse" model. This expression refers to anything considered to be ridiculously simple in nature and requiring an I.Q. of 73 to understand. It consists of three parts, as shown in Fig. 1-1.

FIGURE 1-1 A Communication Model (Stage I).

Arranged in this way, these components tell us little more than the words themselves. We haven't the foggiest notion of how they relate (if at all) to one another. To compensate for this deficiency, let us add a few arrows (Fig. 1-2).

FIGURE 1-2 A Communication Model (Stage II).

Now we are able to perceive a sense of movement from left to right [that is, a speaker (SENDER) is communicating something (MESSAGE) to someone (RECEIVER)]. Next, if we want to indicate that the sender has gotten a response (FEEDBACK) from the receiver, how could that be done? Watch (Fig. 1–3)!

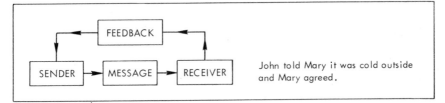

FIGURE 1–3 A Communication Model (Stage III).

Thus far, our model seems to be on safe ground and not likely to frighten off even the most timid student. Just how long this will last is difficult to say.

Messages do not mysteriously pass from a sender to a receiver. They require pathways (CHANNELS). Consequently, our next alteration will cause our model to look like Fig. 1–4.

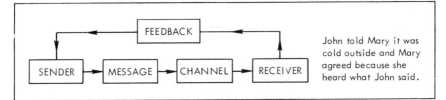

FIGURE 1–4 A Communication Model (Stage IV).

We must pause here and do some explaining. When you see the word sender in a model, you are not always sure what kind of a sender it is. For all you know it might be an animal, plant, or computer. Or, perhaps you might be shocked to learn that the sender you automatically assumed was a male, turned out to be a female. Any one of these qualifications could make a serious difference in the outcome of a communication. Such items as age, health, race, religion, occupation, attitudes, values, and beliefs should also be considered as variables. Figure 1–5 incorporates these characteristics.

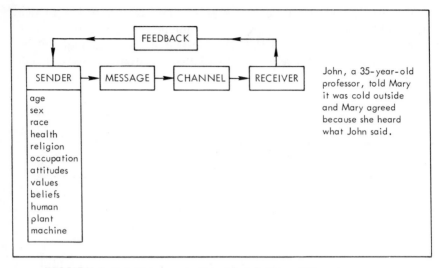

FIGURE 1–5 A Communication Model (Stage V).

Next, it must be established that messages don't mystically fly from the mouth of a sender to the ear of a receiver. The message must be put together in the sender's brain (ENCODING) and interpreted by the receiver's brain (DECODING). Incidentally, all of the characteristics indigenous to a sender also pertain to the receiver. Now look at our slightly pregnant model (Fig. 1–6).

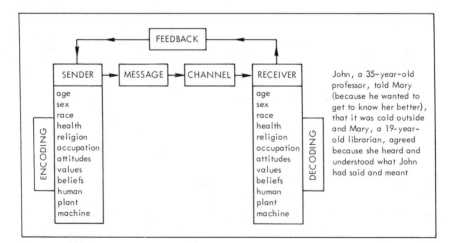

FIGURE 1–6 A Communication Model (Stage VI).

Assume, if you will, that the MESSAGE in the preceding model was verbal. Could it take any other form? Yes, it could be nonverbal or vocal. These distinctions must be plugged into our model. While we're at it, why not expand the word CHANNEL to include seeing, hearing, tasting, touching, and smelling. Our model seems to be getting a little cluttered, doesn't it?

Communication never occurs in a vacuum. When John says hello to Mary, it happens at a given time, in a given place, and under a specific set of circumstances. This setting is an example of a CONTEXT in which a communication takes place. Another ingredient that must also be added to our model is NOISE or INTERFERENCE (for example, static on your radio, snow or lines on your television, airplanes overhead, or a baby crying in the next room). Now look at our model (Fig. 1–7).

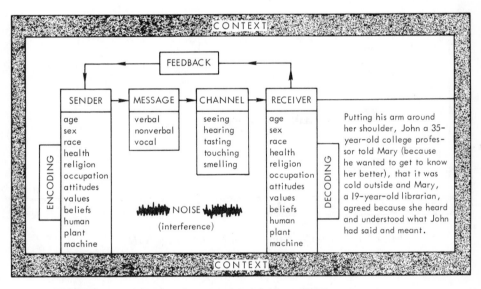

FIGURE 1–7 A Communication Model (Stage VII).

With a minimum of effort you should be able to see how easily any well-intentioned model-maker could get carried away. Aware of the danger of continuing with our model, we can either stop here or press our luck until all hope of its being understood is lost. Let's chance it.

Although the component of FEEDBACK has already been introduced into our model, mention was not made of the FEEDBACK we get from ourselves (INTERNAL FEEDBACK) as compared with that which we receive from others (EXTERNAL FEEDBACK). For example, while making a speech, you get internal feedback from the dryness in your mouth, tightening of your jaw muscles, or "butterflies" in your stomach. At the same time, you are receiving external feedback from your audience in the form of applause, boos, dead silence, or dirty looks. Now, with the reader's permission, to dramatically show the effects of overloading a communication model, Fig. 1–8 presents "the kitchen sink."

You have just seen how a communication model evolves; hopefully you are now less fearful of it. Also, you should have a better understanding, on

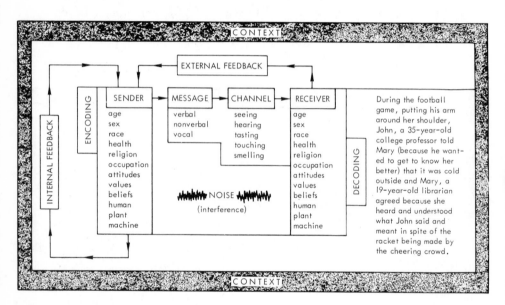

FIGURE 1–8 *A Communication Model (Stage VIII).*

a step-by-step basis, of the role each component of a communication model plays in the interpersonal process. Now, to further round out your exposure to communication models, several other kinds will be presented and explained.

A number of communication models employ symbols as well as words. These symbols (1a, 2b, 3) drive off many readers because insufficient time is taken to decipher them. Their meaning often remains obscure. Notice your reaction to Fig. 1–9, a model of nonverbal communication containing symbols.

Only when the application of a model is explained in everyday language

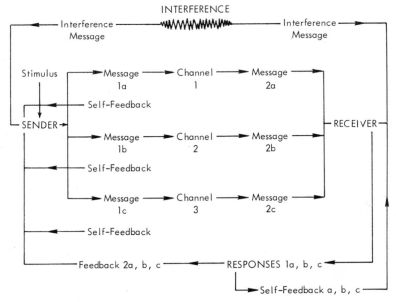

FIGURE 1-9 A Communication Model.[1]

does it take on some familiar meaning. To illustrate this, let us talk about Fig. 1–9 in terms of John and Mary mentioned earlier. Look at the model and locate the SENDER who, for our purposes, will represent John. Notice that he is sending not one, but three MESSAGES (1a–1b–1c). This could be confusing—unless you realize that in practically all of our communications with others, we send more than one message at a time. And, since this is a nonverbal communication model, John may be sending three nonverbal messages to Mary. MESSAGE 1a could represent John putting his arm around Mary (touching); MESSAGE 1b a silly grin on his face (facial expression), and MESSAGE 1c an exciting cologne he is wearing (smell). Mind you, all three of these messages are being sent by John to Mary at the same time (his touch, facial expression, and smell).

Next you will notice that this model presents three CHANNELS (1–2–3). In order for Mary to become aware of John's touching her, Mary's sense of touch must come into play; therefore, CHANNEL 1 will travel over the sensory apparatus responsible for tactile sensation. CHANNEL 2

[1] Figure 1–9 is reprinted from *Nonverbal Communication* by Abne M. Eisenberg and Ralph Smith. Copyright © 1971 by Bobbs-Merrill Co. Reprinted by permission of Bobbs-Merrill Co.

will involve Mary's visual perception of John's silly grin; and CHANNEL 3, her sense of smell. Now concentrate if you will on MESSAGES (2a–2b–2c). If you will accept the fact that the messages sent by John in the form of his touch, facial expression, and smell may not be interpreted in exactly the same way by Mary, we are in good shape. This, then, is the significance of the model's listing another set of messages. It simply indicates that the messages a sender sends are not necessarily interpreted as the same messages a receiver gets.

Finally, you will notice the term FEEDBACK—once as just plain FEEDBACK (2a–2b–2c), and again as SELF-FEEDBACK (a–b–c). As you probably already know, the term feedback refers to whatever is returned to a sender in response to the message he has sent out. In this case, we are dealing with the FEEDBACK 2a, 2b, 2c being received from Mary in response to John's touch, facial expression, and smell, and the SELF-FEEDBACK a, b, and c being returned to Mary on the basis of her own responses to John. Put another way, Mary is not only aware of her reactions to John's messages, but also to the fact that she is responding to them. The item labeled INTERFERENCE, as the word implies, refers to the surrounding noise in which the aforementioned nonverbal communication takes place.

The next model worthwhile considering was created by Wiseman and Barker. It describes the intrapersonal process by which we communicate with ourselves (see Fig. 1–10).

The most unique characteristic of this model is that it portrays both the *speaker* and the *receiver* in the same body. By so doing, it illustrates what happens when someone communicates with himself. In constructing their model, Wiseman and Barker had to decide two things: (1) what components it should include, and (2) how these components should be organized. Notice the labels they use. Recognizable at once is the distinction made between the stimuli arising from outside of the subject (EXTERNAL STIMULI) and those arising from within the subject (INTERNAL STIMULI). Thoughts that race through your mind, while sitting quietly, are examples of INTERNAL STIMULI, whereas those reaching you from your surroundings are EXTERNAL STIMULI. The word RECEPTION applies to the ability of your sensory apparatus to pick up these stimuli (seeing, hearing, tasting, touching, and smelling). DISCRIMINATION refers to the process by which certain stimuli are allowed to stimulate thought. Beneath a conscious level, insignificant or weak stimuli are screened out without your ever being aware of them. REGROUPING signifies the method by which order is made out of the chaos that would result if incoming stimuli were admitted and processed in a helter-skelter manner. SYMBOL DECODING represents the way in

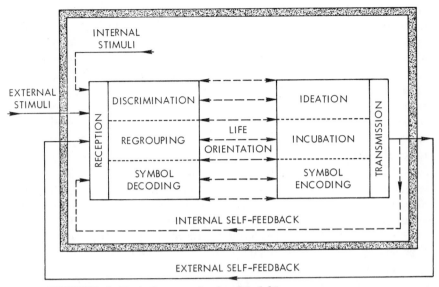

FIGURE 1–10 *A Communication Model.*[2]

which raw stimuli are transformed into thought symbols. All of these incoming data are then played against your LIFE ORIENTATION, constituting all that you have ever experienced, past and present. IDEA-TION in this model denotes the process by which your thoughts become organized. After your brain seizes upon an idea, immediate action may not follow. INCUBATION refers to this period of time during which you "mull things over." When you are ready to express yourself, you must ENCODE your thoughts into a symbolic form which others will recognize as meaningful and understandable. A final effort consists of TRANS-MISSION, wherein you physically communicate using either speech, or gesture, or both.

Suppose, now, that we translate the contents of this intrapersonal model in terms of John and Mary.

Looking at the model, notice that a distinction is made between IN-TERNAL and EXTERNAL stimuli. It simply separates what is going on outside of John and Mary from what is going on inside them. (In case you have forgotten the definition of the word *stimulus*, it refers to anything capable of eliciting a response.) Returning to John and Mary, we next encounter the word RECEPTION. It denotes the ability of their nervous systems to effectively pick up impressions from their inner and

[2] Figure 1–10 is reprinted from *Speech-Interpersonal Communication* by Gordon Wiseman and Larry Barker. Copyright © 1967 by Chandler Publishing Co. Reprinted by permission of Chandler Publishing Co.

outer worlds through the use of their senses (seeing, hearing, tasting, touching, and smelling). In our scene between John and Mary, each was fully aware of what was happening. John knew he was touching Mary when he put his arm around her shoulder, and Mary was conscious of the fact that he was doing it. This same principle applies to everything that went on between them. DISCRIMINATION is next. It concerns the ability of their nervous systems to accept, reject, or hold in abeyance stimuli emanating from the other. For example, if Mary found John appealing, her senses would honor those stimuli generated by him, and reject those from the fellow next to him. Then, via the process of RE-GROUPING, John's qualities, still in the form of raw stimuli, would be sorted into collections on a priority basis according to the needs they filled for her. At this point, John exists in Mary's consciousness only as a "feeling" based upon certain stimuli. To provide John with a recognizable identity, Mary's nervous system must translate these raw stimuli into thought symbols. This is called SYMBOL DECODING. Once this has been accomplished for both John and Mary, these symbols must be processed through their respective LIFE ORIENTATIONS. Here, all their attitudes, values, beliefs, biases, and prejudices will be confronted. If the symbols of each are able to survive this processing, IDEATION WILL FOLLOW. This is the stage where some of the ideas John has about Mary, and she about him, come to life. Each is now a meaningful reality for the other. The only question that remains is, will they act on their impressions? The INCUBATION period takes care of that. John may ask Mary for a date that very moment, or perhaps may wait a week. Put simply, it refers to that period of time between what John and Mary *think about each other* and what they actually *do about each other*. If John should decide to ask for that date immediately, he will have to ENCODE a suitable message—put it together in his head ("Mary, would you like to have dinner with me tonight?"). And finally, if he has the courage to say it to her out loud (rather than cowardly to himself), TRANSMISSION will have taken place.

In practice, you should be able to reduce any good communication model into understandable terms. If not, the problem may be due to: (1) unfamiliar terminology, (2) disinterest in the subject, (3) unclearly depicted relationships between its components, (4) unnecessary or excessive ingredients, or (5) unwarranted assumptions made by the model-maker.

In the next two models, see if you can figure out how they could apply to John and Mary. The first of these models, conceived by Stephen Toulmin, is used in the field of argumentation and borrows its orientation from our judicial system. It is shown in Fig. 1–11.

SAMPLE TOULMIN MODEL

SUPPORT (evidence)   *CLAIM* (conclusion)

Jill is one of Jack's   (therefore)
sisters.   ⎯⎯⎯⎯⎯→   Jill now has red hair

WARRANT   *REBUTTAL*

Any of Jack's sisters may   (unless)   1. Jill has dyed her hair.
be taken to have red hair.   ⎯⎯⎯⎯⎯→   2. Jill's hair has turned white.
                                           3. Jill has lost her hair.
                                           4. Jill is John's half sister.
                                           5. Jill is a mutant.

BACKING

On account of the fact that
ALL of his sisters have previously been observed to
have red hair.

HOW TO USE THE TOULMIN MODEL IN AN ACTUAL ARGUMENT

Step 1   The advocate should establish exactly what it is that his opponent is claiming. ("Capital punishment should be abolished." "Jill now has red hair.")

Step 2   After determining the claim that is being advanced, find out what evidence is being presented in support of such a claim. After all, a claim without evidence is worthless.

Step 3   At this stage, a warrant must be introduced. A warrant is informa- tion that justifies linking the claim with its supporting evidence. Referring back to our sample model, you will see that simply claiming that Jill now has red hair along with the fact that she is one of Jack's sisters is of no significance whatsoever. The warrant therefore introduces the basis for such a progression. It can be said this way, *since any of Jack's sisters may* be taken to have red hair ⎯⎯→ Jill is one of Jack's sisters ⎯⎯→ *therefore* ⎯⎯→ Jill now has red hair.

Step 4   But this may still be insufficient evidence for some. You now must provide the backing for the argument. Backing is additional evidence that reinforces the warrant. The model can now be read like this: since any of Jack's sisters may be taken to have red hair ⎯⎯→ *and* ⎯⎯→ Jill is one of Jack's sisters ⎯⎯→ on account of the fact that all of Jack's sisters have previously been observed to have red hair ⎯⎯→*therefore* ⎯⎯→Jill now has red hair.

Step 5   This, the rebuttal, is a critical element of the model. It attempts to either deny or cast doubt upon the conclusion or claim made by your opponent.

FIGURE 1–11 *Argumentation Model.*[3]

[3] Figure 1–11 is reprinted from Stephen Toulmin, *The Uses of Argument* (New York: Cambridge University Press, 1958).

The Toulmin model has several attractive features. Among them are its simple and direct approach, its omission of symbolic forms, and its effectiveness as an operational tool in the field of argumentation.

The second model dealing with levels of feedback in relation to the art of listening comes to us from Barker (Fig. 1–12). See how well you can grasp his meaning.

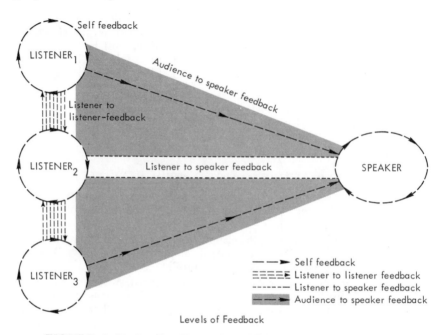

Levels of Feedback

FIGURE 1–12 *Another Type of Model.*[4]

Based upon what you now know about models and their construction, how about trying your hand at building one of your own? Space has been provided in Fig. 1–13. You will soon discover whether you fall into the class of model-makers who *overexplain* or those who *underexplain*. When you are finished, trade models with a classmate and evaluate each other's workmanship.

Now that we know how models are born, the various forms they may take, and the purpose they serve in the communicative process, the next logical step is to look at the types of communication likely to be conveyed by these models. It is important here for the reader to understand that

[4] Figure 1–12 is reprinted from Larry Barker, *Listening Behavior* (Englewood Cliffs, N.J.: Prentice-Hall, Inc., 1971), p. 108.

FIGURE 1–13 *Your Own Communication Model.*

the term communication (as it is used in this text) involves more than speech. Communication should be taken (a) to allow for both a sender and receiver to exist in the same body, (b) to exist beyond language as we know it, (c) to include interactions with subhuman and nonhuman forms, and (d) to allow for feedback from a receiver to employ a code different from that used by the sender. So that you may see the various types of communication that will be covered, check over Fig. 1–14.

TYPES OF COMMUNICATION

I. *Intrapersonal*	II. *Interpersonal*	III. *Extrapersonal*
Verbal	Verbal	Man—Animal
Nonverbal	Nonverbal	Man—Plant
Vocal	Vocal	Man—Object
Olfactory	Pseudoaffective	
Tactile	Phatic	
Pharmacogenic	Terminal	
Cathartic	Metaphysical	
	Mediational	
	Irrational	
	Instrumental	
	Olfactory	
	Tactile	
	Pharmacogenic	

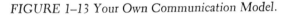

FIGURE 1–14 *Classification of the Types of Communication.*

TYPES OF COMMUNICATION

I. Intrapersonal Communication

That process by which people, either consciously or unconsciously, communicate with themselves on a verbal, nonverbal, or vocal level.

Verbal intrapersonal communication
The act of either thinking, writing, or talking to oneself. EXAMPLES: meditating, diary keeping, rehearsing a speech.

Nonverbal intrapersonal communication
Communicating with oneself through the use of body movements and gestures. EXAMPLES: making faces in a mirror, exercising, pacing back and forth.

Vocal intrapersonal communication
Communicating with oneself through the use of extralinguistic sounds. EXAMPLES: grunting, groaning, crying, laughing, moaning, humming, or sighing.

Olfactory intrapersonal communication
The act of smelling areas of oneself. EXAMPLES: articles of clothing, underarms (to detect whether your deodorant is effective).

Tactile intrapersonal communication
The act of touching or handling oneself. EXAMPLES: nail-biting, thumb-sucking, masturbation, hand-wringing, nose-picking, or ear-lobe pulling.

Pharmacogenic intrapersonal communication
The act of altering communication with oneself through the use of various drugs that either speed up, slow down, or significantly modify behavior. EXAMPLES: tranquilizers, antidepressants, hallucinogens.

Cathartic intrapersonal communication
The process by which inner hostility and tension are released through verbal, nonverbal, or vocal means. EXAMPLES: screaming, cursing, throwing a tantrum.

II. Interpersonal Communication

". . . the process of one individual stimulating meaning in the mind of another individual by means of some kind of message."[5]

Verbal interpersonal communication
Any interaction in which the medium of exchange employs words, either spoken or written.

Nonverbal interpersonal communication
The act of sharing meaning, intentional or accidental, through the use of body language (kinesics).

[5] James C. McCroskey, Carl E. Larson, and Mark Knapp, *An Introduction to Interpersonal Communication* (Englewood Cliffs, N.J.: Prentice-Hall, Inc., 1971), p. 2.

Vocal interpersonal communication
Any interaction in which there is an exchange of extralinguistic signals. EXAMPLES: yawning, burping, giggling, gagging, snickering.

Pseudoaffective interpersonal communication
Situations in which an individual's nonverbal behavior contradicts his verbal behavior. EXAMPLE: Someone claims that he feels great but looks like hell, or claims that he is not in a hurry while drumming his fingers on a desk and restlessly tapping his foot.

Phatic interpersonal communication
Any verbal interaction consisting of what is commonly known as small talk. EXAMPLE: "Hi Larry, what's new, how's mother, father working, see ya!"

Terminal interpersonal communication
A verbal transaction in which a statement is made for which no intelligent answer is possible, nor is one warranted. EXAMPLE: Imagine that you have just run out of cigarettes (if you smoke) and darted into a diner for a pack. After you deposit your change into a cigarette machine and pull the Lucky Strike lever, out comes Pall Mall. Annoyed, you search out the manager and explain exactly what happened. His reply, "That can't be, Mac!" represents terminal communication. It has come to the end of the line and is usually self-limiting; there is nothing to be gained from arguing the issue. Other replies characteristic of this type of communication are (1) "Oh yeah!" (2) "Sorry fellah, there's nothing I can do about it," (3) "I'm only following orders, mister."

Metaphysical interpersonal communication
Any interaction wherein an exchange of information takes place between man and sources beyond his immediate conceptual world may be designated as metaphysical communication. EXAMPLES: seances, transcendentalism, extrasensory perception, demonic possession.

Mediational interpersonal communication
A form of communication in which a middleman is used by either a sender or receiver to relay information. EXAMPLE: When two people are angry at each other and refuse to talk to one another directly, they avail themselves of a mediator—someone who, without actually being involved, acts as a verbal go-between.

Irrational interpersonal communication
Any exchange in which logical discourse is either partially or completely absent. Not exclusively limited to psychotic or psychoneurotic individuals, it is frequently found among so-called normal people. EXAMPLE: Certain lovers' quarrels occasionally become irrational.

Instrumental interpersonal communication
Those communications from which something happens. EXAMPLES: "Shut the door." "Eat your cereal." "Give me a drag on that cigarette."

Olfactory interpersonal communication
While man's smell is not as indispensable to his survival as it is among certain lower forms of life, he seems to do his fair share of sniffing. The sale of perfumes, deodorants, mouthwashes, and various odoriferous soaps bears witness that olfactory communication plays more than a

casual interpersonal role in societal living. Actually, all this form of communication amounts to is people-smelling-people.

Tactile interpersonal communication
Any type of communication employing the sense of touch. EXAMPLES: hand shaking, kissing, hugging, fighting.

Pharmacogenic interpersonal communication
The use of such drugs as heroin and a wide variety of mood modifiers which are capable of altering a person's communicative process. EXAMPLE: "What's wrong, Phil, you sound kind of strange?"

III. Extrapersonal Communication

The process by which man communicates with animals, plants, and/or inanimate objects.

Man—Animal
Any interaction between man and animal wherein the receipt and transmission of verbal, nonverbal, or vocal information results in a perceptible motoric display deemed meaningful to one or both communicators. EXAMPLE: Asking a trained dog to give you its paw and having it respond appropriately. (See Chapter 4.)

Man—Plant
Any interaction between man and plant wherein the receipt and transmission of verbal, nonverbal, or vocal information results in a perceptible behavioral display (for example, variations in growth, reproduction, metabolism, or irritability) by the plant and is acknowledged as meaningful by man. EXAMPLE: Telling your plants how beautiful they are and how much you love them, and having them respond by looking even more beautiful than before. (See Chapter 4.)

Man—Object
Any interaction in which man, treating an inanimate object as either a sender or a receiver, assigns some personal significance to the cognitive and/or behavioral consequences (real or imagined) derived from it. EXAMPLE: Talking to a car that is cold and won't start, and having it start. (See Chapter 4.)

SUMMARY

Because of man's inborn curiosity, his insatiable desire "to know," this chapter has referred to him as a compulsive message hunter. In an effort to establish some sort of relationship between man and information, the chapter you have just read has stressed three points: (1) messages, under no circumstance, should be restricted exclusively to words; (2) communication models are indispensable to an understanding of the communicative process and can be approached in a painless manner; (3) the serious student of communication has at his disposal not one but many different types of communication from which to choose according to his personal and public needs.

Man's growing need for deeper and more meaningful communication with other members of his species is becoming progressively more difficult to ignore. No longer satisfied with two-, three-, and four-word utterances such as "How's your old lady?" "Wanna Coke?" and "See ya around" (referred to in this chapter as mini-messages), his message hunger occasionally drives him to pay for communication, such as dial-a-friend, dial-a-shoulder, professional counseling, or group discussions. In a time-driven society where "hurry, hurry" are watchwords and people either don't give a damn or won't take the time to listen, understanding the role played by messages is of grave importance.

Endeavoring to place messages in an even more utilitarian perspective, we have plugged them into a variety of communication models. Starting with an almost indecently simple form of model, we added components, one-by-one, until a reasonably sophisticated level was reached. From this process the reader should have acquired a clearer understanding of the communication model and its purpose—that is, to (1) present its components, (2) demonstrate their relationship to one another, and (3) diagrammatically illustrate their operational significance.

Last, three major classifications of communication were given: *intrapersonal, interpersonal,* and *extrapersonal.* Subsumed and defined under each heading were those forms found most commonly in use along with some not so common. Since this list is by no means exhaustive, it can only be expected to provide a basis for preliminary insight and a springboard for further investigation into communication in a more expanded sense.

CHAPTER 2

DIMENSIONS
OF
THE SELF

INSIGHTS

After reading this chapter you should have a clearer understanding of:

- *the various forms your SELF can take.*
- *why the SELF you see in your mirror is not necessarily the same as the SELF others see.*
- *how the way you perceive your SELF can affect your communication, not only with yourself, but with others.*
- *the different ways, if you wanted to, you could alter your SELF.*
- *how your environment, both before birth and after death, can influence your SELF.*
- *those aspects of the SELF that are often driven underground, and hidden from view.*

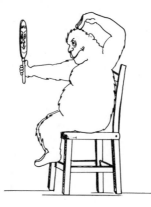

Few of us can cope with a clear and undistorted image of ourselves. Like the photographer who touches up his final prints, we, too, "touch up" other people's impressions of us. Perhaps we are all three people: who we think we are; who others think we are; and who we think others think we are. To these one might facetiously add—who we really are. Some of the common areas in which we perform this "psychological tailoring" include age, height, weight, and intelligence. Expressions like the following illustrate how we manipulate our internal and external environments as a means of survival:

"Don't tell me I look as old as Dennis."
"Come on, Don, I'm taller than that shrimp brother of yours."
"You must be kidding, I'm at least 20 pounds lighter than John."
"Can you believe that moron sitting over there is my boss?"

Negative perceptions of who we are, like virulent viruses, can infect most communications. Imagine a student suffering from a deflated SELF. You might hear him say, "Let's face it, I'm a born loser. Anything I have ever tried never worked out." Or, "I'll ask him for a 'C' but I'm sure he will refuse." Compare these with the remarks of someone having an inflated sense of SELF. He would probably say, "I'm the best student in his class," or "I'll definitely pull an easy 'A' in this course." Obviously, the SELF resident in each of these students contributes substantially to both how and what they communicate to others.

Children who have been continually "put down" by their parents—negatively reinforced in almost everything they have done—often fulfill the prophecy. When a youngster spills milk at the breakfast table or scratches the family car accidentally, it is wrong to say, "You are a bad little boy" or "a naughty little girl." Condemning the child instead of the act, if repeated often enough, can seriously damage the child's sense of SELF. This, in turn, can affect future communication as well.

You need not go outside your family circle to find a variety of SELFS. Whenever the clan comes together at weddings, wakes, bar mitzvahs, and communions, certain relatives can be relied upon to air their favorite SELF. When Uncle Charlie begins his familiar refrain, "When I was in the army during the big war . . . ," the family winces and thinks, "Here we go again with Uncle Charlie and World War II." Or, perhaps an Aunt Lucy will grace the occasion with her favorite size-9 SELF: "When I was your age, I was a size 9 and could eat all of you under the table without gaining an ounce." All of us have someone like Uncle Charlie or Aunt Lucy in our families whose rhetoric is organized around and deeply rooted in a past SELF—someone they used to be and refuse to let die a natural death. Rehearsing these bygone SELFS provides some people with a sense of security and a feeling of psychological well-being. During a lifetime, we all accumulate an assortment of SELFS which we may choose to revive from time to time.

EVOLUTION OF THE SELF

"How did you arrive at your present conception of yourself?" How would you answer this question? Probably by giving your name or the kind of work you do (doctor, lawyer, teacher, student). See how differently people answer this question. Some invariably, tell WHAT they are and insist that it also communicates WHO they are. Webster helps clarify the issue in a reference to Who's Who. It is put this way: (1) who the important people are; (2) a book or list containing the names and short biographies of the prominent contemporary persons of a country, city, profession, etc. Such a definition demonstrates an awareness of coupling WHAT a man is with WHAT he has done with his SELF.

Historically, men were identified in more than one way: by their place of origin or their trade (Jesus of Nazareth, Saul of Tarsus, John the Fisherman) or according to their father's name (David, son of Saul; Isaac, son of Abraham). Further, men were identified by some character trait (Richard the Lionhearted, Alexander the Great, Ivan the Terrible). In each case, beyond the mere utterance of his name, insight was given into the man. Today, most men do not have such qualifiers associated with their names. Consequently, it frequently becomes necessary to ask the person to whom you have just been introduced, "What do you do, or what are you?"

Nowadays, a growing number of people are experiencing a sense of alienation, a lack of individuality—"an identity crisis." Such an attitude has made the search for SELF a popular pastime, as witnessed by the number of encounter, sensitivity, and discussion groups that have cropped up lately—a pursuit that appears to warrant attention.

Your SELF does not remain static. It is constantly undergoing change, mirroring past, present and future happenings. Together, these reflections, both in and out of consciousness, are critical to the formation and evolution of your SELF. And, since the paramount objective of communication is to express what you think and feel, your SELF must be understood.

One final point. Your SELF is not limited to your lifetime. There are cases in which it was initiated before you were born; this is your *prenatal SELF*. Then, after death, your *postmortem SELF* will be born.

The Prenatal SELF

Parents-to-be often discuss their forthcoming blessed event. Some speak in generalities, others compulsively dwell on the most miniscule details. Items such as the baby's sex, room decor, education, playmates, wardrobe, and future mate are deliberated with mathematical precision. It is interesting to speculate how many children would want to be born if they knew of these plans beforehand.

Whereas in most instances such anticipations are innocent and harmless, they can, under certain circumstances, prove dangerous. Imagine those who have their hearts set on a son and then, as fate would have it, are delivered a daughter. Shocked and disappointed, they might, consciously or unconsciously, raise her "as though" she were a son. Here a female child is welcomed into the world by a male pre-natal SELF, conceived in the minds of her parents before she was born. Such a distortion can, if continued, precipitate an identity crisis in later life.

The Postnatal SELF

This SELF begins at birth and ends with death. During its tenure it passes through a succession of phases: baby SELF, child SELF, adolescent SELF, teenage SELF, adult SELF, middle-age SELF, and senior-citizen SELF. Each could be considered a life in itself, fully endowed with the joy, pain, and suffering that gives it direction and meaning. Family photograph albums, memory boxes, and diaries all chronicle stages in the evolution of the SELF.

To what extent can the SELF influence your communication with others? Should having to tell someone to stop talking like a child have special meaning? If so, what? Is it relevant that psychologists and psychiatrists take serious notice of how a person communicates? Simply put, it seems that how an individual communicates his internal state could be a fairly good barometer of his mental posture.

Graduating from one SELF to another is an accumulative process. As each SELF emerges, instead of cancelling out preceding SELFS, it joins them in a combined state. Competent hypnotists have been reputed to regress a subject and thereby reveal a past SELF. Many of us can voluntarily revive a characteristic of a prior SELF (baby talk, tantrums, and so on). It is important to remember that no SELF stands alone. All are affected, directly or indirectly, by those which have preceded it. For example, imagine you are leaving your mother's house after a family visit. You are a married man, 29 years old, and have two children. Kissing you goodbye, she tells you to button up your coat and put on your scarf. Automatically you comply. Which SELF is she talking to and which SELF is responding? Obviously, as some mothers are apt to do, she has not succeeded in turning loose your childhood SELF. To her, it will never fully disappear, regardless of how old you get to be. But such behavior is not restricted to parents. It infiltrates our communication with all those who are close to us. We appeal to that SELF in others which best meets our needs and avoid those which threaten them.

The Postmortem SELF

Wills, epitaphs, and eulogies apply to people who have died. They communicate to the living the attitudes, values, and beliefs the deceased held when alive. Communication between the living and the dead may be characterized by plaques, cornerstones, monuments, and building wings. Ancient civilizations to this day communicate through their art, architecture, and statuary: the cave paintings at Lascauz, France (c. 15,000–10,000 B.C.), the great pyramids at Giza (c. 2500 B.C.), Apollo from the Temple of Zeus at Olympia (c. 460 B.C.).

Being forgotten seems a fate few people are willing to accept, and one that some manage to escape. Take the postmortem SELFS of Socrates, Aristotle, Michelangelo, Leonardo Da Vinci, Mascagni, and Puccini. In their words, art, and music, they live today—years after their physical death.

How much can you learn about a person's postmortem SELF by knowing his dying words? Does knowing that Winston Churchill's last words were "I am bored with it all" tell you anything about the man?[1] Or consider Benjamin Franklin's epitaph for himself:

[1] Appeared in New York Times, Feb. 1, 1965, p. 12.

The body of Benjamin Franklin, Printer, (Like the cover of an old book, its contents torn out and stript of its lettering and gilding), Lies here, food for worms; But the work shall not be lost, for it will (as he believed) appear once more in a new and more elegant edition, revised and corrected by the author.[2]

Here are a few more:

Life is a jest,
and all things show it,
I thought so once,
but now I know it.—*John Gay, poet (1685–1732)*

Now I am about to take my
last voyage, a great leap in
the dark.—*Thomas Hobbes, philosopher on his deathbed, 1679*

Under the wide and starry sky,
Dig the grave and let me die;
Glad did I live and gladly die,
And I laid me down with a will.
This be the verse you grave for me:
"Here he lies, where he longed to be;
Home is the sailor, home from the sea,
And the hunter home from the hill."[3]—*Robert Louis Stevenson, engraved
on his tombstone.*

Fascinated by the communicative implications of an epitaph, this writer, over several semesters, gathered from black and white students samples of how they would like to have their epitaphs read. Examine them and see what conclusions you reach.

Black Students

Here lies the mother of the first lady president. Black at that.

Here lie the remains of a failure in everything.

Here lies a Faithful mother of 10
Beloved wife
Whose Deeds will live on
through the centuries.

Here lies a brilliant scholar in all fields, too bad he was never understood.

White Students

Love and peace to all Mankind.

What a pity. What she might have been.

He ate what was set before him.

To rest . . . we hope.

Died at the age of 97 at the hands of a jealous husband.

Here lies a man whose life should not be mourned, but to be learned from; Life for him was worthwhile

---

[2] Henry C. Lewis, ed., *5000 Quotations for All Occasions* (Garden City, N.Y.: Garden City Books, 1945), p. 76.
[3] *Ibid.*, p. 76.

Here lies a woman dedicated to the betterment of herself and of other people, particularly children.

Here lies _____, who dedicated her life to educating the children of Jamaica, N.Y. May she rest in peace knowing it was not done in vain.

1949–2049
Here lie her

Here lies a man who dedicated his life to curing sick people. May he rest in peace.

Here lies a sweet, quiet, yet contributive human being to this world. Her work, nor the wonderful memories of her, held the world over, will never be forgotten but will linger on from generation to generation.

Here lies _____, he was a big man, a mighty big man.

Here lies an unknown person who tried.

because he did what he felt had to be done, and believed in it.

She lived till she died.

Born as no-one
Died as no-one
But lived as someone
Dear and beloved

Born 1948–1999

Thanks, Oh Lord, for permitting to live on your creation for being part of it; But next time you feel like creating something with people on it, please let me be the first one here. I never believed in things that way, so I'll be ready for that serpent.

Here lies _____;
she tried hard.

He was born,
He lived,
He died,
He lives.

The world will not be the same.

Were you not looking at this stone, you may have been stoned with me.

To die in peace was to live in vain.

Conclusions drawn from these epitaphs must be those of the reader. They have been reproduced *exactly* as they were written by students. However, interest permitting, one might examine them from the standpoint of their positive or negative attitudes. You will notice that some are failure-oriented; others, success-oriented. Also, suggested in them is the need to either serve or be served. Speaking advisedly, these epitaphs should not be used as a basis for any reckless and irresponsible inferences.

Communication is time-binding, welding together past, present, and future in an ongoing process. Your prenatal SELF (how you were conceived before you were born); your postnatal SELF (how you are being perceived during your life); and your postmortem SELF (how you will be remembered after you are dead) all contribute to your better understanding human communication in an ever-changing world.

THE PHYSICAL AND PSYCHOLOGICAL SELF

Are you satisfied that others see you as you see yourself? Stand in front of a full-length mirror and take a long, studied look. Would you consider yourself tall or short, over- or underweight, attractive or unattractive, distinguished or plain? To what extent do your physical attributes influence the opinion you hold of yourself? Your impressions could be crucial to your interaction with others.

People's attitudes toward their bodies vary. Physicians describe patients coming to them with a painful leg. However, instead of referring to the extremity as "my leg," they say, "the damn thing is killing me, doc." After recovering, they quickly reclaim the healed limb. Parents whose children misbehave refer to them as "those rotten kids"; but, when they are little angels, "Our kids."

In the chapters ahead you will learn that people have the option of viewing themselves either as a "whole" or in parts. Boulding[4] feels that we behave in relation to the images we hold of ourselves. A lovely story makes this point. There was a young girl who was ugly and very lonely. She lived in New Orleans and the Mardi Gras season was approaching. Finding her brooding and determined not to go, a friend suggested that she visit a mask-maker and have a beautiful mask made. Reluctantly she agreed. At the Mardi Gras, to her amazement, many handsome young men pursued her. Finally, one of them fell deeply in love with her and she with him. Petrified at the thought of unmasking when the Mardi Gras was over, she was tempted to run away. Resisting, she found herself face-to-face with the moment she dreaded. He removed his mask first and, as she imagined, he was extremely handsome. It was now her turn. As he reached over to undo her mask, she died a thousand deaths inside. Finally it was done. He looked tenderly into her eyes filled with tears and said, "God, but you are beautiful!" Obviously, the SELF she saw was not the same SELF he saw.

Approaching this theme from another direction, did Mrs. Einstein share her bed with and keep house for the same SELF that gave the world $E = mc^2$? Was it the same SELF that Napoleon's armies followed at Waterloo that Josephine loved? Obviously, these women perceived their men differently from the way they were perceived by their students and soldiers.

Body types also play an important role in your communication with others. Some people actually dislike their bodies—especially certain parts (big nose, protruding ears, large breasts, underdeveloped genitalia, and

---

[4] Kenneth Boulding, *The Image* (Ann Arbor: University of Michigan Press, 1956).

so on). In some cases they actually hate them. Consider the social implications of such an attitude. How does one avoid the negative effects upon
the SELF produced by such physical rejections?

Could you imagine what it would be like to have a duplicate of yourself, "made in Detroit," an android? It would walk like you, talk like you,
think, feel, and smell like you. In every particular it would be exactly like
you with one exception: it would be "man-made." What characteristics,
aside from the fact that you were identifiable as a male or a female, would
enable your friends and loved ones to identify this android as you? What
makes your SELF distinctively you? Would you reveal or conceal this
information? Is it your imagination, or are fewer and fewer people willing
to disclose things about themselves? Are they reluctant because SELF dis-
closure makes them more responsible for their behavior? Is the trend,
though on perhaps a low key, toward anonymity? Revealing one's identity
these days does suggest an element of risk. There are people who literally
take refuge in such anonymity—the phone caller who refuses to give his
name, the witness to an accident who leaves the scene before being identified. Thousands appear to enjoy being "a face in the crowd"—a silent partner to the spokesman airing their views, while they remain unthreatened
in the sanctuary provided by an anonymous SELF.

ALTERATION OF THE SELF

If you could alter the design of your body, how would you do it? Would
you have an extra pair of eyes in the back of your head, some extra fingers
on each hand, or perhaps two stomachs: one for nutrition and one for
pleasure eating? For centuries, people have employed various means of
altering the SELF. In some cases it was surgical; in others it was by
ingesting herbs or other medicaments having special effects upon the
body. Less heroic procedures involved applying cosmetics to parts of the
body or modifying the mode of dress. In addition to fulfilling requirements
dictated by social, hygienic, and religious mores, the majority of these
alterations of the SELF were used to make an individual more beautiful.

But how can altering the SELF affect communication with others? An
example of the "weight watcher" clearly illustrates this. Being, let us say,
70 pounds overweight forces an individual to wear certain types of
clothes, walk in a certain manner, and talk about subjects common to
overweight people (food, recipes, diet doctors, and so on). Once the
weight is lost, these characteristics usually become lessened. These behavior modifications are frequently reflected in the communication process.
Thus, to be more aware of the role of the SELF in communication, it is

necessary to familiarize oneself with some of the ways a SELF can become altered.

Surgical Alteration

Depending upon a culture's conception of beauty, parts of the human anatomy are altered. In some situations the changes are temporary; in others they are irreversible. Some practices of the western world include: capping teeth, shortening noses, drawing back the ears, increasing or decreasing breast size, surgically trimming away excess fat, lifting the skin on the neck and face, or transplanting hair onto bald heads. Among the more primitive peoples, practices include: filing teeth into various shapes, inserting wooden plugs into the lips, scarifying the skin according to specific designs, and bandaging the feet of female babies. One of the more interesting (though repulsive to the western mentality) is skull moulding.

Three somewhat extreme methods (voluntary or involuntary) of altering a SELF are sterilization (by tubal ligation or vasectomy), castration, and transsexual surgery. The attitude of the public toward these procedures is curious. Voluntary sterilization has been, and continues to be, considered a mortal sin by the Roman Catholic Church. Conversely, others, because of the population explosion, regard it as a courageous and socially commendable act. It wasn't too long ago that the mere mention of the word sterilization drew looks of disdain and mortification. Today, it is natural and acceptable in some circles to openly mention that you have had a tubal ligation or a vasectomy. Castration, in contrast, has not come that far. It is more shocking and decidedly not something one shouts from the rooftops. Two historical situations come to mind with regard to castration. One involves the eunuch, whose ancient role was to guard the sultan's wives; the other, the castrati, who were males castrated when young so as to retain their soprano voices for singing.

The most recent means of altering the SELF is by transsexual surgery. For anatomical reasons, this surgical procedure is currently limited to transforming males into females. Perhaps, in the future, the female will also be able to avail herself of this conversion. Candidates are generally males whose identification is female. Some have claimed they feel like a woman trapped in a man's body. Christine Jorgenson was probably the first publicized case in which a man was surgically converted into a woman. Since then, many others have followed his (or her) lead.

Biochemical Alteration

Many substances, if injected or ingested into the body, are capable of altering the SELF. Without going into extraneous pharmacological detail, some of the more familiar biochemical agents are:

Hallucinogens: mescaline, peyote, L.S.D.
Opiates: morphine, hashish.
Amphetamines: Dexedrine, Benzedrine.
Tranquilizers: Miltown, Librium, Valium.
Hormones: thyroid, estrogen, testosterone, pituitary extracts, corticosteroids.
Barbiturates: Nembutal, Seconal.

These drugs, to varying degrees, either speed up, slow down, or alter certain body functions. The extent will depend upon an individual's psychological and physiological susceptibility. The hallucinogens, for instance, can precipitate auditory and visual hallucinations by altering the biochemistry of the brain. For the person who's SELF is down, "ups" (Dexedrine, Benzedrine) might be the choice; if the SELF is up, "downs" (Nembutal, Seconal) may be the option. Add to these the tranquilizers which some people have already adopted as a way of life. Not only do they pop them when under stress, but also at the mere hint of forthcoming stress a week or two away.

Last, there are those who suffer from what might be called "the Ponce de Leon Syndrome." They are in search of the fountain of youth and believe they have found it in hormone therapy. By taking regular injections of estrogen or testosterone, they have persuaded themselves that the aging process has been halted, or at least slowed down. The result: an externally unchanging SELF.

Today's pharmaceutical offerings make possible a variety of ways to biochemically alter your SELF. "Next, please—what is your pleasure?"

Cosmetic Alteration

As though chemical and surgical tampering with the SELF were not enough, painting, plucking, bleaching, baking, dowsing, and oiling must be added to the list of ways some people commit "cosmetic assassination." One wonders if it is simply a matter of conforming to social norms, or an outgrowth of deeper psychological motives; to what extent can inferences about personality and character be made on the basis of how the SELF is altered cosmetically?

Hollywood makeup men have been transforming faces in films for decades in order to communicate the illusion of various images. Pioneers such as Helena Rubinstein and Elizabeth Arden have enabled millions of women to alter their appearances through the use of cosmetics. Small eyes can be made to look bigger, eyebrows crop up where none exist, wrinkles are made to disappear—all ways of altering the SELF with cosmetics. Machinations like these, however, must be considered in context, not in isolation. For example, the flaming red lipstick on an 11-year-old girl carries a different connotation on the lips of a hard-core prostitute. Thus, whether we are considering the implications of plucked eyebrows or bleached blond hair, each must be viewed in relationship to the other determinants of the SELF.

Some women flatly refuse to communicate until they have "made up their faces" in the morning. And, just as there is protocol dictating how and what one should say on a specific occasion, there is comparable protocol regulating the use of cosmetics. The manner in which the SELF is altered cosmetically seems to be bound up with certain well-defined social, psychological, and cultural mores. Therefore, how people think, look, and feel is frequently communicated by how they use cosmetics.

Sartorial Alteration

According to Dr. Jean Rosenbaum, a Colorado psychiatrist, "When you're selecting clothes, you're choosing a kind of substituted body."[5] It seems to raise the age-old question of whether clothes make the man. Does how you dress affect your behavior, or does your behavior affect how you dress? Anyone who has spent time in an institution (such as army, orphanage, or military academy) remembers the feeling of sameness. For some, it was a problem trying to assert individuality amidst hundreds of look-alikes. We dress differently depending upon the circumstances or the special occasion, and we fully recognize the social consequences of not being appropriately groomed. Some people rank their personal appearance at the top of the list; others couldn't care less about how they look. In both cases a "nonverbal statement" is made; they cannot not communicate.

The Prince and the Pauper by Mark Twain illustrates the relationship between clothes and the wearer. Although the Prince and the Pauper exchanged clothes, they still retained their private SELFS. The way they walked, talked, and held themselves eventually betrayed their true identities. At first glance, many were fooled; only careful observation disclosed the inner man. Part of the problem is knowing what to look for.

In truth, a number of people intuitively detect these contradictions in the SELF in everyday life. For example, there are individuals of humble beginnings who, through good fortune or just plain hard work, have accumulated large sums of money. Unfamiliar with the nuances and protocol of upper-class living, though expensively dressed, they can be detected by some as *nouveau riche*.

Clothing plays a greater nonverbal role in communication than many people are willing to concede. Testing this premise, nude marathon en-

---

[5] *Long Island Press*, October 22, 1973, p. 11.

counter groups have recently challenged the role clothes play in our lives. Investigators have noted that participants' immediate reactions to nudity fell into seven categories:

I. A sense of pleasure derived from the freedom to look at other peoples' bodies and be looked at.

II. A personal sense of comfort, exhilaration, and freedom.

III. The desire to touch and experience skin contact and a sense of being inhibited in this respect.

IV. Pleasure arising from the sense of group closeness and the relaxed expressions on the faces of the other participants.

V. A sense of naturalness of the nude condition, and a feeling of relief at not having reacted inappropriately.

VI. The experience of being high or unable to sleep for most of the remainder of the night.

VII. The sense of concern about one's physical body when comparing it with other members of the group.[6]

On the assumption that you have never attended a nudist colony or participated in a nude encounter, ask yourself whether you would do so, and list your reasons for such an attitude:

I WOULD NOT ATTEND A NUDE ENCOUNTER OR NUDIST CAMP BECAUSE:

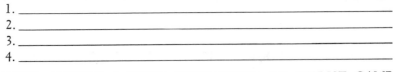

I WOULD ATTEND A NUDE ENCOUNTER OR NUDIST CAMP BECAUSE:

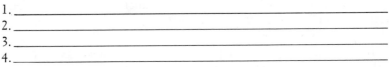

Those who have attended nude encounters report a decrease in their feelings of alienation, greater warmth, greater openness, and increased feelings of aliveness. Such reactions beg the question, "Are clothes an asset or liability to interpersonal communication?" Perhaps by removing the stereotypes that various forms of dress conjure in the public mind, we can better comprehend the deeper SELF within us. With or without

[6] Leonard Blank, Gloria B. Gottsegen, and Monroe G. Gottsegen, eds., *Confrontation* (New York: Macmillan, 1971), pp. 231–32.

clothes, it seems determined to make itself known through any and all available channels.

Psychological literature mentions an interesting condition involving clothes called transvestitism. It deals with people who, like transsexuals, have an identification problem. They enjoy wearing clothes of the opposite sex. While a certain amount of preference in clothes is manifested among "normal" people, they are not considered antisocial unless they go to extremes. The full-blown transvestite satisfies this criterion.

Prejudging people on the basis of their dress is commonplace. Not long ago, men who wore hats were considered either incredibly rich or credibly poor; those with suspenders—not too sure of themselves and not trusting of others; those who wore suede shoes in broad daylight—charming; while those who wore loafers—of sound judgment and pressed for time.[7]

Even wearing glasses is subject to bias and prejudice. Thornton studied how people judged subjects wearing glasses on photographs and in person. On photographs, those wearing glasses were rated more intelligent, more industrious, more honest, and more dependable. Those who were observed in person (with glasses) were also rated more intelligent and more industrious but not more honest.[8]

Although conclusions drawn on the basis of these data must be cautiously made, one might justifiably speculate that how people dress has the capacity to alter their SELF and directly or indirectly alter the way they communicate.

THE PATHOLOGICAL SELF

Semantically, the word *pathological* should be approached with care. Although its popular meaning usually goes unchallenged, most dictionaries assign it synonyms such as abnormal, irregular, atypical, aberrant, and deviant. Thus a stage is set for the pathological SELF.

In the waking or dream state, people have imagined themselves as other people. A compelling book, film, or play can easily produce enough empathy in a susceptible SELF so as to temporarily displace it. This normal tendency, if uncontrolled and carried to an extreme, can graduate into a pathological SELF. For example, in a psychiatric condition known as delusions of grandeur, the patient perceives himself as someone of exceedingly high status. While there are various forms of delusions, only those in which the subject believes himself to be someone else are intended here. Despite being presented with evidence to the contrary, these

---

[7] Joseph Rosner, "Unmask the man," *Mademoiselle*, May, 1956, pp. 122–23.
[8] G. R. Thornton, "The effects of wearing glasses upon judgments of personality traits seen briefly," *Journal of Applied Psychology* 28 (1944), 203–7.

people have entertained the false belief that they were God, Jesus Christ, the Virgin Mary, Napoleon Bonaparte, and so on.

A story is told about a man who visited a mental hospital. While waiting for visiting hours to begin, he struck up a conversation with a patient sitting nearby. After 15 or 20 minutes of what seemed to be perfectly rational discussion, the visitor stood up to leave. Thoroughly persuaded that the patient was as normal as he was, he said, "Well, I hope to God that you will soon be leaving this place and resume a normal healthy life with your family." The patient, looking him squarely in the eye, replied, "God cannot help me—I AM GOD." As you can see, a pathological SELF is not always easy to detect. It may lie well concealed beneath layers of perfectly normal-sounding communication and may only be diagnosable by a well-trained professional.

Some years ago, there was a film in which the leading character, Walter Mitty, suffered from flights into fantasy. In all matters he appeared normal, save one: from time to time his SELF would manifest a change of identity. On one occasion, by sleight of mind, he would see himself as an ace pilot in World War II, on another, a major in the Foreign Legion. While these excursions from SELF-to-SELF harmed no one, they presented serious difficulties for his fiancée, who was somewhat overwhelmed trying to keep up with him. Another case involved a girl with three separate personalities whose story was told in a motion picture entitled *The Three Faces of Eve*. Finally, there was the story of the Great Impostor. It seems there was a young man who derived psychological satisfaction out of successfully deceiving experts in the various fields he invaded. He impersonated such people as a college professor, a prison warden, and a naval surgeon. Perhaps the reason people are inclined to believe such impostors is because they so thoroughly immerse themselves in the SELF they are pretending to be that others are unable to detect even a trace of self-doubt. Pirandello[9] was probably onto this when he wrote, *Così È (Se Vi Pare)*, which means, "You are, if you think you are."

A final pathological SELF concerns a ventriloquist and his dummy. It seems the ventriloquist suffered from the delusion that his dummy had a separate identity, was evil, and was out to destroy him. After years of mental anguish, he built up enough courage to do away with the dummy once and for all. One morning he picked it up by its legs and smashed it against the wall. It broke into a thousand pieces and fell to the floor. The ventriloquist, feeling reborn, smiled with a new sense of freedom. As he opened his mouth to shout "Hosanna," guess whose voice came out? IT WAS THE VOICE OF THE DUMMY.

Communication is a powerful tool by which the "inner man" can make

[9] See Luigi Pirandello, *Così È (Se Vi Pare)* in *Three Plays by Luigi Pirandello* (New York: Dutton, 1922).

himself known. In this light it must be regarded as a diagnostic instrument as well. Furthermore, the relationship between an individual's self-image and the statutes of limitation he places upon what he can or cannot do, can or cannot be, often becomes a self-fulfilling prophesy; *what he fears will happen*—happens. A differentiation must always be made between the resident SELF and the pathological SELF.

THE CULTURAL SELF

Repeating: the SELF must be approached in some sort of context. We do not exist in a vacuum but in relation to people, places, and things. Culture is the milieu into which we are born and, like a sculptor, it gives shape, form, and meaning to the raw SELF. "No matter how different people are, they share a common humanity."[10] And, whether engaged in conflict or cooperation, it is their communication which unites them. Beyond certain genetic determinants, much of what influences us culturally is outside of our awareness.[11]

Consider the claim, "It isn't so much what we don't know that hurts us, but the thousand and one things we do know that ain't so." As children, we were inundated with countless *shoulds* and *should nots*. Too young and innocent to understand and evaluate them in perspective, we grew up, not because of them, but in spite of them. Now, as adults, we occasionally find ourselves behaving in ways difficult to understand, their explanations long-steeped and secreted in a kind of "cultural catechism."

A housewife who has just baked a cake that failed exclaims, "I can't understand it, everything I put into it was good." Likewise, parents whose children have failed often issue this same lament: "Everything we put into them was good." Culture, like a mother and father, imparts to its children a wide assortment of values drawn from magical, mystical, scientific, and religious systems of knowledge.[12] How they turn out, unfortunately, depends upon more than simply "putting good things into them."

The way we see the world is not necessarily how it is in any absolute sense but rather how we are trained to see it. Take, for example, the question of beauty. Millions of Americans are compulsive about making themselves beautiful, their homes beautiful, their children beautiful.

[10] Abne M. Eisenberg and Joseph A. Ilardo, *Argument, An Alternative to Violence* (Englewood Cliffs, N.J.: Prentice-Hall, Inc., 1972), p. 110.
[11] A. L. Davis, ed., *Culture, Class, and the Disadvantaged* (Chicago: Center for American English, 1969), p. 21.
[12] Judith Willer, *The Sociological Determination of Knowledge* (Englewood Cliffs, N.J.: Prentice-Hall, Inc., 1971).

Department-store counters throughout the nation groan with beautifying agents. Newspapers, magazines, and television commercials literally saturate the public mind with the importance and necessity of beautification.

This cultural obsession with beauty begins at an early age. Experimenters Berscheid and Walster[13] feel that in the classroom, children quickly learn to recognize the role played by "how one looks." In a class where a disturbance has occurred, the teacher is more likely to accuse the unattractive child than the attractive one. Later on, physical attractiveness may be the single most important factor in determining popularity among college-age adults. It is regrettable that any child need be born into a culture which openly and often cruelly favors one physical appearance over another.

Other forms of cultural biases capable of overtly or covertly affecting the SELF are inferred by the following clichés:

1. Daddies work—mommies cook, clean, and have babies. (social role)
2. The family that prays together, stays together. (religion)
3. Boys who have premarital sex are admired; girls are ostracized and labeled immoral and loose. (morality)
4. Never kick a man when he's down. (ethics)
5. All work and no play makes Jack a dull boy. (philosophy)
6. When money talks, everybody listens. (economics)
7. America, love it or leave it. (nationalism)
8. A sound mind in a sound body. (health)

Stereotyping, mentioned earlier, also takes its cultural toll. It is the situation in which some characteristic of an individual or group is singled out and used to characterize the entire class. Whereas references may occasionally be flattering, they are usually pejorative. Do these sound familiar to you?

All Italians smell from garlic
All Latins are good lovers
All Arabs are filthy
All Polish people are stupid
All Jews are loudmouthed and rude
All Irishmen are drunkards
All Blacks have rhythm
All Puerto Ricans carry knives
All Germans are antisemitic[14]

[13] Ellen Berscheid and Elaine Walster, "Beauty is best," *Psychology Today* V (March, 1972), pp. 43, 46, 74.
[14] If you know of some stereotypes that were omitted here, please write them in the margins of this page.

Cultural prescriptions should be given special attention when analyzing the SELF. A cultural cue, such as how far people stand from one another in conversation, conveys an interesting meaning. In South America, people stand closer than in North America.[15] Reacting to a *distance cue* like this without knowing its cultural context could give the wrong impression. An American, used to "keeping his distance" in conversation, might offend a South American. Conversely, the South American might, out of ignorance, be considered excessively rude and aggressive by the American. Thus, understanding one's cultural SELF makes communication at all levels more effective. Neglecting it could be disastrous.

SUMMARY

If the reader has experienced the full impact of this chapter, a rethinking of the role of SELF in an interpersonal situation should have occurred. Not only was the critical importance of understanding your own SELF vigorously pronounced, but also the SELF on the opposite end of a communication. Emphasis was also placed upon the idea of the SELF not being a time-bound phenomenon; it exists before birth (the prenatal SELF), during life (the postnatal SELF), and after death (the post-mortem SELF). The concept of a prenatal SELF (as used here) applies, not to the unborn child, but rather to those characteristics assigned it by its parents-to-be. This same admonition concerns the postmortem SELF. It derives its characteristics from the living, not the dead. If a man dies unnoticed, without a family or will, and is buried in an unmarked grave, will he have a postmortem SELF? In both instances, whether before birth or after death, all matters pertaining to communication must be decided by the postnatal SELF.

Following some examples of dying words, a description was then advanced of the ways in which one could alter the SELF surgically, biochemically, cosmetically, and by the manner of dress.

Next, a pathological SELF was proposed and the forms it could take. Examples included Delusions of Grandeur, the Walter Mitty Syndrome, the Great Impostor, the Three Faces of Eve, and the case of the Ventriloquist and His Dummy. These distortions of the SELF were then complemented by a set of cultural determinants capable of influencing the SELF. The chapter concluded with the admonition that one must constantly be on guard against those obstacles to effective communication which grow out of cultural prejudices and misunderstanding.

[15] See Edward Hall's *Silent Language* (Garden City, N.Y.: Doubleday, 1959).

CHAPTER 3

INTRAPERSONAL COMMUNICATION

INSIGHTS

After reading this chapter you should have a clearer understanding of:

- *why being able to communicate with yourself could be so important.*
- *what goes on inside your body when you communicate with yourself.*
- *the different ways people can and do communicate with themselves.*
- *how unfair it is to write off people who talk to themselves as being "flaky" without knowing more about them.*
- *the role communicating with oneself plays in terms of building better mental and physical health.*
- *how the nature of our senses limits our perception and, by so doing, our intrapersonal communication.*

While the preceding chapter focused on the ways physical and psychological alterations of the SELF might affect a communicator's outer world, this chapter will emphasize the communicator's inner world. In fact, a fitting credo for this section might be, *In order to make your inner and outer worlds harmonize, you must take an equal interest in both.* A study of intrapersonal communication lends itself to this task.

DEFINITION OF INTRAPERSONAL COMMUNICATION

Intrapersonal communication is a process by which people, either consciously or unconsciously, communicate with themselves on a verbal, nonverbal, or vocal level.

WHY STUDY INTRAPERSONAL COMMUNICATION?

If we are ever to truly understand how to communicate effectively with others, we must first learn how to communicate with ourselves. From childhood, most of us were brainwashed into believing that the *First*

Law of Survival in this world is learning how to get along with others. Learning how to get along with yourself was hardly ever mentioned. Soon we learned that successful communication with oneself was an indispensable tool which none of us could afford to be without. This left us with the question of how to do it.

On the surface it appears simple; you lie down in bed, close your eyes, and indulge in some intrapersonal communication. But what do you say? How do you answer some of the difficult questions that often come up?

What you discover all too quickly is that intrapersonal communication can be constructive, destructive, or just a hopeless exercise in futility. Consequently, it is extremely important that when you look inward, you have a good idea what you're looking at, and what you're looking for. Be reminded, however, that not everyone can handle what he discovers. In many cases, uncensored intrapersonal communication requires not only a readiness, but maturity and courage as well. Occasionally, it is like witnessing an automobile accident; you want to look and not look at the same time. Surely you have had the experience of thinking something you didn't want to think about. And the more you tried to exorcise the unwanted thought, the more it remained.

One thing is perfectly clear: whenever you are communicating with someone, you are, at the same time, communicating with yourself. For example, as this page is being written, the author is engaging in intrapersonal communication; he thinks to himself and then writes. You, in turn, read his words and, if they trigger any meaning, another intrapersonal process of communication is initiated within you. Obviously, the more sensitive an author is to the intrapersonal processes of his reader, and the reader to those of the author, the more effectively meaning will be shared.

A last, but certainly not least important, reason for studying intrapersonal communication concerns what we believe. Essentially, what we think about in our inner world is a reflection of what we think about in our outer world. The main differences do not revolve around *what* we think about, but *how* we think about them. To illustrate this concept, let us consider for a moment how Man used to think about what went on inside his head.

Prehistoric skulls with holes in them have been dug up in various parts of the world. Anthropologists tell us that the practice of drilling holes in the skull (called trephining) was performed to let out the demons thought to be responsible for producing an individual's illness.[1] Thus, if someone was observed talking to himself, it was thought that he was communicating with a demon or spirit inside his head.

[1] Kenneth Walker, *The Story of Medicine* (New York: Oxford University Press, 1955), p. 23.

At the beginning of this century, Sigmund Freud introduced a new family of residents to the human skull (including Ego, Superego, Id, Libido, Subconscious, and Unconscious). So enthusiastically were these psychological constructs (ideas or perceptions) received by the general public that they were soon believed (by certain naïve laymen) to physically exist in the body on the same basis as the liver, spleen, or gall bladder. As a result, if someone were observed talking to himself, instead of blaming some mischievous demon or spirit, the blame conveniently fell on a fractured Ego or the stirring of a restless Libido.

Rounding out the second half of the twentieth century, society, a trifle bored with Egos and Ids, found itself fascinated by another approach to the contents of Man's skull. Operating under the banner of *physiological psychology*, this school of thought took off in still another direction. It reasoned that what goes on inside Man's skull could, and should, be explained in physiological terms. To wit, it pressed forward in hot pursuit of such constructs as brain codes, neurological pathways and centers, biochemical regulators, and the effects of certain surgical procedures on brain tissues. Thus, twice removed in theory from demons and spirits, it no longer was necessary to explain the phenomenon of talking to oneself in terms of a fractured Ego or a restless Libido.

In sum, whether your belief-system supports demons and spirits, Egos, Ids, or faulty brain physiology, the importance of intrapersonal communication must not be ignored. Through it, we are afforded the option of becoming either our own best friend, worst enemy, or a perfect stranger. Ultimately, the fate which befalls us depends largely on how we relate to ourselves. WHY STUDY INTRAPERSONAL COMMUNICATION— because it is a starting point or baseline to which all forms of communication must adjust.

There are three modes by which you can communicate intrapersonally: *verbally, nonverbally,* and *vocally.* A brief description of each follows.

MODES OF INTRAPERSONAL COMMUNICATION

Verbal Mode

Two ways people communicate with themselves are by *talking* and *writing.* Rankin,[2] in 1929, did a study which disclosed that adults spent 32 percent of an average day talking and writing. Twenty-eight years later,

[2] P. Rankin, "Listening ability," *Proceedings of the Ohio State Educational Conference's Ninth Annual Session* (Columbus, Ohio: The Ohio State University, 1929), p. 172–83.

Breiter[3] performed a similar study on housewives and found that 35 percent of their days were spent talking and 7 percent writing. Whereas both of these studies referred to interpersonal communication, this chapter restricts itself to a form of communication (intrapersonal) that is much more difficult to determine. Unless science develops some kind of a mind-reading machine, we cannot just barge into people's minds and jot down what percent of their day is spent in intrapersonal communication. Instead, we remain obliged to accept statements as to how much time they say they spend communicating with themselves.

When we memorize a speech, learn lines for a play, or simply think out loud, we are engaging in intrapersonal communication. Out of curiosity, how do you personally feel about people who talk to themselves while walking down the street or sitting on a bus? Do you write them off as "flaky" or do you extend them the courtesy of having a good reason for doing it? What percentage of the people who talk to themselves (out loud) in public would have a rational excuse for doing it if asked? Have you ever been caught talking to yourself? What was your excuse? Practically all of us have at some time had some such experience as the following: You leave your home or apartment, walk a block or two, and remember that you forgot something. Then, after going back and getting it, you hear the phone ring; the call distracts you, causing you to leave the house again without whatever you forgot the first time. A block away you stop dead in your tracks, remember that you did it again, and say in an audible voice, "Oh my god, I did it again! I must be getting senile." Just as these words leave your lips, a neighbor rounding the corner overhears you. Suddenly, you become keenly aware of how it feels to be caught talking to yourself.

Now how do you feel about people who talk to themselves? Do you think people should be encouraged to talk to themselves out loud in public if they feel like it? Gagné and Smith[4] had something to say on this subject. They discovered that if we vocalize our thoughts, they are likely to be sharper, more systematic, and easier to follow. Also, that when the 14- and 15-year-old boys they were studying were required to *verbalize* —that is, to think out loud to themselves—during problem-solving, they performed better than boys that did not.

The verbal mode of intrapersonal communication may occur in two forms: *overt* and *covert*. Thus far we have been discussing the *overt form* —talking to yourself out loud. A perhaps more common type is the

[3] L. Breiter, *Research in Listening and Its Importance to Literature*, Unpublished master's thesis, Brooklyn College, New York, 1957.
[4] Robert M. Gagné and Earnest C. Smith, Jr., "A study of the effects of verbalization on problem-solving," *Journal of Experimental Psychology* 63 (1963), 12–18.

covert form—talking to yourself on the inside, sometimes referred to as inner speech. Most studying for examinations involves covert intrapersonal communication. Either slumped over your desk, stretched out on your bed, or hidden away in some special place, you recite your lessons over and over again to yourself without making a sound. Some students get the most mileage out of their studies using the overt method, others the covert method; still others find combining the two most rewarding.

One of the more interesting examples of covert intrapersonal communication occurs while a conversation is in progress. Chances are it has happened to you. Imagine that you are having a discussion with one of your classmates about a wild weekend you both had. While he is talking, and you are looking him squarely in the eyes, your mind suddenly shifts gears and you find yourself involved with what might in this situation be called a covert para-intrapersonal communication—a silent conversation with yourself on a topic completely different from the one you are engaged in with your friend. Occasionally such a side-trip is detectable by a certain look in your eyes, prompting the other person to ask, "Are you listening to me?"

Written intrapersonal communication may also take either an overt or covert form. If whatever is written is read by anyone other than the person who wrote it, it should be considered as overt. If its content remains exclusively known to the person who wrote it, it should be considered covert. A well-kept diary is a classical example of covert intrapersonal communication; it remains strictly personal until such time as its owner chooses to disclose its contents. Only then does it become overt.

Probably one of the most useful purposes of verbal intrapersonal communication is to release tension. In psychological jargon, it is called *catharsis*—letting off steam, so to speak. The next time you accidentally smash your finger with a hammer, notice the difference in how you feel when you shout certain expletives, and when you remain silent. It might be worthwhile mentioning here that one of the major objectives in psychoanalysis is to get the patient to convert his covert intrapersonal communication into the overt form. In some way, being able to hear (out loud) a thought that had been kept silent may make some kind of an attitudinal difference toward the management of its content and meaning.

Nonverbal Mode

Close your eyes, remain perfectly still, and "feel." What part of your body are you most conscious of—your legs, hands, face, or perhaps something inside you? Unless you have been trained or have trained yourself to *tune in* on the countless intrapersonal nonverbal messages your body generates daily, you are being deprived of a valuable and frequently unnoticed definition of yourself.

For example, did you know that each system of your body, in addition to serving its normal biological purpose, may also serve as a vehicle for the psychological stress so often associated with everyday living. In some instances, suggests Arieti,[5] mental unrest is transformed into muscular activities (such as twitching, tics, and the like). Other forms of displaced intrapersonal transformations of stress include digestive irregularities, difficulty in breathing, raised or lowered blood pressure, frequency of urination, or perhaps just an old-fashioned skin rash. According to Eisenberg and Smith,[6] only a small proportion of our thoughts find expression in either verbal or iconic form. The greater proportion are retained internally and are either stored in a memory bank or expressed through one or more of the biologic systems just mentioned.

Becoming sensitive to one's own nonverbal intrapersonal communication can be either an asset or a liability. Behaving as an asset, it enables you to enjoy a more total sense of self, allowing you to experience identifiable feedback from all parts of your body. This is especially important to the professional athlete who depends heavily upon maximum coordination and split-second timing. As a liability, it can best be seen in the hypochondriac who, excessively preoccupied with the way his body is functioning, pays too much attention to the nonverbal cues he receives intrapersonally.

On countless occasions each day we petition our bodies for information —an effort to keep in touch with ourselves. When you awoke this morning, how did you know that everything was O.K. inside your body? Subconsciously, you probably ran a routine check on such matters as: (1) are my eyes working properly, (2) do my ears hear, (3) will my legs support me, or (4) can I feel all the parts I went to sleep with the night before? Satisfied that all was well on the basis of the nonverbal cues that were intrapersonally transmitted, you proceeded with the business of living. But not all of us are equally sensitive to these signals. For example, when final examination time rolls around on campus, nonverbal intrapersonal communication seems to reach epidemic proportions. Their nervous systems teeming with activity, certain susceptible students experience a wide range of strange feelings (such as a lump in the throat, cramps in the stomach, sweaty palms, or a dryness in the mouth). Others, less conscious of their nonverbal behavior, bite their fingernails to the quick and rest-

[5] Silvano Arieti, The Intrapsychic Self: Feelings, Cognition, and Creativity in Health and Mental Illness (New York: Basic Books, 1967).
[6] Abne M. Eisenberg and Ralph R. Smith, Nonverbal Communication (New York: Bobbs-Merrill, 1971), p. 59.

lessly pace back and forth. When their behavior is brought to their attention, they often say, "Gee, I didn't realize I was doing it. I guess I must really be nervous."

There are still other individuals who entertain an almost constant need to know how they look. Many spend more time than they would care to admit peering into a looking glass. With meticulous care, they examine themselves in great detail. Then there are those who find themselves preoccupied with their moving parts—wiggling their fingers, shrugging their shoulders, doing a deep knee bend from time to time. In the rare case, such a person performs these movements ritualistically, and they become an indispensable part of his lifestyle. The majority of us, fortunately, require only a modest amount of nonverbal feedback from our bodies in order to experience a sense of well-being. Only when this need becomes distorted or exaggerated is there a basis for concern.

Vocal Mode

The next time you, a friend, or member of the family moans or groans, sighs or cries, laughs or giggles, remember that you are witnessing examples of vocal intrapersonal communication. All are messages we send ourselves. Children at play are excellent sources of these extralinguistic sounds. Sitting by themselves in a corner, they can often be overheard simulating automobiles racing by, airplane crashes, and animals of every description. Unfortunately, the process of growing up (in our culture at least) demands that the majority of these vocal modes of intrapersonal communication be suppressed and treated as unbecoming the behavior of a mature adult.

To show you how a form of vocal intrapersonal communication can serve as a means of self-help, hear this. At a German University, a story is told about a very distinguished professor. It seems that each afternoon at about 3:00 P.M. he would religiously drive out into a nearby forest, remain there for approximately half an hour, and return. His students, dying to know what he did out there every day, decided to follow him. Here is what they saw. Arriving at a clearing, he would get out of his car, remove his coat and hat, open the collar of his shirt, and—LET OUT THE LOUDEST SCREAM HE COULD MUSTER. Then, in reverse order, he would return to the university. The explanation which accompanies this story is that he was by nature a quiet and introverted person who felt many things but let few of these feelings out. His daily scream acted, for him, as a catharsis—a safety valve enabling him to maintain his psychic equilibrium.

If you find the study of the sounds people make interesting, try monitoring your own for a day. Whereas their deeper psychological significance lends itself to a variety of interpretations, it is the superficial relationship of these sounds to *what you are doing* and *how you are feeling* that should warrant your attention. To start you in the right direction, list below some of the private sounds you know you make:

1. _____ 2. _____ 3. _____ 4. _____ 5. _____

If you are having some difficulty understanding what is being asked for here, imagine this scene. You have been running around all day and are really exhausted; what kind of a sound do you hear yourself making as you fall limply into your bed? Now think of yourself as being very, very thirsty and finally drinking a cold glass of Coke, beer, or chocolate milk. What kind of a sound do you hear yourself making under these circumstances? All things being equal, you should now have a better idea of what is involved when we speak of vocal intrapersonal communication.[7]

Without at least a superficial knowledge of how your senses operate, an understanding of verbal, nonverbal, and vocal intrapersonal communication is virtually impossible. Not only must you be familiar with the different types of senses that exist in the body, but with how they relay information from one place to another. Thus, to provide you with the necessary insight, let's begin with your own sense of self.

A SENSE OF SELF

When someone tells you that he feels "funny inside," what do you think it means in physical terms? Our vocabularies are chock full of expressions intended to reflect our sense of self. Here are a few to which you can add some of your own:

1. I'm just not myself today.
2. I feel so alone.
3. I feel so unreal.
4. _____
5. _____
6. _____

Obviously, to attempt a translation of these psychological states into physically identifiable components would be a monumental if not im-

---

[7] The term *vocal* is being used here to describe how extralinguistic sounds are capable of taking on their own meaning. In the next chapter, under the heading of *paralanguage*, its expanded use will include its function as a verbal modifier.

possible task. The best of poets would be hard pressed to describe in words of any kind, not to mention physical terms, the emotional condition we know as "being in love." In the final analysis, all we have to go on in order to test the validity of someone's saying, "I am in love" is the fact that they have said it. Furthermore, we are obliged to assume that their senses do not deceive them. People are prisoners of their senses; if their senses malfunction, the people malfunction.

This raises an interesting question: just how much should we trust our senses? Should they be trusted blindly or understood to be governed by certain physiological statutes of limitation? How do you feel about people who are willing to bet enormous sums of money on what their senses tell them? Did you know, for instance, that our eyes register only a very narrow range—roughly waves of between 800 and 390 millimicrons length (one millimicron is 1/1,000,000 millimeter, or 1/25,000,000 of an inch)—and that all other radiation is invisible to us? Add to this limitation of sight our limitation of hearing. We can hear no sound, strong as it may be, that vibrates fewer than fifteen or more than 20,000 times a second.[8] In spite of these data, most of us continue to have implicit faith in our senses—that is, our SENSE OF SELF. The legions of people who, based upon what they have seen or heard, will swear up and down that it is absolutely true are endless. "I saw it with my very own eyes" or "I heard it with my very own ears" are claims familiar to us all. Even more familiar is how indignant so many of these people become when the accuracy of their sense perceptions is challenged. Why they insist upon treating their senses as infallible is a question that shall have to go begging for an answer elsewhere. Perhaps if we took a look at some of the limitations imposed upon the sensory world (also known as *the unwelt* [oon-velt]) of certain other organisms with which we share space on this planet, we will gain a better insight into our own SENSE OF SELF.

Two completely different creatures, a bird and a caterpillar, are perched on the branch of a tree. Both have the same environment, but each lives in its private outside world. The bird keeps glancing about with its keen little eyes. Nothing that takes place on the highway or the nearby field escapes its watchful attention. It sees the bird of prey that circles high in the sky and the tiny mouse that rustles in the foliage below. The caterpillar, however, is unaware of all this activity. Nature has given the caterpillar a few quite rudimentary eyes, which can do little more than determine the direction from which the rays of the sun are coming, and whether the day is bright or cloudy. Moreover, the caterpillar is totally deaf, whereas for the bird, the air is filled with voices, among them the

[8] Wolfgang von Buddenbrock, *The Senses* (Ann Arbor: University of Michigan Press, 1958), pp. 9–10.

call of its own kind. The bird, on the other hand, is oblivious of certain distinctions that are vital to the caterpillar. To the bird it means absolutely nothing whether it is sitting in an oak, a linden, or a birch tree. But for the caterpillar there is a world of difference between the specie of one tree and another, for the leaves of one it considers a delicacy, while it would starve to death rather than eat as much as one leaf of another. So, you see, each form of life has its own unique outside world.[9]

But man is neither bird nor caterpillar. He is infinitely more complex. As an indication of this complexity, consider that his brain consists of over 13 billion cells; that if its folded cortex (the thinking portion) were spread out flat, it would cover more than two square feet (an area almost as large as the front page of your newspaper); that the brain of a five-week-old embryo has already advanced two hundred million years or more; that the Empire State building would not be large enough to house a computer with as many tubes as there are nerve cells in the brain—and that it would take Niagara Falls to cool it.[10] Thus, whether man, bird or caterpillar, an environment exists only in terms of the mechanism which perceives it.

Intrapersonal communication appears to draw its boundaries from our senses and the limitations they impose upon us. Our nervous system can process only the information it has the capacity to register, directly or indirectly. For example, whereas an animal will react to fire when confronted by it, Man is capable of experiencing this same reaction at the mere mention of the word "FIRE"—especially if it were shouted in a crowded theater. Hence, Man can intrapersonally modify his sense of self through direct contact with his environment and, indirectly, through the magic of the spoken word. Nevertheless, to succeed at any level, he must have the full support of his nervous system, a system that will now be explained.

NEURAL MONITORS

Few people realize that the expression, "I'm a bundle of nerves" accurately corresponds to the way things are in our bodies. Without nerves, we would be unable to move or feel; if we were not a bundle of nerves, life as we know it could not go on. Obviously, a thorough knowledge of the nervous system requires extensive training and study. This section of the text does not entertain such a goal. It does, however, seek to apprise the reader of its overall function and how it enables Man to coordinate his

[9] *Ibid.*, pp. 10–11.
[10] John Pfeiffer, *The Human Brain* (New York: Pyramid Publications, 1962), pp. 8, 12, 38, 238.

internal and external environments. To accomplish this, at least a basic familiarity with the nerves which monitor stimuli from our inner and outer worlds is necessary. Only by diligently studying these monitors can we even begin to appreciate some of the unique changes the body must make in order to survive, in the classroom as well as in the streets.

External Monitors

Physiological psychologists have demonstrated a growing interest in the mind-body relationship, their primary concern being to develop better ways of studying the nervous system and, by so doing, to enrich our understanding of the intrapersonal or intrapsychic process. The watchwords in this endeavor are *observation* and *experiment*.

As early as 1953, electrodes were implanted into human patients' brains. Different areas of the brains of several hundred patients were then stimulated, producing such sensations as: ease, and relaxation, joy, and great satisfaction. The stimulation of other brain centers caused patients to report feelings of: anxiety, restlessness, depression, fright, and horror.[11] These experiments encouraged other experiments now in progress.

From all appearances, however, any hope of understanding the agony which overcomes the mind and body of a person with a real-world problem such as speech fright will encounter many obstacles and require a heaping tablespoon of patience and tender loving care.

Picture yourself standing in front of a class ready to deliver a required speech. Your senses are alive with activity. Your neural monitors pick up stares from your classmates (sight); your teacher's voice saying, "You may begin now" (hearing); smoke from the cigarette being smoked in the first row (smell); that parchmentlike feeling in the mouth (taste); those sweaty and cold hands (touch). Taken together, you are indeed a *bundle of nerves*. All of these impulses, upon reaching your brain from the world around you, do not simply cease and desist. They can, and frequently do, reflexly cause other things to happen. Nausea, dizziness, palpitations of the heart, weak or knocking knees, butterflies in the stomach, and a sudden urge to urinate are commonplace among frightened speakers. Naturally, not everyone suffering from speech-fright manifests these particular symptoms. Much will depend upon how the individual is "neuroned"—that is, how his particular nervous system operates. Be aware that your nerves, aside from any genetic influence, are affected by such determinants as age, health, climate, ecology, conditioning and diet. Any one, or a combination, of these factors has the capacity to alter the physiological be-

---

[11] Dean E. Woolridge, *The Machinery of the Brain* (New York: McGraw, 1963), pp. 132–33.

havior of your nerves, with effects ranging from moderate discomfort to outright hysteria.

Internal Monitors

In addition to external monitors, you are also endowed with widely distributed internal monitors. Their job: to keep you posted on changes occurring within the body. Lack of an accurate and reliable communication between your internal and external monitors could result in a nervous breakdown.[12]

Wherever you are right now, close your eyes and raise your right arm above your head. Can you tell exactly where your arm is in space? Is it directly overhead, to the right, left, backwards, or directly in front of you? How do you know this? It is because of the proprioceptor nerves located deep in the muscles of your arm and shoulder. Whenever there is a change in joint position or tissue tension, these nerves are automatically fired and provide you with feedback—thus helping you remain spatially oriented.

Growing up, we all developed degrees of good and bad posture. In the military, drill sergeants are forever shouting, "Chest out, stomach in, shoulders back." For the average soldier, this becomes a conditioned reflex. In civilian life, without that drill sergeant on your back, postural integrity is found to vary from person to person. Whatever posture you assume on a daily basis becomes your postural norm.

If you will, please stand for a moment. This is probably your "postural norm." If you lean forward 10–15 degrees, you will feel awkward and experience a desire to straighten up. In someone with bad posture (a person who has been bent over for years), such a bent forward position may go unnoticed. His brain has accepted this posture as "normal"—for him. We all receive different messages from our internal and external monitors and, as a general rule, they take the line of least resistance. Ironically, this seemingly innocent bit of information is overlooked by most people. In fact, more often than not, people who walk and stand erect can't for the life of them understand why anyone has bad posture. A cartoon in a popular magazine once showed a man and his wife preparing to go out for the evening. Incidentally, the man was a hunchback. The caption over the wife's head read, "Please George, when we get to the party, will you please try and stand up straight?" A similar case involved a man who, as a result of a prior nerve condition, was numb on the left side of his face. He felt

---

[12] The term *nervous breakdown*, as used here, should not be taken to mean a breakdown in the traditional psychiatric sense but rather, a lack of harmony within the body resulting from neurological imbalance.

absolutely nothing on that side. When he ate, food particles often remained on his face without his being aware of them. To his misfortune, when he went out socially with strangers who were unfamiliar with his condition, he was written off as a slob at the dinner table. Naturally, after learning of his problem, they displayed the appropriate sympathy and courtesy. This dilemma, as you shall soon see, goes well beyond poor posture or crumbs of food on a cheek. It strikes at the very heart of the intrapersonal process.

Proprioceptors are a continual source of feedback from our mechanical as well as muscular systems. They contribute to the self-expression felt by the fat person, thin person, or the muscular person. Each senses a different SELF. Readers who are "weight watchers" know what this means. After losing 20 to 30 pounds, a new SELF emerges with which one must become reacquainted. A slogan well known among overweight people is "Inside every fat person there is a skinny one crying to get out."

Leaving proprioceptors, we move to the internal monitors which line the viscera (any of the bodily contained organs—usually referring to those found in the abdominal cavity, such as liver, spleen, gall bladder, and so on). You would be astonished at how many people are almost totally ignorant of what is inside their body, nor do they seem to give much of a damn. Would you believe that people have been known to come home from the hospital after surgery and not know what was removed from their bodies? Ask a few and see if the charge is not absolutely true. What is so incredible about this is that these same people would be furious if you dared invade their homes and, without their permission, take something. Yet, seemingly cool as a cucumber, they sign a release permitting a surgeon to remove a part of their body and neglect to ask what was taken out. Again the reader is urged to take more than a casual interest in his inner world as well as his outer one.

Return now to that picture of you standing in front of your class ready to give your speech, and speculate as to the condition of your internal monitors. Imagine that before coming to class you had (1) a hot dog with mustard and sauerkraut, a juicy slice of pizza and a chocolate shake for lunch; (2) a big fight with your mother about going away for the weekend; (3) convinced yourself that you were going to flunk this speech course. With all this gnawing at your innards, how do you think it might affect your intrapersonal communication? Unless you have a cast-iron stomach and nerves of steel, the possibility of overloading your nervous system is excellent. Anxiety and apprehension alone often give rise to such symptoms as nail biting, hand wringing, fidgeting, purposeless body movements, hair pulling, clothes fixing, finger drumming, and toe tapping. Add to these the hot dog, pizza, the fight with your mother, and the fear of flunking the course, and you have some real cause for concern. Each of these disturbances, to say nothing of them all together, can certainly shake up your internal monitors.

Internal monitors are named according to the function they perform —whether they respond to chemical changes, light, touch, or pressure. For 24 hours a day, 7 days a week, 12 months a year, every year of your life, these monitors (without interruption) feed information into your nervous system—information that provides a foundation for your self-awareness.

Monitors do not remain static. Different people have different peak periods—that is, times when they are most productive and energetic. They are either "larks" or "owls." The *larks* are most productive during the early morning hours and are rather lazy at night; the *owls* find it difficult to get up in the morning and reach their peak at night.[13]

As age advances, monitors lose some of their vitality. Vision dims, hearing fades, smell and taste wane. Cigarette smoking, vitamin deficiency, and disease also can affect the performance of these monitors. Coupled with these physiological and pathological inequities, cultural determinants should be included, since "body and culture mutually control one another."[14] The yogi, conditioned from childhood, is able to tolerate walking on hot coals; the jungle native, extreme heat; the Eskimo, cold; the Hunza, extremely high altitude. Each has been successful in adjusting to the demands peculiar to his culture. Another consideration is that the sensations produced by stimuli (heat, cold, pain, altitude) are not interpreted at the periphery, but when they reach the brain. That is to say, the impulses initiated by these stimuli are carried to the brain as common currency, and there, meanings are assigned. Sometimes our monitors fool us, as in the case of dry ice producing the feeling of heat instead of cold when it is applied to the skin.

While most scientists are fully aware of how man is being saturated with stimuli from the mass media, some have expressed special interest in the consequences of *sensory deprivation*—a phenomenon in which the effect of too little rather than too much stimulation is studied. Experiments involving the prevention of subjects from seeing, hearing, and feeling external stimuli have been performed and their results recorded and analyzed.[15]

[13] Gay Gaer Luce, "Understanding body time in the 24-hour city," *New York Magazine* (November 15, 1971), 39–43.

[14] Loren Eiseley, *The Immense Journey* (New York: Random, 1957), p. 132.

[15] J. C. Lilly, "Mental effects of reduction of ordinary levels of physical stimuli on intact healthy persons," in *Research Techniques in Schizophrenia*, Psychiatric Research Reports 5 (Washington: American Psychiatric Association, 1956), pp. 1–9.

Some years back the reactions of newborn babies in a hospital nursery were observed in relation to the way nurses handled them. Generally, it was believed that infants usually cry for two reasons: (1) when they are hungry and (2) when they need their diapers changed. However, in addition to these basic needs, researchers hypothesized that babies that were held, hugged, and cuddled fared better than those who were not. Following this hunch, "proxy mothers" were brought into the nursery, their function being to manually cater to some and not others. Results indicated that the infants who were extended more physical contact by the proxy mothers cried less and generally seemed more tranquil.

While such a conclusion is far from the last word on the subject, the study did spark an interest in the effects of *too much* and *too little* stimulation of the human organism. The coming of space travel then provided the perfect medium for further investigation of the subject. Away from the Earth's gravitational pull, our nervous systems become exposed to a variety of new and different kinds of environmental stress—among them, sensory deprivation. Some of the symptoms that have been associated with it are: (1) an intense desire for extensive sensory stimuli and bodily motion, (2) increased suggestibility, (3) impairment of organized thinking, (4) oppression and depression, and (5) in extreme cases, hallucinations, delusions and confusion.[16] In some cases a deficiency in external stimulation causes an individual to compensate from within through self-induced stimulation. In this way, a sensory equilibrium in the body is maintained. What happens is that people suffering from stimulus hunger become, in effect, their own "stimulus pushers."

Based upon the foregoing, behavior does not seem to be influenced solely by a bombardment of our internal and external monitors with a given amount of stimuli, but also by the manner in which our nervous systems integrate them.

INTEGRATORS

The term *integrators*, as used here, denotes those nerves which connect millions of other motor and sensory nerves in the central nervous system. Technically, they are referred to as connecting, internuncial, or intercalated neurons. But, for the purpose of simplification, we shall call them integrators.

Perhaps a few visual aids will help to maneuver these nerves into a more understandable perspective. Figure 3–1 is a schematic drawing of a motor nerve.

[16] P. Solomon et al., "Sensory deprivation: a review," *American Journal of Psychiatry* 114 (1957), 357–63.

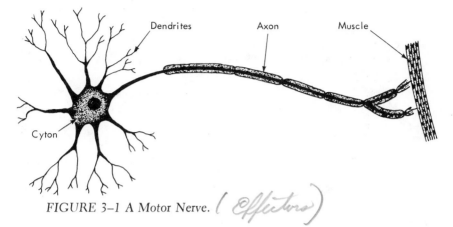

FIGURE 3–1 A Motor Nerve. (*Effectors*)

Now examine Fig. 3–2, a drawing of a sensory nerve:

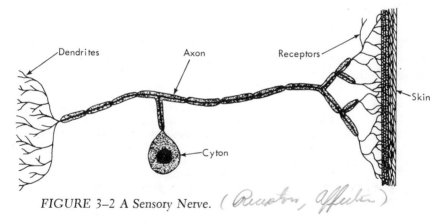

FIGURE 3–2 A Sensory Nerve. (*Receptors, Affectors*)

Proceeding on the assumption that these two simple drawings have created no anxiety in the reader, here is what they mean. The sensory nerves (or internal and external monitors as we have been calling them) are responsible for conveying information as to how we "feel." The motor nerves make it possible for us to move our bodies about. Figure 3–3 shows how a sensory and motor nerve look when they are joined in the body. Notice that the point at which they meet is called a synapse (see p. 58).

This might be a good time to ask a question concerned with the operation of your body. What is a "reflex arc"? Most students insist that they have heard of it but are hard pressed for a definition. It shall soon become apparent that, while not knowing the location of your liver is excusable, being ignorant of what a reflex arc is could represent a real barrier to under-

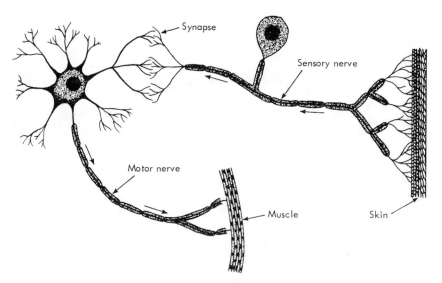

FIGURE 3–3 A Synapse between a Sensory and Motor Nerve.

standing the nature and function of integrator nerves. Therefore, to avert such a dilemma, here is a workable antidote requiring some of your imagination:

It is 3:00 A.M. and you are in a sound sleep. Startled by an unexpected ringing of the telephone, you literally jump out of bed and hurry to answer it before it wakes the entire household. But, as fate would have it, not only is the phone in the hall but, as you are about to reach it, you step on a tack. Naturally, unless you sleep with your shoes on, you are barefooted. Like a shot, you leap into the air and blurt out the appropriate remarks—/*#@&/#*, etc. Such a reaction involves the reflex arc (Fig. 3–4 p. 59).

As the point of the tack penetrates the skin on the sole of your foot, the sensory nerves found there are stimulated. Impulses are immediately sent to your spinal cord in the lower part of your back. From there, at incredible speed, a synapse is made with motor nerves (or effectors) which, in turn, release a volley of nerve impulses that pass down your leg and activate the muscles in the area. The Result: they contract, and suddenly you and the tack have parted company—all this through the courtesy of the reflex arc.

This, obviously, is only a very small part of what happens when someone steps on a tack. Usually, heart and respiratory rates are increased, pupils become dilated, adrenalin is released into the blood stream, muscle tone and blood pressure are elevated, and so on. Over and above these

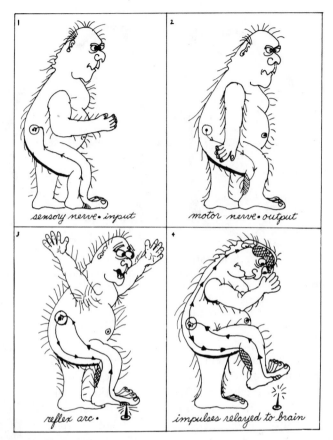

FIGURE 3–4 A Reflex Arc.

purely physiological responses, there are certain psychological questions such as: (1) who would call at 3:00 o'clock in the morning, (2) why was there that lousy tack on the floor, and (3) why didn't someone else in the house get up to answer the phone? For you to have experienced all of these thoughts, countless neurological connections had to be made in your brain and spinal cord. Most psychology students will remember this kind of neural activity in relation to the S-I-R (stimulus-integration-response) mechanism.

Throughout the central nervous system, acting as administrators of our internal affairs, are these "nerve bridges" which not only modify what we think and feel, but also how we behave. Figure 3–5 is a diagram showing a thick band of these integrator fibers called the corpus callosum. Their function is to transmit information from one hemisphere of our brain to the other.

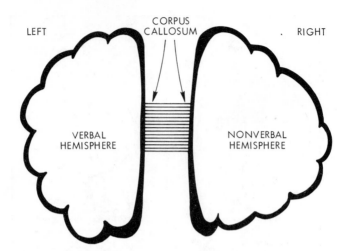

FIGURE 3–5 A Schematic Cross Section of the Brain. The surgical cutting of the corpus callosum constitutes the principal factor in what has recently come to be known as "split-brain studies." [See The Brain Changers; Scientists and the New Mind Control by Maya Pines (New York: Harcourt Brace Jovanovich, Inc., 1973).]

All of the material presented thus far occurs in the spinal cord where integrators make those connections necessary for everyday reactions to our internal and external environments. Your attention should now be directed to the brain, wherein an enormous amount of neurological activity goes on continuously. Millions of tiny nerves, whose purpose is to organize, store, and translate data into codes capable of sustaining an individual's psychological survival, travel in every direction. Any accidental or willful tampering with their structural or functional construction has the capacity to alter behavior. Figure 3–6 illustrates some of the ways these integrators may be affected (see p. 61).

Led by pioneer Roger Sperry, professor of psychology at California Institute of Technology, a great deal of research has been done on split-brain studies with monkeys, cats, and human beings. Essentially, the interest of those experimenting in this area focuses on how the brain stores and codes information. One of the working hypotheses shared by these researchers is that the right and left hemispheres of the brain are not the same. For example, they regard the right side as the "nonspeaking" hemisphere and the left hemisphere as "verbal, analytical, and dominant." Some of the questions that have been raised include: (1) Are the two halves of our brains integrated into a single soul? (2) Is one hemisphere

FIGURE 3–6 Modes of Behavior Modification.

always dominant over the other? (3) Do the two persons in our brains take turns at directing our activities and thoughts?[17]

One thought prevails throughout these studies—that our behavior is modified by the manner in which these various types of integrative fibers connect specific sectors of the brain and relay information to others. Further, that accidental or deliberate alterations of their structure could have a discernible effect upon our behavior.[18]

[17] Maya Pines, "We are left-brained or right-brained," *The New York Times Magazine*, September 9, 1973, pp. 32–37.
[18] Keep in mind that the research in this area is comparatively recent and thus extremely tentative at this point. It does, however, seem very promising for the future.

Until now, the majority of scientific research has treated such emotional states as anxiety, frustration, confusion, and indecision as psychological phenomena. The trend, as you have probably gathered, has veered in the direction of physical phenomena. As in the case of the split-brained studies, it might almost be accurate to say, "I've changed my minds," or, "I've got half a mind to . . . ."

We have entered a time in history when dissatisfaction with one's self is no longer hopeless. Formerly, an individual whose personality suffered a change causing him to become unhappy, disillusioned, and riddled with fears was written off as a loss. Today, an artificial personality can be created or a slightly bruised one patched up. Not only can our exterior be altered, but our interior as well. It is no longer necessary for anyone to suffer in silence—to commit "intrapersonal suicide." Society, recognizing the importance of keeping the inner man well ventilated, appears to have adopted a new philosophy: LET IT ALL HANG OUT. Skeletons closeted for years are now invited to come out, be examined, and be counted. In fact, there are circles in which it is considered "chic" to disclose some deep dark secret, fear, or guilt. However, if turning oneself inside-out is to become fashionable, some careful thought must be given to how it can be done with a minimum of risk and a maximum of benefit. This brings us to a consideration of the EFFECTOR nerves.

EFFECTORS

Every cell in the human body is limited to three responses to any stimulus: (1) acceleration, (2) deceleration, and (3) alteration. No matter what the stimulus is, both man and his cells are bound by certain structural and functional limitations. You can speak faster, slower, or differently; walk faster, slower, or differently. Similar alternatives are diagnostic of disease. In diabetes the pancreas produces too little insulin; in hyperthyroidism the thyroid gland produces too much thyroxin; in cancer the cells manifest abnormal growth and function. If we extend these alternatives to include the effects of drugs, it boils down to the same three consequences: they either speed up, slow down, or alter cellular activity. Even the practice of psychotherapy does not escape this basic formulation. Patients are observed to manifest either an increase, a decrease, or a change in their behavioral patterns.

While these references to therapy and disease are not directly related to communication, they do tangentially help us with our understanding of "normal" behavior. At random, now, turn your thoughts back to any recent social gathering at school. You should be able to recall the behavior of some friend or colleague. Verbally, nonverbally, or vocally, he may have behaved in some deviant fashion. To accomplish any of these behaviors, he employed either *voluntary* or *involuntary muscles*—the voluntary muscles being those over which he could exert conscious control, the involuntary muscles being beneath a conscious level and regulating such functions as heartbeat, digestion, circulation, respiration, and glandular action. While engaged in interpersonal communication, neither communicant can know for certain what is going on in the other person's head. Individually, each enjoys the exclusivity of a private "sense of self." It is only when these intrapersonal activities trigger certain body movements and gestures (voluntary and involuntary) that we can take the liberty of making inferences about a person's character or personality. In short, the only readily available barometer of someone's intrapersonal state seems to be muscular behavior. Standing side by side, the genius and the moron are difficult to tell apart as long as they are both prevented from making any muscular displays. Without cues from muscular behavior, judgments about an individual's internal state are extremely difficult to make.

The problem is not, however, insurmountable. During the dawn of medicine, physicians had only a cursory understanding of how the body operated internally. Except for the information they gained from human dissection, the rest was garnered largely through trial and error. They had no electron microscope, electrocardiogram, fluoroscope, sphygmomanometer, or any of the other modern diagnostic equipment. As far as they were concerned, man's inner world was steeped in myth and magic. Today, with the advent of medical electronics, we can not only look more deeply into ourselves but also exercise certain new forms of self-control. One of these is called BIOFEEDBACK.

Assume for a moment that you have high blood pressure and would very much like to lower it without taking drugs. Under biofeedback training, you would be hooked up to an instrument which monitors your blood pressure. If it increases, a little red light goes on—if it decreases, a green light goes on—if it remains stable, a yellow light goes on. In this fashion you are kept informed, through biofeedback, of the level of your blood pressure as long as you remain attached to the machine. Through trial and error, you discover that when you think peaceful and quieting thoughts, your pressure drops; when you think violent thoughts, it goes up. After a little practice, you find that you can exert reasonably good control over your blood pressure.

Some very promising results have recently come from a team of researchers at Harvard Medical School. In a clinical study, seven patients with high blood pressure were trained to lower it by themselves through the use of biofeedback training.[19] Numerous other reports like these can be found in the literature, describing how subjects were able to affect their heart rates, oxygen consumption, skin resistance to electricity, alpha rhythm in the brain, and muscle relaxation using biofeedback methods. Similar results have also been achieved through transcendental meditation, yoga, operant conditioning, or just plain "talking to oneself."

There is one important point to remember, and that this chapter should have driven home. Unless you keep the lines of communication with yourself open, someone in the future may have to be called in to repair them.

SUMMARY

Reading this chapter should not only have clarified certain misconceptions about intrapersonal communication, but also reinforced any prior appreciation of how important a role it plays in interpersonal communication.

After intrapersonal communication was defined (as conceived in this chapter), a plea was made for its inclusion in any and all interpersonal transactions. And, to insure against such an omission, a physiological look was taken into the body of a communicator while communicating with himself, as well as with others.

Using three familiar modes of intrapersonal communication—*verbal, nonverbal,* and *vocal*—as springboards, we explained how one arrives at a sense of self. Heavy emphasis was placed upon the importance of not relying on one's senses without at least a superficial understanding of their nature and limitations. From this theme, a discussion was developed of how a communicator's perceptions are translated into actions.

Next, the reader was introduced to his nervous system and how, specifically, certain nerves are responsible for receiving and transmitting information to and from the inner and outer worlds. These include *internal monitors,* which police the inner world, *external monitors,* the outer world, and *integrators,* serving to connect those nerves carrying incoming impressions with those carrying outgoing impressions. Lastly, *effectors* are nerves which make possible behavioral responses to both worlds.

The chapter winds down with references to biofeedback training, transcendental meditation, yoga, operant conditioning, and just plain talking to oneself as ways of facilitating self-control—all forms of intrapersonal communication designed to improve one's mental and physical health.[20]

[19] Gerald Jonas, *Visceral Learning: Toward a Science of Self-Control* (New York: Viking, 1973), p. 118.
[20] Get to know yourself better, you're all you've really got.

CHAPTER 4

EXTRAPERSONAL
COMMUNICATION

INSIGHTS

After reading this chapter you should have a clearer understanding of:

- *the extent to which people seriously communicate with
  animals, plants, and inanimate objects.*
- *why communication should not be a strictly people-to-
  people transaction.*
- *how richly our lives are bound up with nonhuman forms and
  the means we employ to communicate with them.*
- *the many ways the Atomic Age has forced us to communicate with machines.*
- *why certain individuals who have become disenchanted with
  mankind have turned a good measure of their attention to
  animals and plants.*

Many writers use the term "communication" as synonymous with "influence," as in the sense that any response to any stimulus involves "communication." Thus, communication in its most primitive form is said to occur whenever an organism (however automatically or unconsciously) responds to its environment. Advocates of this view make no distinction between the influential behavior of either animate or inanimate objects as parties in the process. The ability to engage in the communication process in this elemental manner is thus not limited to humans, since presumably lower forms of animal (and plant) life can respond to their ENVIRONMENTS in "meaningful" (as inferred by humans, at least!) ways.[1]

This chapter deals with the somewhat unorthodox subject of extrapersonal communication. It refers to those interactions which take place between man and animals, plants, and inanimate objects. The mere suggestion that extrapersonal communication should be considered a separate type of communication will probably encounter some resistance in certain quarters of the public mind. Let's face it, people who claim to communicate with their pets, plants, and cars are usually met with a patronizing smile or a raised eyebrow.

[1] From Robert Goyer "Communication Process: An Operational Approach," in *Perspectives on Communication*, ed. Carl E. Larson and Frank E. X. Dance. Milwaukee: Speech Communication Association, 1968, p. 21.

The process of communication immediately becomes suspect when it strays from a people-centered approach. It is interesting to speculate on exactly what grounds communication with nonhuman forms should be predicated; or a still better question might be, "What role, if any, should such communication play in our lives?" People seem to fall into four general categories with regard to extrapersonal communication: (1) those who accept the idea of man communicating with animals, but not with plants and inanimate objects; (2) those who accept the idea of man communicating with animals and plants, but not with inanimate objects; (3) those who accept the idea of man communicating with animals, plants, and inanimate objects; and (4) those who are so anthropomorphically chauvinistic that they flatly refuse to accept the idea, to say nothing of the act, of man communicating with anything other than his own species; these people feel that communication is a "strictly human, people-to-people affair."

Many people throughout the world find communicating with their pets and plants more gratifying than communicating with human beings. Others, at the outer limits of society, have become so disenchanted with mankind that they have turned all of their mental and physical attention toward inanimate objects. They become compulsive collectors of stamps, coins, butterflies, guns, pipes, dolls, and various other bric-a-brac who spend practically "all" of their waking hours involved with these objects. Each constitutes an extreme expression of extrapersonal communication.

Loneliness is universal. We have all been touched by it to varying extents. Stories about a famous actress of the silent film era who turned recluse illustrate the effects loneliness can have on communication. The scene is a familiar one. She lives alone in a big house filled with countless photographs, news clippings, records, costumes, and an assortment of cats, dogs and birds—a house full of memorabilia symbolizing a bygone era. Living in the past, she communicates verbally, nonverbally, and vocally with each of them. One day she might slip into a costume she wore in a favorite film and, for a little while, relive the moment; or she might thumb through several dozen old pictures. With a wide variety of *inanimata* from which to choose, she indulges in what is being referred to here as extrapersonal communication. Having withdrawn from the present, she, vicariously, bathes in the past.

In the anticipation that reactions to this chapter will not be unanimous, it might be wise to raise certain objections at the outset. The first deals with whether or not communication can exist between a *sender* and *receiver* employing different *codes*. Is it imperative that my dog and I use an identical symbol system in order for us to communicate? Obviously not. If I say, "Spot, give me your paw" (verbal code) and he responds by raising his paw and licking my hand (nonverbal code), communication appears to have occurred. The second question pertains to a phenomenon known as FEEDBACK. In plain language, this term refers to those *cues an encoder perceives as being emitted in response to him.*[2] Taken together, the licking of my hand (nonverbal feedback), the wagging of his tail (also nonverbal feedback), and his big brown eyes looking soulfully up at me all constitute forms of positive feedback. The use of the gestural language of the deaf by Washoe the chimpanzee, and the monitored clicking sounds made by Peter the dolphin (both to be described shortly) also qualify as bona fide types of feedback.

Extrapersonal communication encounters a little more resistance when it moves into the world of plants. Again the same objections arise (the absence of a shared code or symbol system and the nature of the elicited feedback). Since the anatomy and physiology of plants is different from that of man, it would be sheer nonsense to expect them to talk or wag their petals. However, since they are living things just as we are, they can communicate through variations in their growth, ability to reproduce, metabolism, and degree of irritability. Hence, the code used by plants seems inherent in their structure and function. The feedback from them, likewise, seems to utilize these same biological manifestations as components of their symbol system.

The final unit of this chapter will undoubtedly attract the greatest amount of resistance. In truth, while to some it might represent a highly charged emotional transaction, communicating with a car, photograph, mink coat, or piece of statuary cannot be considered communication in the accepted sense. Since both a shared code and the element of feedback, as we know it, do not seem to exist, extrapersonal communication between man and object will have to remain open to some rather lively argument.

Having made these opening remarks and hopefully whetted the reader's appetite, let us proceed to explore how people feel and behave toward a form of communication with nonhuman entities—animals, plants, and inanimate objects. Perhaps it will also precipitate a redefining of the word COMMUNICATION.

DEFINITIONS OF COMMUNICATION

To sharpen the meaning of the term *extrapersonal communication* in the reader's mind, here are some popular definitions of the word "communication." Included in each of these definitions are the key terms which help

[2] John R. Wenburg and William W. Wilmot, *The Personal Communication Process* (New York: John Wiley, 1973), p. 128.

convey their central meaning. They will be boxed so as to set them apart from the body of the definition.

EXAMPLE:
Communication is a ⬚process⬚ in which a
⬚message⬚ is ⬚transmitted⬚ .

Definition I
Communication means that ⬚information⬚
is ⬚passed⬚ from one ⬚place⬚ to another. . . .
In most communication ⬚systems⬚ the
⬚source⬚ of the information is a
⬚human being⬚ . From his ⬚past experience⬚
and ⬚present needs⬚ and ⬚perceptions⬚
this source has information to pass on to
others.[3]

Definition II
. . . the connecting thread appears to be the
idea of ⬚something's⬚ being ⬚transferred⬚
from one ⬚thing⬚ , or person, to another.[4]

Definition III
Communication: the
⬚discriminatory response⬚ of an
⬚organism⬚ to a ⬚stimulus⬚ .[5]

Definition IV
Communication: a "meeting" of
⬚meaning⬚ between two or
more ⬚persons⬚ .[6]

Definition V
. . . we sometimes slip into the error of
thinking that ⬚all communication⬚ must
be verbal communication.[7]

[3] George A. Miller, Language and Communication (New York: McGraw, 1951), pp. 6–7.
[4] A. J. Ayer, "What is communication?," Studies in Communication (London: Martin Secker and Warburg, 1955), pp. 12–13.
[5] S. S. Stevens, "A definition of communication," Journal of the Acoustical Society of America, XXII (1950), 689.
[6] Reuel L. Howe, The Miracle of Dialogue (New York: Seabury Press, 1963), pp. 21–22.
[7] Andrew W. Halpin, Theory and Research in Administration (New York: Macmillan, 1966), pp. 253–54.

Definition VI

… *the* | *process* | *of one*
| *individual's stimulating* | *meaning in*
the | *mind* | *of another individual by*
means of a | *message* |.[8]

Definition VII

Communication is a generally | *predictable* |,
| *multilevel* |, | *continuous* |, *and*
| *always-present* | *process of the* | *sharing* |
of meaning through | *symbol* |
| *interaction* |.[9]

Definition VIII

Communication: a process involving the
| *selection* |, | *production* |, *and*
| *transmission* | *of signs in such a way as*
to help a receiver | *perceive* | *a meaning*
similiar to that in the | *mind* | *of*
the communicator.[10]

Definition IX

Communication is the interpersonal
| *dissemination* | *of meaningful*
messages | *in a society* |.[11]

Definition X

Communication is a term used to refer
to | *any dynamic information* |
sharing process.[12]

Granting that one accepts these definitions, even provisionally, what boundaries for communication do they supply? One impression to be drawn is that communication need not be limited to humans. Also, the character of the message does not necessarily have to be verbal. Where the source

[8] James C. McCroskey, *An Introduction to Rhetorical Communication, The Theory and Practice of Public Speaking* (Englewood Cliffs, N.J.: Prentice-Hall, Inc., 1968), p. 21.
[9] Gail E. Myers and Michele T. Myers, *The Dynamics of Human Communication* (New York: McGraw, 1973), p. 12.
[10] Wallace C. Fotheringham, *Perspectives on Persuasion* (Boston: Allyn & Bacon, 1966), p. 254.
[11] Edward L. Brink and William T. Kelly, *The Management of Promotion* (Englewood Cliffs, N.J.: Prentice-Hall, Inc., 1965), p. 49.
[12] Theodore Clevenger, Jr., "What is communication?" Task Group Letter No. 2, NSSC Committee on Extant Theory, *Journal of Communication* 9 (March, 1959), 5.

is involved, such synonyms as *thing, person, individual, mind,* and *communicator* are offered. Substitutes for the *message* include: *information, something, stimulus,* and *behavior.* Interchangeable with the word *channel* are *passed, system, transferred, transmits,* and *disseminates.* Finally, other designations for a *receiver* remain essentially the same as those used for the sender (or source). Although *feedback* was conspicuously absent from all of the definitions of communication just cited, its role in the context of extrapersonal communication must not be overlooked.

These variations appear to warrant extending our conception of communication to include animals, plants, and inanimate objects. On the strength of such an assumption, this chapter will continue its efforts to persuade the reader to reconsider accepting this amended version of communication.

Amended definition of communication:

*Communication is that process which (1)
can exist beyond language as we know it,
(2) allows for both sender and receiver
to occupy the same body, (3) includes
subhuman and nonhuman forms, (4)
recognizes feedback from a receiver
employing a code different from that used by
the sender.*

COMMUNICATION BETWEEN MAN AND ANIMALS

Historically, Man has displayed some rather definite attitudes toward animals. Depending upon the time, place, and circumstance, he has used them for sacrificial purposes, objects of worship, beasts of burden, experimental subjects in the name of research, household pets, and entertainment. In each case Man in some way has communicated with animals (on the basis of our expanded definition of communication).

Just as there are people with green thumbs who are gifted with the ability to make things grow, there are those who have a "way with animals." Wherever they go, animals are drawn to them. By comparison, there are individuals who harbor a downright hate for animals, which the animals can usually sense. While few of these inferences can be scientifically validated, they provide a convenient basis for some of the generalizations made in the past.

A classic relationship between man and animal can be seen in certain families without children. Dogs and cats have been known to play the role of children, and the process becomes symbiotic: each serves a felt need of the other. Not all animals, however, lend themselves to such relationships. Cats are believed by some to be less suitable because they are more independent than dogs, and whatever care and attention they do require must be rendered "on their terms." Conversely, dogs appear more willing and better able to tolerate human idiosyncrasies than cats. It is this writer's understanding that psychiatry has recently been added to the practice of veterinary medicine. Wouldn't it be interesting to eavesdrop on a clinical interview between a veterinary psychiatrist and a basset hound or French poodle?

People communicate with animals verbally, nonverbally, and vocally, depending upon the animal's structural and functional makeup. Parakeets, parrots, and mynah birds fascinate people because of their ability to mimic sounds and voices. Jokes about talking birds have, for years, provided story tellers with humorous material. Communicating with animals who lack this ability to speak causes a shift of emphasis in the direction of nonverbal and vocal communication. Aside from the dog who nonverbally sits up and begs, gives its paw, or plays dead, there are those who vocally howl along with you when you sing certain tunes. Then there is the cowboy who, on thousands of feet of film, has provided moviegoers with various examples of man-to-horse communication. Legend also has it that some cowboys of the Old West spent more time communicating with their horses than with people.

What is there about certain animals that causes particular people to prefer them to humans? Could it be that some of these animals are more affectionate, faithful, loyal, sensitive, and loving than humans? In a recent class in group discussion, a strange topic arose. It dealt with the question of marrying out of one's species. At first, most of the students found the subject absurd and refused to participate. Others appeared to have a perverted curiosity and wanted to explore the topic further. A consensus finally prevailed and the discussion got under way. The first step was to list those items which the majority of the class agreed were necessary for a "good marriage." To everyone's surprise, with the exception of sexual intercourse and childbearing, criteria like loyalty, respect, affection, devotion, sympathy, protectiveness, and love could all be supplied by the average pet in good standing. After a while, the topic seemed to attract a larger following than it had at the outset. Although the entire discussion was performed with "tongue-in-cheek," it proved to be both novel and exhilarating.

Myths about gods and demigods who were part man, part animal reach far back in time. Among those worshiped by the Egyptians was *Anubis*, who was supposed to care for the entombed and perform the part of the conductor of departed spirits. He was represented as having the body of a man with the head of a jackal. Another was *Horus*, the sun god, with the head of a hawk and the body of a man. Among the Greek gods was *Pan*, son of Hermes, who was a noisy, merry god with the horns and hoofs of a goat. The centaur—half man, half horse—was also greatly romanticized by the Greeks. Our physical and psychological involvement with animals goes deeper than many of us realize. We seem divided into two camps: (1) those who consider man little more than an animal with a highly developed forebrain, and (2) those who think that man is endowed with something extra such as a soul or spirit. Freud, in his psychoanalysis of dreams, devotes considerable space to the role animals play in our psychic world. Among these, he speaks of how children, brothers, and sisters are symbolized in dreams as little animals or vermin. He also proposed that male symbols occur as reptiles, fishes, and serpents.[13] These are but a few of the animals he assigns to man's mental menagerie.

Evidence of our preoccupation with animals often crops up in our language. Try this exercise and prove it to yourself. Complete each of the following phrases by writing whatever pops into your mind. Then, compare your answers with other members of your class:

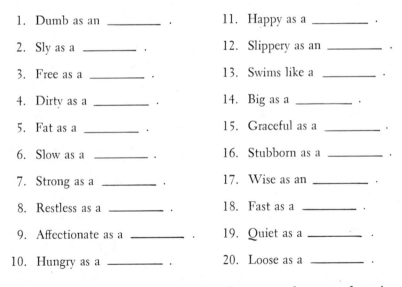

1. Dumb as an _____ .

2. Sly as a _____ .

3. Free as a _____ .

4. Dirty as a _____ .

5. Fat as a _____ .

6. Slow as a _____ .

7. Strong as a _____ .

8. Restless as a _____ .

9. Affectionate as a _____ .

10. Hungry as a _____ .

11. Happy as a _____ .

12. Slippery as an _____ .

13. Swims like a _____ .

14. Big as a _____ .

15. Graceful as a _____ .

16. Stubborn as a _____ .

17. Wise as an _____ .

18. Fast as a _____ .

19. Quiet as a _____ .

20. Loose as a _____ .

If we add to these the countless children's nursery rhymes and stories, such as Alice in Wonderland, Androcles and the Lion, Tarzan of the Apes, you should get at least an inkling of how perfused our lives are with animals.

13 *A General Introduction to Psychoanalysis*, ed. Joan Riviere (New York: Perma Giants, 1949), pp. 137–39.

For children, communicating with animals represents an integral part of their reality which does not always disappear upon reaching maturity. Many adults continue to enjoy cartoons and films in which animals communicate with people, such as Cinderella and all her little animal friends, Alice in Wonderland talking with the white rabbit and the Cheshire cat, or Pinocchio chatting with Jiminy Cricket.

Another aspect of our behavior toward animals concerns using them as food. Our sensitivities will allow us to eat certain animals and not others. There is a perfectly revolting little story which, though probably untrue, makes its point with regard to the eating of animals. It seems an American couple were traveling through China just after World War II and stopped at a restaurant to eat. Unfamiliar with the language, they were completely at the mercy of the natives. After finishing their dinner, they wanted a few scraps for their pet poodle. Unable to make themselves understood, they resorted to some good old-fashioned sign language. With great care and precision, the husband first pointed to their pet, then to his mouth, and then to the dish on the table. After several demonstrations the waiter's eyes suddenly opened wide, a smile jumped to his face, and he gingerly scooped up their little pet and disappeared into the kitchen. Satisfied they had finally communicated with the waiter, the couple patiently waited for the return of their dog and a doggie bag filled with the scraps they had requested. About ten minutes passed and the waiter returned carrying a large tray with a lid on it. As he placed it on the table before them and proudly raised the lid, the woman promptly passed out cold! That's right, you guessed it, there on the tray in a special sauce . . . . There's no need to go any further, you know what happened. It seems that in China, dog (as well as cat) stimulates rather than depresses the appetite.[14]

Now pretend that you are a world traveler and seated in an international restaurant serving foods from all corners of the Earth. Look over the menu on page 75 and decide what you will order when the waiter comes over to serve you. Remember, price is no object—the other fellow is picking up the check.

If you are like most Americans, the items listed in the menu will prompt you to say, "No thank you" to the waiter and simply order a cup of coffee or tea. The object lesson here, once again, is that even the word descriptions of culturally different foods are enough to turn you, as well as your stomach, away.

As if this were not enough, Man has used certain animals in the treatment of disease. During the seventeenth century, for example, one of the

---

[14] To the best of this writer's knowledge, it is against the law for any establishment to sell or serve dog or cat. During wartime, or perhaps when there was a scarcity of food, the practice probably prevailed. For further information, contact the Chinese Embassy.

M-E-N-U

Appetizers

Hummingbird tongues dipped in rose honey	2.75
Cubed snake en brochette in spicy sauce	3.25

Entré

Braised calf brains	8.95
Baked dog stuffed with apples, raisins, and almonds	8.50
Poached goats eyes	7.75
Stuffed mountain oysters	7.95
Kangaroo Bourguignon	12.00
Baked baby birds in herbed lemon sauce	10.95
Unborn monkey (must be ordered 24 hours in advance): price according to weight	

Dessert

Crisply fried baby bees and ants dipped in chocolate	4.00
Grasshoppers and locusts with golden honey	3.00

Wine

Egri Bikaver (bull's blood)	half bot,	8.25
	whole bot,	14.00

less pleasant concoctions was oil of puppies made by cutting up and boiling two newly born puppies, with earthworms, in oil. This [it was claimed] cured paralysis and was a nerve tonic.[15] The history of medicine jingles with similar remedies that would stagger your imagination.

In health or disease, our behavior toward animals subconsciously betrays a subliminal trace of animalism in us all. Such expressions as "John, you behaved like a beast last night," or "What an animal Herbie turned out to be," suggest not only a preoccupation with animal-like behavior, but a tendency to consider it a liability rather than an asset. Accusing someone of behaving like an animal could be taken as an insult to animals by some people. Anatomical descriptions such as webbed feet, pigeon-toed, chicken breasted, and canine teeth all reinforce the belief that we still cling to a facet of our self-image that is animalistic.

A famous case illustrating this unwillingness to be equated with animals was the Scopes Trial or Monkey Trial, as it was called. In July of 1925 in Dayton, Tennessee, a young school teacher named Scopes was dismissed for teaching Darwin's theory of evolution—that man descended from the

[15] Richard Mathison, *The Shocking History of Drugs* (New York: Ballantine Books, 1958), p. 66.

apes. According to Tennessee law, it was considered illegal for any teacher to espouse an explanation of man's creation conflicting with the *Bible* version. The case drew worldwide attention to the extent that the famous trial lawyer, Clarence Darrow, offered to defend young Scopes. For the prosecution the brilliant orator, William Jennings Bryan, stepped forward. Dayton teemed with activity. People packed the courtroom, holding up signs and banners caricaturing man's descent from the apes. After some intensive examination and cross-examination, Scopes was found guilty and fined. A thrilling play entitled *Inherit the Wind* was presented by Herman Shumlin in association with Margo Jones at the National Theatre, New York City, April 21, 1955, based on this trial.

Today, nearly a half century later, man has revised his attitude toward animals somewhat. No longer does he arbitrarily consider them unintelligent and the object of his whim. Through research, he has learned that certain animals are capable of moderately sophisticated levels of intellectual activity. However, before any communication with them could be attempted, specific considerations had to be entertained. For example, how close in size was the brain of the animal? Man's brain weighs approximately 1700 grams compared to the chimpanzee with 375 grams, the dolphin with 1700 grams, and the elephant with 6075 grams. Other factors include: (1) the physical structure of the animal's body and brain, (2) its possession of a language of its own, (3) whether it could learn our language if necessary, (4) whether it came from an environment similar to ours, and (5) whether its vocal apparatus was able to reproduce human sounds. In many ways, the chimpanzee qualifies nicely. According to distinguished scientists such as Dr. Grafton Elliot Smith, "No structure found in the brain of the ape is lacking in the human brain; and, on the other hand, the human brain reveals no formation of any sort that is not present in the brain of the gorilla or chimpanzee."[16] In only one area is the chimpanzee deficient—its vocal apparatus. Not only is its apparatus different from ours, but its vocal behavior differs as well. While the chimpanzee does make many different sounds, they generally occur during periods of great excitement and tend to be situation-specific. In fact, undisturbed chimpanzees are usually silent.

In a book entitled *Ape in Our House*, Keith and Cathy Hayes tell about the time they took a baby chimpanzee named Vicki into their home and treated her as a human child. Using modern techniques, they spared no effort teaching Vicki to speak human sounds. Unfortunately, in six years, Vicki was able to make only four sounds which approximated English words. In one respect, however, the chimp is extremely desirable—in its ability to gesture, which figures prominently in its normal behavior. Taking

[16] Geoffrey H. Bourne, *The Ape People* (New York: Putnam, 1971), p. 318.

advantage of this characteristic, Professors Allen and Beatrice Gardner, at the University of Nevada, decided upon an experiment which consisted of trying to teach the chimpanzee the gestural language of the deaf. The chimpanzee's name was Washoe and its age was between 8 and 14 months. As a criterion of acquisition, the Gardners chose a reported frequency of at least one appropriate and spontaneous occurrence each day over a period of 15 consecutive days. By the end of the twenty-second month of the project Washoe displayed 30 of the signs listed in the accompanying chart (Fig. 4–1)—to which four more were added that did not meet the criteria. At the completion of the study, Washoe displayed at least 28 of the 34 signs listed on at least 20 days. Further, she was able to transfer signs (for example, from the dog sign to the sound of barking by an unseen dog) and use signs in combination with other signs. It would be most interesting to see whether an average college student, using only those signs mastered by Washoe, could get through a typical day on campus. Think of each sign in an imaginary context and speculate as to the difficulties that might arise.

Still another chimpanzee named Lana deserves our attention. At the Yerkes Regional Primate Research Center associated with Emory University, she is rapidly learning how to read and write with the help of a computer. When Lana presses large colored keys on which there are different geometric forms, symbols flash overhead on a screen, reproducing their English equivalents on a teleprinter in a nearby room. For example, if she pressed the symbol for M & M chocolates, a piece of the candy would drop from a vending unit. A next stage required that before pressing the M & M key, she first pressed the please key, and then the period key. Failing to hit all three keys in the proper sequence would deny her the candy. This was not all. Lana was then taught to press such verb keys as give and make before allowed to have her reward. Soon she was constructing entire sentences. To test her ability to read the overhead screen, her tutors would flash incomplete sentences and Lana would be obliged to punch out the correct completion. When they tried to trick her, she would press the period key which would automatically clear the computer and the screen. Psychologist Duane M. Rumbaugh of Georgia State University speculates this way: "Perhaps one day Lana or another chimp can act as an interpreter between their world and ours,"[17]—a living example of extrapersonal communication in the making (see pp. 78–80).

In contrast to the chimpanzee, the dolphin is able to mimic the human voice rather well. Look at the marked similarity between the oscillographic recordings of the human voice and those of the dolphin (Fig. 4–2).

[17] "Lessons for Lana," Time 103:9 (March 4, 1974), 74.

FIGURE 4-1 Signs Used Reliably by Chimpanzee Washoe Within 22 Months of the Beginning of Training.[18] The signs are listed in the order of their original appearance in her repertoire (see text for the criterion of reliability and for the method of assigning the date of original appearance).

Signs	Description	Context
Come-gimme	Beckoning motion, with wrist or knuckles as pivot.	Sign made to persons or animals, also for objects out of reach. Often combined: "come tickle," "gimme sweet," etc.
More	Fingertips are brought together, usually overhead. (Correct ASL form: tips of the tapered hand touch repeatedly.)	When asking for continuation or repetition of activities such as swinging or tickling, for second helpings of food, etc. Also used to ask for repetition of some performance, such as a somersault.
Up	Arm extends upward, and index finger may also point up.	Wants a lift to reach objects such as grapes on vine, or leaves; or wants to be placed on someone's shoulders; or wants to leave potty-chair.
Sweet	Index or index and second fingers touch tip of wagging tongue. (Correct ASL form: index and second fingers extended side by side.)	For dessert; used spontaneously at end of meal. Also, when asking for candy.
Open	Flat hands are placed side by side, palms down, then drawn apart while rotated to palms up.	At door of house, room, car, refrigerator, or cupboard; on containers such as jars; and on faucets.
Tickle	The index finger of one hand is drawn across the back of the other hand. (Related to ASL "touch.")	For tickling or for chasing games.
Go	Opposite of "come-gimme."	While walking hand-in-hand or riding on someone's shoulders. Washoe usually indicates the direction desired.
Out	Curved hand grasps tapered hand; then tapered hand is withdrawn upward.	When passing through doorways; until recently, used for both "in" and "out." Also, when asking to be taken outdoors.
Hurry	Open hand is shaken at the wrist. (Correct ASL form: index and second fingers extended side by side.)	Often follows signs such as "come-gimme," "out," "open," and "go," particularly if there is a delay before Washoe is obeyed. Also, used while watching her meal being prepared.
Hear-listen	Index finger touches ear.	For loud or strange sounds: bells, car horns, sonic booms, etc. Also, for asking someone to hold a watch to her ear.

18 Allen Gardner and Beatrice Gardner, "Teaching sign language to a chimpanzee," Science 165 (August 15, 1969), 668–69, Table 1. Copyright 1969 by the American Association for the Advancement of Science.

FIGURE 4–1 (Cont.)

Signs	Description	Context
Toothbrush	Index finger is used as brush, to rub front teeth.	When Washoe has finished her meal, or at other times when shown a toothbrush.
Drink	Thumb is extended from fisted hand and touches mouth.	For water, formula, soda pop, etc. For soda pop, often combined with "sweet."
Hurt	Extended index fingers are jabbed toward each other. Can be used to indicate location of pain.	To indicate cuts and bruises on herself or on others. Can be elicited by red stains on a person's skin or by tears in clothing.
Sorry	Fisted hand clasps and unclasps at shoulder. (Correct ASL form: fisted hand is rubbed over heart with circular motion.)	After biting someone, or when someone has been hurt in another way (not necessarily by Washoe). When told to apologize for mischief.
Funny	Tip of index finger presses nose, and Washoe snorts. (Correct ASL form: index and second fingers used; no snort.)	When soliciting interaction play, and during games. Occasionally, when being pursued after mischief.
Please	Open hand is drawn across chest. (Correct ASL form: fingertips used, and circular motion.)	When asking for objects and activities. Frequently combined: "Please go," "Out, please," "Please drink."
Food-eat	Several fingers of one hand are placed in mouth. (Correct ASL form: fingertips of tapered hand touch mouth repeatedly.)	During meals and preparation of meals.
Flower	Tip of index finger touches one or both nostrils. (Correct ASL form: tips of tapered hand touch first one nostril, then the other.)	For flowers.
Cover-blanket	Draws one hand toward self over the back of the other.	At bedtime or naptime, and, on cold days, when Washoe wants to be taken out.
Dog	Repeated slapping on thigh.	For dogs and for barking.
You	Index finger points at a person's chest.	Indicates successive turns in games. Also used in response to questions such as "Who tickle?" "Who brush?"
Napkin-bib	Fingertips wipe the mouth region.	For bib, for washcloth, and for Kleenex.
In	Opposite of "out."	Wants to go indoors, or wants someone to join her indoors.

FIGURE 4-1 (Cont.)

Signs	Description	Context
Brush	The fisted hand rubs the back of the open hand several times. (Adapted from ASL "polish.")	For hairbrush, and when asking for brushing.
Hat	Palm pats top of head.	For hats and caps.
I-me	Index finger points at, or touches, chest.	Indicates Washoe's turn, when she and a companion share food, drink, etc. Also used in phrases, such as "I drink," and in reply to questions such as "Who tickle?" (Washoe: "you"); "Who I tickle?" (Washoe: "Me.")
Shoes	The fisted hands are held side by side and strike down on shoes or floor. (Correct ASL form: the sides of the fisted hands strike against each other.)	For shoes and boots.
Smell	Palm is held before nose and moved slightly upward several times.	For scented objects: tobacco, perfume, sage, etc.
Pants	Palms of the flat hands are drawn up against the body toward waist.	For diapers, rubber pants, trousers.
Clothes	Fingertips brush down the chest.	For Washoe's jacket, nightgown, and shorts; also for our clothing.
Cat	Thumb and index finger grasp cheek hair near side of mouth and are drawn outward (representing cat's whiskers).	For cats.
Key	Palm of one hand is repeatedly touched with the index finger of the other. (Correct ASL form: crooked index finger is rotated against palm.)	Used for keys and locks and to ask us to unlock a door.
Baby	One forearm is placed in the crook of the other, as if cradling a baby.	For dolls, including animal dolls such as a toy horse and duck.
Clean	The open palm of one hand is passed over the open palm of the other.	Used when Washoe is washing, or being washed, or when a companion is washing hands or some other object. Also used for "soap."

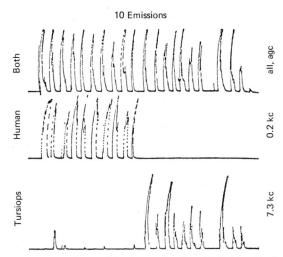

10 Emissions

Both — all, agc

Human — 0.2 kc

Tursiops — 7.3 kc

FIGURE 4–2 Oscillographic Record of a Dolphin Exchange Showing Ten Bursts of Sound Emitted by the Human Matched by Ten Bursts of Sound Emitted by the Dolphin.[19]

The upper trace shows all of the sounds emitted by both the man and the dolphin; the second trace, those by the man only; the lower trace, those emitted by the dolphin. It is to be noted that the delay between the end of the human presentation and the beginning of the dolphin reply is of the same order of magnitude as the interburst silences in the human presentation. This is a selected portion of a very long experiment in which numbers of bursts of sound emitted by the human were varied from 1 to 10 and the replies of the dolphin were from 1 to 10. [See J. C. Lilly, "Vocal mimicry by the dolphin," *Science* 147 (1965), 300–301.]

Paradoxically, whereas the chimpanzee more closely approximates man with regard to structure and environment, it lacks the vocal ability to reproduce the human voice; the dolphin has this capacity, but lacks the structural and environmental compatibility with man. Nevertheless, communication with both has been attempted and has met with reasonable success.

Margaret Howe, who lived in a tank with a dolphin named Peter, engaged in a dialogue with him over a period of two and one half months. Figure 4–3 is an attempt to transcribe portions of the tapes she made during her vocal interactions with Peter Dolphin. It is not an effort to accurately describe the exact sounds made by the dolphin, but rather to show the progress, over a period of several months, that took place between the human and the dolphin in a pupil-teacher relationship.

The transcription method is set up as follows:

1. Two lines are read at a time, as in a staff of music. One line is MH (Margaret Howe), and the other line is PD (Peter Dolphin).
2. The symbol c is used to designate a click, whistle, or any other form of "delphinese." Thus a series of clicks may be written ccccccc. An exact count of the clicks is not represented here, and cccccc does not mean six clicks . . . it simply means a series of clicks.
3. The symbol x is used to designate a humanoid sound made by the dolphin which is *not a clear enough humanoid to accurately describe phonetically.* This is a humanoid attempt by the dolphin.
4. When the humanoid attempt is clear enough to be written phonetically in English, it is described as best as possible. Thus "oie" may be an attempt at "boy" . . . without the "b."
5. Instructions to Peter spoken by MH are in lower case, and words to be copied by Peter are in capitals. Thus, "Peter, please say HELLO MAGRIT."
6. Brief summary notes follow each transcription.
7. These transcriptions are of only the airborne sounds as they are recorded on the tapes. All underwater sounds are kept out of this account.

THE MIND OF THE DOLPHIN

Sample Seven Months before 2½-Month Experiment
(November 3, 1964)

```
MH   SPEAK GOOD   SPEAK GOOD BOIE       Good, Peter, good!
PD                  cccc              ccccxx xx

MH   Now you're going!   Yes,                    SPEAK
PD                      cccccccccxxx ccccccccccxxx  ccccccccxxoi

MH   Good boy!  SPEAK GOOD BOIE   SPEAK GOOD BOIE.
PD                cccc            xx
```

Dr. Lilly (JCL) has just arrived and Peter is taking a break to see what's happening.

```
MH   SPEAK      GOOD BOIE      Good boy. (JCL in background)
PD   cccccccccc          cccc xx xx

MH   Did you hear that?    Speak GOOD BOIE          SPEAK
PD                        cccc  c c c c c c c c c c ccccc

MH   GOOD BOIE    SPEAK GOOD      (Giggle)     yes, come on,
PD              xxx           xxxxx        oii

MH   take a fish       (JCL voice in background) MH and JCL chat.
PD         xxxxxxcccc
```

FIGURE 4–3 Vocal Exchanges Between Teacher and Dolphin.

```
MH   SPEAK GOOD BOIE   SPEAK GOOD BOIE       (JCL in back-
PD              xx              ccc              xxx
MH   ground) Who is that, Peter? (JCL voice) Come on . . . SPEAK
     GOOD BOIE
PD
MH   (JCL voice) SPEAK        GOOD BOIE
PD               cccccccc              ccccc
```

1. Repetition of SPEAK GOOD BOIE by Margaret over and over, an attempt to get Peter to respond in humanoid.
2. Peter responds mainly in delphinese clicks . . . only a few humanoids.
3. Peter often speaks (clicks) while Margaret is still speaking.
4. Lesson is interruptible . . Peter and Margaret are not "meshing gears" . . . there is a rather loose structure to the lesson.

Sample Six Months before 2½-Month Experiment

```
MH   Sssssshhh I AM SUCH A GOOD BOIE
PD                     cccccccxxxxccc ccxxxx xxx xx (shrill)
MH   No, Peter, sssshhh. SPEAK GOOD       No, no. Shhhh SPEAK
PD                     xxxxxx (shrill)
MH   GOOD BOIE FOR FISH        shhh DO NOT PLAY
PD               xxxxxcccxx (shrill) cccc      ccccccccccccccc
MH   shhhhhhh, Peter, DO NOT PLAY    Yes, sshhhh SPEAK GOOD
PD               cccccxxxxxccxxx xxx
MH   BOIE      SPEAK GOOD BOIE           John, that telephone
PD   cccccc xx cc              xxxx (shrill)
MH   is ringing. SPEAK FOR FISH GOOD BOIE    HELLO ELVAR
PD                     ccccxxxx (weak)
MH   HELLO ELVAR            SPEAK AND EAT
PD            c ccc xxx lo xxx        xxxx cccccc xx (shrill)
MH   No no, sssssshhhh    ssssshhhh  SPEAK AND EAT      SAY
PD            c c c x x x c c c x x x      xxxxxx cccccxxxx   C
MH   GOOD BOIE     SAY GOOD BOIE        ssshh come on,
PD            CCCCCCC          ccccccccccccccccccxx    xxxxccxx
MH   I MUST SPEAK FOR FISH   I WILL SPEAK AND EAT NOW
PD               xxxxx cccc xxx      ccccc     ccc xxx (shrill)
MH   sssshhhh, no Peter            I WILL SPEAK AND EAT
PD            ccccxx (shrill blasts)        cccccxxxxx (shrill)
```

1. Peter is still doing a lot of delphinese clicking.
2. He is beginning to give a few more humanoids, but these are in the form of shrill blasts.
3. He still interrupts Margaret and vocalizes while she speaks.

Five Months Previously (January 5, 1965)

```
MH   AIR OWN EMM    SAY NO ETCH EIM     SIGH IT ARE
PD   cccc cc        cc xxx xx           xx cc xxx
```

FIGURE 4–3 (Cont.)

MH	I'll go from lesson eleven back into lesson
PD	xxxx ccc xxx

MH number eight   listen   TOI   OIT   OICH
PD   ccc xxxx cc xxx   c c   c c xxx cc

MH CHOIE OIT   COIE OIT COIE TOIE
PD   c c c c ccccc xxxxx xxxx   xxxx ccc xxxxx

MH say GOOD BOIE GOOD BOIE   OIEZ ZOIE OIS CHOIE
PD   ccc xx   xxxxx ccc xxx

MH   OIE Peter, say BOIE . . . GOOD BOIE   I AM A
PD ccc xxxxx   xxxxcccxxxxx   ccc

MH GOOD BOIE   SPEAK GOOD BOIE   TOIE
PD   c c c c c xxxxx cccc xxxx   ccc xxxx xxx

MH OIE SOIE ROIE   OIE say OIE   GOOD
PD   cccc xxxxx ccc xxx c c   xxxx c

MH BOIE·   OIM MOI LOI OIT   OIL   murmur
PD   cccc xxxx ccc   cxxxx   xxxxx

MH OIL LOI ROI OIK   Listen . . . OIL LOI ROI OIK
PD   ccc xxx ccc xx   xx oi xx c

MH OIZ ZOI OIS CHOI   (murmur) OIL LOI ROI OIK
PD   xxx ow xxx   xx xx xxx xxx xxxx

MH say GOOD BOIE nope . . . GOOD BOIE GOOD BOIE (high)
PD   ccc xxx xxx   xxxxxxxxx

1. Peter is giving more and more humanoid responses. Still some clicks.
2. Peter interrupts occasionally, but is getting a nice sense of listen, speak, listen, speak.
3. Words used by Margaret are from a nonsense syllable list designed to present combinations of sounds to the dolphin.

MH Peter, say HELLO yes . . . say GOOD BOIE . . . GOOD BOI . . .
PD   ccxxxx xxlo

MH Come on, Peter, say GOOD BOIE Nice. English, Peter, pronounce.
PD   xxxccxxxccxxx xx xx

MH Say MARGARET . . . come on MA No! Listen. MARGARET Not
PD   cccvv xx   xxxxx xxc

MH very good say HELLO That's better say HELLO MARGARET
PD   ccc   xxaw baw   cccc

MH   uh uh . . . listen, listen HELLO MARGARET   nice
PD cccxx uh uh uh   awxxx e

MH nice   listen listen listen say HELLO GOOD BOY
PD   awxxxx ccccc c c c c c c c c   cc c ccxxxw aw xxx

MH We are going to speak English yet, Peter . . . say HUMANOID . . .
PD

MH HUMANOID No! That's not right. Say . . . BALL   No! Listen
PD   xxxxx   awxxx

FIGURE 4–3 (Cont.)

MH   Listen, listen   BALL   O.K. HELLO   uh uh uh
PD   cccccxxx   cccccccxxxxaw   cc uh uh
MH   listen listen HELLO   Uh uh Peter, I don't mean to bore you
PD   cc   xxxxxxxx
MH   but you say it right and then we'll go on. Hmmm? You didn't say it
PD
MH   right. Now listen. HELLO   Pretty good, pretty good.
PD   xxxx xx   ccccxxx
MH   n'uh un uh now listen, listen listen listen Peter sssssh, say
PD   c c c c c c c   c c c c c   xx
MH   MARGARET uh uh no! Wrong MARGARET.
                        Peter! That's noise!
PD   ccc uh uh uh xx uh   uh uh uh xxx

1. Peter still clicks, but mainly humanoid.
2. Some of his humanoids are beginning to shape into English sounds.
3. Peter still interrupts Margaret, but occasionally hushes when told to.
    Whole lesson is shaping up.

After Ten Days of Living Together Twenty-four Hours per Day (*June 8, 1965*)

MH   Say . . . MAGRIT   all right   ssssssh   listen listen no!
PD   ccccc xxx xxx   xxx xxxx   x x x x x x x x x x
MH   Listen! Listen, Peter! Listen no! Listen Peter! sshhhh
PD   xxx   xxxowxxxxxxxx xxxxxxxx xx
MH   HELLO MAGRIT   GOOD BOIE GOOD BOIE Come on . . .
PD   xxx   xx   xxxx xxxxx
MH   Listen, listen. no no no . . . say GOOD BOIE
PD   xxxx xxx xxxxxx   xx xxxxbxxxxxxxx
MH   Peter! Listen to me! Now stop it! no! no! no! Listen
PD   x x x x x x x x x x x x x x x x x x x x x x
MH   Peter, shhhh shhhh   say GOOD BOIE   Oh, he just won't
PD   x x x x x x x x x x
MH   listen to me. HELLO thank you, that's good. MAGRIT   all right
PD   xxx   ccccxxx xxxx
MH   I Am   all right GOOD BOIE   all right no, listen, no no no no
PD   axxx xxx   xxx Bxxx xxx   xxx x x x x x x x x x x x x
MH   shhhh listen   listen   listen Peter   HELLO   no, he's just
PD   x x x x x x x   x x x x x x x   x x x x x
MH   getting HELLO   HOW ARE YOU?   No, not very good, Peter.
PD   xxxxxxxxx   xxxxxx   xxxx xxx
MH   HOW   Listen, Peter, no no no no ssshhhh . . .
PD   xxxx xxx   xxxx x x x x x x x x x x x x x x x x x

1. Peter replies in almost solid humanoids. Very few clicks.
2. He has lost his beginning sense of conversation . . . again, he interrupts
    Margaret. He speaks at the same time.

FIGURE 4-3 (*Cont.*)

3. Time is spent trying to get him to listen . . . hush.

After Sixty-three Days and Nights (August 10, 1965)

MH MAGRIT   All right, listen . . . BALL   Peter . . . BALL
PD   xxx xxx   xx xx   x xx xx
MH BALL   Yes. Say TOIE FISH   listen . . . TOIE FISH   murmur
PD   xxaw   aw   xxx xxx
MH come over here, Peter. Say BO BO CLOWN   Let's do it again.
PD   xxx xxx xxx
MH Pronounce, Peter BO BO CLOWN   nice. KI NI PO PO
PD   xxo oh xxx   xx xx xx xx
MH Listen . . . KI NI PO PO   That's better. murmur MAGRIT
PD   xx xx xx xoh
MH   Listen, MAGRIT   No . . . MAGRIT   No, Peter.
PD xx xx xx   xx xx xx   xx xx ee
MH Listen, MAGRIT   MAGRIT   better. Say HELLO MAGRIT
PD   xx xx xx   xxx xxx
MH   Pronounce, Peter. HELLO MAGRIT   That's
PD xxx xxx xxx xxx   xxx ohh aaa xxx
MH better, Peter. Say BO BO CLOWN   Listen. BO BO CLOWN
PD   xxx xxx   xxx xxx xx
MH Listen . . . BO BO CLOWN   Listen, Peter, BO BO CLOWN
PD   xxx xxx ownxx   xx xx xx

1. Peter no longer clicks or gives any delphinese responses.
2. Peter listens, speaks. When he is wrong, Margaret can hush him and start over.
3. Peter improves in giving back the same number of sounds that are given to him.
4. Peter is able to make parts of his words understandable.
5. Less is controlled, progress can be seen and heard during even such a short segment.

After the Experimental Period Is Finished (October 8, 1965)

MH Now you think, Peter, 'cause you used to do this. Listen. BA BEE
     BLOCK
PD
MH   Yes! (clapping) That's better. Now do the other
PD   mxx xxx
MH one. Say . . . BA SKET BALL   No, BA SKET BALL
PD   xx   xx xx xx   xxxx xx xx
MH Better. shhh! MAGRIT   No. It's EMMMMMM (ends with a
PD   xxx   xxx xxx
MH kiss on Peter's head) say . . . MMAGRIT no, not EH. It's MMM.
PD   eh xxx

FIGURE 4–3 (Cont.)

FIGURE 4–3 (Cont.)

MH   Eh . . . MMM MMMMMM MMAGRIT   Yes! Yes! (clapping)
PD   (softly) Mxx xxx

MH   That's an EM. Let's do it again. Say . . . MMAGRIT   Yes, that's
PD   mxxx xxx

MH   better. (clapping) Good! Say . . . BALL   No, not MAGRIT.
PD   xxx xxx

MH   BALL with a BEE. Say . . . BALL   Yes! BAWL! Good! Say . . .
PD   baww

MH   MMAGRIT   No . . . not EH.   MMMMM. MMMMM.
PD   eh xxx

MH   MMAGRIT   Yes . . . that's better . . . that's better, Peter . . .
PD   mxx xxx

MH   Good! Yes, you can muffle it (clap)
PD

1. Note that Margaret syncopates "baby block" and "basketball" and Peter learns to follow this.
2. Note Peter speaks out of turn and is immediately hushed in lines seven and eight.
3. Note Peter, for the main part, is responding with humanoids, the right number with usually a good pitch and inflection. Margaret begins to demand more . . . working on enunciation. Special sounds.
4. The lesson is controlled and formal, and the give-and-take of learning, teaching, speaking, and listening is established so that progress can be seen.

These experiments in communicating with Washoe and Peter Dolphin are but two of several now in progress. Minds that have been closed to the possibility of inter-species communication are now beginning to admit light. Scientists such as John Lilly caution us against being unprepared to communicate with nonhuman intelligent forms and to seriously consider the kinds of people such contact will require, the type of training they will need, and the brand of motivation best suited to it. Films such as *Planet of the Apes*, *Birds*, and the *Helmstrom Chronicle* should not be glossed over too casually if we are to successfully meet the challenge of a rapidly changing age.

COMMUNICATION BETWEEN MAN AND PLANTS

If you thought talking with animals had the capacity to attract frowns and raised eyebrows, try talking to plants. The world-renowned expert on plants, Jerry Baker, has some very definite ideas on our relationship with them. He insists they have feelings and will produce for people they like and pout and be stubborn with those they dislike. He encourages us to name our plants and learn their language so that we can carry on conversations with them, compliment them, and tell them we are glad to have them staying at our house.[20]

Back in 1969, Cleve Backster created quite a stir with an article he wrote in *National Wildlife*. He attached a lie detector to the leaf of a plant and it showed reactions similar to those of a human being. In subsequent experiments, Backster discovered that plants are hooked into some kind of telepathic communication system and that they are highly sensitive to people, to the destruction of animal life, and to threats to their own well-being.[21] While Backster's vocation is teaching policemen and other interested parties how to operate a lie detector, his avocation is pure research into the secrets of Nature. He has made speeches at Yale to audiences of linguists on nonverbal communication, at M.I.T. on plant sensitivity, and at Dartmouth and North Carolina to biologists and botanists.

One of his most unusual experiments involved the murder of a plant. In Pavlovian style, he asked six of his polygraph students to participate. One of them was chosen to murder a plant. His identity was kept a secret from Backster. The crime was committed with only another plant as a witness. Backster then attached a polygraph to the surviving plant and paraded the six suspects into the room, one by one. Five of them caused no noticeable reaction in the plant witness; but, when the killer entered the room, the needle on the polygraph went wild.[22] Surprisingly, the plant's psychogalvanic reflex (PGR) reaction resembled that of a human subject undergoing emotional stimulation.[23] Dr. Fergus Macdowall of the Plant Research Institute (Ottawa, Ontario) claims that, "As biological organisms, we share some biochemical mechanisms as well as cell structures with plants and other forms of life. . . ."[24] Of course, it is far too early for any firm conclusions to be drawn concerning communication between man and plant. Observations, however, have begun to infiltrate scientific literature, causing a reduction in the amount of skepticism.

A popular form of plant research that has caught the fancy of serious researchers such as Prof. T. C. N. Singh, Head of the Department of Botany at Annamalai University (Annamalainagar, India) and Dr. Pearl Weinberger at the University of Ottawa, as well as high school and college students, is the study of the effect various forms of music and the

[20] Jerry Baker, *Plants Are Like People* (New York: Pocket Books, 1971), pp. 73–74, 246–47.
[21] "Startling new research from the man who 'talks' to plants," *National Wildlife* (October–November, 1971), pp. 21–22.
[22] *Ibid.*, pp. 22–23.
[23] "Do plants feel emotion?" *Electro-technology* (April, 1969), p. 27.
[24] "Thought provoking," *Avant Gardner* 2:10 (March 1, 1970).

sound of the human voice has on plant growth and behavior. Here are a few examples:

> Crops of tobacco, sweet potato, and petunia grew better when exposed to thirty minute applications of music and other instruments. . . .
>
> Seed of winter wheat subjected to continuous tones of 5,000 cycles/second grew two and one half to three times larger.
>
> Sound percussion transmitted through the earth was effective: performing the "Bharat Natyan dance without trinkets on ankles" made marigolds grow 60% taller and flower 14 days earlier.[25]
>
> A gentle stroking of the leaves of Bryonia dioica (bryony vine) for a short period each day was sufficient to reduce both leaf size and internode length. Upon chromatographing extracts of the plants, it was discovered that auxin levels in the touched plants were less than in the untouched plants.[26]

It is unlikely that any of these reports will make believers out of non-believers. All they might hopefully do is confront the reader with some of the data accumulating in the field of plant research and, in particular, communication between plants and humans.

Before leaving Nature's handiwork, consider, if you will, the extent to which the world of plant life has permeated our language. We not only find millions of people who have "plant names" but countless other references to plantlike qualities in humans.

People with plant names:

1. Iris
2. Lily
3. Rose
4. Daisy
5. Holly
6. Buttercup

Plant characteristics that have been assigned to people:

1. Milton is as tall as an *oak*.
2. Danya's skin is *lily* white.
3. At 14, little girls begin to *blossom*.
4. Beverly sure doesn't let any *grass grow* under her feet.
5. People don't like to have their lives *uprooted*.
6. Mary Ann's career is just beginning to *branch out*.

[25] "Notes on harmony and theory," *Avant Gardner* 2:6 (January 1, 1970).
[26] "Tactile tactics," *Avant Gardner* 3:21 (August 15, 1971).

7. No matter what happens to Eric, he always comes away *smelling like a rose.*
8. Evelyn doesn't like to *beat around the bush.*
9. A *wallflower* is to be understood, not pitied.
10. Billie is anything but a *shrinking violet.*

Perhaps you would like to try and complete a few plant-related expressions:

1. She's the _____ of his eye.
2. She has skin like _____ and cream.
3. At times of crisis, he is as cool as a _____ .
4. They are as alike as two _____ in a _____ .
5. In time, we should be able to _____ out the troublemakers.
6. Money is the _____ of all evil.
7. The way he has been acting lately, I think he has gone _____ .
8. Life is just a bowl of _____ .

COMMUNICATION BETWEEN MAN AND INANIMATE OBJECTS

Imagine that it is time to register for next semester's classes and you are confronted by a strange choice: a human teacher or an android.[27] Which would you choose? Aside from your decision's being influenced by the nature of the course involved, do you have a preference?

Most students reason this way. If the course is mathematics, physics, or chemistry, they might consider the android. If it were philosophy, literature, public speaking, or poetry, they would prefer the human. These reactions came as somewhat of a surprise to this writer. Somehow, he had the distinct impression that what bugged students most about human teachers was their tendency to be arbitrary and capricious when it came to grading, assignments, and classroom treatment. One would think that by choosing an android, all this hanky-panky would disappear. Because the android would be totally automated, it would be logical, rational, and fair at all times; the students would always get *exactly what they deserved.* Well, needless to say, this last remark literally scared the shoes off most of them. The greater majority were perfectly willing to take their chances with a fellow *homo sapien* in spite of the risk.

Public opinion toward machines has changed considerably since the days of the horseless carriage, Bell's talking machine (telephone), and the

---

[27] An *android* is an automaton resembling a human form.

Wright brothers' flying machine. Our lives have become so cluttered with machines it is sometimes difficult to tell when the machine leaves off and man begins, or vice versa. Furthermore, too frequently, the machine is afforded more credibility than the man. A recent incident at a supermarket illustrates this point. A man inserted the correct change into a cigarette machine and pushed the Winston button. Out came Tareytons. On relating what happened to the manager, he replied, "That can't be. If you pushed the Winston button, then you get Winston." The manager either could not or would not entertain any explanation other than the fact that the customer pushed the wrong button; end of discussion.

On most college campuses, computers figure out a student's program. Each semester, a percentage of poor souls are driven out of their skulls not only by computer errors but also by the unshakable faith the people who operate them have in their infallibility. Whatever the computer does, is likened to an act of God. If the computer says you are a sophomore, YOU ARE A SOPHOMORE. Obviously, the computer is trying to tell you something and you're not listening. Then, after it is discovered that the computer actually made the mistake, the entire matter is dismissed nonchalantly with the quip, "We're not all perfect, you know."

Children of the sixties have been blessed with two things: *television* and *teaching machines*. Still in diapers and with pacifiers in their mouths, babies throughout the country are parked in front of T.V. sets and exposed to everything from breakfast cereal to the tribal dances of the Northwest Melanesians. After five or six years of this brainwashing, these tots are relocated to classrooms where teaching machines take over the conditioning process. Finally, after a dozen more years of these "machine mammas," adulthood arrives and the following ritual might begin.

Awakened by the buzzing, humming, ringing, or chiming of an alarm clock, groomed by an electric toothbrush, water pick, shaver, or hot comb, fed by an electric coffee maker, toaster, blender, or can opener, and entertained by radio or television, a city dweller begins an average day. At work, other machines take over the ongoing process of mechanizing mankind. Lord only knows how many people have sat in a stalled car, late for work or class, and cursed the damn thing into oblivion. Did it help? Of course not. Occasionally, out of fairness to the car, if you did speak softly and sweetly to it, it started. It reminds one of the computer named "Hal" that took over the space ship in *2001—A Space Odyssey* by Arthur Clark. Here was a situation in which the machine which man built took control over him. Our society may now be very near to such a dilemma.

The toy industry has also entered upon the scene. Stroll into any large toy store and be shocked at the number of things children can buy that "talk." Just pull a string and almost everything in the store talks (except the manager when you want a refund). And, as though talking were not enough, there are now dolls that communicate nonverbally by dancing, crying, urinating, gestating, growing hair, crossing their eyes, and throwing up. Then, to top it off, they eat a colored gel that passes through a tube into their disposable diaper.

Automatic answering machines have also reached epidemic proportions. Most businesses already have them and more and more private homes are installing them every day. But, perhaps you've noticed some mixed reactions to them. While most people have accepted them in their stride, there are some who will not, under any circumstances, talk with a machine. As soon as they realize they are talking to a box of nuts, bolts, and wires, they angrily slam down the receiver, arguing that man is becoming obsolete and, little by little, machines are taking over the country.

One form of retaliation to this mechanistic movement is the "group." Encounter, sensitivity, discussion, therapeutic, cultural, educational, religious, and organization cliques have multiplied by the thousands, protesting the depersonalization of man by machine—their contribution being to help resuscitate a rapidly waning sense of brotherhood and, in the process, hopefully awaken the dignity in us all.

A great many things that happen in everyday life lack the benefit of scientific validation. This chapter, in part, qualifies as one of these happenings—particularly, the section dealing with man's communicating with plants and inanimate objects. Although some scientific research has trickled through in relation to work done with chimpanzees and dolphins, even less with plants, and virtually none with regard to inanimate objects, we should still be able to discuss these phenomena while we are waiting for scientific corroboration. For instance, to what extent do you, or the people you know, talk to inanimate objects? Would you believe that there are individuals who talk to their cars, television sets, photographs of their favorite movie stars or vocal group, and statues? Children are particularly well known for their extended conversations with dolls and toy figures. These, of course, are but a few of the more orthodox objects of human communication. There are a vast number of others that seldom are aired in casual conversation. A student of this writer once admitted to bidding her apartment "goodbye" every morning when she left for school and greeting it with a warm "hello" on her return. A friend named Pete, at a local luncheonette, quietly confessed that he talked to his grill, toaster, and slicing machine. Like naughty children who have misbehaved, he scolded them when they failed to work properly. Loyal and devoted fans of certain daily soap operas on television become so involved with the story that they occasionally join in the dialogue. Widows who have lost a husband whom they loved dearly have been reported to kiss as well as converse with photographs or paintings of the deceased. So you see, while communication theorists have not as yet seen fit to recognize extrapersonal communication between man and inanimate objects, reality dictates otherwise.

Communication, like blood, is necessary for survival, whether it be with animals, plants, or objects. However, since our senses are limited, we know very little about the world we inhabit. Other forms possessing different sensory mechanisms are aware of information we lack. Thus, whatever we can learn from them favors our chances of survival. On the strength of this insight alone, extrapersonal communication becomes both a social and biological imperative.

SUMMARY

Whether or not one agrees with the ideas advanced by this chapter, it will have achieved its purpose if the reader has come to realize that communication is not an exclusively people-to-people transaction. A concerted effort was made to drive home the point that, to certain individuals, communicating with animals, plants, and inanimate objects is a perfectly normal and vital part of their lives.

We have noted that people fall into four different groups: (1) those who feel that man can communicate with animals but not with plants and inanimate objects; (2) those who feel man can communicate with animals and plants but not with inanimate objects; (3) those who feel man can communicate with animals, plants, and inanimate objects; (4) those who are so anthropomorphically committed that they adamantly reject the idea of man's communicating with anything other than man; that is, they insist that *communication is a strictly human phenomenon.*

If the chapter sparked any controversy, its cause could probably be traced to definitions of the word "communication." Therefore, to semantically clear the air, ten conventional definitions were cited and their key terms isolated and grouped on the basis of common meaning.

The greater part of this chapter concentrated on people's attitudes and behavior toward animals, plants, and inanimate objects. The textual material was accompanied by illustrative examples. These included references to animals in the contexts of myths, therapeusis, analogy to people, food, and research. Likewise, similar illustrations were given in connection with plants and inanimate objects.

If one central idea had to be picked from this chapter, it would be that extrapersonal communication must be considered along with any study of intrapersonal, interpersonal, and mass communication. Man can no longer afford the luxury of standing alone on this planet. His senses are limited and supply him only partial information about the world he inhabits. To survive, he must learn to share impressions from his environment with other forms of life. This chapter encourages thinking in this direction.

AUTHOR'S NOTE

Although you have finished reading this chapter, some of you may still have a reservation or two about its relevance, particularly with regard to communication between man and animal. As a postscript, then, here are a few more choice items:[28]

Did you know that:
There are humans who are hypochondriacs for their pets—people who phone their veterinarians and have their dogs bark into the receiver because the animal seems to have a hoarse voice and they'd like an instant diagnosis.

Did you know that:
The number of family-owned dogs in the U.S. has increased by 36 percent since 1964 and cats by 13 percent.

Did you know that:
A Park Avenue matron has a separate room for her pet parrot equipped with television and hi-fi.

Did you know that:
Many people have religious ceremonies for their deceased pets with ministers, priests, and rabbis officiating.

Did you know that:
Harry the Grasshopper is buried at the Bide-A-Wee Memorial Park in Wantagh, Long Island, next to President Nixon's best friend Checkers.

Did you know that:
On certain pet gravestones the inscription reads: "My dogs—here lies part of me," "Our Baby," and "Our beloved little boy."

Did you know that:
In Mahway, New Jersey, there is a pet hotel with efficiency and studio apartments, executive and master suites with wall-to-wall carpeting.

Did you know that:
A lot of people are opting not to have children, or perhaps they can't have children, but they still have to deal with the frustration of childlessness.

[28] Reported by Claire Berman, "A member of the family," *The New York Times Magazine*, Oct. 7, 1973, p. 15.

They will love their own animals, as a parent loves his own child but not all children.

Did you know that:
There are 410 pet cemeteries and crematories in the U.S.

And, for the *pièce de résistance,* a student in one of my classes informed me that her dog had a *bar mitzvah* celebration (a religious ceremony conferred upon a Jewish boy when he reaches the age of thirteen). If you own a pet and think you can top this, list in the spaces below some of the ways you communicate with your pet.

1. _____   2. _____

3. _____   4. _____

5. _____   6. _____

CHAPTER 5

NONVERBAL
MESSAGES

INSIGHTS

After reading this chapter you should have a clearer under-standing of:

- *the extent to which you do communicate without words.*
- *how your physical structure affects your nonverbal messages.*
- *the manner in which how you behave contradicts what you say.*
- *the various ways of knowing how to use nonverbal com-munication can enhance your relationship with the people you care about.*
- *how difficult, and often impossible, it is for you NOT to com-municate.*
- *why anyone who ignores the nonverbal aspect of communi-cation is robbed of a powerful means of persuasion.*

The meaning of each communication is to be found neither in words spoken, nor in the actions, but in both, understood in relationship to one another.[1]

Words such as nonverbal communication, body language, and kinesics have infiltrated popular usage. Newspaper articles, magazines, books, and professional journals have all begun to talk about this new and interesting dimension of human communication. But is it new? Consider the words of Edward Sapir written twenty-five years ago:

> We respond to gestures with an extreme alertness and, one might say, in accordance with an elaborate and secret code that is written nowhere, known by none, and understood by all.[2]

Since then, this so-called elaborate and secret code has received more than casual attention by several researchers and its study has commenced to bear fruit. If you haven't heard these terms yet, you will shortly—in fact, right now!

Sponsored by the hue and cry, "We're not communicating," WORDS and ACTIONS have entered into open competition with each other.

[1] Abne M. Eisenberg and Ralph R. Smith, Nonverbal Communication (New York: Bobbs-Merrill, 1971), p. 5.
[2] Edward Sapir, "The unconscious patterning of behavior in society," in David Mandelbaum, ed., Selected Writings of Edward Sapir in Language, Culture and Personality (Berkeley: University of California Press, 1949), p. 556.

There is a widespread belief that when people stop talking, they stop communicating. Nothing could be further from the truth, and it shall be the expressed purpose of this chapter to dispel such a notion. More correctly, the opposite may be true—when people stop talking, they first begin to communicate.

As mentioned earlier, we live in a speech-centered society; from childhood, most of us have been taught the importance of being able to get up on our feet and talk. Do you recognize this scene? You are at a party and, for some reason, you don't feel like talking. Without fail, someone strolls over and says, "What's the matter, aren't you having a good time?" For some spurious reason, he cannot seem to understand how anyone can be having a good time and not be talking.

This preoccupation with the spoken word has also invaded our judicial system. Unless a court stenotypist is specifically instructed by an attorney or judge to enter into the transcripts of a trial a witness' body movements, posture, or gestures, they go unrecorded. While everyone in the courtroom is fully aware of a witness' fidgeting, frightened look, and slumped body position, these nonverbal messages will be entirely missed by anyone reading the transcripts. Words, it seems, are thought to possess greater credibility than actions.

A number of today's youth show signs of losing their patience with words. They argue that an ever widening "communication gap" exists between what is SAID and what is DONE and that this hypocrisy has not only contaminated governmental agencies, but their homes as well. With WORDS, their parents are overheard to deplore all forms of addiction, but not with ACTIONS. Blithely, they smoke, drink, and gamble as though such behavior were totally unrelated to addiction. The same double standard is applied to drugs. Ask the average person if he takes drugs and the answer will usually be, "Certainly not!" Then, ask if he takes aspirin, bicarbonate of soda, tranquilizers, or sleeping pills, and he openly admits to doing so. One explanation is he doesn't consider these medicines to be drugs in the same way as heroin or L.S.D. This, admittedly, is a sweeping generalization having only limited application. But, simply because a great number of youth believe the allegation to be true, their voices should not go unheard. What they seem to be saying is, "Don't TELL me what to do—SHOW me!"

Our environment abounds with opportunities to pit WORD against ACTION. In an average day, except for those whose work requires a great deal of talking, the majority of us use more gestures than words. Ray Birdwhistell, a pioneer in the field of kinesics, estimates that the average person speaks words for a total of 10 to 11 minutes a day, with the standard spoken sentence being about 2.5 seconds in duration. This raises an interesting question. Will people in A.D. 2000 be talking more or less than we do now?

There are times when WORDS appear to carry a greater social risk than ACTIONS; they are situation-specific. Most college students soon realize the danger hidden in an innocent question or comment made in class. A girl raises her hand and asks: "Professor, is it true that Socrates was an ugly man?" The professor answers, "Young lady, if you had read your assignment and paid attention in class yesterday, you would know the answer to that question." Put in her place and thoroughly embarrassed in front of her classmates, she vows never to ask another question. This "conspiracy of silence" goes even deeper. Some students have learned that if you keep your mouth shut, sit toward the rear of the room, and get assignments in on time, it is not too difficult to pull a grade of C or perhaps a B—. This formula, of course, will not work in classes where verbal participation is required (group discussion, debate, acting, and so on). The need to watch what we say has increased considerably during the past decade. Although the war cry is "Get involved," how it should be done without running into difficulty is frequently left unspecified.

Many will find this chapter picking up where spoken and written language leave off. If you will reread its opening quotation, this should not be the impression imputed to nonverbal communication. As a rule, the majority of body movements and gestures are interpreted in terms of words and thus become verbal phenomena. There are, however, many cases in which these phenomena remain physiological. Let me explain.

Insofar as the human nervous system is equipped with more sensory than motor nerves, input exceeds output. Consequently, our nervous system is generally bombarded with more information (stimuli) than it can comfortably manage. Granting that an expansion of one's awareness is basically desirable, it occasionally produces certain side-effects. Which of us has not known the frustration of being fully aware of a situation and not being able to do a darn thing about it, or the panic of knowing the answer to an examination question and being unable to find the words with which to answer it? Muscular tension is the handmaiden of anxiety and, regardless of the circumstance, insists on being of service—if not in the form of verbal communication, then through biomuscular or biomechanical communication.

I. M. Sechnov, the father of Russian physiology[3] and teacher of Pavlov, was of the opinion that *there can be no thought without some muscular action.* Phrased differently, regardless of the individual's psychic state— loving, hating, longing, or whatever—it is coupled with both voluntary and involuntary muscular activity. Increased heart and respiratory rates,

---

[3] I. M. Sechnov, *Reflexes of the Brain* (Cambridge, Mass.: M.I.T. Press, 1965).

elevated blood pressure, or altered muscle tone are but a few of the physiological manifestations which can be triggered by the mind. *In short, chained to each thought is some form of muscular activity.*

Human speech is but one channel through which muscular energy can be released. It has been contended by some authorities that the human organism cannot totally "conceal" emotion—that emotion denied expression in one channel finds another outlet.[4,5] Physical movement provides one of the most convenient alternatives. Members of both civilized and uncivilized societies are familiar with the value of "working off" feelings of frustration, irritation, anger, and hostility through physical exertion. Any nervous system suffering from an overdose of stimulation from its environment must find a means of siphoning off the surplus energy it produces. Failing to do so could mean IMPLOSION. Energy turned inward, or implosion, is the result of verbal messages that cannot find an outlet through ordinary channels. Asthma, hypertension, ulcers, and migraine headaches are some of the conditions which frequently result from these blocked verbal avenues. Of course, these are pathological states and not within the purview of this text. Its domain is the more natural alternatives open to individuals whose verbal systems are either undernourished, underexercised, or simply require nonverbal supplementation and/or reinforcement.

This chapter aims to help move the reader toward a better understanding of how and why nonverbal communication can enrich interpersonal communication.

STRUCTURE AND FUNCTION

"As is the mind, so is the form."

"Aristotle himself criticized the 'Platonists' . . . for their 'separating' of the structure they had discovered from experienced things, from what 'we see.' "[6] Not unlike the ongoing contest between words and actions, a similar confrontation has existed through the centuries between STRUCTURE and FUNCTION. Nonverbal communication is but a by-product of this rivalry.

Joseph Gall (1758–1828) made an effort to correlate STRUCTURE

---

[4] P. Ekman and W. V. Friesen, "Nonverbal leakage and clues to deception," *Psychiatry* 32 (1969), 88–106.

[5] A. Mehrabian, "Nonverbal betrayal of feeling," *Journal of Experimental Research in Personality* 5 (1971), 64–73.

[6] John H. Randall, *Aristotle* (New York: Columbia University Press, 1960), p. 296.

with FUNCTION. Though crudely, he attempted to formulate relations between conformations of the skull (bumps on the head) and personality traits. Called *phrenology*, his approach enjoyed considerable popularity outside of scientific circles and lasted for over a hundred years. One of Gall's activities included visiting prisons and studying the heads of pick-pockets. He came to the conclusion that the particular bump they shared indicated excessive "acquisitiveness." His strategy was simply to select people with some outstanding psychological characteristic and search for a concomitant bump on the skull. The accompanying phrenological chart (Fig. 5-1) shows a variety of "bumps" and the meanings he assigned to them.

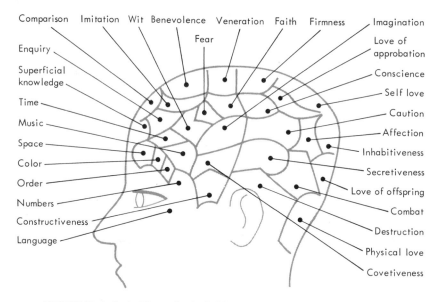

FIGURE 5-1 A Phrenological Chart.[7]

Though the merit of Gall's anatomical work was recognized by his colleagues, he was denied membership in the French Academy of Sciences because of his association with phrenology. His labors, nevertheless, were not in vain. Physicians, such as the famous Paul Broca, took up his localization banner—that of the relationship of structure to function. Broca, through a lucky accident, discovered what is now accepted as a "speech

[7] William N. Dember and James J. Jenkins, *General Psychology* (Englewood Cliffs, N.J.: Prentice-Hall, Inc., 1970), pp. 117–18.

center" in the brain—a small, delimited region of the cerebral cortex that controls linguistic behavior.[8] The search for correlates was on.

Investigators, both legitimate and illegitimate, began to study all manner of human attributes. Some read palms (chirognomy—the study of character and psychological dispositions; chiromancy—the prediction of fortunes, past and future events, and the general course of an individual's life);[9] some read faces (physiognomics[10]—the study of judgments pertaining to character and mental qualities based upon facial features); some read handwriting (graphology—the study of handwriting as it relates to the writer's character, aptitude, and so on). These are just a few of the better-known structural correlates of human behavior.

If a "will to live" could be attributed to nonverbal communication, contemporary evidence suggests such a will. Despite the ridicule and deprecation it has incurred from the so-called "scientific community," some clear signs of rebirth are now available. The first of these since Gall came from a researcher named W. H. Sheldon, whose interest came to rest on variations in the human physique. He referred to the process of judging body types as somatotyping, classifying the human form into three kinds: endomorph (a fat individual), mesomorph (a muscular individual), and ectomorph (a skinny individual). These types are illustrated in Fig. 5–2. Each is rated on a scale ranging from 1 to 7. To rate yourself, according to Sheldon's classification, stand without clothes in front of a full-length mirror. If you are frankly overweight, give yourself a full 7 for endomorphy. If you are pretty solid under a layer or two of fat because you exercise, give yourself a 4 or 5 for mesomorphy. And since you are obviously not skinny, give yourself 0 for ectomorphy. Taken together, your classification according to Sheldon's method is a 7–4–0[11] (see p. 104).

Several years later, Sheldon came out with a book based on the study of 200 men whose lives and adventures were followed for approximately eight years (from 1939 to 1946). He described them as cases of youthful delinquency and of precocious down-and-outism. Again basing his investigations upon the premise that BEHAVIOR IS A FUNCTION OF STRUCTURE, he produced data which continue to this day to attract considerable interest. In his preface, he pleads for a ". . . biologically

---

[8] Ibid., p. 119.
[9] Fred Gettings, The Book of the Hand (London: Paul Hamlyn, Ltd., 1965), p. 10.
[10] M. E. Mitchell, How to Read the Language of the Face (New York: Macmillan, 1968).
[11] W. H. Sheldon, Atlas of Man: A Guide for Somatotyping the Adult Male at All Ages (New York: Harper & Row, 1940); The Varieties of Human Physique (New York: Harper & Row, 1940); The Varieties of Temperament (New York: Harper & Row, 1942).

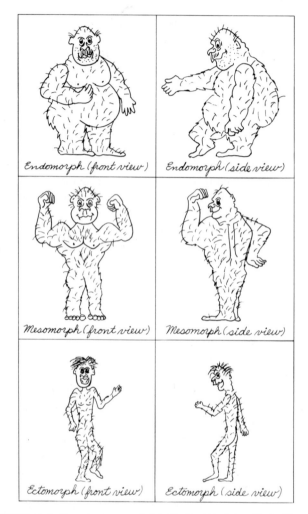

FIGURE 5–2 *Somatotypes—A Method of Judging Body Types.*

oriented psychology and psychiatry in place of the essentially theological orientation underlying all the current social institutions . . . one taking for its operational frame of reference a scientifically defensible description of the structure (together with behavior) of the human organism itself.[12]

Also interested in the structure-function relationship was the famous Harvard anthropologist Earnest A. Hootoon. Based on a study of 15,000 subadult males incarcerated in ten states, he published his impressions of the anthropology of the American criminal. Offered with a careful apology

[12] William H. Sheldon, *Varieties of Delinquent Youth: Introduction to Constitutional Psychiatry* (New York: Harper & Row, 1949).

for the art work he used to describe the various types, he cautions that they are not to be taken as portraits, nor even composites, but only as mosaics of facial features and proportions. The reader should find interesting the examples given here (Figs. 5–3, 5–4, 5–5).

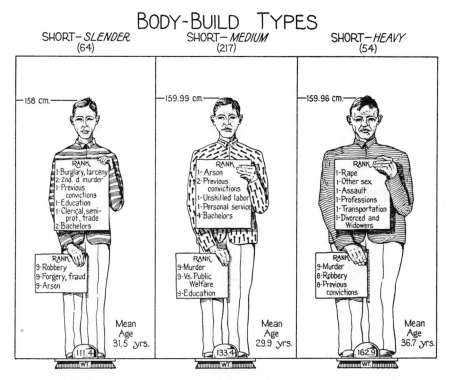

FIGURE 5–3 *Short Body Build Types* (*Figures 5–3, 5–4, 5–5 reprinted from Earnest A. Hootoon, Crime and the Man (Cambridge, Mass.: Harvard University Press, 1939), p. 98, by permission of the publisher.*)

Fully aware of the danger of overreaction, Hootoon strongly advised: ". . . you must not imagine that any single criminal of a given classification resembles the drawing made to illustrate the anatomical peculiarities of that class and none have all of them." One particular generalization made this writer's ears tingle: ". . . short, fat men rape; short, thin men steal; tall, thin men kill and rob; tall, heavy men murder and forge."[13]

Kretschmer[14] added his classification of the *athletic type* (in connection with crimes of violence); *asthenic type* (petty thievery and fraud); *pyknic*

---

[13] Earnest A. Hootoon, *Crime and the Man* (Cambridge, Mass.: Harvard University Press, 1939), p. 98.

[14] Ernest Kretschmer, *Körperbau und Charakter*, 21/22 Auflage (Berlin, Göttingen, und Heidelberg: Springer Verlag, 1955), Chap. 17, pp. 331–57.

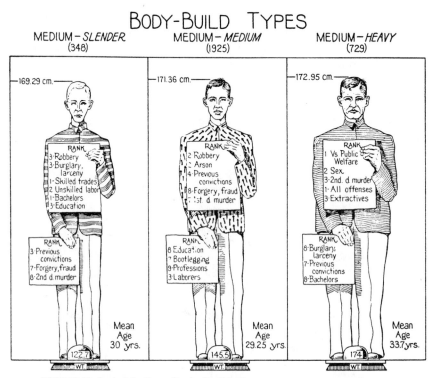

BODY-BUILD TYPES
MEDIUM – *SLENDER*   MEDIUM – *MEDIUM*   MEDIUM – *HEAVY*
(348)   (1925)   (729)

FIGURE 5-4 Medium Body Build Types.

type (also deception and fraud); and *dysplastic or mixed types* (associated with offenses against decency and morality, and also those involved with violence).

The course set by these men is clear, and Vold said it well: "Where essential inadequacy is present, the inadequacy is well-reflected in observable structure of the organism."[15] The question still remains as to how it is reflected, and the most reliable method of studying it.

Spanning approximately one hundred and fifty years and enjoying only a tepid reception, the works of Gall, Hootdon, Kretschmer, Vold, and Sheldon remain landmarks in the infant world of nonverbal communication. Poaching on the outskirts of science for another dozen years, nonverbal communication was again revived by Ruesch and Kees,[16] who rendered it a modern debut—this time, within the confines of propriety. Again it failed to "catch on" in the public mind. As though shackled to

[15] George B. Vold, *Theoretical Criminology* (New York: Oxford University Press, 1959), p. 73.
[16] J. Ruesch and W. Kees, *Nonverbal Communication* (Berkeley and Los Angeles: University of California Press, 1956).

BODY-BUILD TYPES

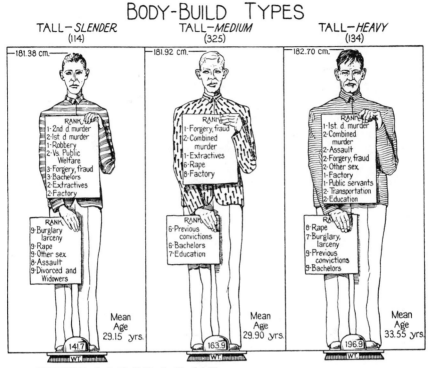

FIGURE 5-5 Tall Body Build Types.

some unwritten code regulating the acceptance of a new idea, nonverbal communication continued to receive only marginal attention. The 1970s, however, was a turning point. A paperback by Julius Fast entitled *Body Language* took the public by storm. Several million copies were sold. The book described, in nontechnical language, how the attitudes, values, and beliefs people held could be revealed by how they stood, sat, walked, dressed, used their hands, and so on. Soon, newspaper and magazine articles began to appear bearing references to nonverbal communication. Even the renowned mime, Marcel Marceau, jumped on the bandwagon by billing himself as "The world's most famous nonverbal communicator." So enthusiastically has the subject caught on that colleges and universities have not only incorporated it in existing courses but, in some instances, offer it as a separate course. In sum, *it has become fashionable to nonverbally "read" people.*

"*Funny, you don't look like a . . . .*"

Do you judge others by how they look—or by what they say about themselves? Imagine meeting a friend on the street who looks positively horrid. When you ask her how she feels, she answers, "Great!" Which message are you inclined to believe, the verbal or nonverbal one? "Generalizing, we can say that a person's nonverbal behavior has more bearing than his words on communicating his feelings to others."[17] If, for any reason, a person doesn't happen to look the way he says he feels, his credibility steps into serious jeopardy. For example, how willingly do you think movie and theatre-going audiences would accept as believable a cross-eyed physician, a 300-pound rodeo rider, or a severely bowlegged flamenco dancer? Conceding that such individuals might be experts in their field, their popular image would be tarnished by these structural deviations.

Here is a quiz designed to test your attitude toward the relationship between the way people look and how they claim to feel.

Quiz

Complete the following statements according to your impressions of how these people *should* look:

1. A typical accountant is _____ .

2. A typical alcoholic is _____ .

3. A typical librarian is _____ .

4. A typical college professor is _____ .

5. A typical "dirty old man" is _____ .

6. A typical kindergarten teacher is _____ .

7. A typical whore is _____ .

8. A typical cab driver is _____ .

9. A typical short order cook is _____ .

10. A typical neurotic is _____ .

11. A typical social worker is _____ .

12. A typical traveling salesman is _____ .

13. A typical musician is _____ .

14. A typical opera singer is _____ .

15. A typical nun is _____ .

[17] Albert Mehrabian, *Silent Messages* (Belmont, Calif.: Wadsworth, 1971), p. 44.

After filling in the blank spaces, have a friend do likewise on a separate sheet of paper; then list those responses most common to each question. Be careful to include ONLY physical characteristics, such as body type (fat, muscular, skinny), type of body movements (slow, medium, fast), vocal quality (volume, pitch, rhythm), clothing (style or substance), and special traits. Then discuss why each of you assigned these particular characteristics to these socially held roles.

A person's physical structure not only dictates function but also offers the opportunity to make certain assumptions pertaining to that function. To what extent do you think a seasoned football coach could pick those most likely to succeed from a lineup of freshmen trying out for the team? Can experts in dance, voice, or theatre make judgments solely on the basis of structure? Confessing that there are athletes who don't look like what they are nor what they do, the majority seem to share a structural common denominator (6'7" tall basketball players, 5' tall jockeys, and so on).

ANATOMICAL DIFFERENCES

Although we all look alike structurally, there are some differences that can have a significant effect upon our biomuscular communication.[18] While textbooks on human anatomy confirm that men and women have essentially the same number of muscles, the size, shape, origin, insertion, and action of these muscles can vary.

If you have an opportunity, visit your library and check out a copy of *Gray's Anatomy*,[19] a standard text used in medical schools. Turn to the section on myology (the study of muscles) and notice, after a description of each muscle, the variations it mentions. The *risorius*, for example—the muscle which retracts the angle of the mouth as in smiling or grinning—is reported to vary greatly, be absent, doubled, or greatly enlarged. Then, find the *dilatator naris posterior* and *anterior*—the muscles which dilate the nostrils. They, too, are reported to vary in size and strength, or may be absent.

Should your curiosity extend beyond facial muscles, you will find these same variations exist throughout the body. You will discover, in fact, that the way people look and how they behave is subject to anatomical differences over which they have little or no control. Thus, the professor or student who "looks mean" may well be one of those individuals whose

[18] *Biomuscular communication:* messages transmitted by body movements and gestures.
[19] *Gray's Anatomy,* ed. Charles Mayo (Goss, 27th Ed.) (Philadelphia: Lea Febiger, 1962), pp. 418–19.

anatomical construction consists of muscles that are either larger, smaller, or attached differently than in you or me. Or, the entire muscle might be absent in them. Any nonverbal impressions not taking these factors into consideration should be treated as incomplete.

BIOMUSCULAR COMMUNICATION

Years ago there was a song, "Every little movement has a meaning all its own." While it might be true, some qualification seems necessary. Any body movements or gestures which contribute meaning to an orally de- livered message should be considered as *purposeful*, and those which de- tract, *purposeless*. Imagine yourself at the front of the room delivering a speech and unconsciously rocking back and forth. Although this motion could understandably relieve your nervous tension, it usually makes your audience nervous and detracts from your speech. If, on the other hand, you were to tremble while describing an old woman opening a letter from her son, it would enhance your speech. In each case, the way you move in relation to the words you speak will dictate whether they will be *pur- poseless* or *purposeful*.

Years ago a trend existed in which students obliged to deliver speeches were given certain instructions by their teachers. They went like this: "Stand still, look at some fixed spot in the rear of the room (usually a clock), speak *loudly*, *clearly* and *slowly*." Like robots, students delivered stilted speeches to bored classmates. It was almost as if they were penal- ized for sounding or looking alive. Teachers who subscribed to this method, however, should not be condemned without explanation. Their *raison d'être* possessed some validity. Since a form of quiet desperation is fre- quently associated with having to deliver speeches, students, naturally, tend to fidget! Also, wanting to get the speech over with, they rushed through it like a dog with its tail on fire. Looking at the clock is a device intended to keep the speaker from reading his speech from a paper and never looking up at the audience.

If you had a speech teacher named Francois Delsarte (1811–1871), his recommendations concerning your body movements and gestures might have been quite different than those just described. He has been referred to as the *Father of Elocution* (the art of public speaking) and was con- sidered the most original teacher of his time. Believing that "gesture is more than speech," it is understandable why Beloof[20] considered Delsarte to be a pioneer in what is now referred to as the science of kinesics. An

---

[20] Robert Beloof, *The Performing Voice in Literature* (Boston: Little, Brown, 1966), p. 70.

example of how his work has been interpreted can be seen in old silent movies and melodramas, where normal gestures were jerky and grossly exaggerated. Villains invariably twirled their big, black moustaches and moved across the stage and screen with their capes held in front of their faces and their bodies in a slightly hunched-over position. Heroes stood tall with their chests out and their eyes open wide. Heroines clutched their hands over their hearts at the sight of the hero and cringed in the presence of the villain. Delsarte sought to learn Nature's way, not by hit or miss but through the scientific method of observation. He collected enormous amounts of data, even dissecting corpses and observing inmates in insane asylums. He tried, according to his biographer Ted Shawn, to observe human beings in every aspect and condition of life and death, normal and abnormal.[21] It was Delsarte's adoption of what he took to be the scientific method of observation and classification that made it possible for his untalented followers to make something mechanical out of the system.

Perhaps the most efficient way to learn the art of gesture is by observing those who have mastered it. The probability is high that their every body movement will be purposeful and consonant with their every word—*body and mind in perfect synchrony*. A most helpful way of improving bio-muscular communication is to become familiar with your own kinesic personality. Notice such items as your hand movements, facial expressions, foot and leg behavior, and postural attitude. Then ask, "In what way does each of these movements contribute to or detract from what I am communicating verbally?" Assume that you are an "ear lobe puller" or a "chin stroker." How do these actions affect those watching and listening to you? There are public speakers who play with or fondle pens, pencils, books, keys, and papers while they speak. Many are not even aware they are doing it. *The first step toward improving your kinesic behavior is to bring your subconscious nonverbal actions to a conscious level.* It is remarkable how many people are shocked when they see themselves on television or film for the first time and exclaim, "Is that really me?" The average person has but only a vague inkling of his kinesic personality—that is, his kinesic SELF. Once he is aware of it, a new dimension of the SELF appears upon the horizon.

MYOKINETIC RHYTHMS

There are two types of myokinetic rhythms, *hyperkinetic* and *hypokinetic*; most people have a tendency to lean toward one or the other of these

[21] Ted Shawn, *Every Little Movement* (privately printed, 1954).

extremes. The hyperkinetic type does everything quickly, while the hypo-kinetic one does everything slowly. Thus, were they to marry one another, a good measure of their lives would probably sound like this:

Hyperkinetic Husband: "Honey, will you hurry up, we're late!"

Hypokinetic Wife: "What's the big hurry—where's the fire, we have plenty of time."

Failing to recognize someone's myokinetic rhythm (body tempo) could cause a serious communication breakdown. For example, people who are fast talkers are frequently intolerant of those who talk slowly, and vice versa. A teacher who speaks rapidly usually has little patience with students who take forever to get a statement out of their mouths. The same applies to the slow-talking teacher, who becomes somewhat unglued in the presence of a hyperkinetic type. In short, human compatibility will often depend upon an individual's myokinetic rhythm. Surprisingly, many people who are hyper- or hypokinetic are unaware of it. They are, however, quick to notice this trait in others. A common scene witnessed in any reasonably busy restaurant is the hypokinetic waiter and the hyperkinetic customer. The result needs no explanation. At school, a similar dilemma occurs when a hyperkinetic professor clashes with the hypokinetic student. In each situation, the consequence is generally the same. Unless one of them is willing to accommodate the other, a communication breakdown is not far behind.

While a particular myokinetic rhythm is usually irreversible, it can be modified—slowed down or speeded up—by a mood, martini, or, perhaps a tranquilizer. Should you meet a friend whom you knew many years ago and who was extremely hyperkinetic, the chances are that he or she will still display that same body-tempo. Among children, mothers often climb the walls when they have a hyperkinetic child. In desperation, they pray for a way to get the kid to sit still for a few minutes instead of being in a state of perpetual motion.

A golden rule of human communication should then include the realization that people have, in addition to anatomical differences, varying myokinetic rhythms over which they have little or no control. Nonverbal interpersonal compatibility will depend upon an understanding of these differences.

BIOMECHANICAL COMMUNICATION[22]

According to Hewes, "A whole complex of factors—anatomical, physiological, cultural, environmental, technological—is involved in the evolu-

[22] *Biomechanical communication:* messages conveyed by body positioning or posturing.

tion of the many different postural habits that peoples of the earth have assumed." He also suggests that of the more than 1000 different steady postures available to man, the postural choices he makes are largely culturally determined.[23] (See Fig. 5–6.)

This chapter has already indicated that structure is a cardinal determinant of function and, according to the thinking of Julius Wolff, a German anatomist (1836–1902), function can alter form.[24] Thus, it is possible that how an individual conducts himself biomechanically represents a grossly underestimated source of information. Sensitive to this oversight, many investigators have recently turned their attention in its direction. James, one of the earlier researchers into the question of posture and its implications, after a series of experiments with variously arranged mannequins, concluded that "postures do give clues to attitude, and that the placement of the trunk and head contributes most to interpretations of postures."[25] Despite the many journal articles that followed, the role and the relevance of these postural cues in communication still remain open to conjecture. Once more, posture as a form of nonverbal communication takes a back seat to words.

Are you familiar with these expressions?

> *Position* is everything in life.
> *Stand* up to him.
> Don't just *sit* there, do something!
> *Lie* back and enjoy it.
> I would *bend over backwards* for him.
> How can you just *turn your back* on the business?
> Just how *low* can a person *stoop?*
> Boy, am I in a *slump*.

All of these clichés draw at least part of their meaning from a postural attitude. Regardless of how much importance one assigns to body positioning, it does seem to play a definite role in the communicative setting. Even the position of your body, while reading this page, is invested with some meaning—you are tired, interested, in a hurry, annoyed, or whatever.

Before we go any further with this discussion of posturality, an important misconception must be set right. Posture is, by no means, restricted to the upright position. While some of us, if pressed, will agree that our

---

[23] From "The anthropology of posture" by Gordon Hewes, *Scientific American* 196 (February, 1957), 123–32. Copyright © 1957 by Scientific American, Inc. All rights reserved.

[24] W. A. Newman Dorland, *The American Illustrated Medical Dictionary*, 21st ed. (Philadelphia: Saunders, 1950), p. 786.

[25] W. James, "A study of the expression of bodily posture," *Journal of General Psychology* 7 (1932), 405–436.

POSTURE TYPES are shown in this sampling from the classification scheme of Hewes. The figures numbered 301 through 306 (*top
row on this page*) are common resting positions; by contrast, the
arm-on-shoulder postures of the next four figures are found mainly

among western American Indians. In the next row are variations
of the one-legged Nilotic stance, found in the Sudan, Venezuela
and elsewhere. Chair-sitting (*third row*) spread from the ancient
Near East, but the Arabs there have replaced it with floor-sitting

FIGURE 5-6 Variations in Posture.[23]

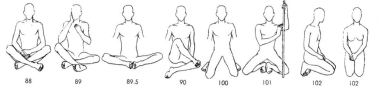

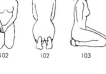

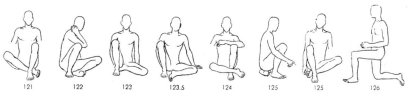

postures (*fourth and fifth rows*). Sitting cross-legged (*top row on this page*) predominates south and east of Near Eastern influence. Sedentary kneeling postures (102 *to* 104) are typically Japanese; sitting with the legs folded to one side (106 *through* 108) is a femi- nine trait, a rare exception being the male Mohave Indians. The deep squat (*fourth row on this page*) is uncomfortable for adult Europeans but replaces the sitting posture for at least a fourth of mankind. The last two rows show various asymmetrical postures.

FIGURE 5–6 (Cont.)

connotation of posture includes both seated and recumbent positions, the general public does not. If someone accuses you of having "bad posture," the probability is high that you will think only in terms of the standing or upright position. Seated and recumbent postures are seldom primary considerations in this society.

Another popular misconception about posture is that it is always a still or motionless state. Posture in motion is rarely considered. This phenomenon may be observed at a dance where a young man or woman displays an impressive sitting posture but, getting up and dancing, create quite a different picture. In motion, the person's posture might be that of someone with "two left feet". Posture, if it is to be studied seriously, must be conceived in both a static and a dynamic context.

Though an awareness of the sitting and recumbent postures does not generally enter into the traditional concept of posture, people spend the majority of their lives in these positions. Seldom do the seats on long-distance buses, planes, and trains fail to recline. The straightback chair is swiftly becoming a topic of discussion among archeologists. Comfort is the watchword of the Western World, and comfort translated into physical terms means *horizontality*. Why stand if you can sit, and why sit if you can lie? This seems to be the modern postural philosophy most of us live by. Visit any well-stocked furniture store and see the kinds of chairs, couches, and beds now in use. They, if Julius Wolff (cited earlier) is correct, are prognosticators of how our postures will look in the future. Sometimes, one gets the feeling that modern furniture makers have never seen a human being. Rarely do they make but tokenistic allowances for our structural differences. Tall, short, fat, or skinny—all must adjust to the furniture, not the furniture to them. Like clothing, people should have their furniture made to measure. It is painful to imagine the structural discomfort a student over six feet tall experiences having to sit in one of those ridiculous one-armed chairs currently used in most college classrooms. Unable to cross his legs from right to left without considerable effort, he often suffers in silence.

Adding insult to injury, think for a moment of how the industrial revolution has affected our postures. Each of countless machines operated by men and women demands the assumption of certain body positions. Multiply these positions by 20 years on a job and what have you got— distortion: kyphosis (round shouldered), scoliosis (curvature of the spine), lordosis (sway backed), and muscles developed more on one side than the other. In time, it may become no task at all to identify a person's occupation by his posture.

Stepping from an industrial to an academic milieu also permits certain postural inferences. At school, there is hardly a student who does not register an immediate impression of a teacher on the first day of class, based upon his posture. The teacher with the chest forward, shoulders back, and head held high creates a different image from the one who scurries into class with the shoulders hunched over and head down. Conversely, the teacher, looking over a new class of students, gets some feedback from their postural attitudes. Mehrabian's studies have produced a striking and consistent finding that males, in this culture, assume more relaxed postures than do females.[26] This introduces another dimension of the postural complex to be considered—the degree of relaxation or tension inherent in a given posture. Consequently, whether standing on a diving board preparing to do a double front somersault with a half twist, sitting in the dean's office waiting for him to chew you out, or coming face-to-face with a mugger at 2:00 A.M.—your state of relaxation or tension may be communicated by your posture. Experimental observations in this culture have shown that body relaxation is a very important, though subtle, indicator of status. When two strangers meet, the more relaxed individual is probably accepted by both as being of higher status.[27]

Wherever you go, relaxed or tense posture can act as a source of advertisement, with you as the product. Freud phrased it beautifully when he said, "He that has eyes to see and ears to hear may convince himself that no mortal can keep a secret. If his lips are silent, he chatters with his finger tips; betrayal oozes out of him at every pore."[28] Perhaps that explains why so many psychiatrists and psychoanalysts prefer to seat themselves outside the patient's view so as to deprive them of any nonverbal feedback from each other. How many patients do you think would be able to sit face-to-face with their doctors, 24 inches from nose to nose, and openly communicate their problems? If messages can truly leak from every pore, it would take an enormous amount of self-control to prevent such leakage under the best of circumstances.

Still another aspect of posture is its biomechanical range. Every joint in the body is classified as either synarthrodial (immovable), amphiarthrodial (partially movable), or diarthrodial (completely movable). Those which are movable and involved with regulating posture possess a physiological range of motion. For purposes of illustration, let us take anteflexion (forward bending) and retroflexion or extension (backward bending) of the trunk. Further, assume that maximum forward bending is 90 degrees and backward bending 30 degrees. Somewhere between the two extremes

[26] A. Mehrabian, "Significance of posture and position in the communication of attitude and status relationships," *Psychological Bulletin* 71 (1969), 359–72.
[27] E. Goffman, *Encounters: Two Studies in the Sociology of Interaction* (Indianapolis: Bobbs-Merrill, 1961).
[28] S. Freud, "Fragment of an analysis of a case of hysteria (1905)," *Collected Papers*, Vol. 3 (New York: Basic Books, 1959).

is what is known as one's basal posture. Deutsch[29] contends that "every individual has a characteristic basic posture to which he returns whenever he has deviated from it." It is this basic or neutral posture that others use as a yardstick by which to judge us. In effect, it behaves as a "postural indicator."

Most people are impervious to their postural idiosyncrasies. Many would not recognize someone walking down the street or standing on a corner with their identical posture. It is curious how people psychologically "doctor up" their personal stance or gait and vehemently reject being likened to someone who stands or walks peculiarly. "Are you kidding—me, walk like that? You must be joking." This is not an uncommon reply. On the whole, people's postures are essentially the same, deviating only slightly from one to the other. However, within this subtle range of differentiation, a biomechanical marker is often manifested. Whether it is a policeman, doctor, politician, professor, prostitute, or criminal, there are people who claim to be able to pick them out of a crowd. Surely you've been to a party and noticed someone across the room whom you could swear was one of the aforementioned. Yielding to the lure of generalization, there are a vast number of seasoned criminals who would bet their bottom dollar that not only can they spot a "cop" at twenty yards, but also can smell one as well. Surely you have, at some time, fallen prey to the temptation of labeling a stranger as perhaps a doctor or a prostitute? Of course you have.

Sometime, when you have an hour to spare, sit in the waiting room of any hospital. You will notice that the nurse at the desk permits certain people to pass without questioning and stops others. Try to guess the criteria she uses for making these judgments. Dismiss, for a moment, those men and women who are either wearing hospital uniforms or who are regular employees (whom she knows on sight). Be concerned only with those who are unknown to her. Could posture have anything to do with her instantaneous determinations of who should or should not be allowed to pass? Do you think, for instance, that a doctor from out of state or from another country would be stopped? Might not his psychological sense of being a doctor and feeling at home in a hospital be reflected in his posture? Similar posture-typing occurs with policemen who, though out of uniform and off duty, still carry themselves with an air of authority —a certain bearing that most people seem to equate with the position they hold. In short, to the trained eye, posture may serve as an excellent means of identification.

[29] F. Deutsch, "Analysis of postural behavior," *Psychoanalytic Quarterly* 16 (1947), 195–213.

A last, but not least important item to be kept in mind regarding posture, is whether it is *regional* or *systemic*.

Regional Posture

Regional posture applies to specific parts of the body, such as the head, trunk, or extremities. Apart from how the rest of the body is carried, regional postures are judged on the basis of their individual positionality. Among your friends, how many hold their heads straight while talking to you; how many hold them cocked to one side? (See Fig. 5–7.)

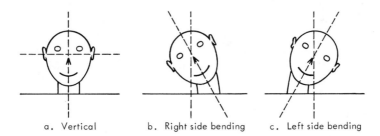

| a. Vertical | b. Right side bending | c. Left side bending |

FIGURE 5–7 Head Postures: (a) vertical, (b) right side bending, (c) left side bending.

Another example of regional posture involves the way the arms are held. Brachial[30] attitudes may consist of arms folded across the chest, hands clasped behind back, one or both hands placed on hips, or arms simply hanging limp at the sides. All these postures, naturally, exclude those resulting from disease.

Systemic Posture

The word systemic refers to postures assumed by the entire body. A postural deviation often goes unnoticed until someone draws attention to it: "Hey, did you know that you have a funny walk, or that you lean to one side when you stand?" Only by becoming aware of the nonverbal statement your posture makes can you even begin to cope with people's reaction to it. For a quick *personal postural check-up*, stand in front of a full-length mirror (with or without clothes) and observe these check points:

1. Are your ears the same height?
2. Are your shoulders the same height?

[30] Brachial—referring to the arms.

3. Are your arms of equal length?
4. Does your waist go in to the same extent on each side?
5. Are the spaces between each arm (at elbow level) and your waist of equal distance?
6. Are your hips the same height?

A structural imbalance involving any of the above may suggest a postural distortion capable of affecting how you sit, stand, lie, or move.

A story has been circulated about a bank robber who capitalized on his knowledge of posture and its effect upon people—specifically, that people generally avoid direct eye contact with cripples. Realizing this, he bought himself one of the orthopedic boots worn by people with a club foot. Thus, armed with a gun and wearing the orthopedic boot, he successfully held up a number of banks. Almost consistently, witnesses were able to do little more than identify him as a man with a crippled foot.

To experience the full impact of posture and the type of feedback it is able to yield, try assuming one of the following postures on campus for an hour or two. Be alert and carefully notice such things as eye contact, distance kept, verbal comments, facial expressions, and the degree of touching you experience.

EXERCISE: *Postural Ploys*

1. Head cocked up, down, or to one side.
2. Trunk bent forward, backward, or to one side.
3. Reduced or increased stride.
4. Very upright or slumped sitting posture.
5. Walking with toes pointing inward or outward.
6. Walking with or without a bounce to your gait.

The kinds of feedback you receive should give you some idea of the role posture plays as a source of nonverbal messages.

Microecology[31] (proxemics)

Accept, if you will, that *space communicates*—that by familiarizing yourself with its language (proxemics) you can make a significant contribution to any interpersonal relationship you might have. Put this book down for a moment and notice the space around you. Such a request usually meets with not only a puzzled expression but also the question, "Exactly what am I supposed to be looking at, or looking for?" The normal tendency is to simply move your eyes from object to object or from person to

---

[31] Edward Hall, *Hidden Dimension* (Garden City, N.Y.: Doubleday, 1966), p. x.

person in a random fashion. Only through the process of intellectual concentration does any deeper meaning tend to arise.

Edward Hall, the famous anthropologist and pioneer in the field of proxemics, is firmly convinced that making man more keenly aware of the space he maintains between himself and his fellows and that which he builds around himself in his home and office will elevate his self-image, intensify his experiences, and diminish his sense of alienation.[32] Hall strongly feels that space does communicate and we had best learn to use and understand it more profitably.

Like Pavlov's dogs who salivated at the sound of a bell, there are people who become anxious, nervous, apprehensive, and begin to sweat profusely whenever anyone comes too close them. Others do not appear to mind such sociopedality (excessive closeness) and remain inordinately calm in a packed bus, train, or elevator. In fact, some people actually derive pleasure from such an experience.

Surrounding each of us is an invisible and personal "bubble" which, when invaded, tends to elicit a particular response. Actually, what it does is provide a readily accessible method of determining an individual's "degree of approachability." Should you, perchance, wish to test the size of your bubble, simply notice how close (measured in inches) you will allow strangers to come to you before feeling a sense of discomfort and psychological uneasiness. The size of your bubble will vary according to: (1) your own physical size, (2) the physical size of the other person, (3) mood, (4) personality, (5) race or culture, (6) prejudice and bias, (7) time of day or night, (8) previous relationship, (9) visual acuity, (10) social setting, (11) geographic site, and (12) climate. Even though the size of your bubble may range from 18 inches to 4 feet (depending upon the circumstances), it will assume a mean size that will be characteristic for you.

For those having a researcher's curiosity, guessing the size of other people's bubbles might prove an amusing pastime. Whose bubble do you think would be larger, the mathematics or the English teacher's; or would you care to speculate as to the size of a psychology, sociology, economics, or foreign language professor's bubble? Regardless of how many people you survey, they will all manifest some form of response, ranging from no response at all to outright antagonism. You may elicit remarks such as "What the heck do you think you're doing!" or "What's the matter with you?" Other reactions to an invasion of people's bubbles include the indictment that (1) you want something from them, (2) you feel sexy, (3) you want to whisper something to them, or (4) you are nearsighted. Parents, when their bubbles are invaded by their children, frequently

---

[32] *Microecology*—a synonym for the term *proxemics*.

think they want money, keys to the car, or permission to get an apartment of their own.

Living and nonliving things occupy space. In the laboratory, the space occupied by various substances will vary in relation to their mass, morphology, and specific gravity; in the garden or field, corn will consume more vertical space than pumpkins, whereas pumpkins consume more horizontal space than corn. Each uses space according to the matter and manner of its existence. Animals (in their natural habitat) also manipulate space or territories in relation to their feeding, mating, and nesting practices. Man is no exception. The only serious difference is that he not only is willing to kill in the name of space, but also passes endless laws to insure against its mismanagement and abuse. Hardly a period in history is free from an occasional blood bath over some land dispute. Signs reading: STAY OUT, NO TRESPASSING, KEEP OUT, PRIVATE, KEEP OFF, NO EN-TRY, CLOSED, VIOLATORS WILL BE PROSECUTED, all bear witness to man's preoccupation with the importance of space.[33] The discussion to follow deals with some of the ways SPACE communicates nonverbal messages.

As a result of overpopulation, crowding has become a way of life. With precious few exceptions, anyone who lives or who has lived in a large urban center knows the feeling of helplessness and futility of waiting in lines. Lines to board buses, planes, trains; lines to get into restaurants, movies, plays, and closed-out classes; lines to get a hot dog at a beach in the summer, or to pay for an item in a local department store. For many, this ritual has reached epidemic proportions. Although some of us have acquired a partial immunity against the psychological trauma it produces, there are rugged individualists who flatly refuse to knuckle under and have their "bubbles" invaded. For them, three alternatives remain: (1) continually get into fights with people wherever they go, (2) avoid places where there are crowds and lines, or (3) stay home and read a good book or watch television.

The dangers of overpopulation and crowding should not be underestimated. An experiment by Calhoun performed on Norway rats produced some observations which, if by analogy extended to man, provoke some rather frightening speculation. Calhoun noted that with plenty of food and no danger from predators, rats in a quarter-acre outdoor pen stabilized their population at about 150. He then designed another experiment which he called a "behavioral sink." In it, he maintained a stressful situation through overpopulation while three generations of rats were

---

[33] Even the innocent act of moving too far over on his wife's side of the bed might cause a restless husband to be charged with trespassing—daring to use more than his allotted amount of space.

raised. The results were startling. Some withdrew from social and sexual intercourse; others began to mount anything in sight. Patterns of courtship were totally disrupted and females were pursued by several males. Neat nest-building became nonexistent and young rats were either stepped on or eaten by hyperactive males. Males fought over dominant positions near eating bins and violated all territorial rights. These same hyperactive males began to run in packs. Pregnant females had frequent miscarriages and only one-fourth of the 558 newborns in the sink survived to be weaned. Overall, aggressive behavior increased significantly.[34] While studies like this have not been conducted with human subjects, certain behavioral similarities seem to exist.

From about the age of 5 or 6 most children, if they complete a college education, spend slightly more than two decades in classrooms of various types. It might be a good idea to look at these classrooms a little more closely from a proxemic standpoint. Do the spatial conditions in which students must learn serve as assets or liabilities? Surprisingly few teachers (students for that matter) complain about the classrooms in which they must spend so many years of their lives. True, there is the traditional hue and cry about class size and inadequate facilities, but rarely specific protests concerning the internal architecture and geography of the physical classroom itself—floor space, window space, number and types of chairs and tables, blackboards, lighting, ventilation, arrangement, and so on. Perhaps we had best enlist the aid of value engineers. Value engineering is an organized effort to attain optimum value in a product, system, or service, by providing the necessary functions at the lowest cost. To be more exact, it is a selective process whereby all available alternatives are considered and the best are thoroughly examined before a course of action is chosen.[35]

Many designers reject the idea that what is believed to be an optimal environment has a single static form. Architect Raymond Studer[36] advocates servo-environmental systems, which respond to changes in behavioral input. Recognizing that the needs of a physical structure undergo changes in time, he argues for a dynamic system capable of accommodating such changes. Most people are unaware that while many new schools are being built to accommodate spiraling enrollments, their classrooms do not differ appreciably in structure. Rectangular in shape, they consist of chairs in rows, teacher's desk and chair at the front, windows lining one wall, and

34 J. B. Calhoun, "Population density and social pathology," *Scientific American* 206 (1962), 1939–48.

35 John W. Greve and Frank W. Wilson, eds., *Value Engineering in Manufacturing* (Englewood Cliffs, N.J.: Prentice-Hall, Inc., 1967), p. 3.

36 Raymond Studer, "On environmental programming," *Arena* (May, 1966), 290–96.

blackboards at eye level. Before the invention of electricity, chairs were arranged in rows for two reasons: (1) they allowed for a maximum of natural light, and (2) it was easier for the school janitor to clean between the seats. Unfortunately, arranged this way, all that students saw and all that they now see are the backs of the heads of their classmates. The teacher, in presenting her lesson, has the benefit of eye contact from all members of the class, while the student who answers or asks a question has only her eye contact. This factor alone, from the standpoint of effective learning, justifies a rethinking of certain proxemic practices. Investigator Fitch[37] rejects the view that a classroom environment should remain fixed throughout a given day. Contesting the premise that an ideal room is at 72 degrees temperature, humidity 50 percent, 60 foot-lamberts illumination at desk top, and 45 decibels of sound, he submits that a student needs less heat in the afternoon than in the morning, more oxygen and less humidity by the end of the day, as well as greater sound levels in the afternoon than in the morning. These, it should be remembered, are physiological considerations which make little or no allowance for a student's psychological needs.

Did you know that in the average classroom a teacher has approximately 50 percent more space to move around in than any of the students? Educators have for too long ignored the psychological implications of students' being bunched together like grapes. From the student's visual perspective, the world is cluttered, disorganized, and full of shoulders, heads, and body movements. The teacher, according to Sommer, hovers overhead like some giant helicopter ready to swoop down to ridicule or punish any wrongdoer.[38] Many teachers, sensing the gross injustice of this classroom arrangement, have converted, wherever possible, to learning "in the round." The only hardship growing out of this change in seating seems to affect the teacher of the next class who, preferring the traditional format, must return the chairs to their original positions. Hard data notwithstanding, any student or teacher who has experienced both forms of environmental engineering will testify that the old and outmoded arrangement of students produced these symptoms: decreased feelings of individuality, dampened desire to ask questions, reduced listening levels, more cheating, limited participation, and, in general, an atmosphere of dehumanization.

One of the popular myths which has circulated in education for years deals with where students choose to sit in a classroom—for example,

---

[37] James M. Fitch, "The esthetics of function," *Annals of the New York Academy of Sciences* 128 (1965), 706–14.
[38] Robert Sommer, *Personal Space* (Englewood Cliffs, N.J.: Prentice-Hall, Inc., 1969), p. 99.

interested ones in the front rows, those who engage in unacceptable activities (such as reading newspapers, sleeping, and gossiping) in the back rows, quick-escape artists on the aisle, "voyeurs" near the windows, and those in search of anonymity, unobtrusively secreted in the center toward the rear. Needless to say, a confirmation or denial of such a myth is not readily available. Any teacher or student could easily supply examples in support of either view. Most class distributions do, however, seem to consist of zones containing people who behave differently.

While all this talk about space and how things are arranged may seem rather obvious, just the reverse is true. Recall the number of day-to-day experiences which involve position. Isn't there an expression, "Position is everything in life?" This cliché seems to make sense. Just thinking about whether you should be the first or last to give a speech; the seating arrangement at a wedding, making it a success or a failure; the position in which you hold a golf club, baseball bat, pistol, knife and fork; the positioning of furniture to make a room look more or less spacious; or having your coffee with or at the end of a meal heightens one's appreciation of the vital role space can play in our lives.

There are innumerable other situations in which space is relevant. Every institution, whether it be a hospital, prison, college, orphanage, or old age home, has its space-oriented folklore. That is, certain territorial imperatives, if violated, can produce serious repercussions. Hospitals go to great lengths to keep certain kinds of patients separated; regulars in a prison yard to establish their status by standing in certain places; geriatric patients in nursing homes to defend their usual "place" in the solarium; papa, when his son or daughter takes his seat at the dinner table; and students when someone takes a seat they have been occupying for a half semester. The degree of importance that should be placed on space as a source of nonverbal communication is debatable. What should not be debated, however, is the role of space being omitted from any analysis of the communicational process.

HAPTIC COMMUNICATION[39]

The word *haptic*, derived from the Greek (haptomai), means "I touch." Haptic communication, therefore, refers to the LANGUAGE OF TOUCH.

[39] The decision to substitute the word *haptic* for tactile was prompted by William M. Austin's section on nonverbal communication in *Culture, Class, and Language Variety*, ed. A. L. Davis (Urbana, Ill.: National Council of Teachers of English, 1972), p. 146.

For centuries thinkers have, arbitrarily and capriciously, divided people into pairs: those who have moustaches and those who do not; those who play the oboe and those who do not; those who like comic books and those who do not. To these, let us presumptuously add those who *touch* and those who *do not touch*. To be realistic and fair, the concept of touching should include:

1. WHO is doing the touching and WHO is being touched.
2. REASONS for touching.
3. ZONES of the body being touched.
4. WHEN and WHERE touching occurs.

Who Is Doing the Touching

There are people you know or have known that compulsively touch everyone and everything. In fruit stores and markets, they are the culprits for whom the proprietors post signs: PLEASE DON'T SQUEEZE THE TOMATOES. In parks, they find the newly painted bench irresistible—especially if there is a sign which reads: WET PAINT. These *touchophiliacs* do not stop at fruits and vegetables or wet paint; they also include humans as fair game. When they walk, sit, or stand near you, they physically seek to commandeer the very space you are occupying. Touching, tapping, poking, shoving, guiding, pushing, patting, rubbing, pawing, and pulling are the unmistakable characteristics by which they can be recognized. In addition, the diagnosis of a touchophiliac is clinched when you hear him say, "Who me? I never do that!"

People, like animals, seem to be either *contact* or *noncontact* types. Some contact animals are the walrus, hippopotamus, pig, bat, parakeet, and hedgehog; while noncontact ones include the horse, dog, cat, and rat.[40] Although the extent to which most humans touch each other varies according to the situation, there seems to be a tendency (in most cases) for the "touchers" to touch and the "nontouchers" not to touch. This desire to handle things may be detectable in early life. Certain children cling to their mothers like leeches, while others are content to sit by themselves and play in a corner. Thus, the touching-type child and its affinity for this particular form of communication may be significantly affected by the manner in which it is raised. In some families, touching is a free and everyday occurrence. In others, it is virtually nonexistent.

Who Is Being Touched

With regard to the touchable and untouchable types, have you ever noticed certain people whom you would not dare touch and others who

---

[40] Hall, *Hidden Dimension*, p. 13.

have such a "welcome mat" demeanor that you would not hesitate to put your arm around their shoulders? It is difficult to articulate why we have these insights about people's approachability and touchability. All most of us have to go on is a "feeling" which can rarely be explained.

One determinant of an individual's touchability is the sensitivity of his nervous system. Some are so hypersensitive that being touched unexpectedly causes them to literally jump. Others possess nervous thresholds that are so high it would take a mini-mugging to get them to respond. Contrary to popular opinion, these people cannot easily change their manner of responding. In the majority of cases the response is reflexive and so quick that they haven't time to reflect upon the action. It can, however, be modified somewhat through conditioning. The ballerina, for example, needs to condition herself to accept the manner in which her partner must hold her in order to execute certain lifts. Likewise, the actor, engaged in a torrid love scene, must not allow physical contact to detract from his concentration on the dialogue. In both instances, responses to being touched must be subjected to a stringent discipline of the mind.

Extending beyond normal limits, depending upon your definition of normal, there are certain pathological conditions involving exaggerated haptic appetites. One of these is masochism—the desire to be touched abusively (beating, kicking, slapping, whipping, and the like). In contrast, there is sadism, wherein psychosexual gratification is derived from the administration of such physical abuse. A relevant term used in science, symbiosis, aptly fits what has been referred to as a sado-masochistic relationship. Simply, it is a situation in which both parties, by the very nature of the roles they play, fulfill the other's haptic needs. In this particular case, the need is to touch and be touched in a very special way.

M. F. A. Montagu cites many animal and human studies to support the theory that haptic satisfaction during infancy and childhood is of fundamental importance to the subsequent healthy behavioral development of the person.[41] This raises three questions: (1) Are there children who do not receive adequate tactile stimulation? (2) Is it true that today's parents hug, kiss, and handle their children less than their grandparents did?[42] (3) Do modern parents consider spanking vulgar and obsolete and spend relatively little time with their children in physical play? Children raised in orphanages have been observed to be apathetic and listless and reported to receive minimal, if any, physical contact; schizophrenic children have

[41] M. F. A. Montagu, Touching: The Human Significance of the Skin (New York: Columbia University Press, 1971), p. 188.
[42] This may be due to the fact that many immigrants who arrived in this country at the turn of the century had to live in crowded quarters; sometimes three and four children slept in a single bed, the natural consequence being a good deal of touching. Today, the trend is for each child to have not only his own bed but his own room.

been reported to be deprived of handling and mothering as infants.[43] According to Frank,[44] denying or depriving a child of these early tactile experiences may compromise his future learning—speech, cognition, symbolic recognition, and capacity for more mature tactile communication as an adult. Could such a deficiency in being touched be responsible for the recent popularity of sensitivity groups and games in which considerable importance has been placed on the ability to touch and be touched without fear?

Experts in the field seem to agree that haptic codes are culture-specific and often cause certain customs to be labeled as strange or unnatural. It has been said that Americans are "hung up" on not being touched. A ride on any densely crowded means of public transportation should convince even the most devout skeptic of its truth. Many an inadvertent or truly accidental contact between strangers has led to a fight.

Packed like sardines, the residents of any urban center stand in silence on buses and subway trains during rush hours either looking blankly out into space or buried deeply in their newspapers. Bodies, uncomfortably pressed against one another, dread the experience in unison. This same dilemma does not occur, however, among the Arabs, who have a much higher tolerance for crowding in public spaces and conveyances than Americans and northern Europeans. According to Hall,[45] people of the Arab world play by an entirely different set of rules when it comes to being touched. Their tendency to shove and push each other in public places and to feel and pinch women would not be tolerated by any self-respecting Westerner. In the Western world, a person's outside is synonymous with his inside. To touch either his clothes or skin requires permission, if you are a stranger. For the Arab, the location of the person, in relation to the body, is quite different. The "person" exists somewhere deep inside the body. Consequently, they do not consider being touched on the outside as an invasion of privacy. There is no such thing as an intrusion in public. Public is public for the Arabs.

Reasons for Touching

One of the most reliable ways of determining that you exist is to touch or pinch yourself. For most people, this method is adequate proof. Others require additional evidence, such as verification by another person whom they accept as existing via a birth certificate or an affiliation with some

[43] Mark Knapp, *Nonverbal Communication in Human Interaction* (New York: Holt, Rinehart and Winston, 1972), p. 110.
[44] Lawrence K. Frank, "Tactile communication," *Genetic Psychology Monographs* 56 (1957), 209–55.
[45] Hall, *Hidden Dimension*, pp. 156–57.

established idea, act, or deed. What kind of proof do you require that you exist? Is touching enough, or would you have to resort to some deep phenomenological means? While you are thinking about that, here are some of the reasons people touch:

EXAMPLES:

Touching for Pleasure
1. Bathing.   2. Sexual gratification.   3. Certain sports.

Reader's example: _____

Touching for Profit
1. The healing arts (medicine, dentistry, etc.).   2. Massage.
3. Prostitution.   4. Hairdressing and cosmetics.

Reader's example: _____

Touching to Attract
1. Child pulling on mother's skirt to get her attention.
2. Tapping someone who has dropped something.
3. Poking a friend in the ribs to alert him to something happening on the screen during a good suspense movie.

Reader's example: _____

Touching to Distract
1. Having a friend or relative kiss, hug, or tickle you while you are trying to concentrate on reading a good book.
2. Being nudged repeatedly on a crowded bus or train while engaged in a serious discussion with a friend.

Reader's example: _____

Instrumental Touching
1. Being pulled back on the curb by a good Samaritan when you absent-mindedly begin crossing a street against the light.
2. Helping a blind person do something or go somewhere.
3. Being shaken by your mother to get up and go to school.

Reader's example: _____

Religious Touching
1. Being baptized.   2. Being circumsized.
3. Having ashes applied on your forehead on Ash Wednesday.

Reader's example: _____

Salutatory Touching
1. Hand shaking.   2. Kissing.   3. Hugging.
4. Back slapping.   5. Pinching or patting on the cheek.

Reader's example: _____

Palliative Touching
1. Stroking the forehead of someone with a headache.
2. Neck rubbing for tension release.
3. Briskly rubbing hands of someone who feels chilled.

Reader's example: _____

Punctuative Touching
1. Poking the person to whom you are talking in order to make a point: "Listen, wise guy, I'm talking to YOU!" (The poke is coordinated with the word YOU.)
2. Being pushed from the rear as you hear the words, "Go ahead, Lenny, ask him."

Reader's example: _____

Zones of the Body Being Touched

Most children, after exploring their little bodies during the first year of life, soon discover that certain zones hurt when touched and others feel good. Erotic areas quickly earn top priority in the child's emerging sensitivities. Masturbation, for too many years, has been treated as a taboo and warned against in most households. Old wives' tales about this haptic form of self-indulgence has been associated with such fates as going blind, crazy, or to hell. Only in recent years has the medical profession volunteered the view that it is not so much masturbation that is harmful, but rather the GUILT often accompanying it. The puritanical attitude toward touching oneself in any of the commonly labeled "erotic zones" continues to echo: "No, no!"

If, as the animal data suggest, contact is the primitive language of love, then extensive physical contact may be, indeed, the natural or primordial sedative or tranquilizer—without the dangerous side effects of pharmaceutical compounds. From even a passing glance at current psychoanalytical literature, it seems that the role body accessibility plays in nonverbal communication demands more serious attention than it has received heretofore.

One imaginative investigator recognized the crucial role haptic communication plays in everyday living and made some interesting observations. He watched pairs of people engaged in conversation in coffee shops in San Juan (P.R.), London, Paris, and Gainesville (Fla.) and counted the number of times one person touched another at one table during a one-hour sitting. The scores were: for San Juan, 180; for London, 0; for Paris, 110; and for Gainesville, 2. He made similar observations in mental hospitals in the United States where, as a matter of policy, physical contact of any kind between professional staff and patients and among patients is discouraged. By contrast, at the French hospital he visited, physical contact was deliberately encouraged and seen as an important aspect of rehabilitation.[46]

During the past decade, Parent-Teacher Associations across the country have discussed the pros and cons of introducing into their regional schools a course in sex education. After much heated debate, both private and public (on radio and television), in those municipalities where it was accepted and incorporated into the curriculum, it was predominantly restricted to the physiology of sex. Rarely, if at all, was there any mention of the erotic zones to be manually stimulated for maximum excitation. Body positions facilitating optimal skin contacts were also conspicuous by their absence. In consequence, references to "biologic zoning" in the twentieth century still remain members in good standing of that well-known organization called "Unmentionables, Inc."

When and Where Touching Occurs

Each culture dictates its own touching protocol. Consider one of the oldest forms of human contact—hand-holding. Although a young man and woman attending the same school may hold hands privately and break no rule of propriety, they may be in violation when they hold hands in the same class during a lecture. The act of kissing is also subordinate to certain unwritten social codes dependent upon where it is done. Though it is a popular public pastime in America, it is an exclusively private act of lovemaking in the Orient which, if performed publicly, arouses disgust. In Japan, it is necessary to censor it out of the major portion of love scenes in American-made movies.[47]

Most of the rules governing the location of various touching practices are predicated upon context. For instance, a middle-aged couple seeing a pair of teenagers feverishly kissing and hugging each other in a corner booth of a restaurant, might say, "Why can't those kids do their smooching somewhere else instead of where people are eating. Don't they know there's a time and place for everything and this is neither the time nor the place."

Those who have traveled through Europe must be acquainted with the reputation Italian men have for pinching female American tourists. It has even been suggested in certain quarters that some women who go there

---

[46] S. M. Jourard, "An exploratory study of body-accessibility," *British Journal of Social and Clinical Psychology* 5 (1966), 221–31.
[47] Weston La Barre, "Paralinguistics, kinesics, and cultural anthropology," in Thomas Sebeok et al., eds., *Approaches to Semiotics* (The Hague: Mouton, 1964), p. 199.

are actually offended if they aren't pinched at least once. The point is that while in Italy this particular brand of touching may be both tolerated and a national hobby, it does not enjoy the same poetic license in the United States.

The relationship between people's moods and their touching tendencies is important. The touching behavior of most winners on television quiz shows almost invariably demonstrates this phenomenon. At least 8 out of 10 female winners kiss or hug the master of ceremonies (or anyone in sight, for that matter).

Leaning toward the negative, more sorrowful situations also precipitate an increase in touching. To comfort those grieving the death of a loved one, friends and relatives embrace more readily and render whatever physical support they deem appropriate to the occasion. Haptic conduct during wartime, where survival is the prime objective, causes the majority of people to band together emotionally and spiritually—as well as physically.

We all engage in two types of scratching: OVERT and COVERT. Before going further, it should be noted that all self-respecting animals, when they have an itch, scratch! This is not the case with Man. He must not only take into careful consideration the part of his body that itches but also where he is at the particular time of itching.

Overt scratching, bluntly speaking, refers to satisfying an itch in any part of the body except the genito-anal region. All other areas are considered public domain and may be scratched to one's heart's content. The genito-anal zone requires more deliberation. Scratching etiquette, with the exception of the breast area, is the same for men and women. Outside of the aforementioned areas, both sexes enjoy unrestricted privileges to scratch whenever and wherever they wish. An itch in a forbidden zone can be dealt with overtly by indirectly getting at it with a handbag, umbrella, pencil, pen, or book; or, covertly, one may withdraw to some secluded corner and, with lightning speed, "sneak-a-scratch." Under no circumstance should anyone allow himself to be caught doing this because it can be exceedingly embarrassing.

A System of Haptic Notation

Recognizing the need for a method of recording observed or experienced haptic communication, William Austin conceived the following system or code (see Fig. 5–8). On the right are the receptors—those parts of the body being touched; on the left are the parts doing the touching. The lines arranged vertically indicate the amount of pressure being exerted. Example: $(-)$ for slight pressure, $(=)$ for medium pressure and $(\equiv)$ for heavy.

The number of lines arranged horizontally represent the number of repetitions executed. Example: = = = indicating three touches of medium pressure.

After examining Austin's sample haptic notations, try to decipher the hypothetical touching situations in Fig. 5–8 using his notation system.

Code	Meaning
p = = > l sh	two rather heavy pats by the palm on the left shoulder
p — > r k	one light touch of the palm on the right knee (left versus right is probably nonsignificant)
f ≡ > j	a punch in the jaw
fn — > lo a	a fingertip touch on the lower arm (a "woman's touch")
el — — > el	two slight nudges of one elbow against someone else's
ft — > ft	a foot nudge (generally under the table—"discontinue that line of talk" or "watch the card you're going to play")
kn = > st	a fairly heavy knuckle touch (mock fist) in the stomach ("You old so-and-so!")
k — > k	a knee nudge, for people sitting side by side
pp = > ha	both palms covering another's hand with some pressure
kn — — — > up l a	repeated light taps of the knuckle on the left upper arm; a warning
lp — > ck	a light kiss on the cheek

FIGURE 5–8 Touching Situations.[48]

To be sure that you understand, take a moment to transcribe into code the following haptic incidents:

Meaning	Code
1. A heavy knee kick to the jaw	1. _____
2. Three light kisses on the hand	2. _____
3. A heavy elbow to the stomach	3. _____

From the information presented thus far, there is good reason to believe that in the near future, once satisfactory notation systems have been de-

[48] William M. Austin, "Nonverbal communication," in *Culture, Class, and Language,* ed. A. L. Davis (Urbana, Ill.: National Council of Teachers of English, 1972), pp. 151–52.

veloped in kinesics, proxemics, and haptics, there will be nonverbal stenographers trained to record extralinguistic communications.

PARALANGUAGE

"It's not what you're saying that offends me, but how you're saying it."

This one statement tells exactly what paralanguage is all about. George Trager, in a more sophisticated manner, does the same thing with a definition.

> When language is used it takes place in the setting of an act of *speech*. Speech ("talking") results from activities which create a background of VOICE SET. Against this background there occurs a range of cues employing the vocal apparatus. There are VOCALIZATIONS that characterize, qualify, and segregate how you speak, and VOICE QUALITIES that modify it further. Together these are referred to as PARALANGUAGE.[49]

Perhaps arranging his meaning differently will help.

PARALANGUAGE

VOCAL QUALITIES

PITCH (spread, narrowed)

RANGE (vocal lip control)

ARTICULATION (forced, relaxed)

RHYTHM (smooth, jerky)

RESONANCE (resonant, thin)

TEMPO (increased, decreased)

VOCALIZATIONS

CHARACTERIZERS

laughing

sobbing

crying

moaning

whispering

clearing the throat

yelling

sniffing

QUALIFIERS

intensity (too loud, too soft)

pitch height (too high, too low)

extent (drawl, clipping)

SEGREGATES

uh-huh

shh!

silence

[49] George L. Trager, "Paralanguage: A first approximation," in *Studies in Linguistics* 13 (1958), 1–12.

Paralanguage in Practice   .

Since the credo of this text is *functionality*, this discussion of paralanguage will be arranged so it fits a familiar setting: the classroom. Imagine it is the beginning of a new semester and you are on your way to class with a new teacher. For our purposes, exclude those teachers with whom you have taken previous courses. *Target:* the completely strange teacher.

Eliminating the scramble for correct buildings, floors, and rooms, you breathlessly arrive at, let us say, Room 285. Seated near a window (as is your custom), you patiently wait for the teacher to arrive. Several of the usual questions circulate through your brain: (1) will it be a male or female, (2) young or old, (3) good-looking or ugly, (4) interesting or boring, (5) understandable or incoherent, (6) informative or a B.S. artist, (7) easy or hard grader, (8) good or bad speaker. While questions 1 through 7 are of potential importance to the success or failure of any course, this section on paralanguage addresses itself to number 8—the good or bad speaker.

It is 9:00 A.M. and the teacher walks into the room. Instantly, your senses begin to monitor all data emanating from him, rational and irrational. By the end of the period, you have come away with the traditional "first impression." Naturally, the basis for it will be multifaceted. We, however, will focus solely on his *speech delivery*. There is an expression, "The operation was successful, but the patient died." Its meaning applies here: "The lecture was successful, but the student didn't learn a thing!" Our task—to discover whether certain paralinguistic agents may have been responsible for your reactions.

Most people tend to equate a low, deep voice with sophistication and sexiness. Knapp[50] mentions that some speech scientists talk of a "vocal neurosis" from which many radio announcers, salesmen, receptionists and lawyers suffer. Its major symptom—the pursuit of the low, deep voice. If your teacher happens to have a low and deep voice, you might easily (consciously or unconsciously) impute to him the associated attractive traits. Some of the other characteristics that have been assigned to speakers (though somewhat less consistently) on the basis of their vocal quality are (1) enthusiastic or apathetic, (2) energetic or lazy, (3) extroverted or introverted, (4) honest or dishonest, (5) law-abiding or criminal, (6) healthy or sickly.[51] Think of a teacher you have had who was enthusiastic. What kind of a voice did he have? Now reflect upon one who appeared

[50] Mark L. Knapp, *Nonverbal Communication in Human Reaction* (New York: Holt, Rinehart and Winston, 1972), p. 151.
[51] D. W. Addington, "The relationship of selected vocal characteristics to personality perception," *Speech Monographs* 35 (1968), 492–503.

lazy and low on energy. What type of voice did he have? *You are now thinking in paralinguistic terms.*

In an effort to discover the relationship between vocal expression and emotional meaning, Davitz[52] conducted an unusual experiment in which he had speakers express ten different feelings by reciting letters of the alphabet. They were then recorded and played to judges who were asked to identify the emotions expressed by choosing from a list of ten emotions. Davitz concluded that regardless of the techniques used in this type of inquiry, all studies of adults, thus far reported in the literature, agree that emotional meanings can be communicated accurately by vocal expression. Although findings like these might whet the appetite of the serious student of public address and interpersonal communication, a modicum of restraint is in order. A *dictionary of emotions* defined in paralinguistic terms is still a long way off. This, of course, should not preclude making a tentative judgment of a teacher's emotional disposition on the basis of his vocal personality. The danger in such a practice is that it often leads to sweeping generalizations that are grossly unwarranted.

Veering off in a slightly different direction, consider a teacher's speech speed. Understand that the normal rate of speaking is between 125–190 words per minute (wpm). Does how quickly or slowly a teacher speaks make any difference in your comprehension of what he is saying? It should. Some experts feel that speeds of over 200 wpm begin to show signs of decreased comprehension, while others place the level of decline between 275 and 300 wpm. Indications are that the average preferred speed is about one and one-half times normal speed.[53] What would you do if, on the first listening, a teacher manifested a speech speed of between 240–280 wpm? Would you drop the course or brace yourself for some muddled and fuzzy comprehending?

The credibility of a teacher is next on our agenda. Will the information he give you be reliable? Sereno and Hawkins suggest, "As nonfluencies increase, ratings for a speaker's competence and dynamism decrease. . . ." Nonfluencies, according to these researchers, include "ah, sentence change, repetition, tongue slip and stutter."[54] How do you rate a teacher's credibility in relation to his nonfluencies? Does his delivery suffer from any of these, and, if so, how badly? This writer recalls some classroom pranksters who, upon encountering a teacher using multiple *ers* and *ahs* and *uh-huhs*, would count them to see how many he would deliver in one period.

---

[52] J. R. Davitz, *The Communication of Emotional Meaning* (New York: McGraw-Hill, 1964), p. 23.
[53] D. B. Orr, "Time compressed speech—a perspective," *Journal of Communication* 18 (1968), 288–92.
[54] K. K. Sereno and G. J. Hawkins, "The effect of variations in speakers' nonfluency upon audience ratings of attitude toward speech topic and speakers' credibility," *Speech Monographs* 34 (1967), 58–64.

Hesitations or *pauses* in speech patterns also come under the jurisdiction of paralanguage. Most of us normally "speak in chunks." The important question is, "How large are the chunks and what happens in between them?" An analogy could be made to eating. Some people bite off more than they can chew and spend the following half minute trying not to choke or suffocate. Others nip off tiny bits of food and, like white mice, chew in miniscule volleys of rapid jaw action. The interval between mouthfuls also varies. Some NEVER can be found with an empty oral cavity, shoveling spoonful after spoonful, forkful after forkful, in uninterrupted cadence from plate to palate. These same rhythmic patterns appear to occur with speech.

Take notice and you will find there are two types of pauses: *filled* and *unfilled*. It is the unfilled hesitation or pause that can drive some of us up a wall. The average unfilled hesitation or pause (complete silence) usually lasts from one to two seconds. What would you do if one of your teachers produced pauses lasting from eight to ten seconds? Could you tolerate them? When you were in public school, do you remember the tendency certain teachers had of assuming that you didn't know the answer to a question if you hesitated in answering it? The proverb, "He who hesitates is lost!" was invented for these teachers. If, on the other hand, your hesitations or pauses were filled with ers, *ahs*, and *uh-huhs*, the indictment against you was revised to read: unclear, confused, and disorganized.

A more tolerant attitude toward these paralinguistic phenomena rationalizes them as having either a physiological or psychological explanation. However, regardless of how one approaches their diagnosis or management, a major hope is that should you get a teacher who manifests these extralinguistic vocal elements, they will not interfere with your learning or final grade. It seems that paralanguage, like a sleeping giant, is of little or no consequence until it affects you personally. Thus, since chance does favor the prepared mind, it might behoove you to pay closer attention in future to the vocal behavior of others as well as your own.

EYE-CONTACT

If you are looking for a hobby, this book enthusiastically recommends "people watching." It requires no special equipment save a pair of working eyes, no financial expense, and it can be indulged in practically anywhere. Granting that "people watching" usually incorporates a survey of the entire person, here it will be restricted to eye-contact.

Few parts of the body have received more attention from poets, painters, and songwriters than the eyes. While we can measure blood pressure with a sphygmomanometer, cardiac function with an electrocardiogram, brain activity with an electroencephalogram, we have no way of measuring the interpersonal messages dispatched by our eyes. So important are they to human communication that whenever someone's identity is to be protected, only the eyes are covered (Fig. 5–9). Medical texts classically illustrate this practice when showing patients with various diseases.

FIGURE 5–9 Concealing a Patient's Identity.

Each day we engage in dozens of people-watching encounters with strangers, family, and friends. And, while they last but a second or two, their meanings may vary from the very innocent to the deeply profound. Great loves have been known to begin with little more than a fleeting glance, whereas men have been killed for looking at one another the wrong way (whatever the "wrong way" means). What is there about the way certain people "look" that elicits feelings of being liked or disliked? Argyle and Dean tell us that when two people like one another, they establish eye-contact more often and for a longer duration than when there is tension in their relationship.[55] Perhaps you have noticed this phenomenon in some of your classes, where a professor looks at those students whom he likes more frequently than those whom he dislikes. Or, have you noticed among your friends that those who are more dependent upon you for reinforcement tend to maintain more eye-contact than those feeling less need for reinforcement? Exline and Winters'[56] research corroborates this tendency.

A variety of the studies dealing with eye-contact have started to confirm many of the common-sense impressions and observations we have been experiencing all our lives. For example, one study reveals that people tend to increase their eye-contact with those from whom they seek recognition or approval;[57] another, dealing with eye-contact among group members, reports that those who spent the most time looking at their fellow dis-

[55] Michael Argyle and Janet Dean, "Eye-contact, distance and affiliation," Sociometry 28 (1965), 289–304.
[56] R. Exline and L. Winters, "Affective relations and mutual glances in dyads," in Affect, Cognition and Personality, ed. S. Tomkins and C. Izard (New York: Springer, 1965), pp. 319–30.
[57] J. Efran and A. Broughton, "Effects of expectancies for social approval on visual behavior," Journal of Personality and Social Psychology 86 (1972), 29–33.

cussants (looking and listening while the person was speaking) saw themselves as having more influence than those who spent less time looking at the speakers.[58] All of the experimental research, however, does not cover such familiar terrain. Hess, for instance, discovered that the pupils of homosexual males will dilate (become larger) when they are shown pictures of other males; whereas heterosexual males will manifest the same response when shown pictures of females.[59] This phenomenon raises the question of whether or not an individual's pupillary responses might be considered an index of his attitudes (that is, they dilate in response to positive experiences and constrict in response to negative ones).

Turning now from the experimental to the experiential, let us wonder together about the different kinds of "looks" people display (such as sexy, shifty, evil, jealous, suspicious, hypnotic, antagonistic, dirty, and wise-guy). If you can think of a few more, write them in the spaces that follow:

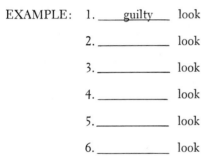

EXAMPLE: 1.____guilty____ look

            2._____ look

            3._____ look

            4._____ look

            5._____ look

            6._____ look

What is there about being "looked at" in a certain way that drives some people crazy and others into a state of smug satisfaction? If you had a dollar for every fight that began with "And what the hell are you looking at!" you could probably retire twice over. It is amazing how many daily communications take place on an exclusively visual level. Stop and reflect for a moment about the different types of interactions you have had personally that functioned on a purely eye-contact basis. Consider such exchanges as those you have had with some of your teachers, your Mom or Dad at home, or your boss at work. Estimate how accurately these glances represent how you think or feel in a particular situation. Now, before con-

[58] R. Weisbrod, "Looking behavior in discussion groups," unpublished report cited by M. Argyle and A. Kendon in "The experimental analysis of social performance," in Advances in Experimental Social Psychology, ed. L. Berkowitz, Vol. 3 (New York: Academic Press, 1967), pp. 55–98.

[59] E. H. Hess, A. L. Seltzer, and J. M. Shlien, "Pupil Response of Hetero- and Homosexual Males to Pictures of Men and Women: A Pilot Study," Journal of Abnormal Psychology 70 (1965), 165–68.

tinuing, make a value judgment as to the importance of eye-contact in human communication.

Rationale for Eye-Contact

One of the best ways to fully appreciate the importance of eye-contact in communication is to engage in a group discussion while you are blind-folded. If this exercise is successful, you should be able to agree or disagree with Knapp on the different conditions he claims are influenced by eye-contact: whether we are seeking feedback, whether we need certain markers in conversation, whether we wish to open or close the communication channel, whether the other party is too near or too far, whether we wish to induce anxiety, whether we are rewarded by what we see, whether we are in competition with another or wishing to hide something from him, and whether we are with members of a different sex or status.[60] Essentially, these items cover the major reasons why people engage in eye-contact with one another, plus those personality characteristics that are woven into them. Try and think of one practical situation which illustrates each factor mentioned by Knapp. (A few have been filled in to help you along.)

1. Seeking feedback _____

2. Need for conversation marker _____

3. Open or close communication channel *Looking away from someone because he bores you.*

4. Other party too near or far _____

5. To induce anxiety *The way a teacher looks at the student he knows is unprepared..*

6. Rewarded by what we see _____

7. In competition _____

8. Wishing to hide something _____

9. Member of a different sex *The way a guy looks at a pretty girl.*

10. Member of a different status _____

Types of and Reasons for Eye-Contact

Eye-contact may be either purposeful (overtly or covertly intentional) or purposeless (completely lacking intentionality), and the gaze may be

[60] M. L. Knapp, Nonverbal Communication in Human Interaction (New York: Holt, Rinehart and Winston, 1972), p. 138.

Direct gaze

Downward gaze

Upward gaze

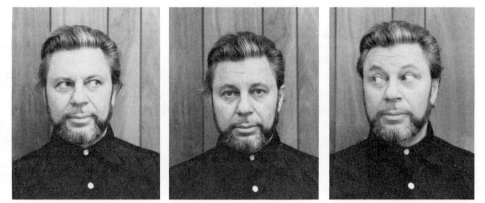

Left lateral gaze   Vacant gaze   Right lateral gaze

FIGURE 5-10 Variations of Gaze.

classified as: (1) direct, (2) upward, (3) downward, (4) right or left lateral, and (5) vacant. Figure 5-10 illustrates each of these.

Basically, people give six reasons for looking at one another: to *attract*, *acknowledge*, *distract*, *reject*, *intimidate*, or *explore*. Here is how each occurs in everyday life.

1. *Eye-Contact to Attract*
   Boy- or girl-watchers use their eye-contact to attract members of the opposite sex.
2. *Eye-Contact to Acknowledge*
   While conducting an oral quiz, a professor frequently, through eye-contact, acknowledges the student with her hand raised (indicating that he knows that she knows the answer) and passes to another

whose eyes register panic and reek with signs of NOT knowing the answer.

3. *Eye-Contact to Distract*
   Some students feel frightfully upset having a professor stand nearby and watch them while they are taking a final examination.

4. *Eye-Contact to Reject*
   Being interviewed for a job and having a personnel manager reject you with his eyes and say, "We have several more interviews. Don't call us, we'll call you."

5. *Eye-Contact to Intimidate*
   Two people simultaneously see a parking space. After glaring at each other for a moment, one yields because of an intimidating look—that wide-eyed look on the face of a person capable of doing almost anything for a parking space.

6. *Eye-Contact to Explore*
   The physician, while conducting an examination, looks searchingly at his patient for signs and symptoms incidental to making a diagnosis.

The Value of Eye-Contact

Are you aware that the better the eye-contact, the better the listening? Have you noticed that if you look off into every direction except that of the person to whom you are talking, you seriously reduce the extent to which he listens? Recall, if you will, the teacher who walks into the classroom, shuffles some notes, and, never looking up, lectures without interruption for a straight fifty minutes. If, perchance, he should look up, his gaze unfailingly bypasses the class and lights on such important items as ceiling fixtures, light switches, outdoor activities, or a hangnail on his index finger. This, fortunately, is an extreme case, not encountered too often. Had he spent these same fifty minutes engaging members of his audience in closed-circuit eye-contact, the attention and listening levels probably would have been higher, there would have been more nonverbal feedback from individual students and a greater sense of cohesiveness, increased comprehension and retention of the subject matter, more decorum, and a heightened interest in the lecture. For optimal face-to-face communication, eye-contact is an indispensable ally for speaker and listener alike.

CLOTHING—HAIR—ODORS—BAUBLES—BANGLES —BEADS

People can be compared with letters: they are contained in envelopes (clothes), sent, received, and bear messages. When you receive a letter, how much are you able to tell about the message inside by looking at the envelope? Is its importance hinted at by being REGISTERED, SPECIAL DE-LIVERY, AIR MAIL or FIRST CLASS; quality by its rag content; formality by whether it is addressed in longhand or imprinted; biases by special stamps or stickers; and, finally, love content by its color or fragrance? All, to varying extents, communicate something about what is contained in an envelope.

Steal a moment from whatever you are doing and look at your own envelope. What do you think it tells about you (the message)? (1) Are you important or unimportant? (2) Are you of good quality? (3) Are you formal or informal? (4) Are your biases showing? (5) Are you a loving person?

> Clothes . . . to the wearer . . . represent an effort to control the reactions of others, and to the observer, they are the means by which individuals can be socially classified.[61]

What is your candid opinion of the cliché, "Clothes make the man"? Many youth of the 60s took umbrage at it as an absurdity subscribed to by people over thirty. *En masse*, they began doing "their own thing" and, in the process, alienated numerous mothers and fathers. Throughout the land, voices of frustrated parents could be heard saying, "If you don't take off those dirty dungarees, wash yourself, and put on a regular pair of shoes, you're not coming with us." Unmoved, thousands of teenagers ignored their plea, convinced that the letter in the envelope (the person in the clothes) was more important than the clothes. As the 60s drew to a close, telling the difference between a boy and a girl became increasingly more difficult.

Then, adding insult to injury, *unisex clothes* appeared on the scene. The expression, *clothes make the man*, had to be amended to read, *clothes make the person*, then amended again to read *the same clothes make the man and woman*. Attire seemed to be feverishly caught up in a new "revolution in fashion."

One of the most telling blows struck by youth involved the question of HAIR. For some reason, when young men let the hair on their heads and faces grow, society fell to its knees. Adults, when asked what it was about long hair that upset them, answered in bits and pieces: "They look unclean—wild—degenerate—unkempt—they just look terrible!!!" Shopkeepers refused to admit them, business and industry would not hire them, and professional schools rejected their applications once they saw their admission photos. All this furor because of hair, hair, and more hair.

---

[61] Eisenberg and Smith, *Nonverbal Communication*, p. 107.

Professor Guthrie,[62] a zoologist at the University of Alaska, recently did some research on the subject of human hair. He asks: "Why do people react differently to men with beards than to those without them?" And, "What is the function of pubic and underarm hair, eyebrows, beards, and long head hair?" Opposite to, but not in conflict with, the anatomical and biological opinion that hair in these places may serve some survival purpose, Guthrie subscribes to the view that "the beard, for example, seems to have developed as a way for adult males to intimidate each other; that the most successful way of achieving high rank in society is through intimidation or threat." Have you ever had the experience of waiting in your car for a traffic light to change and casually looking at someone in the car next to you? What do you think determines the length of the eye-contact? For most people, it is the "look" on the fellow's face. It could range from an innocent "love-your-fellow-man" expression to one that is angry, sad, annoyed, impervious, happy, or antagonistic. Guthrie argues that there are advantages and disadvantages to both concealing and revealing emotions, and that one of the major questions humans continually ask themselves is, "How much of myself should I reveal to others?" Is it also possible that the man in the next car is sporting a look on his face of which he is unaware. It might be a question of anatomical variance—which, you will recall, is a situation wherein either bone structure or facial musculature is atypical. This, in itself, can cause someone to look angry or bored and not be either.

Specifically, certain parts of the human face are responsible for threat: eyes (staring), nostrils (flared), eyebrows (tightly drawn together and downward), mouth (tense, with teeth bared), jaw (protruding, with musculature contracted). On the clean-shaven face, all of these features are open, clearly visible, and easily "read" by others. This kind of identification becomes increasingly difficult as the head hair is permitted to grow long, eyebrows get bushy, a mustache is cultivated, and a lush, full beard is grown. As a result of all this foliage, facially linked emotional indicators are blocked from view. This "masking" of emotional content, Guthrie feels, is responsible for people's feeling differently in the company of men with lots of hair on their heads and faces.

A good many of our attitudes, values, and beliefs are communicated by what we wear or don't wear, whether it be a rhinoceros tooth, a rhinestone in the navel, black nail polish, army boots, or a dueling scar neatly displayed on the right cheek. They make it possible for others to tell at a glance who we are, what we are, and what we stand for. Americans are devout button, badge, and emblem wearers. Name the cause and a dozen

---

[62] R. D. Guthrie, "The evolution of menace," *Saturday Review of Sciences* 1:4 (April 28, 1973), 22–28.

buttons will spring from nowhere, ready to be pinned, glued, or sewn on the first passerby.

Few things produce greater feelings of security and calm than uniformity. What woman, in her right mind, can resist smiling approvingly at twin boys or girls, dressed alike and propped up in their carriage. Parades are known for their ability to excite people from eight to eighty with their columns of humans, all dressed alike, marching to the booming sound of a brass band.

John T. Malloy believes so strongly that clothes make the man that in 1970 he became America's first "wardrobe engineer." A veritable B. F. Skinner of haberdashery, Malloy felt that clothing can be chosen to produce conditioned responses in others, and he turned his hypothesis into a business. His services were sought by men in all walks of life who wished to alter their images. He left nothing to chance—everything he chose for his clients was well thought out and deliberate—an excellent example of sartorial nonverbalism. Clothes certainly seem to have "made" Mr. Malloy.

Another instance of the relationship between self-image and grooming occurred at the detention center of the Massachusetts Department of Youth Services. The Clairol Company, operating on the premise that if you "look good," chances are that you will feel good and perceive your environment more favorably, decided to try an experiment. With the cooperation of Jay Paris, director of the detention center, nine teenage girls between 13 and 16 were used as subjects. Some of the reasons for their incarceration were prostitution, drug abuse, attempted suicide, and truancy. When asked if they felt beautiful, they all shouted, "NO!" With the help of Daniel Kelly of Continental Coiffeurs (a chain of ten salons in Massachusetts), the girls were started on a four-week grooming junket. Their hair cut and styled, faces brought into line with the latest in cosmetic fashion, and exposed to the fundamentals of poise and social graces at the famous John Robert Powers Finishing School, they emerged transformed—on the outside anyway. Now the question was, "Will such external changes affect their internal state?" Naturally, any conclusions based upon such an experiment should be drawn with at least one raised eyebrow. Director Paris did, however, come away with this comment: "It's really exciting to see their reactions. You very rarely see such a change in the girls in a matter of four or five hours." He went on to say, "The object of the program is to get the girls to feel a little better about themselves . . . to give them that added confidence so they'll allow other professionals to help them cope with the problems—emotional or otherwise—that got them into trouble."[63]

[63] Ginny Pitt, "Grooming improves delinquents' self-image," *Long Island Press*, January 26, 1974, p. 5.

Color is another form of nonverbal communication that has fascinated man for thousands of years. Traditionally, colors have been associated with personalities, character traits, and values. For instance, red is often coupled with passion, courage, cruelty, justice, and health. It was not too long ago that the barber-surgeons advertised their profession (surgery) by placing red and white striped poles outside their shops. Barbers, though they no longer perform surgery, still perpetuate this custom.

Like the plants and flowers associated with people mentioned in Chapter 4, there is also a plethora of color preferences in our language. Here are a few:

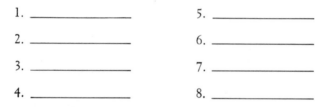

Paint the town red	Black is beautiful
Rose-colored glasses	It's a red-letter day
A scarlet woman	Yellow-belly
Red-hot news	That's white of you
Once in a blue moon	Green with envy
Yell blue murder	A bolt from the blue

If you can think of others, write them in the spaces below:

1. _____   5. _____

2. _____   6. _____

3. _____   7. _____

4. _____   8. _____

We can certainly join in speculation about why doctors and nurses wear white, while members of the clergy wear black—perhaps because white is generally associated with cleanliness and purity, black with unworldliness, immutability, and dignity. The mortician wears black because, nonverbally, it reveals the least, is the most sophisticated, and excites no one.

Clothes-conscious people insist that the colors they wear affect their moods, and vice versa. One student took the study of colors seriously and put them to work. Whenever he handed in a paper or a report, he chose a folder of the color most frequently worn by the teacher. He claimed it had a positive effect upon his grade.

Another nonverbal cue is odor. Whereas many lower forms of life could not survive without their sense of smell, man can. There are several terms the reader should be familiar with concerning the sense of smell: *macrosmia*—a highly developed sense of smell; *microsmia*—a poorly developed sense of smell; *parosmia*—a perverted sense of smell; *anosmia*—a loss of the sense of smell. Although we are all not equally endowed with the same ability to detect and differentiate odors, they play an important role in our behavior. Being able to recognize foul odors given off by food that has gone bad, smoke in the event of fire, or gasoline leaking from an automobile are but a few of the cases in which our sense of smell is important. Beyond these, its value is generally considered to be marginal. The perfume industry, naturally, feels differently. Most women and, now, men would not dream of going out of the house without splashing on a little cologne, toilet water, or perfume. Obviously, the mass media, via television commercials, have made the American viewer paranoid about "body odors." Incidentally, have you noticed the names given to these nose-oriented products: My Sin, Karate, Tabu, Brut, Joy, Skinny Dip, Indiscreet, Intimate, Primitif, Plaisir, etc. Beyond its psychosexual connotations, an individual may adopt a particular fragrance as his or her trademark.

Our lives are intimately bound up with odors. We recall so many people, places, and things by their odors. In contrast, there are the perverted odors hallucinated by the insane and those with epilepsy. An aura, for example, may be represented by an unpleasant odor described as resembling chloride of lime, burning rags, or feathers. Within the boundaries of normalcy, there are also a few odors that find acceptance among discriminating noses, such as leather upholstery of a new automobile, various organic fertilizers, freshly laundered clothes, a newly struck match, lighter fluid, and so on. But, regardless of your preference in odors, all are bona fide, if you like them. List in the blanks below some of your olfactory idiosyncrasies (your favorite odors):

_____   _____   _____

_____   _____   _____

A section on odors would be remiss if it didn't mention some intrapersonal and interpersonal implications. As incredible as it may sound, most people are strikingly unaware of how important a role odors play in our lives. Take the familiar, "Who, me?" syndrome shared by thousands of people whose body and breath odors offend others seven days a week, fifty-two weeks a year.

Moving in for a closer smell, let us consider those odors which qualify a home or apartment as having "house-atosis." Specifically, what are some of the odor producing items that might keep the guest book at your house perpetually unsigned? Do you smoke cigars, burn incense, cook much fish or cabbage—or is there an infant around whose diaper pail is never empty?

On a more personal note, breath odors are commonplace offenders; onion and garlic eaters leading the pack. Then, there are clothing odors which cause some people to smell as if they had just stepped out of a hamper or lived in a locker room. In fact, certain of the newer synthetic fabrics have also been known to produce unpleasant odors after they have been cleaned or washed.

Rashes that flake or weep, gastrointestinal disturbances, infections or inflammation of the teeth and gums, nose and throat problems, genitourinary embarrassment are but a few of the specific odor-producing pathologies having the potential to break down or seriously interfere with interpersonal communication.

So, to be perfectly certain that your checklist of nonverbal messages is complete, do not neglect to include odors among them.

SUMMARY

This chapter commenced by alerting the reader to the growing interest in communication without words—nonverbal communication. We noted also that in a speech-centered society, being able to get up on your feet and talk is "a must." The arguable impression was given that more can be learned about a person by watching his body movements and gestures than by listening to what he says. The reader has been encouraged to draw his own conclusions.

Emotions were then discussed in terms of expression through muscular activity. For instance, if someone is unable to vent his hostility in words, a psychosomatic route might be chosen. Asthma, hypertension, ulcers, and migraine headaches are some of the conditions which can result from blocked wordways.

Next, a quiz was presented that probes the correlation between how a person looks and how he actually is (see page 108). The relationship between structure and function was further explored with regard to phrenology, graphology, chiromancy, physiognomics, and somatotyping. This discussion was rounded off with the observation that people cannot help the way they sit, stand, walk, or move because of certain genetically determined anatomical traits.

A detailed description of haptic communication followed, describing the various circumstances in which people touched one another; where, when, and how they preferred to be touched; and giving a system of haptic notation. This led the reader into an explanation of paralanguage and its use in everyday speech, the effects of variations in clothing, hair, odors, and eye-contact as nonverbal cues to the inner self. Emphasized heavily was the importance of including in any communicational analysis its nonverbal components.

CHAPTER 6

VERBAL MESSAGES

INSIGHTS

After reading this chapter you should have a clearer understanding of:

- *how frustrating it can be to know what you want to communicate and not be able to find the right words.*
- *the basis for the expression, "There are some people who have something to say and others who have to say something."*
- *how arbitrary and capricious Man is in his labeling of people, places, and things.*
- *why the phrase, "sticks and stones can break my bones but names can never harm me" should not be accepted too lightly.*
- *not only how the structure of a verbal message creates a situation in which each element of the message is set in meaningful context with other elements of the message, but also how manipulating such structure and context can distort meaning.*
- *how the words we use are subject, like clothing styles, to whatever is currently fashionable.*
- *the semanticist's caution: THE WORD IS NOT THE THING.*

The ability to give a name to everything often passes for education. It is a common belief that to be able to name something is to know it; to define something is to "truly understand it."[1]

You have already been informed that nonverbal messages frequently act as "stand-ins" for verbal messages. This, however, will not do in a cosmopolitan society. From kindergarten through college and graduate school, compulsory education has jostled us from classroom to classroom, teaching us to label everything in sight and then define it. Examination after examination has tested our ability to "name things." As if this were not enough, television quiz shows and matching games have continued our programming by offering us rewards for correctly identifying people, places, and things. Not knowing the name of something has been unforgivable. Words seem to have taken us prisoner.

Educators and critics of education have bellowed for the past 40 years, "Johnny can't read or write properly." In spite of all the remedial courses in reading and writing that have become available, their benefit seems marginal. The need for competence, with regard to verbal messages, remains in a state of communicational emergency. Entrance and qualifying examinations are still heavily weighted in favor of reading comprehensively and writing tightly knitted essays. Despite efforts to find workable alter-

[1] John C. Condon, *Semantics and Communication* (New York: Macmillan, 1966), p. 30.

natives to these methods of evaluating verbal skills, they continue as the most reliable barometers of a student's academic status and potential. Thus, while the strong silent type might enjoy considerable success in life, unless he learns to manipulate words, his chances of success in a verbal milieu are limited. Actually, the ideal communication is one in which verbal and nonverbal messages are blended into a symbiotic state. Even under these optimal conditions you will find people who say, "*I know that you believe you understand what you think I said, but I am not sure you realize that what you heard is not what I meant.*" You can readily see that communication (verbal or nonverbal), at best, leaves much to be desired.

Verbal messages come in various sizes, shapes, and types. To be effective, you must know what kinds of messages to stock up on, ways and means of delivering them to a receiver, and, once delivered, how to deal appropriately with their consequences. To aid in achieving these goals, the remainder of this chapter will consist of a relatively informal discussion of Man and his symbols.

A VISITOR TO EARTH

What do you think fish think as they glide past each other in the briny deep or birds as they fly through the air or people as they scurry about on the crust of this planet? An extremely inventive writer named Bryng Bryngelson created a Mr. Glub, who claimed to be a reporter for the Venus *Star*, a newspaper published on the planet Venus. Glub, visiting this planet to report on our customs and conditions, made these observations:

> THE EARTH, Nov. 20. What struck me first on my arrival on this planet was the interminable din of human voices. It appears that the periods of silence and meditation required by our laws are wholly unknown here. The people on Earth talk all the time. On several occasions, however, I have observed in the public squares men and women talking when no one seemed to be listening. On inquiring into this curious situation, I was informed that they talk to hear themselves talk. To my question as to what they talked about, the invariable reply was *nothing*. When I asked what nothing was, I was told it is talk.
>
> They have another strange practice here of assembling vast quantities of the talk that is uttered in various places and publishing it in their newspapers and even books. I am informed that if in that form it is not generally read it is only because the people are too busy talking to do much reading. [Here endeth Mr. Glub's dispatch.][2]

[2] Bryng Bryngelson, "Man and his symbol," *The Speech Teacher* 11:2 (March, 1953), 81–82.

It would be an education to hear how certain members of our species would explain to Mr. Glub why we do so much talking and are so preoccupied with it. A psychologist would probably suggest that talking is one of the better ways of getting to know oneself and getting along with others; a physician—talking is an important means by which a patient is able to reveal his symptoms and thereby enable the doctor to treat him; an educator—talking facilitates a pooling of knowledge which, in turn, contributes to societal growth and understanding; a theologian—talking brings Man closer to God's Word and, through it, to serve Him more faithfully. No matter whom Mr. Glub would ask, some kind of an answer would be given. The only person who might give him some trouble would be the semanticist. In order to explain even partially why people talk so profusely, he would have to indicate that "words" do not necessarily mean what they are intended to mean, and the very words he must use to explain this phenomenon also run the risk of being misunderstood. Typically, when it comes to words, most of us conform to Abraham Kaplan's *Law of the Instrument*[3] which states, "Give a small boy a hammer and he will find that everything he encounters needs pounding." Earthlings, like Kaplan's small boy, also find that everything they encounter needs talking about.

For Mr. Glub to grasp our nature more fully, he must realize that the verbal messages we so liberally exchange tend to be rather vague and can be manipulated so that *anything can actually mean anything.* To illustrate this point more clearly, here are a few quotations you might care to interpret without regard to the context in which they were rendered. Churchill, addressing the House of Commons in 1940, said, "*I have nothing to offer but blood, toil, tears and sweat*"; Benjamin Franklin—"*They that can give up essential liberty to obtain a little temporary safety deserve neither liberty nor safety*"; Socrates—"*I am a citizen not of Athens or Greece, but of the world*"; Lincoln—"*That this nation, under God, shall have a new birth of freedom*"; Voltaire—"*I disapprove of what you say, but I will defend to the death your right to say it.*"[4] Each of these verbal messages, by itself, could be interpreted in many different ways; they have no fixed meanings.

Another warning of the dangers inherent in the spoken and written word comes from George Orwell in his prophetic book, *1984.* In it, he describes a conflict between what he calls Oldspeak and Newspeak, involving the relationship between language, thought, and behavior. Essentially,

[3] Abraham Kaplan, *The Conduct of Inquiry* (San Francisco: Chandler, 1964), p. 28.
[4] Lester Markel, "The future of the printed word," *Vital Speeches* (April, 1956), pp. 381–84.

the aim of Newspeak is to narrow the range of thought, so that thought-crime (as he calls it) would be made literally impossible, because there would be no words to express it. Every concept that could ever be needed would be expressed by exactly one word with its meaning rigidly defined and all its subsidiary meanings rubbed out and forgotten. Every year there would be fewer and fewer words, making the range of human conscious-ness a little smaller.

Although the opportunity to pass final judgment on Orwell's talents as a seer will arrive within a decade, our problems of communication will probably remain with us. If, by chance, Orwell is right and we do evolve a "perfect language," what price will we have to pay for it? Is it possible that we have already begun to pay?

VERBALLY COMMITTED

In everyday living, if we misspell, mispronounce, or misuse a word, it is generally excusable or correctable. There is one area, the field of mental health, in which such mistakes are not always so easily reversed. For in-stance, aside from psychotic and psychoneurotic nonverbal behavior, there are specific responses that occur in the minds of most psychiatrists, psycho-analysts, and psychologists when a "suspected" mental patient uses certain language or makes a particular remark.

In the past, a casual conversation over a glass of beer or wine may have prompted some of us to wonder what we would do or say if we were accidentally locked in a psychiatric ward. Dismissing the idea of claiming that you are "normal" and don't belong there, you desperately search for words which would convince your keepers that you are not mentally ill. David Rosenhan, a professor of psychology at Stanford University, was curious to learn just what would occur if this actually happened. Rosenhan and seven of his colleagues decided to conduct an experiment. Each made appointments with a mental hospital admissions office and told the same story: they were hearing voices, unclear voices, that seemed to be saying words like "empty, hollow, and thud." That's all they said—nothing more, no other symptoms, just words. For the admitting psychiatrists in twelve hospitals, these words were quite enough. All seven, including Rosenhan, were tagged with the diagnosis of schizophrenia; the eighth, with manic-depressive psychosis. The diagnoses stuck and the eight pseudo-patients were locked up for 7 to 52 days before being released. Never was their diagnosis questioned by a staff member in any hospital, nor was any released as cured. "In remission" was the uniform final diagnosis on their being discharged.

The team of pseudo-inmates consisted of a psychiatrist, housewife, painter, pediatrician, two psychologists, and a graduate student in psychology. While their experiment was, admittedly, without controls, it revealed much about the nature of psychiatric diagnosis as a self-fulfilling prophecy, about the unchangeable fixity of the diagnostic label, and about the despairing, painful experience of such depersonalizing practices. Here was a situation in which, on the basis of the words used, a group of people were admitted and kept in a psychiatric institution. Even after they left, the words "In remission (not cured)" remained as a discharge diagnosis.[5] Perhaps the chant, "Sticks and stones can break my bones but names can never harm me" should be changed to read, "Sticks and stones can break my bones *and certain names can definitely harm me.*"

STRUCTURE AND CONTEXT OF VERBAL MESSAGES[6]

Before taking up the structure of verbal messages, we will do well to look more closely into what is meant by "structure" and how it contributes to certain effects that are of interest to the speaker.

Perhaps the most significant feature of structure is that it creates a situation in which each element of the message is set in meaningful context with the other elements. Before we see how this applies to speeches, let us see how certain general principles of context operate in a trivial, but instructive, graphic example.

Figure 6-1 is a graphic message containing eight elements. Some of them are quite familiar to you, and none of them is particularly hard to grasp, yet if you were to close the book and try to reproduce all eight, you would find it hard to do so. (You would find it even harder if the first sentence had not emphasized that there were eight elements in the figure.)

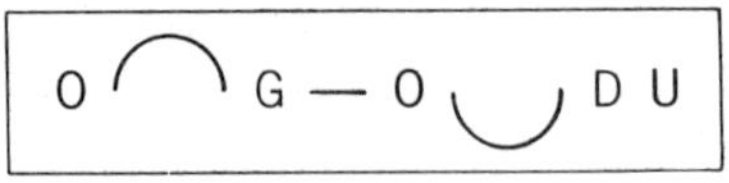

FIGURE 6-1

One reason why Fig. 6-1 is so hard to remember is that it is rather weakly structured. This is not to say that it is entirely unstructured, for

---

[5] David Perlman, "Sane insane sane insane sane insane sane insane," *Saturday Review of the Sciences* I:2 (February 24, 1973), 55–56.

[6] Huber W. Ellingsworth and Theodore Clevenger, Jr., *Speech and Social Action: A Strategy of Oral Communication* (Englewood Cliffs, N.J.: Prentice-Hall, Inc., 1967), pp. 58–63.

it is divided into eight discrete elements (remembering that there are eight makes the task of reproducing them easier), and some of the elements are familiar figures. But they do not create any context for one another.

What might be done to provide more structure for this figure? Let us begin by considering one element in what might be called "zero context" (Fig. 6–2).

$$\boxed{\text{G}}$$

FIGURE 6–2

Standing in isolation, this element appears to us as one of 26 items in our alphabet. Examined closely, it is an arrangement of curved and straight lines; but ordinarily we see it as a thing, the capital "G." Within the context of the letter, the individual lines lose their identity and blend into a single familiar configuration. The letter forms a context for the lines that make it up, but in Fig. 6–2 the letter itself does not appear in any context.

However, let us add a capital "O" following the original "G." Without altering the letter itself in any way, we nevertheless have changed it in some important ways. "G" in "go" is not the same as "G" in isolation; the difference is not in the letter, but in its context. It is perceived as *part* rather than a *whole*. Now, it represents one of two sounds making up the English word, "go" (Fig. 6–3).

$$\boxed{\text{G O}}$$

FIGURE 6–3

But suppose we add another "O" to the two letters we already have (Fig. 6–4). Except to the trained phonetician, who hears a difference

$$\boxed{\text{G O O}}$$

FIGURE 6–4

between the "G" sound in "go" and the "G" sound in "goo," we have not changed the "G" significantly; but we have changed the "O" substantially. Instead of representing a speech sound in its own right, it now combines with the second "O" to represent a completely different sound: its status is changed from that of a *part* (the representation of the "oh" sound in "go") to that of a *subpart* (one part of the representation of the "oo" sound in "goo").

We may carry the same process a step further by adding a capital "D" to the first three letters (Fig. 6–5). Now the original "O" is part

G O O D

FIGURE 6–5

of a different sound altogether, for the "oo" sound is changed from the low front vowel of "goo" to the middle vowel of "good."

Up to this point, each succeeding addition has made a significant new pattern, within the context of which the significance of the old pattern, itself physically unaltered, was changed. Not every addition would produce an equally meaningful result. For instance, we could now add the letter "K" to the four we already have (Fig. 6–6). By adding the "K"

G O O D K

FIGURE 6–6

most readers would say we had produced nonsense; they would find the string of letters "GOODK" meaningless, slightly irritating, and difficult to remember. We would have gotten a different result by adding below the four letters the straight line from Fig. 6–1 (Fig. 6–7). Unlike the "K,"

G O O D
—

FIGURE 6–7

this addition is not particularly irritating. But it is equally meaningless and hard to remember. If one is not looking carefully, it is likely to be overlooked, and it is likely to be regarded as superfluous. However, by adding the remaining elements from Fig. 6–1 in the right configuration, we may endow this line with significance and transform the entire graphic representation into a radically different kind of message (Fig. 6–8). The meaningless line is now a mouth. What were formerly the letters "G" and "D" now appear as ears, and the "O's" are now eyes.

Several important points should be noted concerning the effects of context observed in these figures. First of all, though we ordinarily expect

FIGURE 6-8

complex things to be more difficult to grasp than simple ones, you probably noticed that Figs. 6–2, 6–3, 6–4, 6–5, and 6–8 are about equally easy to recognize and remember, even though each is more complex than those preceding it. This seeming violation of our expectations is explained by the principle that *wherever possible we tend to see familiar patterns as unitary wholes rather than as collections of parts.* Indeed, evidence from perceptual experiments shows clearly that even if some of the elements are left out of a well-known pattern, we still tend to perceive the pattern itself rather than the remaining constituent parts. Since the capital letter "G," the word "GOOD," and the cartoon face all are recognized as familiar patterns, each may be handled as a single unit of perception, memory, and thought, even though the cartoon face contains more information and represents a more complex arrangement of elements than the other figures. Thus, *a familiar whole is recognized and recalled almost as easily as any of its parts.*

No doubt you also found Fig. 6–8 considerably easier to recognize and recall than Figs. 6–6 and 6–7, and very much easier than Fig. 6–1, even though it contains more elements than Figs. 6–6 and 6–7, and exactly the same elements as Fig. 6–1. The differences here are attributable to the same principle: despite its complexity, Fig. 6–8 may be conceptualized as a single entity, but in Fig. 6–7 there are two separate entities to notice (the word and the line), and in Fig. 6–1 there are eight. Individuals will differ with respect to the ease with which they recognize and recall Fig. 6–6, depending upon whether they see it as two elements ("good" + "K") or five ("G" + "O" + "O" + "D" + "K"). This suggests that *difficulty of recognition and recall depend more upon the number of recognizable whole patterns than upon the number of individual elements making up the task.* Thus, a relatively large number of elements may be perceived and recalled more easily than a smaller set of the same elements, if the larger set is composed into a single coherent pattern and the smaller set is not.

Figures 6–1 through 6–8 also demonstrate that *the meaning, significance, or character of an element is determined by its relation to the whole context in which it is embedded.* The context affects not only how we perceive the element, but also how we remember it. If asked to reproduce Fig. 6–8 from memory at a later time, many of us would show the two circles as horizontally flattened ovals   [◯ ◯]   because we would remember them as "eyes," but if asked to reproduce Fig. 6–5, most of us would draw the circles as vertically flattened ovals   [◯ ◯]   because we would remember them as "O's."

As we saw in Figs. 6–1 through 6–5, *an existing pattern may be changed into a new one by adding meaningful elements;* but in comparing Fig. 6–5 with Figs. 6–6 and 6–7, we also observed that *nonmeaningful additions to familiar patterns either destroy the integrity* of the pattern or else are perceived as superfluous.

Everything we perceive has structure and exists in some sort of context. We have just witnessed how the meaning of words can be distorted by altering their internal and external relationships. Now let us see what happens when these very same verbal messages come under the influence of social customs and taboos.

WORDS: Legitimate and Illegitimate

The words that most of us use over a period of time could be subdivided into various classes: (1) those we never speak out loud regardless of the circumstances, (2) those we would write but would not speak, (3) those we would use among intimate friends and family but not among strangers or newly made acquaintances, (4) those we would tolerate others using but would not use ourselves, (5) those we might use in certain places or under certain circumstances but not in others.

Anyone who studies our language and its evolution cannot help being taken by the fact that a great deal of time and effort is spent sidestepping certain words or conjuring up substitutes for them. The traditional "bleep" (or censoring) of various words and phrases on television is a common practice. Children quickly learn which words are permitted and which are forbidden by society. Many children, when frustrated, blurt out some "no-no" just to aggravate their parents. Most fascinating of all is the manner in which we invent stand-ins for the words we cannot handle. Some nurseries for preschoolers require, as part of their admission policy, filling out a form consisting of personal words or sounds. It seems that when a new child is admitted and has to go to the bathroom, he uses peculiar language to describe his physiological needs. For *urination,* words such as pee-pee, wee-wee, sissy, pischy, tinkle, and number I are substituted; for a *bowel movement,* other names include number II, pooh-pooh, ca-ca, or du-du. Aside from being amused, you'd be surprised just how far some people go with the practice of verbal stand-ins. At the risk of offending the more squeamish among us, take the following quiz in substitutional language. You will be astounded at some of the words and expressions other members of your class use.

SUBSTITUTIONAL LANGUAGE QUIZ

Instructions: Supply as many different words or expressions as you can that describe the following:

I. Fluid secreted by the urinary bladder:
_____ _____ _____ _____

II. Material excreted by the bowels:
_____ _____ _____ _____

III. Nose-picking substances:
_____ _____ _____ _____

IV. Sexual intercourse:
_____ _____ _____ _____

V. The sound made from the mouth after eating a big meal:
_____ _____ _____ _____

VI. The act of ejecting material from the stomach after feeling nausea:
_____ _____ _____ _____

VII. Menstruation:
_____ _____ _____ _____

VIII. Being pregnant:
_____ _____ _____ _____

IX. A sudden expulsion of gas from the rectum:
_____ _____ _____ _____

X. Female breasts:
_____ _____ _____ _____

This quiz may disclose language differences that vary not only from person to person but from place to place and generation to generation. People often date themselves by the words they use. Compare your responses with those of someone twenty, thirty, or even forty years your senior. Notice how certain word substitutes hang on while others fade away. Words, like people, have a lifespan and a history. Some that used to be considered illegitimate are now legitimate, while others die from over- or underuse. The mass media, for example, has been responsible for a pronounced shift in the use of our language. Back in the thirties, Clark Gable shocked movie audiences when he used the word "damn" in the film, *Gone with the Wind.* Today, many of the words you inserted in this quiz are freely used in books, plays, and films. The "tell it the way it is" syndrome seems to have swept away much of the need for substitutional language.

DeVito declares that "the importance of a concept is directly related to the number of different terms a language has to express it."[7] Notice how many substitutes or alternative words you listed. Take number ten—female breasts. It would be naive to deny America's preoccupation

[7] Joseph DeVito, *Psychology of Speech* (New York: Random House, 1970), p. 204.

with "the bosom." Do you think it is pure coincidence that virile young men have coined so many different names for these milk-giving appendages? Without effort, several names for the female bust come to mind: water-wings, boobs, knobs, bazooms, and so on. What purpose could so many aliases serve? Why are so many fathers and mothers reluctant to use accurate terminology with their youngsters? Is it any wonder that, on occasion, certain words have been known to intimidate, frighten, and nearly destroy people?

To test the fear-producing potential of words, this author conducted an experiment in one of his classes. It was one week into the semester and the subject was anatomy and physiology of the nervous system. Not only was it a compulsory course (which never fails to precipitate anxiety), it also involved an extensive use of anatomical terminology. To say the very least, students were petrified.

The premise underlying this experiment was that a student could understand a lecture better if it were free from highly technical language. To test its validity, two separate lectures were given. In lecture I, while pointing to various anatomical drawings of the central nervous system on the blackboard, the instructor substituted the word "thing" for each technical word. For instance, while he pointed to the encephalon (the brain), he referred to it simply as "this thing." After completing lecture I, he delivered lecture II in which the correct terminology was used. To give you some idea of how each lecture sounded, they will both be presented as one unit. To read it meaningfully, merely realize that whatever is found in parentheses has had the word "thing" used in its place.

ANATOMY OF A THING

This THING (a neuron) is the functional unit of the nervous system. At one end, there is this THING (a cyton) from which this THING (an axone) projects to end in these tiny little THINGS (terminal arborizations). In your body there are millions of these THINGS (neurons) which connect with each other via these THINGS (synapses).

Your central nervous system consists of this globular THING (the encephalon) contained within this THING (the cranium) and from it passes this THING (the medulla spinalis). Looking like a long cable, it extends downward through this THING (the vertebral column) to your tailbone. At succeeding levels, you will notice these THINGS (spinal nerves) leaving the long cablelike THING (the medulla spinalis) sideways to provide these THINGS (your viscera) with a nerve supply.

Partially contained within these two THINGS (the encephalon and medulla spinalis) is another system consisting of two other THINGS (the parasympathetic and sympathetic divisions of the autonomic nervous system) which automatically regulates bodily functions. One of these THINGS (the craniosacral division) is so named because part of it derives from this THING (the brainstem) and the other part from this THING (the sacrum). The other THING (the sympathetic division) is so named because it originates from this THING (the thoraco-lumbar area).

The basis for judging whether this informal classroom experiment was a success or failure was how well the students understood the lectures. With few exceptions, they seemed to feel that leaving out the highly technical anatomical language in the first lecture enabled them to grasp the relationships more easily. Then, when the technical language was inserted, it was noticeably less disturbing. The reason for this is not clear. What is clear, however, is that unfamiliar words do have the capacity to cloud one's understanding.

To the dismay of many educators, far too many of today's students have been raised in atmospheres where sesquipedality (the use of large words) and books having more than 150 pages were virtually nonexistent—or, worse, were frowned upon. The order of the day again seems to be brevity at all costs. Minds, like muscles, undergo an atrophy of disuse when they do not receive the appropriate stimulation. Consequently, while there should be no need for defining every word over six letters in length, or reducing meanings to "run Spot run," the reality of students' development often dictates otherwise. If words must be substituted for, let it at least be in an upward direction, not downward.

STYLE OF COMMUNICATION

Style signifies the manner in which a man expresses himself, regardless of what he expresses, and it is held to reveal his nature, quite apart from his actual thought—for thought has no style.[8]

In any creative effort, whether baking a cake, making a speech, or teaching a class, the ingredients going into it do little to guarantee its success. Beginners are frequently disappointed when, after putting into one of their projects what they believe to be the right ingredients, it doesn't come off. The young wife whose baking effort failed often insists she followed her mother's instructions to the letter. What was missing? For want of a better answer, perhaps "style" was the missing element.

An excellent example of style at work occurs in the teaching profession. Some educators are thoroughly convinced that a good teacher is one who succeeds in transmitting accurate and reliable information to the student. Their satisfaction seems to begin and end with the student's *getting the*

[8] Paul Valery, "Style," in J. V. Cunningham, ed., and trans. Eugenia Hanfmann and Gertrude Vakar, *The Problem of Style* (Greenwich, Conn.: Fawcett, 1966), pp. 18–19.

material. Regrettably, some extremely qualified teachers hold this view. Semester after semester, their students endure the pain and suffering that comes with having to take a course with someone who bores them to tears.

While various face-saving rationalizations could be offered on their behalf, chances are they simply lack style. Reflect for a moment and think of some teacher you've had who, in your opinion, had style. List, in the spaces below, those ingredients you believe were responsible for it.

Example: spontaneity____   _____   _____

_____   _____   _____

_____   _____   _____

_____   _____   _____

Of the items you have listed, how many are concerned with what the teacher actually taught (the material itself)? Your responses correspond with the majority opinion concerning style if you focused on "the way" the course was presented, not the material itself. Once in a while (paraphrasing Marshall McLuhan's axiom, "The medium is the message") a situation arises in which a speaker says virtually nothing, but does it with extraordinary style. In such a case, perhaps, "The STYLE is the MESSAGE." Great actors have been known to thrill audiences by simply reciting the alphabet; dancers by walking across the stage; opera singers by running through their scales.

Each having its staunch supporters, *style* and *substance* have been engaged in an ongoing feud for centuries. As an interesting aside, the description of nonverbal communication rendered by Edward Sapir more than a quarter-century ago fits style equally well. It reads (substituting the word style for nonverbal communication), "We respond to style with an extreme alertness and, one might say, in accordance with an elaborate and secret code that is written nowhere, known by none, and understood by all."[9] In fact, the impression we make on others frequently is more a consequence of style than of substance. Style, in this context, is able to reveal more about you in the first five minutes of a new acquaintanceship than a ten-page resumé.

CLASSIFICATIONS OF STYLE

Over two thousand years ago, Cicero classified three styles: (1) *plain*— made use of pure and Latin terms, simple and clearly arranged; (2) *moderate*—more forceful, possessing sweetness but little vigor; and (3) *grand*

[9] Edward Sapir, "The unconscious patterning of behavior in society," in David Mandelbaum, ed., "Selected writings of Edward Sapir," in *Language, Culture and Personality* (Berkeley: University of California Press, 1949), p. 556.

—ornate, sublime, dignified, copious, and graceful. A giant step forward into the present gives us five styles conceived by Mario Pei.[10]

Style   I.   *literary-poetical-supererudite*
             EXAMPLE: "Those individuals do not possess any. . . ."

Style II.   *literary-prose-cultured*
             EXAMPLE: "Those men haven't any. . . ."

Style III.   *spoken standard*
             EXAMPLE: "Those men haven't got any. . . ."

Style IV.   *colloquial lower class*
             EXAMPLE: "Those guys haven't/ain't got any. . . ."

Style V.   *vulgar and slang*
             EXAMPLE: "Dem guys ain't git none."

These classifications of style should by no means be taken as the last word. More important than memorizing various subdivisions of style, you should interest yourself in the role they play in living communication. If, in the majority of conversations, most of what is said goes unnoticed, it becomes even more important that you weigh your words and their arrangement carefully so they exert a maximum impact on a receiver.

Speaking and writing styles are not necessarily the same. Characteristics such as volume, stress, pitch, and pauses, so easily achieved in speech, come through poorly in written form. Only a skilled writer can bring words to life on the printed page, and it is generally his style that makes it possible. Have you ever been accused of not actually writing a paper you submitted in class? Where a glaring disparity in style exists between the written and spoken words of a student, "hanky panky" is often suspected. It is rare to find a student who writes papers which are veritable prose, but whose speech, according to Mario Pei's classification of style, qualifies as vulgar and slang.

How an individual can have two different styles at work in the same body remains an enigma. Reasoning logically, if someone can write beautifully, he should be able to speak these same words just as beautifully; at least, one would expect this to be the case. Perhaps you have already had the shocking experience of watching one of your favorite authors being interviewed on television and seeing him "butcher" the English language. Why does this happen? Jot down three reasons you believe might be responsible for a person's having different speaking and writing styles:

REASON I _____
          _____

REASON II _____
          _____

REASON III _____
           _____

[10] Mario Pei, *Language for Everybody* (New York: Pocket Books, 1956), p. 65.

Before leaving styles of communication, we should note that they can change with the growth of an individual. While those characteristics which identify a particular person's style tend to remain, mood swings can, and occasionally do, alter them. Therefore, it is important to remember that what one perceives in another as style, may be a side-effect of some transient mood or attitude and totally uncharacteristic of the person.

SUBSTANCE OF COMMUNICATION: Message Content

Having rendered style its due, and forgetting temporarily how something was said or how the person looked before, during, and after saying it, we turn now to *substance*. We shall dwell on the nature of the *verbal message* and the role it plays in living communication.

"At the sound of the bell, *do not think of an elephant!*" This was the instruction given to a group of students by their teacher. Naturally, they wondered how this was possible and reasoned that by thinking of what you're not supposed to think of, you must think of it. As anticipated by the teacher, the students dismissed it as silly and without meaning. The teacher then read them the following excerpt from the life of Helen Keller (as told by her teacher Anne Sullivan):

> I made Helen hold her mug under the spout while I pumped. As the cold water gushed forth, filling the mug, I spelled "W-A-T-E-R" into Helen's free hand. The word coming so close upon the sensation of cold water rushing over her hand seemed to startle her. She dropped her mug and stood as one transfixed. A new light came into her face. She spelled "W-A-T-E-R" several times. Then she dropped on the ground and asked for its name and pointed to the pump and the trellis, and suddenly turning around she asked for my name. . . . In a few hours she had added thirty new words to her vocabulary.[11]

Again the students were asked how they felt about the instruction of not thinking of an elephant. A discussion finally led to the question, "Can there be thought without words?" What, they wondered, exists inside your head when you think the word elephant? Is it a mental picture of the animal, coded neural impulses, or the letters E-L-E-P-H-A-N-T? As they probed, confusion mounted. They began wondering what happens in the brain during the process of "wondering."

Among the thousands of things man has invented, most valuable are the symbols he can substitute for objects and actions. This made it possible for Helen Keller to experience the thrill of exchanging a single

[11] Helen Keller, *The Story of My Life* (New York: Doubleday, 1954), p. 257.

thought with another human being, to have the mystery of language revealed. Take away our verbal messages and what is left?

Unlike Miss Keller, who was deaf, dumb and blind, there was another celebrated case of a boy, age 10 or 11, found in the forest by French peasants. Known as a feral child (from the Latin word fera meaning wild or untamed), he had the use of all his senses. Though Jean-Marc Itard tried to educate the boy, he was never able to learn more than a few words or communicate in more than the most rudimentary fashion. Francois Truffaut captured this adventure in communication with his film entitled, The Wild Boy.[12] How might Anne Sullivan have fared with this Wild Boy? Could she have taught him language as she did Helen Keller?

Most people, if they were lost and came upon a tribe of natives with whom communication seemed impossible, would eventually resort to drawing pictures. Although pictographs (pictures representing ideas) perform the same symbolic function as words, they possess an additional feature by resembling the object they represent.

Our verbal language is man-made, and the words we use are arbitrary and capricious. Some, however, yield to rationality by imitating the natural sound associated with the object or action (tingle, buzz, boom, clang, hiss, and so on). Others, making up the greater majority of spoken language, are totally lacking in morphological relatedness. (Morphology refers to shape, form, or structure.)

Most words seriously lack a morphological and harmonic relatedness to the things they symbolize. Take the word lunch or pickle. In your wildest dreams, they would fail to conjure in your mind what we know them to actually represent. Children are notorious for making up words and sometimes, at the expense of a perfectly good mother's sanity, they repeat them over and over again. Have you ever tried your hand at neology—making up words? Here are some bona fide dictionary definitions. Make up any word at all that you feel fits its description:

1. _____ : the egg case of certain mollusks and insects.

2. _____ : a strong snuff made from the coarser, darker tobacco leaves.

3. _____ : a female demon or vampire believed to live in ruins and other desolate places.[13]

Many people are emotionally influenced by the sounds words make,

---

[12] Thomas M. Scheidel, Speech Communication and Human Interaction (Glenview, Ill.: Scott, Foresman, 1972), p. 15.
[13] The correct words defined above are: (1) ootheca, (2) rappee, (3) lilith.

especially the names our parents gave us and those we give our children. There must be at least a half dozen names you can't stand—to the point that, when introduced to people bearing them, you find yourself psychologically backing off a little. Subconsciously, regardless of the kinds of words from which we construct our language system, a substantial part of our reaction to them appears steeped in an emotional base. This will become increasingly more apparent as the chapter develops.

LANGUAGE: A Bridge

The relationship between what we think, say, and feel is poorly understood. What is understood, however, is the pressing need for us to get from our thoughts to action. Spoken language provides such a vehicle. Unfortunately, it is far from perfect, and too often it leaves in its wake waves of frustration. Consequently, we have been segregated into three broad classes: (1) those who never get beyond the thought stage, spending the greater part of their lives caught up in fantasy and vicarious preoccupation, (2) those stranded in the verbal stage, endlessly repeating what they are going to do one of these days and never actually doing it, (3) those who reflexly spring into action without thinking about what they are doing or talking about. What we are faced with here are the THINKERS, TALKERS, and DOERS. While, in reality, we are all mixtures of each, there is a pronounced tendency to favor one rhetorical[14] persona more than others.

Crossing the language bridge is not without danger or toll. For some reason, once you have gone beyond the thought stage and verbalized whatever was on your mind, it is impossible to go back. People have said things in anger which they didn't really mean, apologized repeatedly to the injured party, yet never succeeded in being forgiven or freed of the consequences. Even worse than an ill-fated verbal trip over the language bridge is an unpleasant nonverbal one. An innocent act of twenty years ago is occasionally more difficult to live down than a verbal one. Laws in this country reflect some rather definite attitudes toward what people think, say, or do. However, until we have "thought police," there is no jurisdiction over what goes on in our minds. Once these thoughts cross our language bridge into the verbal realm, they become subject to its statutes. Day dreams and night dreams may be literally filled with thoughts of murder, rape, and a dozen other forms of mayhem; but, as long as they remain unspoken, they may continue to enjoy the sanctuary of the mind.

---

[14] In this context, *rhetoric* is intended to include nonverbal as well as verbal modes of communication.

When rebellious thoughts can no longer be contained and, like a pressure cooker, need to let off steam, two choices are open to them: words or actions. From the standpoint of man as a social animal, words seem to be the method of choice. Psychiatrists and psychoanalysts are forever encouraging their patients to "talk it out—get it off their chests." In fact, according to one authority, "All the pharmacopoeia we possess holds no healing potion so potent as speech."[15] The problem is that most of us are woefully ignorant of the survival value inherent in speech. Instead of harnessing its helpful attributes, we tend to compound its shortcomings. Thus, for those who are interested in crossing the language bridge into the remainder of this book, a variety of threatening pitfalls will be cited as well as ways of avoiding them.

Pitfall I—Words 'n' things

There is not one college student who, at some time, has not heard a professor say, "And when you get out into the real world . . . ." One wonders what such teachers think school life is—an unreal world? Millions of words pass from mouth-to-ear-to-pen-to-notebook-to-memorybanks-to-pen-to-examination paper-to-the twilight zone, never to be heard from again. Perhaps this does represent the unreal world, and any similarity between it and the real world is purely accidental. The point being made here is that the symbols or labels we use to represent things are not the things they represent; *the word is not the thing!*

If you take a course in SEMANTICS, expect to deal with the concept of words 'n' things and meanings. (*Semantics* is from the Greek word *semantikos*, meaning "significant.") As a beginning, look at and study Fig. 6–9 on page 168.

Now think for a minute of your room and the things in it (bed, chair, television, radio, and so on). Not one of these words is actually something you sleep in, sit in, watch, or listen to. They are merely the SYMBOLS we use to identify them. In the study of semantics, those things in your room just mentioned are called REFERENTS. The words (or SYMBOLS) you have given them have no meaning in themselves. The only meaning they have comes from those you gave them. *Meanings are in you, not in words or symbols.* Dictionaries do not give REFERENTS, only the meanings various authors have given to words.

Now look again at the triangle in Fig. 6–9. Imagine yourself holding a piece of chalk. The bottom right portion of the triangle marked REFERENT refers to the actual piece of chalk in your hand. The bottom left

---

[15] Charles T. Brown and Charles Van Riper, *Speech and Man* (Englewood Cliffs, N.J.: Prentice-Hall, 1966), p. 30.

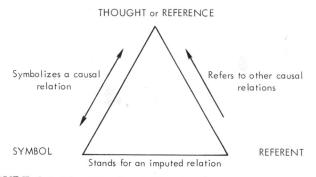

FIGURE 6–9 *The Triangle of Meaning.*[16]

marked SYMBOL refers to the word "chalk." The apex of the triangle marked THOUGHT or REFERENCE refers to the process by which you have brought together in your head the SYMBOL (the word chalk) and the REFERENT (the actual piece of chalk in your hand). You will become a victim of pitfall Number I if you fail to differentiate between the word (symbol), the *thing* (referent), and the *linked state of the two inside your brain* (your reference).

Rx

Whenever using spoken or written verbal language, make it abundantly clear that you fully understand the distinctions existing between a *symbol*, the *referent*, and the *reference*, and, above all, their relationship to one another.

Pitfall II—Ladder of abstraction

Too many conversations involve people talking past one another. While they superficially appear to be talking with each other and using words both understand, this interaction is usually a figment of their imaginations.

   An "abstraction" is the idea or mental picture we get of things (referents) and to which we assign labels (symbols). As you can readily see, the danger lies in the fact that we don't always know what kind of picture a given word has conjured up in someone else's head. As if this were not bad enough, the situation becomes compounded by our realization that we cannot ever know all there is to know about anything; words, at best, call attention to certain aspects of a referent and leave out others.

[16] From C. K. Ogden and I. A. Richards, *The Meaning of Meaning* (New York: Harcourt Brace Jovanovich Inc. and London: Routledge & Kegan Paul, Ltd.), p. 11.

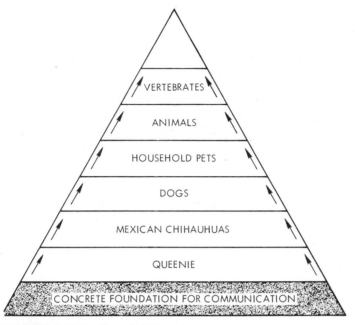

FIGURE 6–10 Ladder of Abstraction.

Language does this—it arbitrarily *includes* and *excludes* referential characteristics (the Principle of Non-Allness).

Putting this concept to work, suppose you were having a discussion with a friend about animals. You own a Mexican chihuahua named Queenie and your friend doesn't have a pet. The word "animal" flashes a picture of your chihuahua in your mind. Having no specific reference, your friend may or may not think of an animal; if he does, he thinks of no particular kind of animal. With this conversation, whatever is said about animals will be based upon each discussant's referent; and all your remarks will be geared specifically to your little Queenie. Unless your friend also links the word *animal* with a Mexican chihuahua, communication is bound to be muddy.

Now, instead of talking simply about "animals" you introduce the adjective "domestic." The conversation immediately rules out all non-domestic animals in the world. If other qualifying terms are added, the degree of abstraction will continue to diminish. When you and your friend agree that the word "animal" will pertain specifically to your Mexican chihuahua, Queenie, you have both climbed down to the bottom of the ladder of abstraction and planted your feet firmly on concrete communication. In reverse, as shown in Figure 6–10, the more one moves up the Ladder of Abstraction, the more unclear meaning tends to become.

R̠

Steer clear of highly abstract terms unless you send up a flare indicating you are not only aware of what you are saying but also in full control of your language. Words such as religion, art, business, transportation, government, love, or education must be qualified so their meanings cannot be mistaken. Remember, the more reckless you are with abstract language, the greater your chances of having a communication breakdown.

Pitfall III—Degree of cogency

The word cogency means "the power to convince." People usually have a variety of opinions about anything and everything. Aside from the *valence* (how strongly they feel about the subject) or the *vector* (the direction in which that opinion exerts influence), it is generally oriented along the continuum shown in Fig. 6–11.

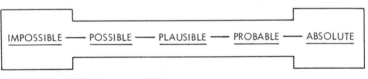

IMPOSSIBLE ——— POSSIBLE ——— PLAUSIBLE ——— PROBABLE ——— ABSOLUTE

FIGURE 6–11 Degrees of Cogency.

If you are talking with someone who buttresses his point of view with the word *impossible*, the likelihood is high that he has a closed mind. If the word *possible* is used in its place, chances are his mind is at least partially open to persuasion. The use of the word *plausible* should make you even more optimistic from the standpoint of open communication. The employment of the word *probability* is, by far, the most flexible and appealing in terms of a free exchange of ideas. However, if the individual uses the word *absolute*, you are back where you started with someone who has a nonnegotiable attitude. Therefore, by noting from which of these verbal building blocks (impossible, possible, plausible, probable, absolute) an individual constructs his language bridge, a responsible estimate of the toll you will have to pay to reach him can be made.

Closely related to users of the verbal constructs just mentioned are three types of people. *Univalued* ones tenaciously adhere to the position that there is only one way to do anything: if you're going to Chicago, the only way to get there is to fly; if you want to lose weight, eat only proteins. Among the *two-valued* types, one hears remarks saturated with either/or, black or white, this or that. For them, there is no middle ground—no grey area. Finally, *multivalued* individuals willingly and patiently accept the fact there is more than one answer to any question, more than one viable solution to any problem. If you are discussing a trip to Chicago with a multivalued person, he will gladly acknowledge that one could get there by plane, automobile, train, roller skates, or pogo stick.

R̰

If one of your personal goals is to dispatch verbal messages which convey meaning, be careful to avoid getting the reputation of being narrow-minded or having tunnel vision. Normal healthy verbal language must be flexible and versatile. The cogency of anything you say will depend upon it.

Pitfall IV—Frozen evaluations

Everything changes—people, places, and things. Unfortunately, many of us are reluctant to accept such change as a fact of life. We are constantly surrounded by signs and symptoms of an unwillingness to honor time— mothers who treat their 30-year-old daughters as if they were still babies, men and women over sixty who dress as though they were twenty-one, teachers who refuse to update their antiquated syllabi, insisting they are still relevant. These are but a few of the ways many of us court the *status quo*—a love for things as they are. To behave as though everything were static and unchanging (frozen, if you please) is to invite problems in communication. The politician who continually exhibits a frozen sense of community must, of necessity, lose out in the long run. At all costs, change should be extended the courtesy of a proper accommodation.

Most seriously hit by frozen evaluations are the people who are victimized by it. A situation which illustrates this is the *PERSONA NON GRATA SYNDROME*. Picture a woman walking down the street with her ten-year-old son. Unexpectedly she meets a friend who asks, "What grade is Eric in now?" Instead of directing the question to the boy (who speaks the language), she directs it to the mother, *as if the boy didn't exist.* Another similar incident occurs when a teenage daughter takes her grandmother to buy a pair of shoes. Not infrequently the salesman will ask, "What size does she wear?"—behaving *as if the older woman were not even there.* These situations epitomize the *frozen evaluation* by inferring that: (a) children never grow up and, therefore, know nothing, (b) once people grow old, they become senile and know nothing. *Conclusion:* They don't exist.

Alfred Korzybski, called "The Father of General Semantics," detected this penchant we have for making frozen evaluations and recommended some prophylactic measures. One of them is called "dating." Instead of loosely referring to people, places, and things, supply each with a DATE which will fix it in time. If you are talking about Democracy, date it perhaps as Democracy^{1944}, Democracy^{1961}, or Democracy^{1970}. If you are talking about your mother, say, mother^{1927}, or mother^{1969}. If you are talking about how you felt yesterday, say, Me^{7} A.M. or Me^{10} P.M.. The practice of DATING will help prevent your communicating "as if" things stood still. It makes us more keenly aware of our responsibility to change.

Another technique is called INDEXING—a process by which the "seen one, seen 'em all" generalization can be averted. In the exact sense, no two things are identical, whether they be snowflakes, leaves, or fingerprints. Imagine being confronted by a dozen leaves, snowflakes, or fingerprints and having to distinguish one from the other. It is by no means easy. Ultimately, the way it is done is by singling out differences—not similarities. Searching out differences rather than similarities conforms with the *principle of nonidentity*. If there is one thing people seem to resent, it is being classified as just another teacher, student, or lover instead of a specific teacher, student, or lover. This immediately prevents generalizing from one teacher, student, or lover to another. Indexing them would depict each as teacher^{1}, teacher^{2}, student^{1}, student^{2}, lover^{1}, lover^{2}, and so on.

Other recommendations caution against the indiscriminate use of *et ceteras*, *hyphens*, and *quotation marks*. An excess of *et ceteras*, for example, could be misleading. While consistent with the principle of non-allness (we can't ever know or say all there is about anything), it could be irresponsibly employed by someone who, not having done his homework, would like to create the impression he did, etc., etc., etc., etc., etc.

A hyphen, like a magician's wand, can create an illusion. Things that are inseparable in reality (mind and body, time and space, structure and function) may be separated verbally through the use of a hyphen.

A vocal inflection cannot always be translated into written form. Quotation marks, to some extent, help make this possible. "When a linguistic formulation is enclosed in quotation marks, reference is being made to the language so enclosed. All formulations not so enclosed refer to something outside themselves. Worded another way, language TALKED ABOUT shall also be enclosed in quotes; language USED shall not be so enclosed. For example: 1) Sky is blue. (I'm talking about that stuff over our heads), 2) 'Sky' has three letters. (I'm talking about a word.)"[17]

In whatever context you use a noun, take special care to avoid treating it as if it had no connotative distinctiveness. For pet lovers, the noun "dog" is quite different from what it is to those who dislike pets with a passion. This admonition, naturally, applies to other nouns as well. There-

---

[17] Robert L. Benjamin, *Semantic and Language Analysis* (New York: Bobbs-Merrill, 1970), p. 11.

fore, if the person with whom you are communicating chooses to ignore or blithely gloss over the *principle of nonidentity* and neglect to index properly, it is perfectly in order for you to draw his attention to it.

With reference to the use of *et ceteras, hyphens,* and *quotation marks,* be very cautious with them because, in the hands of an expert, they can turn any written work completely around and upside down.

Pitfall V—Semantic differential

Not only is there a difference in the words people use but also in the meanings they assign to them. Basically, a word can be looked at either connotatively (your personal understanding of the word) or denotatively (the dictionary meaning). The word *education,* for example, will probably be defined differently by a Ph.D. candidate in literature than by a high school dropout. Or, take the expression, "a good doctor." What, in your opinion, are the qualities "a good doctor" should possess? A survey was once prepared asking this very question. It was circulated among laymen and physicians for the purpose of finding out whether patients defined "a good doctor" differently than the doctors themselves. Laymen felt a good doctor should (1) listen well, (2) not rush his examination or treatment, (3) be kind and honest, (4) not keep a patient coming after he is well, and (5) have a good reputation. The physicians claimed a good doctor should (1) have graduated from a good school, (2) publish scientific papers, (3) be on the faculty of a prestigious medical college, (4) have a successful practice, and (5) be respected by his peers.

Whether the word is education, doctor, politician, beautiful, ethics, or pornography, it is imperative that the meanings assigned it be the same by both parties engaging in the interpersonal transaction. But, how does one go about arriving at a parity of meaning in everyday conversation? What kind of tool could be used to measure the way people feel about certain words? Osgood, Suci, and Tannenbaum,[18] in 1957, came up with a technique called a *semantic differential.* To construct a scale of your own, here is the procedure.

STEP   I.   Decide upon some word or concept toward which you would like to discover people's attitudes. Place it at the top of your scale.

STEP   II.   Draw seven blank spaces across the page and, after marking the center one NEUTRAL, proceed to rank each space to the right and left of it +1, +2, +3 and −1, −2, −3. The

[18] Charles E. Osgood, George Suci, and Percy Tannenbaum, *The Measurement of Meaning* (Urbana: University of Illinois Press, 1957).

plusses and minuses can be placed on *either* side of neutral. So far, your scale should look like Fig. 6–12.

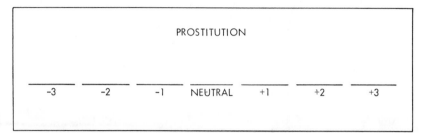

FIGURE 6–12 *Steps I and II in the Construction of a Semantic Differential Scale.*

STEP III. So as to insure greater understanding, you may choose to enter the verbal values suggested in Fig. 6–13 instead of numerical values beneath each blank.

STEP IV. Arrange as many lines of blanks as you wish and, at each end, place words which are polar opposites. Then, the person being tested makes a selection on the basis of how he feels about the word PROSTITUTION and puts an "X" in the proper blank.

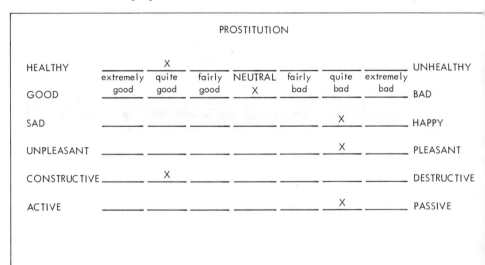

FIGURE 6–13 *Steps III and IV in the Construction of A Semantic Differential Scale.*

Word meanings vary not only from culture to culture but also from subculture to subculture. Osgood and his co-workers found that meanings concentrate themselves around three main factors: *evaluation, potency,* and *activity.* The *evaluation* is expressed in relationships such as good/bad or kind/cruel; *potency* as thick/thin, strong/weak; *activity* as fast/slow or sharp/dull. Naturally, these factors are used according to the word or concept being probed, the nature of the audience being tested, and the particular results being sought.

R

Since many people throw words around as if they were going out of style, it behooves those interested in arriving at their precise meanings to devise a method of screening them. The semantic differential is one such means. It opens to public view the connotations of words behind which people frequently hide. Some hide intentionally; others, innocently or inadvertently.

While it is impractical to carry around a semantic differential form in one's pocket or handbag, the next best thing is carry the concept of it around in one's head. It takes up very little room and is readily available, should the need arise. For example, assume you are having a discussion with a friend about morality and he uses the term *prostitution.* The very sound of this word should instantly trigger the invisible semantic differential inside your head by prompting you to ask your friend for his connotation of the word prostitution. By doing this with any other words or phrases which might be unclear, you will probably avoid succumbing to PITFALL V. Hence, *the prime objective for those seeking to avoid communication breakdowns must include finding out what the other fellow takes certain words to mean before responding.*

If, to this point, you have had the good fortune of successfully crossing the language bridge without stepping into any pitfalls, see now if your verbal skill is equally free of the following liabilities.

VERBAL CRUTCHES

The next time you shop at the market, read carefully some of the labels on the cans and boxes. You will notice, in addition to the primary ingredients for which you are paying your hard-earned money, there are other things in them called *additives* or *preservatives* or *filler.* Even when you buy drugs, over and beyond the pharmacodynamic agent (the stuff that is supposed to make it work), there is often another substance or two included. This tendency to "add things" also occurs in the transmission of verbal messages. We do not mean here those paralinguistic ingredients mentioned in Chapter 5, such as ers, ahs, pauses, stress, volume, and pitch, but rather those actual words or phrases which have infiltrated our language and serve a psychological rather than a linguistic purpose.

These verbal additives shall be referred to here as verbal crutches because they help prop up the sender who has more than a casual need for FEEDBACK. They reassure him that attention is not straying, that his point is being acknowledged, and that what he has to say is of interest to someone other than himself. They include expressions such as, "Look, the Supreme Court has some pretty smart men on it— right? Get what I mean? See my point? Almost every third remark seems to get support from these verbal crutches. Some suffer from the "O.K. compulsion." They are unable to get through a conversation without liberally sprinkling an "O.K.?" here and a "check!" there. Constantly they seek the recognition of knowing you are with them, that you will not go away. The problem is by no means serious. Frequently, such expressions are simply the result of speech trends and untidy verbal habits. But, regardless of their origin, they remain verbal crutches, working the greatest hardship on those obliged to listen. Do you see what I mean? Do you get my point? Are you with me? O.K.? Understand? . . . . What are some of your verbal crutches?

1. _____   2. _____   3. _____

WORDWAYS UNDER CONSTRUCTION

How much of what we know, think, and feel can we translate into words? Just how far can our words carry us? Whether writing a term paper, a thesis, or a dissertation, we must manipulate words skillfully to effect an accurate statement of meaning.

Loosely classified, there are several wordways over which a person can travel in order to express himself:

1. Symbolic or empirical wordways.
2. Intensional or extensional wordways.
3. Inner- or other-directed wordways.

The individual who selects the symbolic, intensional, or inner-oriented route finds meaning in life *indirectly*. Using detours in the form of inferences, presumptions, assumptions, suppositions, similes, tautologies, and metaphors, he navigates himself toward his destination. On a cross-country automobile trip, for example, this type of person would probably have implicit faith in the markings on his maps. He believes that, ". . . because there are certain words there must necessarily be certain 'things' that correspond to them."[19]

Myers and Myers[20] captured the essence of such an individual's lifestyle when they wrote, "A symbolic attitude is very useful and creative as long as we do some checking in the territory to make sure we are not too far off base." They further warn that people who behave symbolically (many of them are great composers, novelists, statesmen, and philosophers) are generally fine unless they become unable to pull back to reality. Talking with them is frequently difficult without knowing the nature of the wordways they employ. Like the biblical scholars who argue the meanings locked in the scriptures, they have been known to suffer at times from tunnel vision.

By contrast, people who travel empirical, extensional, and other-directed wordways seem to find meaning in life more *directly*. They doubt practically everything that cannot be objectively experienced. Carried to the extreme, such behavior can turn them into unbearable nit-pickers who often find themselves denied many of the symbolically beautiful things in life. Did you ever wonder how many scientific and technological advances began in the symbolic rather than the empirical world? Again we should ask, "How much of what we know, think, and feel can be translated into words?"

On one thing you may rely; whichever route to reality you choose, words will be involved in lighting the way. It might also be a good idea to prepare, if necessary, to reroute if certain wordways are under construction, or closed.

PUNCTUATION: Those Funny Little Marks

For a very long time, students of all ages have been plagued by punctuation. While a few have mastered the rules governing these funny little marks, most of them have not. And, like so many other things that are unpopular, these marks have been dismissed as either unimportant, or meaningless, or a waste of time.

Popular belief dictates the myth that educated people know how to properly punctuate whatever they write. It stands to reason—how could they have gotten through college and graduate school without knowing

---

[19] Condon, *Semantics and Communication*, p. 44.
[20] Gail Myers and Michele Myers, *The Dynamics of Human Communication* (New York: McGraw-Hill, 1973), p. 78.

how to properly discipline these tiny little ink marks? Well, there is a story that goes with this myth. It concerns a salty sea captain who, for years, would retire to his cabin each day at three. Secretly, he would take from beneath his bunk a small box in which there was another smaller box. Opening it, he would carefully remove an old and crumpled piece of paper with something written on it. Human nature being what it is, his crew grew progressively more curious as to why he went to his cabin each day at three o'clock. One afternoon, a member of the crew stole into the captain's quarters and opened first the larger box and then the smaller one. Guess what was written on the little piece of crumpled paper? *"Port is left, starboard is right."* Here was a man who had spent more than thirty years of his life at sea and didn't know his port from his starboard. This same phenomenon exists among certain academicians with regard to punctuation.

A college professor, intent on convincing his students that punctuation can make a dramatic difference in meaning, asked them to punctuate the following sentence:

"Woman without her man is nothing."

Before we see how they did it, try it yourself in the space below:

Here's how the men in the class did it:

"Woman, without her man, is nothing."

Here's how the women in the class did it:

"Woman! without her, man is nothing."

Another interesting example of "punctuational hanky panky" is seen in the following two sentences. Compare their meanings.

Senator Jones said, "the governor is an irresponsible fool."

"Senator Jones," said the governor, "is an irresponsible fool."

It soon became unmistakably apparent to every member of the class that by simply moving a comma, a significant alteration could be made in a verbal message. Thus, with a little imagination and a trace of larceny in the heart, it would take practically no effort at all for a clever manipulator to alter the written word for profit or personal gain by juggling around *those funny little marks.*

SUMMARY

After an introduction designed to apprise the reader of how hopelessly "hung up" we are on spoken language, this chapter attempted to validate such a claim. Mentioned first were some observations made by a visiting newspaper reporter from the planet Venus. His assignment: to report on the customs and conditions prevailing here on Earth. One of the things he discovered is that people talk incessantly regardless of whether or not they have something to say (*homo loquens compulsus*—man, the compulsive talker).

Next, the chapter considered the abusive and capricious use of words in relation to mental health. A study was mentioned where several trained individuals, feigning mental illness (pseudo-patients), gained admittance into a psychiatric hospital as patients. The experiment provides a horrifying insight into the consequences of "labeling people." It is one thing to label people sloppy, clumsy, or inconsiderate—but quite another to label them schizophrenic or manic-depressive.

Next we took a microscopic look at words, seeing them to consist of legitimate and illegitimate forms. Examples were given of the ways people sidestep certain words and flaunt others in order to conform with social and moral codes or norms. This theme is extended into the realm of "style," consisting of different levels at which people dispatch their verbal messages (such as the grand, moderate, plain, and vulgar styles). Lessening the magnification, the chapter proceeded to discuss the "substance" of communication with special regard for its evolution as a symbolic form.

Entering the more practical aspects of communication, the reader was guided across a language bridge spanning *thought* and *action* and, along the way, alerted to the existence of certain particularly dangerous pitfalls, plus ways of avoiding them. The chapter then drew to a close by mentioning some of the verbal crutches people use while communicating with each other (such as: Right? O.K.? Do you follow me?) and some of the limitations of language resulting from a lack of suitable or appropriate words or from the personal barriers that cause many of our wordways to be constantly under construction. The ability to reroute meaning was stressed. The conclusion briefly discussed the role punctuation plays in verbal communication and how, in expert hands, it can make or break a speech.

CHAPTER 7

MESSAGES
IN
CONFLICT

INSIGHTS

After reading this chapter you should have a clearer understanding of:

- *the differences between an argument and a fight; an argu-*
  ment and debate.
- *how you can disagree with someone without becoming dis-*
  agreeable.
- *what is meant by the principle of yielding in judo and its*
  application in an argument.
- *the notion that you cannot argue conclusions; only how they*
  were arrived at.
- *the distinction between argument and persuasion.*
- *how to expose your opponent's fallacies.*
- *yourself as an advocate.*
- *the many other factors involved in an argument, over and*
  above the issues themselves, capable of influencing the
  direction of its outcome.

"In an age of polarization and confrontation, argument should be viewed as a useful tool in the marketplace of ideas rather than a stuffy classification of rhetorical principles and devices doomed to stand unread and undusted on some desolate bookshelf."[1]

A PHILOSOPHY OF ARGUMENT

Knowing how to argue in today's world is not a luxury but a necessity. It teaches us not only how to organize and manipulate ideas, but also to defend against being manipulated by them. As children, we were taught to avoid a fight or an argument. Whenever we had a difference of opinion over a toy, some adult always interrupted and said, "Come now, children, don't fight, don't argue—play nicely!" It didn't seem to matter an iota which child was right or wrong. The only thing grown-ups were concerned with was that peaceful coexistence reigned among children. The fact that little boys and girls went to bed each night frustrated seemed of no major importance.

To argue is human. The problem is that too many of us never learn how *to disagree without becoming disagreeable.* Instead of rejecting *what* a person says, we tend to reject *the person* saying it. In this way, many arguments needlessly turn into fights. An example of how civilized people should disagree occurs daily in our courts. Attorneys who were at one another's throats in litigation during an afternoon session often enjoy a friendly supper together that evening.

If not argued properly, conflicting messages may trigger a variety of

---

[1] Abne M. Eisenberg and Joseph A. Ilardo, *Argument: An Alternative to Violence* (Englewood Cliffs, N.J.: Prentice-Hall, Inc., 1972), p. x.

psychologically and physiologically detrimental effects, such as headaches, ulcers, dizziness, and rashes. Have you ever left a party after losing an argument to someone who clearly knew nothing about the subject argued? How can such things happen? Obviously, as this chapter will discuss shortly, there is more to winning than being right.

Where do we learn to argue? In most cases, nowhere! The average person just picks it up along the way without any special training. If you, by chance, have a natural flare for arguing, fine! If not, you run the risk of becoming victimized from time to time. This writer is strongly convinced that compulsory courses in argumentation should be taught in the schools from an early age. A viable alternative to a "punch in the nose" must be made available to every youngster—one that will satisfy their individual and collective needs. Unless children are provided with an education that teaches them how to disagree without becoming disagreeable, it has failed in one of its most critical responsibilities.

While arguments over someone's height or weight are easily settled with a ruler or scale, how are the more abstract ones adjudicated—those dealing with such subjects as God, morality, politics, and inferiority complexes? Obviously, some other kind of yardstick is needed.

People have various ways of deciding who is right and who is wrong. The basis for such decisions may include an honest face, a reputation of being right in the past, or the use of sound logic. Yet, step one millimeter outside the knowledge system of the civilized world and you will find other less familiar criteria—the eruption of a volcano, an eclipse of the moon or sun, or even an earthquake. To a member of a primitive society, these phenomena carry the same validity as an honest face, a reputation of being right, or the use of sound logic. Anywhere you go, people are found to have certain very definite criteria for determining who and what are RIGHT or WRONG. Thus, to argue with the native of Kenya or Wollomombie, the storekeeper in Hughesville, Pennsylvania, or the farmer in Thermopolis, Wyoming, you must acquaint yourself with the criteria they use in establishing validity.

Although modern technology has made our lives easier physically, it has not done as well psychologically. As long as tranquilizers and antidepressant drugs remain on the market, we still need help. One chronic thorn repeatedly pricks the sides of people who suffer psychologically: the need to be right. Regardless into which corner of society you look, someone is always lurking there making judgments; whether it is a clergyman, parent, teacher, policeman, boss, older brother or sister, all seem to busy themselves evaluating whatever you say, do, or think as either RIGHT or WRONG. For some of us, life is a continuum of argument after argument, and, to survive, we must learn the rhetorical art of self-defense.

In many ways, argumentation is similar to judo. The object is to throw your opponent. The major difference is that in judo, the means are physical, whereas in argumentation they are rhetorical. In both, the unprepared mind suffers a disadvantage. Thus, whether one is engaged in the art of judo or of argumentation, a plan, a strategy, a modus operandi, or a philosophy is indispensable to success.

In 1882 Jigoro Kano, the founder of judo, discovered the principle of "maximum efficiency, minimum effort." He reasoned that intelligence, in addition to strength, was necessary to throw an opponent. This same strategy can and should be applied to argument. The use of loudness, verbiage, and imposition, while sometimes effective, negates Professor Kano's principle. It consumes too much energy. Instead, the technique of "yielding" should be used. In judo, when someone bigger than you attacks, rather than resisting, you should pull the attacker in the direction in which he is already moving. In this way, you take advantage of the forward motion he had already initiated and add to it the force supplied by your pull. In effect, you yield, not resist. This same principle can be successfully applied to argumentation.

As a rule, your opponent launches a battery of reasons why his position should be accepted. You, in return, are probably busy trying to refute them. In a restaurant, bar, street corner, or classroom, the pattern is generally the same. People become engaged in a shouting contest and are totally impervious to what the other person is saying. More often than not, the outcome of the argument differs little from its beginning. Neither party has significantly altered the other's point of view. Committed to the notion that yielding is a sign of weakness, each feverishly resents having to give even an inch of ground. In fact, many people believe that being rigid and tenaciously sticking to your point is a sign of strength, not weakness. Such a view, however, gains no support from the philosophy being posited here.

Authorities in the field of argumentation caution that *one cannot argue conclusions, only how they are arrived at.* At this very moment, hoards of people are walking around with their heads chock full of conclusions for which they have not the slightest foundation. Prejudice, biases, and stereotyping characteristically lack foundations and, as such, are particularly vulnerable to the yielding technique. Pretend that at lunch yesterday a friend said, "As far as I'm concerned, you can take the entire jury system in this country and dump it in the ocean." Let us try to find out your friend's basis for such a conclusion. Rather than your running off at the mouth with spontaneous counter-remarks, probe for more information, with the hope that by being given enough rope, he will hang himself. Do not respond to any of his allegations. Just encourage him to "keep talking." Ask questions such as, "Would you define exactly what you mean by a jury system," or "What, precisely, is your point?," or "Are there any alternative explanations for the way you feel?" Get him to talk as much as possible— to illustrate, explain, and clarify. Most people are inclined to be fuzzy thinkers and, as a result, organize their thoughts poorly. This must be taken advantage of in an argument. Surely you have heard people say, in the midst of an explanation, "What I'm really trying to say," or "In other words," or "Let me put it another way." Each of these clichés is symptomatic of at least a partially muddled mind.

For a number of reasons, modern man seems to be uptight and suffering from a poverty of self-esteem. Often he backs off when confronted by someone who behaves as if he knows what he is doing and where he is going. People have definite reservations about "getting involved." It is this very trait which causes certain radio talk shows to be so successful. They thrive on the defensive nature of many members of their audience. Some moderators are sadistically rude and cruel toward some of their callers. One wonders why on earth those who are so severely browbeaten allow themselves to be so verbally abused. They must enjoy being humiliated. Perhaps the lesson we can learn from these shows is that the professional at the microphone wins arguments largely by "yielding." Rarely is any serious attention given to the issue or question raised by the caller. Instead, the caller's Achilles' heel is exposed by drawing attention to the improper foundations for his conclusions. Only by yielding—letting his caller talk—does the moderator consistently maintain the upper hand.

A word of caution: You cannot use the same strategy with all forms of argument. Again, as in judo, the size, strength, and experience of your opponent must be taken into careful consideration. Naturally, the intercollegiate debate, a courtroom action, or a heated classroom discussion will each require a different tack. Failure comes quickly to the individual who has misjudged the kind of argument he has or in which he plans to become involved.

"The twentieth century is literally strewn with such terms as dialogues, talks, and arbitration. Beneath each lies the implied purpose of avoiding violence by settling differences equitably . . . . If man is to live out this century, he must restrict his disagreements to words, not fists, clubs, or guns. In short, we plead for a nonviolent approach to controversy—a shift in the focus of conflict resolution toward a greater reliance upon the strategy of argument as an alternative to violence."[2]

[2] Eisenberg and Ilardo, Argument, p. 136.

DISTINCTIONS TO BE MADE[3]

A.   *Between an ARGUMENT and a FIGHT*

The terms "argument" and "fight" are frequently used interchangeably. This is unfortunate; some distinctions should be made between them.

Broadly speaking, a "fight" is characterized by (1) closed-mindedness, (2) a degeneration of language into its more vulgar form, (3) raised voices, (4) elevated blood pressure, and (5) physical abuse; plus an outcome of either a *stalemate* (no progress made in either direction) or *alienation* ("I'll never speak to you again!").

Socially, fights are regarded as more serious than arguments. In fact, if two calls were to come into the local police precinct, one a complaint of a fight and one of an argument, the fight generally would be given a higher priority.

Since most fights are counterproductive, it is extremely important, whenever possible, that they be converted into arguments. By so doing, *compromise* ("Alright, I'll go to the party, but we will come home early") is made possible rather than stalemate or alienation. Psychologists, social workers, family and student counselors are forever being saddled with the task of converting fights into arguments. At least, by so doing, they reduce the probability of personal injury, help clarify issues, and increase the amount of productive interpersonal communication. It should also be stressed that a sound argument in which both sides are given ample opportunity to express themselves provides the best guarantee that messages in conflict will be equitably resolved with dignity and to the satisfaction of all concerned.

A final distinction must be made: *fights* are subjectively oriented, while *arguments*, as conceived in this chapter, are objectively oriented. Put another way, in a *fight*, people tend to say what they think and feel without regard for external opinions. In contrast, the person in an *argument* tends to say what he knows and to draw upon the knowledge of others who are more qualified. Another method of determining whether you are engaged in a fight or an argument is by the number of times the words I, ME, or MY are used as compared with THEY, THEM, and IT. If the preponderance favors the I, ME, and MY, you are probably in a fight; if the leaning is toward THEY, THEM, and IT, it is probably an argument.

People, like pressure cookers, must be allowed to let off steam. To do this effectively, the words whose emotional meanings most closely align themselves with the SELF work best (I, ME, and MY). Those which

---

[3] Since *arguments, fights, debates,* and *persuasion* are all art forms and not examples of pure science, any distinctions made here between them will necessarily be semantically vague and open to more than one interpretation.

are more impersonal (THEY, THEM, and IT) generally fail to achieve the needed degree of catharsis (the act of letting off steam).

The distinctions being made here between an argument and a fight are by no means conclusive, nor are they easily made in practice. There is much overlapping. Our purpose will have been accomplished if the reader simply is able to recognize that, with practice, most fights are convertible into arguments—and that developing the skill to argue effectively is both a sanity- and civilization-saving device.

B.   Between an ARGUMENT and a DEBATE

A fight requires no special training, unless, of course, you are a professional. This is not the case with an argument and even less so with a debate. Both, being man-made arts, come with written and unwritten rules. Table 7–1 lists some of the characteristics of each which will enable you to differentiate them.

Distinction	Argument	Formal Debate
1. Rules	1. Few	1. Many
2. Topic	2. Not clearly stated	2. Clearly stated
3. Time	3. Unregulated	3. Regulated
4. Emotionality	4. Moderate to high	4. Low
5. Location	5. Anywhere	5. Prearranged
6. Evidence and proof	6. Generally non-logical	6. Logical
7. Psychological side effects	7. Moderate to many	7. Few
8. Decision	8. By advocates or audience	8. By judge(s)
9. Positions taken	9. Ill-defined and subject to change	9. Predetermined and agreed upon
10. Language level	10. Low to moderate	10. Moderate to high
11. Preconceptions	11. Many	11. Few
12. Purpose	12. Personal pleasure, principle, or satisfaction	12. Competition

TABLE 7–1 Distinctions Between an Argument and a Formal Debate

From these distinctions, a conclusion easily arrived at is that formal debate is a highly structured and disciplined form of argument and that a good deal of overlapping exists between the two. What, then, is the importance of knowing the difference? Perhaps it is simply a definitional exercise with which educated people should be, at least, casually familiar.

C. Between ARGUMENT and PERSUASION

Again we run into a semantic bog from which few emerge clear-minded. One pair of experts set the stage for this discussion by suggesting that:

> Most popular definitions of argument make it part of the area of persuasion, with its function that of influencing belief and action. While it is true that the eventual findings of argumentative analysis will be used to influence others, it is not true that this is the purpose of argumentation. Argumentation itself does not seek to persuade anybody of anything.[4]

In and out of bounds, authorities continue to feed us definitional aids—some focusing on the *intent* of persuasion and argumentation, some on the *process* by which goals are reached, some predominantly on the *goal* itself. For example, McBurney[5] describes argumentation as a method of analysis and reasoning providing bases for belief and action, and persuasion as the process of influencing human behavior (attitudes, opinions, overt acts) through the use of oral and written communication or the academic discipline in which applied rhetoric and psychology are studied.

McBurney, in these remarks, stresses the process and goals of argumentation and persuasion rather than their intent. Muehl,[6] in contrast, thinking in terms of intent, tells us that the "aim" of the persuader is not to change an individual's conviction to another but rather to weaken the pull that is drawing him one way and strengthen the pull to the desired direction.

Hance[7] helps us considerably by detecting ground common to both argumentation and persuasion with regard to the goal each seeks—that is, to present the merits of a proposition in order to secure acceptance. Argumentation, he claims, proceeds to achieve this end through the use of logical cogency, while persuasion proceeds through mind changing.

Once upon a time, professional literature dichotomized argumentation (to convince) and persuasion (to persuade), and both enjoyed the widespread reputation of being distinct concepts and processes. In recent years, however, some doubters have appeared upon the scene. One of them set out a basis for distinguishing between conviction and persuasion. To convince, he explains, implies no risk of SELF; it is manipulation without

---

[4] Russel R. Windes and Arthur Hastings, *Argumentation and Advocacy* (New York: Random, 1964), p. 24.

[5] J. McBurney and G. Mills, *Argumentation and Debate*, 2d ed. (New York: Macmillan, 1964), pp. 1, 165–66.

[6] W. Muehl, *The Road to Persuasion* (New York: Oxford University Press, 1956), p. 102.

[7] Kenneth Hance et al., *Principles of Speaking* (Belmont, Calif.: Wadsworth, 1962), p. 67.

conviction. To persuade, however, does risk the SELF and does imply commitment.[8]

Since additional opinion on this subject will probably confound more than clarify, an appropriate alternative might be simply to view the terms "argument" and "persuasion" in a pragmatic light.

Imagine you have just received the grade of "C" in an English course which, in your opinion, you didn't deserve. Assuming a "what harm can it do" attitude, you decide to confront your professor and discuss the matter face-to-face. YOUR OBJECTIVE: to have your grade raised by using either argument or persuasion or perhaps a little bit of both. To help you in your plight, you enlist the aid of Aristotle's three modes of appeal: *ethos, pathos,* and *logos. Ethos* is an appeal based upon the status (competence, integrity, good will, attitude, ability, and knowledge) of an individual; *pathos,* upon emotionality (man's drives); and *logos,* on logical and reasoned discourse. Used separately or together, these appeals may be applied regardless of whether you are planning to engage in persuasion or in argumentation. Each, hopefully, will be able to effect a conversion of your "C" grade. The question now boils down to which technique to use on your professor. Will it be:

I. "Gee Professor, I am an honor student, on the Dean's List, and editor of our school newspaper." (ethos)

II. "Gee Professor, I sure wish you would reconsider my grade. My mother is in the hospital, my father just lost his job, and I have 'mono'." (pathos)

III. "Gee Professor, I can't understand why you gave me a C in this course. You gave me two B's and one A— for the papers I handed in, an 80 on my midterm, and a 79 on my final. Doesn't that warrant more than a C for a final grade?" (logos)

If you elect persuasion, it will probably involve more subjectivity → more of the SELF to emerge. Conversely, argument will involve more objectivity → less of the SELF to emerge. Your decision must be arrived at by carefully analyzing both your personality and that of your professor. Whichever tactic presents fewer obstacles should be your course of action.

Further efforts to refine these often illusory distinctions between persuasion and argument would, at this juncture, be of little practical value. Thus, given the existing overlap between argument and persuasion and the tendency for theory to overemphasize the particular and deemphasize

[8] D. C. Bryant, "Rhetoric: Its function and scope," in *Philosophy, Rhetoric, and Argumentation* by M. Natanson and H. W. Johnstone, Jr. (University Park: Pennsylvania State University Press, 1965).

the general, the reader is left with but this word of advice: Choose that method which best serves your needs and with which you feel most comfortable.

A STRATEGY OF ARGUMENT

Using the philosophy of argument just presented as a springboard, we shall now briefly restress its essence and proceed to offer the reader a *modus argumentum*.

Drawing hasty conclusions is a popular pastime endemic to most of the human race. At the slightest sign of an unanswered question, CONCLUSIONS seem to abound from everywhere. While the majority of these conclusions are emotionally, impulsively, and intuitively drawn, a small percentage of them do stand up reasonably well to cross-examination.

When engaged in, or preparing to engage in an argument, the first cardinal rule is to pay special attention to EXACTLY WHAT IS BEING ARGUED. This should include the CONCLUSION or CLAIM being made, the SUPPORT (evidence or proof) behind it, and the REASONING (or glue) which unites the conclusion to the supportive evidence or proof. Soon, a dozen sample units of fallacious arguments will be presented and the reader invited to dissect and analyze them.

Once more, it should be emphasized that in even the most casual conversation, conclusions are frequently advanced without the remotest trace of a sound foundation. There are so many people who expect you to believe what they say simply because they say it! They have become so accustomed to having their remarks go unchallenged that they are shocked when asked to back up their conclusions with some kind of reliable evidence or proof. Feigning a wounded ego, they often retaliate with, "Are you calling me a liar?" or, "Why would I lie to you?" Incidentally, some of these people possess such an imposing and overbearing manner that contesting what they say becomes almost impossible. The pathological liar is a classic example of one who frequently makes outrageous statements which are so believable they are seldom, if ever, questioned.

Parents of the extremely inquisitive or precocious child know the frustration of being asked WHY after every other remark. Reluctant to accept clichés such as *It is God's will!* or *That's the way the government works!*, they appear convinced that adults have all the answers but simply won't share them with children. At school, teachers often experience similar exasperation with the bright student who refuses to accept generalizations without a satisfactory basis. Too young to realize how little Man actually knows, and lacking the sophistication and tact to pursue what is known, the child is often meted out a hostile response he does not deserve. As a result, it is not uncommon to find some of these students labeled as "behavior problems"—and in time they may actually fulfill the prophecy.

Why are so many of us reluctant to admit, "I don't know!" when confronted with a question we can't answer? The young physician and teacher alike suffer from this tendency. Whenever asked a question they can't answer, rather than admit their ignorance, they conjure up some academic or professional mumbo jumbo to offer it in its stead. In all probability, there is a close relationship between what we know and what others think we should know that regulates our behavior under certain circumstances. A defensive attitude, therefore, is not uncommon when one's credibility is threatened.

Assuming that man's Achilles' heel is having to justify or account for his conclusions, we arrive at the second cardinal rule: SEARCH OUT, WEAKEN, TEAR DOWN, AND DESTROY THE BASIS FOR YOUR OPPONENT'S CONCLUSION. Discredit why something is said and you rob it of its impact, its force, its effectiveness.

As a first exercise, consider your gut reaction to this statement:

"*I think our government is infested with communists, kikes, and niggers.*"

The person who uttered these words has obviously arrived at a rather extreme conclusion pertaining to our government and the kinds of people in it. Absolutely no evidence or proof accompanies it. Its sponsor seems to expect that it will be accepted as gospel and without question. Steeped in cesspools of prejudice and bias, conclusions such as this have already reached epidemic proportions and are a threat to us all. Not only must they be recognized and labeled as dangerous to the public good, but a workable strategy of argument must be developed to combat them.

Since only a small segment of a college population becomes involved with formal debate and almost its entire population involved with informal argumentation, it becomes a sociological as well as a psychological imperative that nondebate-oriented students also learn how to defend themselves against the noxious effects of CONCLUSIONS WITHOUT BASIS. Thus, without getting into the ramifications of collegiate debate, what is the most efficient way of supplying the reader with an operationally dependable strategy of argument? It must be uncomplicated, manageable, and effective in a majority of situations. The following approach has been developed to serve such a need.

Someone once asked a famous sculptor the secret of his success. He answered, "I just chip away the unimportant parts." While these may not have been his exact words, their meaning is clear. To be successful in any endeavor requires the ability to separate that which is important from that which is unimportant. This has very special meaning with reference to all arguments. Unless an advocate is able to distinguish between the relevant and the irrelevant, failure is almost inevitable. Once this ability has been mastered, you are ready to zero in on your target—the basis of your opponent's conclusion. Now, let us return to the statement made about people in government.

It would be foolish and a waste of time to parry such a remark with comments like, "Oh yeah, you're full of crap!" or "That's the most ridiculous statement I've ever heard." Unfortunately, this kind of tit-for-tat is widely practiced among individuals untrained in argumentation. Abandon this useless technique at once! It is redundant, and it goes nowhere at top speed. In its place, substitute a few well-chosen and pointed questions. Your opponent should be made to feel your strength through your demands for clarification, illustration, explanation, and definition. Here is the direction in which your argument should move.

What do you mean by "our government"? Are you referring to local, state, or federal government; the government in office back in 1937, 1951, 1969, or the present one? Press your adversary for a satisfactory meaning of "our government." Then attack the word "communists." When using this label, does he mean people who were born in Russia who are now in government service, card-carrying communists, or members of the socialist party? Precisely what meaning is the word "communists" supposed to convey? Next move on to "kikes." Does the connotation apply to all Jews or just certain Jews—for example, orthodox, conservative, reform? Does it apply only to those who were born Jews, or are converts also taken in by the label of "kikes"? Does the stereotype include or exclude Jews who are not circumcised at birth? Just who are the people working in government who are being labeled here as "kikes"?

The last segment of this conclusion singles out "niggers." Again, a battery of questions are necessary to clear the air. Should the label be taken to include only those people whose skins are black or will it also include those whose skins are extremely light (almost white) who are racially classified as Negro? Insist upon clear-cut guidelines for the label "nigger."

Using this method of interrogation, you can seriously weaken the foundation upon which a conclusion is based, or, if you perform with exceptional skill, totally discredit it.

It is now time to consider the third cardinal rule: EXPOSE THE FALLACIES IN YOUR OPPONENT'S ARGUMENT. To do this, you must acquaint yourself with the kinds of fallacies that exist and develop the ability to expose them. As a second exercise, here are some hypothetical conclusions plus the basis upon which each is founded.

YOUR JOB: to discover the fallacies inherent in them. In the vernacular, a fallacy is a case of "wrong reasoning." Below are a series of CONCLU-SIONS and the REASONS upon which they are founded. In each, one or more fallacies will be committed, and you are challenged to identify and expose them before reading the dissection that follows.

An Exposé of Wrong Reasoning

UNIT I

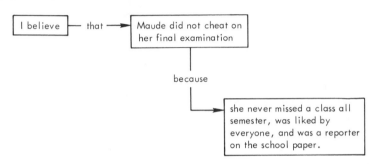

DISSECTION

Even to the untrained eye, this fallacy shines through. Obviously, the reasons used to persuade us that Maude did not cheat on her final examination have absolutely nothing whatsoever to do with the examination. While they are, indeed, admirable traits and warrant separate commendation, they are valueless as evidence or proof that Maude did not cheat. What we find here is an appeal to pity, and the technical name for the fallacy is *argumentum ad miseracordiam*. Be on the alert for this one whenever your adversary drifts away from the specific issue at hand and dwells on emotional matters. Bring the argument sharply back into focus by exposing your opponent's use of this fallacy, and demand that all attention be returned to its central theme: the charge that Maude cheated on her examination.

Another fallacy also creeps into this argument. It is called *non sequitur*, which means, "It does not follow." Although the illusion of relatedness is created, once the question of Maude's cheating is abandoned, a *non sequitur* is committed by mentioning that she was a reporter on the school paper. Attorneys are forever jumping to their feet whenever their opponents even look as if they are going to engage in a *non sequitur* and shouting, "I object, your honor; that is irrelevant and immaterial to this case." In this instance, Maude's being a school reporter had nothing to do with her cheating on the examination.

UNIT II

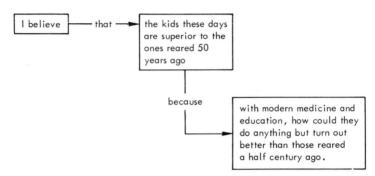

DISSECTION

Parents seem extremely prone to encounter this fallacy when interacting with their teenage children. Without making a value judgment, let it suffice to say that a fallacy has been used called *argumentum ad novarum*. It refers to any situation in which a claim or conclusion is based upon the premise that "whatever is newer, is better." The latest model automobile, the most recently graduated physician, the newest addition to the faculty —all are preferable to the old ones. Television commercials lean heavily on this fallacy by touting products which have just been developed and infer that they are better than the products touted last season. The only possible conclusion which can be drawn about people who employ the *argumentum ad novarum* fallacy is that they not only have tunnel vision but are also rhetorically myopic and bear watching. It is also worthwhile to mention an opposing fallacy—*argumentum ad verecundiam*: that which is older, is better; and experience is the best teacher.

UNIT III

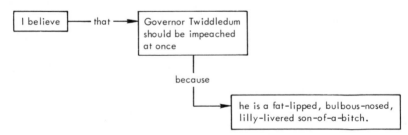

DISSECTION

People lodging this kind of argument must, immediately, be classified as lacking integrity and substance. It is called the *fallacy of psychological* language, and it characterizes the argument which is completely without benefit of evidence or proof. In desperation, its user resorts to emotionally loaded language designed to insult rather than provide a sound basis for an argument. On a rare occasion, it may be found in a rational argument where an advocate senses defeat is inevitable and, frenetically exhibits a verbal "death rattle" filled with language of every description.

UNIT IV

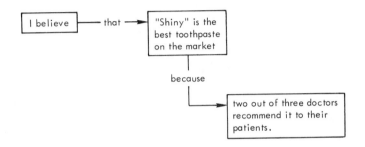

DISSECTION

Aside from bringing a smile to everyone's face, this fallacy does help big companies advertise their product. Although they never tell you how many doctors they had to ask about "Shiny" to get the two out of the three they quote, they compound the felony by failing to tell you what kind of doctors they were. For all we know, they might have been veterinarians, musicologists, pathologists, doctors of divinity, physicists, chiropractors, podiatrists, or psychiatrists—and only by accident, dentists. They also neglect to tell us whether "Shiny" is the *only* toothpaste these doctors recommend, or whether they also recommend other brands, as well. The fallacy committed is called the *fallacy of significance.* Merely claiming that two out of three doctors recommend this or that is of absolutely no consequence unless additional information is made available.

In a similar situation, a dental society claimed that 57 percent of the people in one medium-sized American city had cavities. Such a claim is ludicrous without first specifying how many people in that city *have teeth* and the dental society's definition of a "cavity." Is it anything in which a dentist can catch his pick, or must it be a gaping crater? We must also know the incidence of cavities in other cities for comparison; otherwise, the 57 percent cited is absolutely of no significance. Beware of the isolated statistic without the appropriate supporting evidence, lest you become a victim of the *fallacy of significance.*

UNIT V

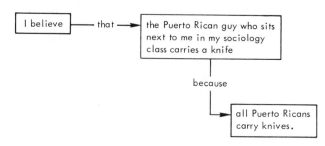

DISSECTION

Positively no *stereotype kit* would be complete without this fallacy. It is the backbone of all prejudice. It enables anyone having the need to put others down, to do so quickly and conveniently. It is the *fallacy of composition*, meaning *what is true of part, is true of the whole*. What more efficient method can you think of that makes it possible for you to deprecate an entire people on the basis of what you think of one of its members? One black has rhythm, they all have rhythm—one Jew is a shylock, they are all shylocks—one Irishman can drink a quart of scotch without batting an eye, they all can—one Chinese owns a laundry, they all own laundries. The list is endless as well as misleading. It strips us of our individuality and axiomatically invests us with the negative characteristics of other members of our class. Hopefully, in a democratic spirit, we should all be judged on our own merits.

The counterpart of this fallacy is the *fallacy of division*, which suggests that *what is true of the whole is true of its parts*. Assign a characteristic to all Frenchmen. Then, find an individual member of that group and assign that same characteristic to him. In Aristotle's syllogistic form, it looks like this:

Major premise: All Frenchmen are good lovers.
Minor premise: Francois is a Frenchman.
Conclusion: Francois is a good lover.

In either case, these fallacies are to be guarded against and exposed at the earliest possible moment. During World War II, Adolph Hitler worked these fallacies overtime against the Jews. No purge or persecutory movement should be without these degenerate tools of human abuse. Adjust your psychic radar so that it will detect both the fallacy of composition and the fallacy of division in your next argument.

UNIT VI

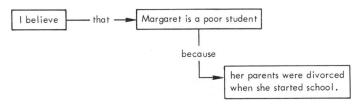

DISSECTION

This is probably one of the most primitive of all the fallacies. Called *post hoc ergo propter hoc* (after the fact, therefore, before the fact), it consists of an argument in which one thing precedes another in time, causing the earlier event to be held responsible for the later one. In the present example, it would appear that Margaret is a poor student because her parents were divorced when she started school; their divorce caused her to be a poor student. Another example is the sequence in which the son of a tribal chief dies immediately after a nearby volcano has erupted. If, in the chief's mind, the volcanic eruption caused the child's death, the *post hoc ergo propter hoc* fallacy was committed. With complete disregard for alternative explanations, people, civilized or uncivilized, seem to find this simplistic causal relationship between events particularly attractive. Circumstantial evidence is known to thrive on this fallacy, especially when it indicts someone for robbery solely on the basis of his being found at the scene of the crime immediately after it was committed. If you require a more personal example, borrow a friend's car and have it break down while you are using it. The chances of your being accused of causing the breakdown are exceedingly high. "Gee, Margaret, it was O.K. until you borrowed it!" is not an uncommon allegation. You know the rest of the story. Both the borrower and the lender solemnly vow never to do it again.

UNIT VII

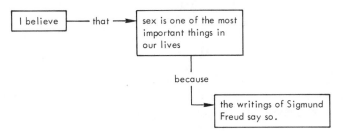

DISSECTION

Any argument whose strength is *exclusively* based upon what some authority has either said or written is open to the charge of the *fallacy of arguing from authority*. It is a very tempting "cop-out" for the person holding to a view totally lacking support of any kind. Some of the phrases its users employ are, "*according to* . . . ," "*authorities agree* . . . ," "*studies indicate* . . . ," or, "*in the opinion of* . . . ."

Coupled with this fallacy, or tagged onto it, is the *fallacy of laudatory personalities*. Its force derives from the premise that people in high places, of substantial position and reputation, can do no wrong. In a film entitled, *Citizen above Suspicion*, a chief of police committed a murder and, in spite of the fact that a long chain of very reliable clues led directly to him, both his staff and the public were adamant against even remotely considering him as a suspect. In their eyes, he was indeed a citizen above suspicion—a most laudatory personality.

To complete a triple threat to right reasoning, here is the *genetic fallacy*, which should not be ignored. It contends that *good people do good things and bad people do bad things*.

In sum, any argument resorting to such fallacies as: (1) arguing from authority, (2) laudatory personalities, or (3) genetics should, unless buttressed by other more respectable evidence or proof, be placed under careful scrutiny.

UNIT VIII

> *Assertion 1.* Why doesn't Marilyn like John?
> *Assertion 2.* Because he bites his nails.
>
>   *   *   *
>
> *Assertion 1.* Why does John bite his nails?
> *Assertion 2.* Because Marilyn doesn't like him.
>
>   *   *   *
>
> *Assertion 1.* Why doesn't Marilyn like John?
> *Assertion 2.* Because he bites his nails.

DISSECTION

This example illustrates the *fallacy of arguing in a circle* and is characterized by two unsupported assertions ("Marilyn doesn't like John" and

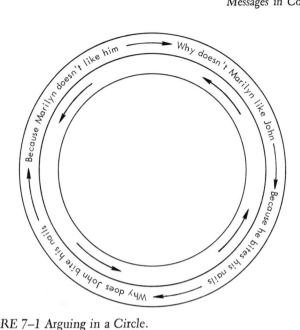

FIGURE 7–1 *Arguing in a Circle.*

"He bites his nails"). Thus, like the dog chasing its tail, it goes around and around (Fig. 7–1).

Note: Don't forget, the same statement cannot serve as both the conclusion and its reason. The two must remain separate and distinct.

UNIT IX

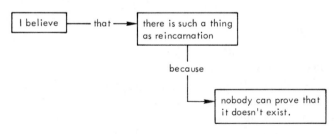

DISSECTION

This argumentative strategy involves the *fallacy of argumentum ad ignorantium.* The person using it hides behind the fact that whatever is being claimed cannot be refuted. As long as the user steers clear of concrete phenomena which can be tested, a substantial margin of safety is enjoyed. In this example, the question of whether reincarnation does or does not exist is patently a nontestable assertion. Challenging someone to refute it is a reasonably secure position to assume. The way to handle such a challenge is to expose the strategy behind it by insisting that a more arguable position be taken instead. A stepping-stone in this direction is to demand some mutually acceptable definitions of the terms *reincarnation, nobody,* and *prove.* Be firm!

UNIT X

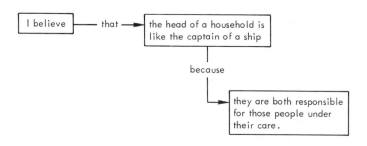

DISSECTION

The use of an analogy makes a comparison between two similar cases by inferring that what is true in one case is necessarily true in the other. Here, the analogy is drawn between the captain of a ship and the head (father, mother, or guardian) of a household. This is a *faulty analogy* for a number of reasons, such as: (1) the captain of a ship is trained to command, whereas the head of a household is generally not trained; (2) a ship is subordinate to Naval Law, a household is not; (3) the number of people involved on board ship and in a household differs substantially; (4) the objectives in each case are not the same.

Defective analogies frequently seek acceptance in arguments where individuals are untrained to recognize and expose them. On the surface, the comparisons presented here seem compatible but, on closer inspection, they disclose inconsistencies which disqualify them. Bettinghaus[9] claims that a "faulty analogy results when two events, structures, or people are not alike in the characteristics being compared or in characteristics relevant to those being compared." Although the reader might inadvertently leave

---

[9] Erwin P. Bettinghaus, *The Nature of Proof,* 2d ed. (New York: Bobbs-Merrill, 1972), p. 136.

this page with the impression that every analogy must contain items that are identical in every regard, substantial similarities often warrant generalizing from one to the other.

UNIT XI

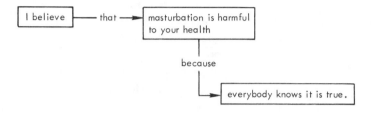

DISSECTION

Few things provide an argument with greater force than having large numbers of people agree with it. Throughout the ages, men and women of foresight and invention have run head-on into the fallacy called *argumentum ad populum*—whatever the majority of people believe is necessarily true because they believe it. Look back at the popular reactions to Columbus' silly notion that the Earth was round; Pasteur's childish prattle about "wee beasties" or germs; or the Wright brothers and their demented ideas about men flying about in the sky like birds. Almost as if they were being compelled by some mysterious guidance system, people are inclined

UNIT XII

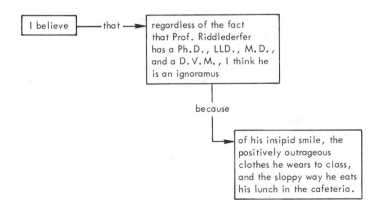

to accept more readily that which is more widely accepted by others. Preying upon this tendency, the advocate who employs this fallacy usually gets away with it because most people lack the intestinal fortitude to stand alone.

DISSECTION

Instead of attacking the integrity of a man through the use of logical proof, this fallacy employs what has been referred to as character assassination or, as it is called in Latin, *argumentum ad hominem*. It has happened to all of us at one time or another. Engaged in an argument in which perhaps you are winning, the other party suddenly shifts the focus of his attack away from the issues and onto you. He might begin by taking pot shots at the city, state, or town from which you came, the way you dress, your education, even the people with whom you associate. His rationale goes like this: if he cannot discredit your argument, he tries to win by discrediting you personally. It is an extremely common ploy and should be exposed the moment it occurs.

In no way should memorizing these fallacies be construed as insurance that you will be able to detect them in an argument. Considerable practice is needed. In addition to becoming a successful "fallacy hunter," you will find other argumentative tactics helpful if winning is your goal. For example, in any contest, whether matching wits in an argument or competing on a ball field, it is essential that a person know his own assets and liabilities. At all costs, avoid over- or underestimating yourself, especially in an argument. And, to guard against such an eventuality, here is a simple quiz which will provide you with additional insight into yourself as either a protagonist or an antagonist.

Before beginning, it is extremely important that you understand the nature and purpose of this quiz. By no stretch of the imagination is it intended to be comprehensive, nor to provide a "sure-fire" formula guaranteed to win arguments. All the questions have a broad base and are subject to scores of intervening variables. For this quiz to be successful, it must (1) confirm many of the things you already know, (2) draw attention to different aspects of things you know, (3) introduce you to certain new dimensions in argumentation, (4) cause you to see yourself more clearly as an advocate, and (5) increase your respect for the fact that the principles of argument extend beyond the realm of logic. After you have finished, each question will be commented on briefly, and a suggestion or two made on how they may be implemented in an argument.

SELF-EVALUATION QUIZ[10]

(Profile of an Advocate)

NAME _____

COURSE _____

SECTION _____

Physical characteristics:

1. *Somatotype:*
   ectomorph ☐   mesomorph ☐   endomorph ☐
2. *Manner of dress:*
   high style ☐   average ☐   unconcerned ☐
3. *Voice volume:*
   loud ☐   average ☐   soft ☐
4. *Speech speed:*
   fast ☐   medium ☐   slow ☐
5. *Haptic behavior (touching)*
   a toucher ☐   a touchee ☐   untouchable ☐
6. *Eye-contact behavior:*
   extensive ☐   moderate ☐   minimal ☐   none ☐
7. *Kinesic behavior:*
   hyperkinetic ☐   hypokinetic ☐   average ☐
8. *Postural attitude preferred:*
   upright ☐   seated ☐   recumbent ☐

Psychological characteristics:

9. *Personality type:*
   introvert ☐   extrovert ☐   ambivert ☐
10. *Intelligence:*
    high ☐   average ☐   low ☐
11. *Open-mindedness:*
    high ☐   average ☐   low ☐
12. *Perception of SELF as an:*
    instigator ☐   aggressor ☐   victim ☐
13. *Ability to stay on subject:*
    high ☐   average ☐   low ☐
14. *Pleasure derived from arguing:*
    high ☐   average ☐   low ☐   none ☐
15. *Tendency to argue:*
    high ☐   average ☐   low ☐   none ☐

[10] Since all responses elicited by this quiz will depend upon whatever circumstances prevail at a given time, only answers of a general nature are expected from the reader.

16. *Lifespan of arguments:*
     short-lived ☐   average ☐   long-lived ☐
17. *Frequency of arguments:*
     high ☐   average ☐   low ☐   none ☐
18. *Tendency to alienate an opponent:*
     high ☐   average ☐   low ☐   none ☐
19. *Type of opponents:*
     same ☐   different ☐   unimportant ☐
20. *Subjects argued:*
     same ☐   different ☐   unimportant ☐

Environmental characteristics:

21. *Proxemic status (interpersonal distance during an argument):*
     less than 6 inches ☐   between 6 and 12 inches ☐
     between 12 and 24 inches ☐   over 24 inches ☐
22. *Location of most arguments:*
     Home:
     kitchen ☐   bedroom ☐   living room ☐   bathroom ☐
     Office:
     your office ☐   someone else's office ☐   hall ☐
     School:
     in class ☐   cafeteria ☐   halls ☐   outdoors ☐
23. *Time most arguments occur:*
     early morning ☐   forenoon ☐   afternoon ☐
     evening ☐   middle of the night ☐
24. *Relationship of arguments to meals:*
     before meals ☐   during meals ☐   after meals ☐
25. *Climatic relationship to arguing:*
     rainy days ☐   sunny days ☐   cloudy days ☐
     any days ☐

SOMATOTYPES (VARIATIONS OF PHYSIQUE)

Have you ever argued with someone having a different somatotype? Assume that you are a typical *ectomorph* and, by conventional standards, short (male—5'1" or female—4'10"). Imagine further that you are having an argument with a typical *endomorph* who, in addition to being fat, is also tall—say 6'4". You wind up looking up at him and he looking down at you. Here, a difference in body type has given the taller individual an argumentative edge. What would you have done if you had found yourself in such a situation? Obviously, a compensatory maneuver is necessary in order to put you both at eye level. Or, better still, maneuver so that you are the one doing the "looking down."

What if you were a thin *ectomorph* arguing with a well-muscled *mesomorph*? Could you tip the scales in your favor? Your scheme must include whatever it takes to neutralize the physical difference either *verbally, nonverbally,* or *vocally*. *Verbally,* make dramatic references to some athletic activity in which you are currently engaged (such as wrestling, karate, weight-lifting); *nonverbally,* display strength by standing tall, fold hands across chest or on hips, and maintain direct eye-contact; *vocally,* lower your voice (if possible), speak less, use shorter sentences (a characteristic of the strong, silent type in films), and avoid the use of "ers and ahs," which are sometimes symptomatic of insecurity and uncertainty.

MANNER OF DRESS

Dress was discussed in Chapter 5, where we used the analogy of your being a message and your clothing an envelope. Also, we noted that a relationship exists between you and your clothes. Placing the analogy in an argumentative context, we can extend it now to include the premise that better-dressed individuals have a slight advantage in most arguments. For the most part, a person wearing cheap and styleless clothes is labeled a failure, one wearing highly styled and elegant clothes, a success. Unfortunately, the basis for making these judgments is too often limited to economics and nothing else.

Social interaction in the business world provides us with a convenient measure of the role dress plays in relation to argument. Picture an exquisitely groomed woman in some large department store having an argument with a salesperson. Now, picture a shabbily dressed woman in a similar situation also having an argument with a salesperson. The section manager has been called and has arrived on the scene. Setting aside the credo, "The customer is always right," which woman do you think has the argumentative advantage? In spite of whose argument has the greater merit, the tendency is to favor the better-dressed individual. Should you take exception to this statement, test it for yourself in the following manner. Get dressed in your finest clothes and stroll into a very chic restaurant. Order a meal and then complain about it to the waiter or waitress loudly enough so you can be overheard by other customers. Notice how you are treated—the tone of voice, posture while speaking, eye-contact, type of language used, and so on. A couple of months later slip into your most awful clothes and visit the very same chic restaurant. Repeat the same scene and dialogue and notice any difference in the way the others behave toward you. Allowing, of course, for the many factors capable of causing this personal experiment to fail, simply going through such a ritual is certain to awaken the realization that the way you dress can affect the direction and outcome of an argument.

The next time you have an argument, take special notice of how you and your opponent are dressed. Then, if another occasion arises where you will be together with this person, make it a point to dress in a markedly different way than you did at your last meeting.

Would you believe that there are people who are intimidated when they are obliged to argue with someone wearing a necktie? An absurd digression brings to mind the case of a student who, upon visiting a nudist colony, had considerable difficulty arguing without clothes. So, you see, clothes, or the absence of them, can, if properly understood as potential tools of argumentation, influence the outcome of your next controversy. Next semester, if you are open to a challenge, dress differently each day for the first week or two of class. Take special notice of how teachers treat you. Engage them in discreet controversy and observe their reactions.

VOICE VOLUME

The more sure of yourself you are, the more forceful your tone of voice will incline to be. The opposite tends to be the case when you are unsure of yourself. "Con men" quickly learn the value of vocal quality when they are making their pitch. Eavesdrop on any random argument and, by the tone of the voice alone, see if you are able to tell who will win or who is winning. Such awareness can become a dependable ally in an argument. Given this generalization, take careful note of your next opponent's voice volume. If it is loud and booming, deliberately shift into low gear and speak softly. This usually disturbs the feedback mechanism of loud talkers and upsets their pattern of thought. Some, thoroughly annoyed, say, "God dammit, can't you speak up? What's with all this mumbling?" If, on the other hand, your opponent happens to be a mumbler, you can have a disquieting effect upon him by raising your own voice volume.

People become accustomed to arguing at a certain sound level. If it is not reached, they will deny that an argument has occurred. Practice varying your voice volume so that you can increase or decrease it without affecting your trend of thought. Try it right now. With the next person with whom you speak, use a much lower volume and watch his reaction. Or, if you prefer, raise your voice. It is incredible how psychologically sensitive many people are to how loudly or softly someone speaks. Are you one of them? Discuss the reasons for this with your teacher or classmates.

SPEECH SPEED

Speech speed usually increases in an argument. This often becomes necessary because each advocate is anxious to "make his point." Because of the rapidity with which most arguing individuals speak, rhythms are established—different rhythms from those found in casual conversation. As a result, the pace of an argument becomes an integral part of it. Could you, for instance, in the midst of an argument continue effectively by speaking at half-speed? Thought-speed and speech-speed are interdependents; when one is disturbed, the entire process may suffer. Thus, a marvelous stratagem to have at your disposal while arguing is the ability to speed up or slow down your "argumental pace" at will. An excellent idea might be to simulate arguments with a friend, each taking turns using different speeds.

HAPTIC BEHAVIOR (TOUCHING)

While touching can be precarious in normal social transactions, it can be especially so in an argument. Remarks such as "Keep your hands to yourself" or "Take your cotton-pickin' hands off me" are traditional precursors to violence. Being aware of people's touching habits can, if understood and manipulated, be an asset in an argument. First, let us agree that physical contact, or the absence of it (sensory deprivation), has the capacity to overtly or covertly affect body-mind states. Second, during an argument when emotional levels soar, those who are touchers touch more and those who are timid about touching touch less. Against this background, speculation suggests that altering this natural pattern can also influence the course of an argument. Perhaps an illustration will help explain.

Imagine that you are in an argument with a compulsive toucher whose every other word is accompanied by a touch on the head, neck, or arm. So habitual has this handling of other people become that he is no longer aware he is doing it. It almost seems an integral part of his argument which, if interrupted, could do serious damage to his power of concentration. What do you think would happen if you returned his touches, one-for-one? Here is a strange phenomenon. Like practical jokers who insult or hurt the feelings of others, they seem unable to tolerate having the same things done to them. Compulsive touchers are, as a rule, output oriented; their nervous systems are programmed to initiate touching, not to be touched. Consequently, when someone haptically exploits them, they tend to overreact. There are, of course, countless other factors capable of modifying this reactive pattern. Experiment with it yourself. In your next argument with a "toucher," touch him back every time he touches you and observe his response. If nothing else, it will come as a surprise to him. For some reason, touchers seldom encounter people who reciprocate in kind—tit-for-tat.

Then there are the "untouchables." The moment they are touched without invitation, they become unnerved. Arguing with such people creates a serious problem for those who are unaware of their untouchability. Inadvertently grabbing such an individual by the arm or around the shoulder could easily alienate him and terminate an argument. Every advocate should be alert to the fact that people have varying haptic personalities which are liable to crop up in an argument. During the first round of an argument, you can frequently tell whether you are involved with a "toucher" or a "nontoucher." If you are dealing with a toucher, make a determination as to the kind of toucher he is—casual, aggressive, compulsive, or whatever. Having made your haptic diagnosis, decide upon which course of action will best serve winning your argument. Whatever you decide, it must accomplish the purpose you should have in mind—to disturb, disrupt, or break your opponent's psychological balance. Depending upon the circumstances, you might elect to ignore your opponent's haptic behavior entirely. The main thing to remember is that physical contact can influence the outcome of certain arguments in susceptible people.

EYE-CONTACT BEHAVIOR

Eye-contact plays a vital role in any argument. Political debates on television have been lost by candidates who were unaware of its importance. The camera, capable of picking up minute eye movements, might easily have prompted the audience to interpret a lateral or downward gaze as admission, submission, or dullness of mind; the direct gaze as confident, authoritative, and victorious.

Practice eye-contact on every occasion: in class, with friends, at home, and at work. The objective is not to stare but, instead, nonverbally to communicate your awareness that others exist. Tell them, with your eyes, that you expect their attention; that is, when you look at them, you expect they will be looking back at you. At first you probably will fail and look away. This is normal and expected. Only through perseverance will this become a dependable tool in argumentation. Using precision eye-contact, make some definite statement to the next person you meet.

As you become more skilful with your eyes, your arguments will also show signs of improvement.

KINESIC BEHAVIOR

The more confident an individual is, the less muscular activity he displays. The opposite is true of the person who lacks confidence. Possessing the self-discipline to keep the body perfectly quiet provides a definite advantage in any argument. Movement is a great betrayer. You must learn to command it, not it you. A good exercise to practice with a friend or classmate is to face each other in a simulated argument and verbally clash without body movement. Sit like a robot and try to argue freely. The objective is not to enter an argument like a ventriloquist's dummy but to control the purposeless movements that untrained individuals are prone to make. Notice the professional athlete's body control when in a contest—steady, regulated, deliberate—no meaningless movement. A disorganized mind is frequently announced by a disorganized body.

POSTURAL ATTITUDE

How a person sits or stands during an argument can reveal how he is faring in the dispute. Losers have the tendency to sit in a slumped position, their heads hung low, limbs flexed. Winners, by comparison, generally are seen with their heads up, shoulders squared, limbs in extension.

Unfortunately, most of us are impervious to body positions. Observe someone you know with his arms folded across his chest or behind his back and ask why he is holding them that way. A common reply is, "Oh, I didn't realize I was doing that." Many of our everyday postural attitudes are subconscious. We move from one to another without becoming aware of them. Creating such an awareness in an argument could be helpful.

Think, for a moment, about the ways you could alter your posture while arguing—not only your standing posture but your seated posture as well. You might lean forward, backward, or to one side; remain perfectly straight; or perhaps alter the position of your arms, hands, legs, or feet. Any one or a combination of these postural modifications could create a different set of psychological cues for your opponent.

Suppose you were losing an argument. Disregarding your basic personality, chances are your posture would reveal signs of your faltering rhetoric. However, if you knew how to convincingly assume a posture of strength, you might be able to manipulate the direction of your argument. Be your own postural laboratory. Experiment by assuming various postures during your next argument and monitor your opponent's responses as well as your own. An excellent rule of posture to remember during an argument is: *flexion is negative, extension is positive.* The moment you feel yourself slumping, "straighten up!"

PERSONALITY TYPE

Popular opinion would probably confirm the view that extroverts have a greater innate flare for argument than introverts. While introverts, how-ever, envy the *joie de vivre* imputed to extroverts, extroverts seem to wind up envying the calm and reserve so frequently imputed to the introvert. Each imagines that the other has an advantage. Extroverts have the reputa-tion of talking too much, introverts—not enough. The question should not be "How can each type acquire the good characteristics of the other?" but rather, "How can each best use his own natural assets and most efficiently cope with his liabilities?"

Let us talk about the extrovert first. His tendency, in argumentation, is to overstate his case. In his zeal to make points, he often denies himself a familiarity with his opponent's point of view. In short, he ends up arguing with himself, so to speak. What he must learn to do is exercise restraint. Make a statement, ask a question, level a charge, and then WAIT PATIENTLY FOR A RESPONSE.

Turning to the introvert, we encounter an opposite dilemma—that of overcoming inertia. The introvert is usually cursed with a difficulty in initiating a line of argument. Since most people are too impatient to wait for a more retiring individual to express himself, introverts are usually overwhelmed and beaten back in most freewheeling arguments. At best, they are successful in getting in a few words or, perhaps, an entire sentence or two. What they must learn to do is make the most out of these opportunities. The stratagems from which to choose include short and direct questions such as, "What's your point?" "How did you arrive at that conclusion?" "Aren't you contradicting yourself?" or "Could you explain that another way?" These are just a few of the questions an intro-vert could inject into an argument. Because of their pejorative nature, they yield the most mileage in a controversy.

INTELLIGENCE

When arguing, it is important to differentiate between a person's intelligence and his formally acquired knowledge. By dictionary standards, someone possessing knowledge is characterized as an individual knowing a great deal about one or more things. This, however, should not be taken to mean that he is able to manipulate this information—a function of the intellect. In contrast, an intelligent person is one who is able to recall pertinent data when needed, manipulate ideas readily, and perceive the relationship between such data. Theoretically, the more intelligent person should be able to do more with fewer pieces of information (using inductive and deductive reasoning)—to see more, generate greater insights, and come to more meaningful conclusions. It should go without saying that anyone who argues who is both intelligent and knowledgeable is a "double threat" to his opponent.

Entirely too many people equate knowledge with intelligence. While extremely unlikely, it is possible for someone to possess a great deal of information (knowledge) on a given subject and not be highly intelligent. However, because large numbers of people have not learned to listen critically, they tend to hear only words. As a result, there are times when they are more impressed by the words they hear than by the way they have been manipulated by someone's intellect. In your next argument, make it a point to ascertain whether the person with whom you are arguing is knowledgeable, intelligent, or both.

OPEN-MINDEDNESS

Paradoxically, many people who claim to be open-minded, aren't. Fruitful argumentation cannot survive without open-mindedness. But, how does one know whether an opponent is truly open-minded? Is it simply a matter of "hearing the other fellow out"? Perhaps it can be better described as a state of mind which honestly recognizes that for every question asked, more than one answer may exist—any of which may be correct. Is the antithesis of an open mind a closed one? In the last analysis, each of these questions leads to VALUES. Most arguments get bogged down because of differences in values and the next fellow's reluctance to accept them, no less honor them.

Can you think of anyone whom you would consider open-minded? What is there about him that makes for open-mindedness? It may have a great deal to do with a person's value system. There are, as we noted earlier, some individuals who are univalued; for example, "There is only one way to get through college and that is to study very hard." Others are bivalued and say things such as, "Look, pal, to get through school you have to be either a good student or a star football player." The multivalued person, when discussing getting through college, might say, "You can get through college in several ways: (1) by studying hard and paying attention in class, (2) by cheating, (3) by establishing friendly relations with certain professors, (4) by finding people who can be bribed, (5) by going to a school which is noted to be a 'breeze'," and so on. Reasonably speaking, can anyone deny that the multivalued person is the more open-minded? Granting this, it would seem only natural for any advocate wanting to engage in constructive and purposeful argumentation, to preoccupy himself with opening his mind by letting in as many alternative thoughts as he can comfortably handle. Purge yourself of tunnel vision—the tendency to think in terms of one question-one answer, one cause-one effect, one sign-one meaning. Any argument hamstrung by such thinking is doomed from the outset; growth becomes virtually impossible. To be absolutely fair, however, one should mention that in certain value systems, a closed mind does not necessarily mean one is incapable of accepting an opposing view, but, rather, that one is satisfied the view being held is correct and elects not to seek further. He recognizes no need for further inquiry. This position also must be respected.

To summarize, then, the advocate approaching any controversy must do so with his mind as "open" or as "closed" as the situation demands.

PERCEPTION OF SELF

For the most part, losers see themselves as losers and winners see themselves as winners. An extreme example is the madman whose perception of self is so absolute and unquestioned that he is remarkably persuasive. Negative thoughts concerning his involvement almost never enter his mind. Numerous figures in history bear out this description. Many have won arguments because of their unswerving faith in themselves and their beliefs. Face it! Any argument you have ever had in which you knew you were right beyond a shadow of a doubt, you probably won. Call it conviction, self-confidence, self-assurance, self-esteem—whatever the symbol, the truth of the matter is that the way in which you perceive yourself is a powerful source of influence upon both you and your opponent.

A fascinating illustration of how powerful self-perception is occurs among skilled actors and actresses. Once they have successfully accepted the personality they will be portraying, a kind of synthesis occurs. This causes the character to "ring true" to the audience because the actor or actress has successfully executed and transferred the perception. This does not mean that the performer's self is lost or sacrificed, only that it has submitted to the one being dramatized. In this sense, the actor and advocate are alike. During every encounter, the advocate must assume a role, and it is determined by his perception of himself as either a winner or a loser. If his perception is faulty, it is more than likely that his argument will follow suit.

ABILITY TO STAY ON SUBJECT

One of the most serious shortcomings of people who argue is their inability to "stay on the subject." While many students do learn, through the valiant efforts of dedicated teachers, how to write a tight composition or term paper, the discipline often fails to carry over into the spoken word. The one luxury a good arguer cannot afford is to have his thoughts wander. A good way to guard against this phenomenon is to silently ask yourself during an argument, "What does what I am saying or thinking have to do with what I am arguing?" This same intrapersonal spot-check also applies to what your opponent is saying: What am I saying, what is he saying, what are we saying?

Although some people are born with the ability to think in an orderly manner, most of us have to learn how to do it. A characteristic growing pain experienced while you are learning this technique is to insist that you are on the subject and that what you are saying is related to the issue being argued. While inside your own head this may be as true as rain, it often succumbs to objective analysis. Ideas are thoughts strung together like beads. If one is not careful, they spill and run madly in every direction.

PLEASURE FROM ARGUING

Inasmuch as there are those who loathe arguing and will do everything in their power to avoid it, there are others who wallow in argument, as happy as a pig in mud. They have the gift of being able to convert the most innocuous conversation into an argument. Such people have an advantage over those who abhor arguing. The way you answer this question (#14 in the quiz) tells how you feel about arguing and how you have conducted most of your life in relation to it. A pathetic situation occurs at a party when someone who loves to argue gets involved with someone who dreads arguing. The consequence is usually that someone comes to the rescue and either assumes the role of the retiring party's attorney or whisks him away to some safe and neutral zone.

One of the functions of this self-evaluation quiz is to prod the reader into consciously labeling himself according to the choices given. To repeat an earlier observation, there are many people who argue continuously and, when confronted with the fact, gingerly deny it. Like touching to the compulsive toucher, it has become such an integral part of their lifestyle that they no longer are aware of it. So, once you are able to say, "I love to argue," or "I hate to argue," you will be ready to adjust your position accordingly.

TENDENCY TO ARGUE

This is a sister question to the preceding one. It, too, focuses on one's attitude toward arguing. A distinction needs to be made, however. Some people would love to argue but lack the courage to do it. Therefore, it is grossly unfair to automatically designate those who actually argue as those with a most pronounced tendency. After all, a tendency denotes an inclination to move or act in a particular direction and not the accomplished act. What this seems to mean is that those who do not actually argue, are not necessarily without the tendency. Perhaps all they need is some encouragement, training, motivation, or positive reinforcement to enable them to come out of a kind of forced retirement and enjoy the mental exhilaration that messages in conflict can provide.

LIFESPAN OF AN ARGUMENT

The most fitting way to introduce the meaning of this unit is to relate a story. There once were two monks who lived in a monastery high in the mountains. Every morning at 5 A.M. they set out to pick berries. One day, while doing this, Brother John noticed a young girl unsuccessfully trying to cross a small stream. By the way she was dressed, it was obvious she was a prostitute. To the amazement of Brother George, Brother John carried the young girl across the stream. Brother George said nothing. Back at the monastery, the noon meal passed and Brother George said nothing. The evening meal passed; still not a word from Brother George. Finally, before retiring, Brother George could no longer contain himself. He turned to Brother John and said, "How could you possibly have carried that young girl across the stream this morning when you knew perfectly well that our Order is opposed to everything she stands for?" Brother John replied, "Brother George, I carried that young girl across the stream at 5 A.M. this morning—YOU ARE STILL CARRYING HER!"

Such a charming story captures the meaning of this segment. There are those of us who carry arguments that are one, three, five, and ten years old. Others have the blessed faculty of being able to "let them go" once they are over. Do you rehearse bygone arguments? If you do, why? Unless you can come up with a sound reason for keeping them alive, bury them once and for all. Past arguments should teach us how to more effectively cope with future arguments. When they can no longer do this, they must be abandoned.

FREQUENCY OF ARGUMENTS

Arguing incorrectly can leave deep wounds and ugly scars. Since the curriculum in most educational institutions does not include adequate preparation for the inevitable arguments ahead, casualties will be many. Have you ever heard someone say, "My life consists of little more than one argument after another." In certain homes where arguments (the incorrect kind) are a way of life, the children come to think of it as the way things are supposed to be. In fact, without all the hollering and shouting, they often wonder if something is wrong.

There is no such thing as the "proper frequency" of arguments. Each individual, couple, and family has its own needs and must fill them according to their individual personalities and values. Argument is one way, a good way, to fill such needs, but most certainly not *the only way*. If it is adopted as a means of conflict resolution, quality and not quantity should be its criterion.

ALIENATING AN OPPONENT

It is very sad to see good friends break up after an argument, especially if it was over something as inane as being late for a date, not returning a lipstick or a ballpoint pen, or switching a television inadvertently without realizing the other person was watching it. You may recall the fallacy of *argumentum ad hominem*, in which an attack is made upon the individual rather than upon what he is saying. This is the major cause of any alienation resulting from an argument. People are, somehow, unable or perhaps unwilling to separate *what* a person says from *who* a person is.

Here is a fine exercise you can do by yourself which will make you more aware of this phenomenon of separating a man from his ideas. Think of someone you dislike with a passion. Naturally, there will be readers who cannot think of anyone they hate. For the purpose of this exercise, they are asked to wait until the rest of us have finished it. After you have singled out the person for whom you can muster the greatest amount of hate, write as many of his good qualities as possible on a sheet of paper. At first, your mind will be blank. Then, with a little patience, some good traits will trickle through. Obviously, your hostility has blinded you to the good traits people who like him so readily see.

If you have a tendency to alienate those with whom you argue, the time has come to ask yourself why. A good course in argumentation might be just what you need in order to find out. Another suggestion is to have a serious talk with someone who, in your judgment, does not alienate people. Find out what he does or does not do and compare such behavior with your own.

TYPE OF OPPONENTS

The people who argue a great deal do not seem to argue with just anyone. Certain individuals seem to have an affinity for each other. Surely you've heard the expression, "Why is it always me?" This is a remark frequently employed by a particular type of person who, strangely enough, is often lured into an argument by another specific type. Recollections of our early schooldays bring to mind the class bully who, if you took the time to notice, only picked on certain types of children. Usually, the kind who gave the bully no resistance and yielded to his every whim were the victims. A similar form of selectivity occurs among adults. Those who are habitual arguers have a knack of ferreting out individuals who satisfy their needs as vulnerable opponents in an argument. They use various buzz words or phrases designed to lure their prey. An example is, "Would you happen to know the depth of Lake Titicaca?" By the way the person answers such an off-beat question, some indication is given as to his suitability as a victim. Not unlike jungle animals who instinctively know which other animals they can bully and which ones they should stay clear of, certain humans seem to possess this same talent.

The one glaring danger involved in arguing with the wrong opponent is that, more often than not, embarrassment or humiliation is the result. None of us likes to be used or abused, and it behooves us to take out whatever safeguards might be necessary to prevent such an eventuality. The best method is early detection. Once you discover that the person with whom you are talking is argumentatively dangerous, either make some excuse and withdraw or adjust your strategy so that he will be put on the defensive. This can be accomplished by saying very little, listening well, and bombarding him with questions whenever you can. It might also be wise to draw another person into the argument so that you divide his attention and thereby give him two targets on which to concentrate instead of one. Remember, each type of opponent thrives on a certain kind of food, which you must be very careful not to become.

Notice carefully the kind of opponents you attract. If, indeed, we are creatures of habit, repeatedly suffering psychotrauma at the hands of a certain type of person, encountering a specific type of opponent can become habit-forming. There are women who fought like cats and dogs with their first husbands, only to marry the same kind of man again. The same phenomenon occurs among men, who remarry carbon copies of the wife they just divorced. For those men and women who did not make the same mistake twice, congratulations!

SUBJECTS ARGUED

Although the things people argue about will vary, there is a noticeable tendency for them to argue the same things over and over again. Whether the issue is politics, religion, education, moral irresponsibility in films, or crime in the streets, the chances of a previously argued topic's being re-argued are very high.

In practically every walk of life, the things people argue about reflect their interests—the things they consider important. Deny the scholar an opportunity to argue the significance of a recent journal article with a colleague, a sports fan the chance to argue who will win the world's series, the housewife, what is going on in the neighborhood, and you strike down a major reason for his or her being. In short, while some people argue for the hell of it, some take the things they argue about seriously. Thus, from a communication standpoint, if you are able to discover what a person enjoys arguing about, engage him on that subject and you are well on your way to a meaningful interpersonal relationship—provided, of course, you are able to disagree without becoming disagreeable.

PROXEMIC STATUS OF AN ADVOCATE

The nose-to-nose distance between you and your opponent may have a definite bearing on how an argument turns out. While some people feel comfortable close up, others prefer standing back. When asked why they assume these distances, they say they feel more comfortable and can argue better.

We noted in Chapter 3 that our senses are interdependent. The comment, "I can't hear you—wait until I put on my glasses!" is not unfamiliar to those who wear glasses. Altered depth perception can influence your ability to argue effectively also. Test for your own "arguing distance." Engage a parent or friend in an innocent argument and, during it, estimate your interpersonal distance. Then, while the argument is in progress, increase or decrease the distance from four to six inches and notice what happens.

The subject being argued can affect an arguing distance as well. The more personal, intimate, or taboo the subject, the closer people seem to sit or stand. The more impersonal and academic the subject, the further apart they remain. This is an excellent nonverbal technique for those who like to argue. Because it is nonverbal, it allows you to very subtly break your opponent's psychological balance and, perhaps, shift the advantage in your direction. To be successful, you must learn WHEN, WHERE, and HOW to adjust your arguing distance.

WHERE MOST ARGUMENTS OCCUR

Every ball club knows that where a game is played can have a potent effect upon its outcome. Arguments also are sensitive to the influence of "location." A simple explanation can be found for family arguments' taking place in the kitchen at mealtime: it is one of the few times they are all gathered together in one place. Furthermore, there is an opportunity for each member of the household to tell the others what he or she is doing in school, at work, at play. Although one would think the kitchen or dining room table an ideal place for exchanging views about things of interest, it often fails. One compelling reason is that parents often feel that when you eat, you shouldn't talk, because it isn't good for your digestion. Others are highly emotional about eating and cannot (or will not) indulge in conversation or arguments, because it distracts them from the food they enjoy.

Think back and you will discover, if you are prone to argue, that your disputes generally occur in certain rooms of the house. Also, as strange as it may sound, people do not argue equally well in every room. Many subscribe to such clichés as *the kitchen is for eating, the bedroom for sleeping, the living room for company, and the bathroom for privacy.* Every room has its function, and to indiscriminantly argue in them is to contradict their intended use. Aside from those who are blasphemous and argue all over the house, the majority seem to prefer one particular room as their "arguing area."

Outside the home, there are also preferred locations in which people argue. The famous admonition, "Not here, not here!" or "Let's go over there!" or "Don't make a scene here!" has, at one time or another, been used by all of us. The question that should spring to mind is, what role does location actually play in an argument? Until research findings become available, you are left to your own devices. In the midst of an argument, cleverly persuade your opponent to move to another location and see if it makes any difference.

WHEN MOST ARGUMENTS OCCUR

Have you ever said, "Why must we start each day with an argument?" or "Why is it as soon as I get home, all hell breaks loose?" When people argue may have something to do with their energy levels. At peak levels, our tolerance is high. Things which would disturb us at a low energy level fail to do so. Few people realize that if they altered WHEN they initiated a controversial subject, it might not produce the same consequences.

Consider your schedule for next semester with regard to time slots. There are certain professors who are delightful at 8:00 A.M. and unbearable at 4:30 in the afternoon (Jekyll and Hyde types). A question asked in an early morning class might be warmly received by such a professor; asked during the afternoon, it might be coldly thrown back at you. Therefore, to disregard the time of an argument is to overlook a very important element.

RELATIONSHIP OF ARGUMENTS TO MEALTIMES

This subject has already been touched upon in our discussion of location. All that might be added is a proverb by Richard Whately (1787–1863): "Never argue at the dinner table, for the one who is not hungry always gets the best of the argument."

CLIMATIC RELATIONSHIP TO ARGUING

From a physiological perspective, weather (temperature, humidity, barometric levels) can and does affect the way our bodies perform. On extremely humid days, some people are absolutely worthless; their bodies virtually come to a screeching halt. As a result, their threshold of irritability drops to a dangerous level; the slightest gesture, the most innocent remark can set them off. Others are affected in the opposite way. Arguments do not occur in a vacuum. We must consider the meteorological climate of an argument as well as its emotional and intellectual climate.

SUMMARY

This chapter, *Messages in Conflict*, has departed somewhat from a traditional approach to argument. Using a two-pronged construction, it first presented a philosophy of argument followed by a strategy for its use. Three key ideas were advanced: (1) you can win an argument by learning how to yield offensively, borrowing from the principles of judo; (2) you cannot—or, rather, should not—argue conclusions, only how they were arrived at; and (3) there is more to winning arguments than "being right."

Also stressed was the belief that too many people think of an argument or arguing in a negative light—as something which should be avoided at all costs. This chapter has taken just the opposite tack; that is, that learning how to *disagree without becoming disagreeable* is crucial to our individual survival.

Without going into the classical aspects of argument, a concerted effort was made to initiate the reader into the world of constructive argumentation on a commonsensical basis and to present it as an excellent means of conflict resolution.

CHAPTER 8

COPING
WITH
AN AUDIENCE

INSIGHTS

After reading this chapter you should have a clearer understanding of:

- *stage fright (also known as speech fright or speech anxiety).*
- *why audiences will or will not choose to believe a speaker.*
- *how to take out insurance that you will succeed as a public
  speaker.*
- *the many things to check out in order to discover an
  audience's X-FACTOR.*
- *how an audience can change radically during the course of
  a speech.*
- *how important it is to think of a speaker and an audience
  as a single unit, each interdependent upon the other.*

We are about to deal with audience analysis—an examination of those characteristics which give an audience personality and are responsible for its behavior. However, before undertaking it, we should pay some attention to a more personal problem—stage fright.

Thousands of students suffer from stage fright and would give anything to be rid of it. Other names by which it has been known are speech fright, speech anxiety, audience and anxiety neurosis. If anything is to be held responsible for a speaker's inability to cope with an audience, stage fright heads the list. For years specialists in the field of public address have argued, "A student should be able to get up on his feet and speak!" Unfortunately, it is a feat easier said than done. So traumatic are its effects that graduating seniors have been found mixed in with freshmen taking the basic speech course—frightened seniors who had run out of ways to avoid taking it. When they were asked the reason for not taking it earlier, they almost invariably confessed they had a morbid fear of getting up in front of a class.

Aside from stage fright, some less complicated elements are involved in a speaker's impression of an audience. The popular conception of an audience treats it as a group of people passively watching or listening to another person or persons perform. Essentially, the flow of information is from performer to audience. Less commonly recognized is the fact that a message flow is moving simultaneously in the opposite direction, from audience to speaker. Expressed differently, the speaker and audience interact freely and should, or could, be treated as a single unit.

So, begging the indulgence of those readers not afflicted with stage fright, we shall spend a little time discussing some of the problems associated with it. Then, with stage fright brought into better perspective, we shall proceed to make a detailed analysis of an audience.

GENERAL REMARKS ABOUT STAGE FRIGHT

In the vernacular, stage fright means being "just plain scared" of getting up in front of people and talking. It refers to the nervousness felt before an audience. Although within normal limits stage fright is commonplace and should not be viewed as unnatural or odd, extreme manifestations require professional attention. Going right to the heart of this condition, we find one important factor—anxiety. Many psychologists and psychiatrists feel that anxiety plays a very important role in almost every form of personality breakdown. Most people suffering from stage fright are completely normal individuals who overreact to a public-speaking situation. With the help of a sensitive and patient teacher, the majority of them succeed in "working through" their problem. A small percentage, however, experience an anxiety neurosis which may require professional assistance.

A centenarian once said to a friend, "What do you mean worrying doesn't help? Anything I ever worried about never happened." Such a statement, in addition to being amusing, is filled with wisdom and might provide the stage-frightened student with a measure of consolation. Any effort to describe in words how a person with stage fright who has to give a speech feels is doomed to failure. It is like trying to describe what goes on in the bowels of a volcano. The important question is not so much what goes on inside the person with stage fright, but what can be done to alleviate it. Do the things he worries about actually happen? If not, then the centenarian was right when he said, "Worrying works!" If, on the other hand, worrying doesn't work, why worry?

Considering the magnitude of this problem, comparatively little on stage fright has turned up in the literature. Most of what has appeared assumes a rather impractical nature. For example, a majority of the suggestions recommend that speakers select a topic with which they are comfortable. Unfortunately, there are many speech classes that do not give the student an option of selecting his own topic. Usually, a list of topics are presented from which he is obliged to choose. Another unrealistic assumption made by many books and articles on stage fright is that anxiety-ridden speakers can analyze their fear, relax, and assume an air of studied nonchalance and self-control. Acquiring insight into a problem doesn't always mean that it has been solved. There are people who, after years of psychoanalysis, have an extraordinary insight into their problem but continue to suffer its effects.

One of the more prevalent charges leveled against people with stage fright is that they fail to make careful and complete preparations of their speeches. This allegation smacks of unfairness. If anything, because a student is apprehensive and anxious, his tendency is to prepare more carefully and completely, rather than less. The charge also assumes that speakers with stage fright have not practiced, prepared, or researched their materials adequately. Seasoned actors and actresses frequently report that in spite of the fact that they walk on stage with their lines neatly memorized, they experience butterflies in their stomachs. At best, the diagnosis and treatment of stage fright has received only tokenistic attention in the literature, and the attention it has received appears to be rather cursory.

Etiology[1]

Most authorities seem to feel that the prospect of facing an audience and being evaluated is a major cause of stage fright. Others speak of a lack of self-confidence, failure to carefully select an appropriate topic, failure to analyze an audience, or insufficient preparation. Let us consider some of the things students suffering stage fright claim causes their anxiety:

1. The audience will laugh at them, or at what they say.
2. They will make mistakes and be humiliated.
3. They will forget what they had planned to say.
4. They will be cross-examined and not be able to handle it.
5. The audience will be bored.
6. The teacher will say something unkind, correct their speech or its presentation.

There are probably other more subtle and personal reasons why aspiring speechmakers panic. Can you add to this list from your own experience?

1. _____

2. _____

3. _____

4. _____

5. _____

[1] *Etiology* refers to the cause of a condition.

Walter and Scott[2] suggest that anxiety and stage fright occur whenever the self is divided so that what a person *is doing*, what he *wants to do*, and what he thinks he *should do* are different things. In the so-called "healthy" person, there is no such strong conflict or division between what he *wants to do*, what he *is doing*, and what he *should do*.

Symptoms

Symptoms of stage fright appear in two forms: *physiological* and *psychological*.

1. *Physiological Symptoms:*
   a. increased muscle tension
   b. disturbed breathing pattern
   c. weakness in the knees
   d. dryness in the throat
   e. elevated blood sugar
   f. elevated blood pressure (occasionally lowered)
   g. hand tremors
   h. excessive perspiration

2. *Psychological Symptoms:*
   a. anxiety
   b. embarrassment
   c. humiliation
   d. persecution
   e. frustration and apprehension
   f. ridicule

Treatment

For the common cold practically everybody and his brother has a secret cure: starve it, feed it, sweat it out, take two aspirins and go to bed, or take several thousand milligrams of vitamin C. The folly of it is that with treatment it takes seven days to get rid of a cold; without treatment, a week. Then, of course, there are those who advocate the "do-nothing approach": just let it run its course and Nature will do the rest.

This same "cure philosophy" has been applied to stage fright. A variety of home-grown remedies are available, ranging from: (a) you've just got to force yourself to get up there and do it, to (b) make believe everyone

2 Otis M. Walter and Robert L. Scott, *Thinking and Speaking: A Guide to Intelligent Oral Communication* (New York: Macmillan, 1962).

in your audience is naked. [The rationale for this one might be very interesting.]

If, as mentioned previously, anxiety is one of the key elements of stage fright, and feeling threatened by an audience creates anxiety, it follows that any means of reducing it might be therapeutically beneficial. For example, many people with stage fright have little or no difficulty speaking before an audience of young children—say, as a Sunday School teacher, camp counselor, or nursery school aide. Why? Because the children represent practically no threat to an adult. Children are smaller, less informed, less mature, and possess less life experience. Under these conditions, the speaker usually feels more secure, less threatened, less anxious. By thinking or imagining that your audience is naked while you are fully clothed, you are psychologically giving yourself an advantage. Naturally, you would tend to feel more secure. In a culture such as ours that is "hung up" on nudity, imposing such imagery upon yourself would probably shift some preoccupation with yourself onto your audience.

The way in which a speaker thinks of himself and his audience[3] is exceedingly important to an understanding of stage fright. Think of an audience as *hostile* and your body will reflexly become tense and develop some of the manifestations mentioned earlier; think of your audience as *friendly* and such symptoms will probably not arise. These psychophysiological mechanisms conform nicely with a prior comment on the effects of worrying. Did you know that the worrying you do before delivering a speech you dread produces exactly the same anxiety that occurs while you are actually giving it? Pragmatically speaking, worrying offers little in the way of help for the person with stage fright.

Whatever mode of treatment you choose, it must be tempered with the realization that it is far from scientific. After a few traumatic experiences of bumbling and bungling through a speech, you should notice that whatever it was that you were afraid of probably "didn't happen." Another consequence of treatment is that you are able to make your way to the front of the room under your own power and get through a speech with less difficulty. The fear may never leave you: all that happens is that you learn to live with it and accept it as your cross to bear. The least desirable effect of certain types of treatment is that your stage fright is made worse. This usually occurs when a frantic student is victimized by a cruel and insensitive teacher who advocates the "sink or swim" philosophy. While such a technique does occasionally bag a success, its track record is hardly a recommendation for standard procedure.

[3] *Konstantin Stanislavsky*—actor, director, and cofounder of the Moscow Art Theatre—heavily stressed *imagery* in his teaching of acting. Performers, through deep concentration, attempted to perceive themselves in various states and forms.

A final consequence of treatment may be no effect whatsoever. In fact, McCroskey,[4] exploring the causes and effects of stage fright, discovered that students so afflicted tended to drop out of the beginning speech course; that students having moderate to severe speech anxiety during the first week of the term had dropped the course by the third week; and that "No course can help if the student is so anxious that he will not take the course." In these terms, it might be wise for someone with more than a casual apprehension to take the course with a teacher from whom "good vibrations" emanate. This can be determined by sitting in on a couple of classes with different teachers. Nine out of ten times a fairly reliable "guesstimate" can be made in a single period. Although this is not a guarantee, it increases the odds of a successful experience.

Again stressing the importance of reducing anxiety in the management of stage fright, one of the more promising methods that has come along is called "systematic desensitization." Here is an explanation of how it works:

> Treatment consisted of seven one-hour sessions, two per week for three and one half weeks, of systematic desensitization for three experimental groups composed of a maximum of five subjects per group. The first session was used to explain the rationale and the procedures of systematic desensitization and the playing of an aural tape recording of deep muscular relaxation instructions. The remaining six sessions were devoted to playing the relaxation tape, until all the subjects reported being relaxed, and the presentations of the items of the speech anxiety hierarchy. Communication of the perceived anxiety by any subject for any item was transmitted to the trainer by the raising of the subject's right index finger, at which time the trainer issued instructions to all subjects to erase the image and concentrate on relaxation. After a brief pause, the trainer again presented the same item. The criterion for successfully overcoming an item was two consecutive presentations (the first for fifteen seconds, the second for thirty seconds) without any anxiety response from any subject. The trainer then presented the next item on the speech-anxiety hierarchy, continuing through the hierarchy until it was completed.[5]

What has been done in this procedure is condition the subject to superimpose on the hearing of an anxiety-producing verbal cue a self-induced state of muscular relaxation. This writer has sought to achieve a similar effect by having members of a class, by prior consent, respond enthusiastically to "anything" a speaker says until (through such positive rein-

---

[4] James C. McCroskey, "Measures of communication-bound anxiety," *Speech Monographs* 27 (November, 1970), 269–77.

[5] James C. McCroskey, David C. Ralph, and James E. Barrick, "The effect of systematic desensitization of speech anxiety," *The Speech Teacher* 19:1 (January, 1970), 32–36.

forcement) he no longer feels threatened, his anxiety threshold becomes raised, and his body assumes a more relaxed attitude.

There is a theoretical principle at work here that deals with psychosomatic behavior. Consider, if you will, this question: "Is it possible for someone whose body is very tense to simultaneously experience a relaxed state of mind?" If your answer is no, here is another related question: "Is it possible for someone whose mind is completely relaxed to simultaneously experience a very tense body?" If your answer is still no, we can proceed.

One of the ways successful business and professional people relax their minds is to relax their bodies. They accomplish this by having a massage, steambath, sauna, hydrotherapy, or physical exercise. All are physical ways of erasing psychological tensions. An inverse approach is employed in yoga, where mental concentration erases tensions from the physical body. The credo of a sound mind in a sound body (borrowed from the ancient Greeks) provides those haunted by stage fright with an excellent perspective. Most forms of treatment, unfortunately, are unidirectional in that they move from mind to body. This chapter counterproposes an interactional approach moving from mind to body to mind.

MINI-EXERCISES TO RELIEVE TENSION OF STAGE FRIGHT

The following exercises are simple and require practically no paraphernalia. They have one express purpose: to siphon off tension-producing energies that interfere with the successful delivery of a speech. You can perform Exercises I, II, and III by yourself. Exercises IV through VII require the participation of an entire class.

EXERCISE I.   Head Drooping

Procedure:

Step 1.   Sitting or standing, close your eyes and "feel."

Step 2.   Try to feel the balance of your head on your shoulders and search for the precise point at which it seems to be weightless.

Step 3.   Now, let it fall smoothly (without a jerk) to a fully forward position. You should feel some pull across your shoulders on both sides. Depending upon your postural habits, you may notice the pull more on one side. This is unimportant here.

Step 4.   Let your head hang free in this forward position for the count of ten. Then, slowly bring it up and backward as far as it will go without strain. Let it remain in this position for the count of five.

Step 5.   Repeat the forward head drooping position and return to the backward position three to four times (each time counting as indicated in Step 4).

EXERCISE II.   Neck Tension Release

Procedure:

Step 1.   Sit in a straight-backed chair.

Step 2.   Place the heels of both hands on your forehead above the eyebrows with the fingers facing upward.

Step 3.   Slowly press your head forward against the resistance of your hands. Maintaining this steady, moderate pressure, count to three and release the pressure without removing your hands from your head. Wait for five seconds and repeat the movement in the same identical manner. Repeat three to five times.

Step 4.   Now, place both hands on the back of your head and interlace your fingers.

Step 5.   Using the same counting procedure as you did with your hands on your forehead, this time exert the pressure by pressing your head backward against your hands. Repeat entire procedure three to five times. (Closing your eyes helps concentration.)

EXERCISE III.   Talking with Yourself

Procedure:

Step 1.   Record your speech on a tape recorder.

Step 2.   While it is playing back, speak along with it while doing the following: (a) standing, (b) sitting, (c) lying, (d) pacing back and forth, (e) simple calisthenics.

EXERCISE IV.   Like Talking to a Wall

Procedure: (performed in class)

Step 1.   After arriving at the front of the room and facing your audience, turn toward the wall.

Step 2.   While talking to the wall, try to ignore the fact that an entire class is sitting and listening behind you.

Step 3.   When you have finished, turn around and have the class turn around in their seats and face the back of the room.

Step 4.   Now, deliver your speech again, facing their backs.

Step 5.   Tell the class some of the things you felt while talking to the wall and ask them to tell you what they felt while you were talking to their backs.

EXERCISE V.   I Don't See Your Point!

Procedure:

Step 1.   From the front of the room, deliver your speech to the class while each member is blindfolded.

Step 2.   Next, blindfold yourself, allow the class to remove their blindfolds, and proceed to give your speech.

Step 3. Engage your class in a brief discussion about their reactions to the exercise.

EXERCISE VI. *It Would Be Better if We Saw Eye-to-Eye*

Procedure:

Step 1. While delivering your speech, maintain eye-contact with each person in the first row, moving slowly from person to person.

Step 2. Next, zero in on the people in the middle row and do the same thing.

Step 3. Repeat your eye-contact exercise with the back row.

Step 4. Your final eye movements should start with the first person on your right in the first row and, in sequence, move from person to person until you have looked into the eyes of every single person in the class.

Step 5. Discuss some of the impressions you and members of the class experienced as a result of your eye-contact.

EXERCISE VII. *Loud—Soft—Fast—Slow*

Procedure:

Step 1. Divide your speech into four parts according to the name of this exercise.

Step 2. Deliver Part One in a loud voice, Part Two softly, Part Three speaking rapidly, and Part Four slowly.

Step 3. Discuss with your class the effects of altering your vocal qualities.

EXERCISE VIII. *Cosí É Se Vi Pare (You Are if You Think You Are)*

Procedure:

Step 1. Dress yourself according to the theme of your speech. For example, if you are giving a speech on the art of cooking, come to class dressed as a chef (apron, big white hat, spatula, and so on).

Step 2. Work your props into your speech so that they become part of it.

Step 3. Discuss whether what you wore made any significant difference in either how you felt giving the speech or how your audience felt while you gave it.

None of these exercises is a panacea. All they are intended to do is make you aware of some variables capable of contributing to or causing stage fright. Knowing something of the mechanism that triggers feelings of anxiety will enable you to cope with it more constructively. For instance, what if you were to learn that eye feedback from your audience can tie your nervous system in knots? Couldn't you wear a pair of sunglasses that let you see out and prevent others from seeing in? While this might not completely solve your problem, it might lessen its intensity.

A speech pathologist once said, "There would be no stutterers if there were no listeners." This might also apply to people who suffer stage fright: "There would be no stage fright if there were no audiences." This raises the question, "Which, in your opinion, contributes more to the condition known as stage fright—the speaker or the audience to whom he is speaking?" The pages that follow may hold at least part of the answer.

AUDIENCE PERCEPTION OF A SPEAKER

A speaker's attitude toward an audience can markedly affect his relationship with it; the reverse is also true. Backstage, actors and actresses can often be overheard asking a member of the stage crew, "How's the audience tonight?" In the past, opera audiences have been known to contain claques[6] of people who were paid to go to the theatre and either applaud or boo. Such an audience can work a serious hardship and, perhaps, even destroy the inexperienced performer.

There are specific ways an audience can transmit its feelings to a speaker. We shall discuss them shortly. In the meantime, it is important to remember that an audience is not a passive blob of humanity to which a speaker addresses himself. Occasionally, on the first day of a new semester, a teacher will find himself standing before a completely new set of faces. If he is sensitive, he will pick up certain vibrations coming from the class. His reputation may have preceded him and his audience is trying to tell him something. If the sentiments of an audience could be known beforehand, a speaker could take the necessary precautions to avoid having them ruin his speech. This is but one way for a speaker to cope with an unfamiliar audience.

GOALS OF AN AUDIENCE

The reason this heading seems strange is that a speaker is seldom aware of an audience's goals until after the fact. Like chemical compounds, audiences are composed of different elements. A knowledge of their nature and behavior can aid the trained individual in making some rather startling predictions about the manner in which it will respond to a speaker or a speech.

Consider a hypothetical audience comprised 97 percent of women between the ages of 65 and 75. An experienced audience analyst coaching

[6] "Class of the claquers," *Time*, January 5, 1962, p. 39.

a speaker on how to best cope with this particular audience would probably point out specific interests common to the majority of its members—
for example, increased social security benefits, ways of combating boredom, relief from the pains of arthritis and rheumatism, and how to arrange seeing one's grandchildren more often. Tactically speaking, being
aware of an audience's goals provides a speaker with blue-chip stock in an
organization called SUCCESS.

Whereas no two audiences are exactly alike, they do share common
characteristics. They usually want:

1. to be spared being exploited by a speaker.
2. to gain something from a speaker's experience.
3. to see some "good" come from the meeting.
4. to realize a sense of personal growth.
5. to feel a contribution has been made to society.
6. to feel needed.
7. to fill the time—alleviate boredom.
8. to sublimate destructive energies.
9. to interact with others on a particular theme.
10. to be entertained.
11. to be heard.
12. to satisfy a curiosity.

Can you think of any others?

1. _____

2. _____

3. _____

WHY AUDIENCES BELIEVE

Most people haven't the foggiest notion how much of their lives are based
upon a blind faith. Take the case of the college student. With a briefcase
filled with assorted notebooks, he moves trustingly from class to class jotting down names, dates, and places, plus a few thousand famous quotations. What percentage of the information he records do you think is
true? Ninety percent, seventy percent, fifty percent? Would it surprise
you to learn that there are people who believe *everything* that is written
in books? Since it is not feasible for them to go out and test the validity
of everything they learn, how are they to separate the wheat from the
chaff?

Most of the difficulty with credibility is not generated by the pure sciences but by the humanities. Observations, judgments, comments, and conclusions dealing with such high-level abstractions as love, morality, religion, ethics, philosophy, and values seem to create the greatest disturbance. Some people are confused but, rather than commit themselves to a particular point of view, take in as much as they can and remain neutral. Others instinctively polarize. Regardless of what they are exposed to, they register an opinion for or against it.

A unique foundation for belief is *charisma*. Historically, it applied to individuals alleged to have a divinely inspired power to perform miracles and render prophecy such as Jesus of Nazareth and Joan of Arc. Adolph Hitler, William Jennings Bryan, Billy Sunday, John F. Kennedy, and Rudolph Valentino are but a few of the more recent of those said to have possessed charisma.[7] Vast numbers of people believed whatever they said and followed them blindly. Wherever they went, audiences sensed that their words rang true.

In addition to this mystical basis for believing, there are also the more traditional criteria that most audiences subscribe to: (1) legitimate credentials from an accredited institution or duly recognized board of examiners, (2) extensive experience in the field in which the individual claims competence, (3) high reputation among a peer group, (4) outstanding and noteworthy accomplishments, (5) extensive publication in his field, (6) an impressive and facile use of the language of his field, (7) affiliation with some prestigious organization.

A perfectly charming story, a true one, is told about a librarian whose credibility suffered instantaneous death owing to the mispronunciation of a word. It seems that a university was to be visited by a V.I.P. in the field of library science. On the day in question, the entire library staff was assembled in the school auditorium to hear this distinguished guest speak on a subject dear to their hearts. Soon, a well-dressed man stepped to the podium and adjusted the microphone. After carefully surveying his audience and allowing a well-measured pause, he said, "Ladies and gentlemen, today I should like to talk to you about liberry science." The audience gasped—discreetly, of course. Absolutely nothing this man could say after his mispronunciation of the word *library* could repair his wounded credibility. It, literally, sealed his fate as far as the audience was concerned.

Some of you may seriously question how such an innocent error in pronunciation could evoke such a dramatic consequence. An explanation is not easily arrived at. Let me put it to you this way. Would you leave your car with a mechanic who had just finished telling you that your

---

[7] The current use of the term *charisma* applies to people having a special kind of personality which draws others to them.

"cabooritor" was busted? Or, would you trust a doctor who said you had a "gold bladder" condition, or that your "prostrate gland was infected"? It all depends upon how rigid your demands are when it comes to believing.

After graduation, students not going to graduate school head for the job market. Armed with a sheepskin, telephone numbers, addresses, and a mind full of field-related jargon, they are off to a series of interviews with strangers knowing considerably more than they do about the area in which they seek employment. As an audience of one, these employers have the responsibility of screening applicants by determining, in part, the credibility of what they say. A popular myth among some applicants is that they can "bullshit" their way through certain interviews. Be reminded that occasional successes here and there do not justify the perpetuation of this myth. More often than not, experts can spot B.S. instantly. See if any of these examples ring a bell.

In researching this subject, the author interviewed several experts in various occupations and professions and asked them this question: "Can you think of any instances in which what someone professing competence in a given field either says or does would expose him as an incompetent or an impostor?" Here are some of their replies:

A. *Professional Steamfitting*: I could detect an impostor by the way he opened a ruler. An authentic steamfitter would snap the entire ruler open with one flick of the wrist. The impostor, or novice, would probably open it segment by segment. Another way of detecting the impostor deals with his actions on a scaffold. He might lean over the edge whereas an experienced man would never do that.

B. *Professional Manufacturer of Plastics*: If someone alleged to know the plastic business were asked what one of those children's beach balls was made of and he simply answered "plastic," I would know he was an impostor. Anyone who knows this business would always identify the particular plastic as either polyethene, vinyl, or polystyrene. He would never just say "plastic."

C. *Professional Typesetter*: Anyone in my business knows about "hot" type (linotype, intertype, monotype) and "cold" type (photocomposition). If I met an individual professing to know my business, I would ask him, "Which is better, hot or cold type?" If he answered, "Hot type, of course. If it were cold, it would not make an impression on the paper." Such a reply would immediately expose such a person as still wet behind the ears.

D. *Practicing Attorney*: If I saw a movie involving a courtroom scene and the judge said to one of the attorneys, "Please approach the bench," I would know at once that the judge was an actor, not a judge in real life.

A bona fide judge would never call just one lawyer to the bench and not the other. Both attorneys are always called to approach the bench together.

E. Professional Teacher of Physical Education: If I saw someone teaching a class a particular dance step or calisthenic movement who did not perform it using the opposite arms or legs, I would know the person to be an impostor. Such things are always done "mirror image style."

The lesson in communication to be learned here is that when relating to an audience (of one or of many), it is important that you pay special attention to little things which could rob you of credibility. Too often, preparation is spent on major issues at the expense of minor ones. Ironically, it is usually a little inconsequential flaw that gives you away.

Unquestionably, the more credible an individual, the better will be his ability to cope with an audience. Once an audience has disenfranchised a speaker, his chances of returning to its good graces are poor. A convenient method of determining the extent to which an audience finds a speaker credible is by the number of times they nod their heads affirmatively. The reason for their reaction should then be given top priority—that is, finding out what causes an audience to nod affirmatively. One way of doing this is to dissect it. The following section does just that.

ANATOMY OF AN AUDIENCE

If a surgeon doesn't know what is wrong with a patient or is not sure of his diagnosis, he will sometimes perform what is known as a laparotomy. It is an exploratory operation—a kind of "Let's have a look-see." Drawing an analogy between a patient and an audience, we derive the heading "Anatomy of an Audience." If something goes wrong between speaker and audience, the cause(s) may be attributable to (1) the speaker, (2) the audience, or (3) a combination of speaker and audience. What we shall now do is dissect a hypothetical audience into as many parts as possible. By so doing, we can acquire a richer understanding of its static and dynamic nature. With due respect to Ellingsworth and Clevenger, who feel that the concept of an audience is an abstraction and that no such creature exists,[8] we shall behave here "as though" it did.

Assume, for a moment, you knew absolutely nothing about art and were shown a painting of St. John the Baptist by El Greco. What if someone asked your opinion of it? Aside from a strictly intuitive response

[8] Huber Ellingsworth and Theodore Clevenger, Jr., *Speech and Social Action: A Strategy of Oral Communication* (Englewood Cliffs, N.J.: Prentice-Hall, Inc., 1967), p. 107.

labeling it good, great, exciting, or unusual, wouldn't you have to know something about art in order to answer? So that you may become better equipped to do this, here are some of the components of an audience and a description of their operational characteristics.

X-Factor

An X-Factor refers to some characteristic of an audience that, if discovered by a speaker, can be used for or against him. If an audience of P.T.A. (Parent-Teacher Association) members were being addressed, the assumption could be made that their X-Factor was a keen interest in education; if it were the Veterans of Foreign Wars, it would probably be patriotism; the B'Nai Brith, world Jewry. With few exceptions, every audience has an X-Factor—an Achilles' heel. Every speaker has the responsibility of finding out what it is.

This X-Factor can make itself known overtly or covertly. Overt manifestations include the use of banners, buttons, and badges (BLACK IS BEAUTIFUL, BUY UNION GOODS, SUPPORT YOUR LOCAL COLLEGE, FIGHT POLLUTION), organizational literature, advertising through the mass media (radio, television, newspapers, films, plays), and the wearing of uniforms. A covertly expressed X-Factor includes any number of organizational characteristics that operate beneath the surface, such as antisemitism, racism, male chauvinism. It should not be assumed, however, that every audience has only one specific X-Factor. On occasion more than one X-Factor may exist on either an overt or a covert level.

Rarely can a speaker enter a room, take one look at his audience, and know its X-Factor. Some detective work is necessary in the form of assumption, inference, deductive and inductive reasoning, and so on. As in analyzing a work of art, the clues are out there in your audience. All you have to do is learn to recognize them.

Age

A young attorney, 29 years of age, was delivering a speech on the philosophy of justice at an annual convention in San Francisco. After he had finished, a 65-year-old lawyer in the rear stood up and said, "Young man, I have been practicing law for the past forty years and I have never heard such utter nonsense." Embarrassed, the young lawyer replied, "Sir, may I respectfully submit that you have been practicing your first year forty times."

For some people, the age of a speaker exerts a pronounced influence upon their judgment. Imagine an audience of college professors, in their forties and fifties, listening to a young professor in her late twenties deliver a paper on the philosophy of teaching. There is little doubt that some of the older professors will be somewhat biased against her solely because of her tender age and relatively limited experience in the field. Therefore, she would be wise to anticipate such a response by saying, "I realize many of you have more experience and I could learn something from studying with each of you. However, since this is not feasible, I would appreciate some of your reactions to the ideas I have advanced in this paper." While she is wholly aware that they may find such a remark somewhat "apple-polishing," it does keep them from rejecting her before they have heard her out.

With the situation reversed, a fifty-year-old professor addressing an audience of young professors should anticipate the charge that "he is over the hill." Immediately, he should declare that a generation gap does exist and that it would be naive to think that what was taught when he went to school was the same as what is taught today. He should also say something such as, "Since our goals are the same, namely to improve the quality of education, perhaps by pooling our resources, we can find some viable solutions together." Again the remarks sound transparent, but, in both instances, they are better said than left unsaid.

The words of Aristotle, spoken over 2000 years ago, are still credible today. Commenting upon the three stages of men (*young men, men in their prime,* and *elderly men*), he assigns to each certain characteristics visible today. To young men he attributes strong passions which are gratified indiscriminantly, sexual desires over which they have little self-control, and inclinations to look at the good rather than the bad because they have not yet witnessed many instances of wickedness. Men in their prime, Aristotle writes, are midway between the young and the old in practically all things. Among elderly men, the pendulum swings in a direction diametrically opposite to that of the young. They have experienced much and learned that life, on the whole, is bad business. They are sure about nothing and undo everything. Being cynical, they see the worst side of everything and tend to suffer from cowardice. They live by memory rather than by hope.[9]

While man may have sustained many changes in lifestyle since Aristotle, his observations on human nature carry as much weight today as they did then. His thoughts on age have certainly withstood the test of time. It would be foolhardy to gloss over age in the analysis of any audience.

[9] *Rhetorica,* trans. W. Rhys Roberts, from *The Oxford Translation of Aristotle,* ed. W. D. Ross, Vol. II (Fair Lawn, N.J.: Oxford University Press, 1924).

Sex

Would you agree that the number of males and females comprising an audience could affect its reaction to a speaker? The Women's Liberation Movement most certainly does. Its members have asserted that although a male pediatrician speaking on the subject of breast-feeding can certainly do a fine job from an objective or theoretical standpoint, an all-female audience listening to him can seldom experience the kind of rapport they would get from a female pediatrician—especially one who has done some breast-feeding of her own. In this same vein, it has been noted that many women who gave birth to their children with the aid of midwives felt psychologically more comfortable than when delivered by male obstetricians. The *sine qua non* in these cases appears to be empathy. Let's face it—people are more comfortable, cooperative, and confident with someone who has "gone through" whatever is being discussed than with someone armed only with theory. Surely you have heard that some drug addicts have had more success rehabilitating other drug addicts than professionals who were equipped with the latest theories and principles but who "never had a fix." This is not to imply that someone has to have cancer in order to treat it, or that you have to be a chicken to know a rotten egg—only that personal experience sure seems to help!

Throughout this text, a clearly male orientation has prevailed. Practically every reference speaks of a *he* this, a *he* that, and a *he* then. Any female reading through could not help but get the impression that the author (1) is unaware that females exist, (2) thinks that females can't read, (3) is a male chauvinist pig. But, whatever the reason, most textbooks do tend to employ the collective "he." Some try to get around the lack of a unisex third person singular pronoun through the use of such literary devices as *he/she, one can readily see, many people are of the opinion that,* or *individuals appear to agree that,* and so on.

Taking care not to overdramatize the importance of this sexual identification, by the same token we should not ignore it. The only male in an audience comprised entirely of females or the only female in an audience of males is quick to realize the potential impact the speaker's orientation could have on some thin-skinned individuals. Occasionally a book or film will come along that causes people to refer to it as a "man's film" or a "woman's book." The reason is usually that it possesses some uniquely masculine or feminine quality or storyline.

Whatever your sex, it does have the capacity to modify your reactions, if you are a member of an audience. Figure 8–1 shows a hypothetical situation in which a male speaker is addressing an entirely female audience on the subject of childbirth. He also is addressing an all male audience on the same subject. Using the spaces provided beneath whichever audience you would find yourself in (depending upon your sex), jot down the reactions you think you might have under the circumstances.

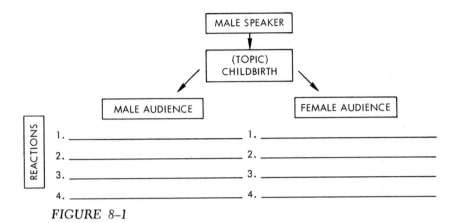

FIGURE 8–1

Size

The number of people gathered together for any reason usually has some special meaning. There are those who walk past a restaurant—peek in through the window and, if the place is either too full or too empty, behave according to how they feel about crowds. Others seem impervious to numbers and will stand in lines for anything, from soup to nuts.

The size of an audience can affect both the speaker and the individuals who comprise it. If you have been in a school play and, on opening night, sneaked a look through the curtain at the size of the house, you understand this point. The smaller the audience, the less enthusiastic the performers. In another direction, few things are more depressing to a teacher than to find, on the first day of class, that only six students have signed up for his class. With a deflated ego, the rationalization process begins. But, no matter how successful he is at rationalizing, the fact remains that only six students signed up for his course.

Switch now from the feelings of a speaker with a small audience to the feelings of members of that small audience. Looking around a classroom and discovering that you and a handful of other students are the only ones registered for a course raises second thoughts: "Why are we the only ones here? Is this course or the teacher really that bad?" Then your rationalizing begins: "Oh well, with such a small class, each of us will get more personal attention and instruction." On the other side of the coin, we have the student gobbled up by an abnormally large class audience. In such a dilemma, students have expressed strenuous objections because of a "lost" feeling: "Just another face in the crowd." Because of this deindividualizing effect, students are often shocked when a passing professor chances to say, "Good morning, Pearl!" or, "Hi there, Dennis, how are you today?" They are astounded that a teacher remembered their names. This is particularly true on some of the larger campuses.

It might also be worthwhile mentioning that young doctors and lawyers have been known to make their waiting rooms smaller rather than larger when first going into practice. The reason is obvious. Four or five people in a small room make an office look busy; the same number in a large one makes it look like business is slow and the practitioner in small demand. Therefore, the size of an audience must be considered in relation to the size of the room they occupy. More will be said about the kind of room later on.

A technique that has been used in coping with oversized audiences has been to break it down, if possible, into smaller units. In this way, feelings of alienation are less, and interpersonal communication seems to flourish more readily.

Again, size is but one characteristic of any audience, and its importance must be weighed in relation to its other characteristics.

Location

WARNING: *Whenever you hear someone say, "Oh, that's all right, any place will do!"—watch out!*

"Where" an audience assembles can be crucial. Professionals spend millions of dollars on the place where they will be seen or heard. If a young and aspiring opera singer or violinist wants to be heard and has to hire a hall in which to do so, nothing could be more ill-advised than to be penny-wise and pound-foolish. If a young artist's funds are low, it would probably be wiser to wait and accumulate a few more dollars than to be heard in an unsuitable hall or auditorium having poor acoustics, uncomfortable seating, antiquated stage and surroundings, and no air-conditioning or heating facilities. The more an audience's senses are pleased, the more receptive they are; the more irritated they are, the less receptive they are inclined to be.

Students are frequently affected by a classroom. Certain rooms invariably provoke moans and groans from those assigned to them. Learning levels seem to be heightened by more attractive classrooms and dampened by ugly ones. If students have a choice, they should exercise it. Student audiences identify with that which contains them. If the room is shabby looking and broken down, the students seem unenthusiastic; if it is bright and alive, they tend to feel likewise. *Repeat:* Avoid, like the plague, the expression, "Oh, that's all right, any place will do." It does make a difference.

Time

To refresh your memory, Chapter 5 suggested that most people are either *owls* or *larks*. The owls are night people who come alive (like Count Dracula) after the sun goes down. The larks do just the opposite and usually fizzle out directly after the evening meal. Audiences are composed of both owls and larks. What worse fate could befall a student who is an owl than having an 8:00 A.M. class, or what worse for a lark than having a late afternoon or evening one? As members of any audience, they are dead weight, doing neither their classmates nor their teacher any good.

Also important to an audience, if several speakers are scheduled to be heard, is the order in which they appear. There has been an ongoing feud among rhetoricians for years concerning the advantages or disadvantages of going on first, last, or in the middle. Regardless of which school of thought you support, the position a particular speaker occupies (the time he/she goes on) does affect an audience. Taking into account such things as owls and larks, attention spans, muscular fatigue from sitting for long periods, and other physiological variables, could help one avoid needlessly sacrificing a perfectly good audience or speaker.

Proxemics

Since the study of proxemics deals with people and places in their spatial relationship to one another, it would be useful to view an audience in that context. To do this, several questions must be considered: (1) How far is the audience from the speaker? (2) What is the angle from which the audience visually perceives the speaker? (3) How far from one another are individual members of the audience? (4) Is the position of the audience fixed or mobile? Each will now be discussed separately.

FIRST: SPEAKER-AUDIENCE DISTANCE

It would be meaningless to speak of an audience's distance from the speaker without noting that each member in an audience usually maintains a somewhat different distance—front row, back row, middle row, and sides. As a result, human sight and hearing being what they are, no two members of an audience experience an identical perception of a speaker. With distances varying in this fashion, visual and acoustic distortions are frequently present. When a speaker looks to the segment of his audience on his right, those on his left are deprived of a full view of his face. Those up front have the benefit of seeing facial expressions that are totally unseen by those in the rear. Stage whispers, breath patterns, and other microphenomena associated with the speaker do not exist for most of the sociofugally[10] positioned members of the audience. In short, speaker-audience distancing could be an extremely important variable in successfully coping with an audience.

SECOND: ANGLE OF AUDIENCE TO SPEAKER

In some auditoriums the listeners are located above the speaker and find themselves looking down on him; others are located below and find themselves looking up. Varying the angle of one's line of vision can alter one's perceptual images. Perhaps operating on a more subconscious level, the feeling some people get when they are "talked down to" differs from being "talked up at." If you are not satisfied that the speaker-audience angle is of any consequence, try this experiment. Have one of your classmates deliver a speech while standing on a desk at the front of the room while the entire class sits on the floor. Then reverse the arrangement by having the speaker deliver his speech while sitting on the floor while his classmates stand VERY CAREFULLY on the seats of their chairs. Excluding the topic of the speech or the caliber of the speaker, analyze how you, as a member of the audience, felt in each position.

THIRD: INTERPERSONAL AUDIENCE-MEMBER DISTANCE

Not too many years ago, to accommodate more passengers, certain airlines squeezed additional seats into a given unit of space in their aircrafts. The result was that people sensitive to "crowding" felt extremely uncomfortable. This situation prevailed until a few companies, realizing that something was not right, expanded their seating facilities. They advertised the option of removing the armrest of the seat next to you if it was not occupied, thus giving you more room.

In the traditional audience setting, if the chairs are movable, the distance between them should be adjusted according to both the topic of the speech and the character of the speaker. The more intimate or taboo the topic, the closer the chairs should be. It seems that when the subject is rather personal, people have a tendency to seek anonymity, to solicit the insulation often provided by crowds. In contrast, a nonthreatening subject such as "A Brief Look at the Rain Forests over Puerto Rico" would justify

[10] *Sociofugal*—increased distance between people; *sociopedal*—decreased distance between people.

having the chairs slightly farther apart than usual. The next time you enter an auditorium and have a choice of seats, notice whether you are sitting one, two, or three seats away from your nearest neighbor. For fun, if there are plenty of seats to choose from, park yourself *right next* to some stranger and observe his reaction.

FOURTH: A FIXED OR MOBILE AUDIENCE

At rallies or outdoor festivities, audience members have the opportunity of either staying in one place or moving about. Observing an audience from a platform reveals currents of movement. People tend to shift themselves from one place to another. The barker at a carnival or on a midway tries to hustle the people in his audience to move from the rear to a more intimate position down front where he can really ply his trade as a pitchman. Occasionally, people down front become annoyed by this captivelike feeling and move to the rear out of range.

Any audience or speaker who understands what can be achieved by manipulating people in space is endowed with added "coping insurance" against breakdowns in communication.

Geography

Anyone who makes his living performing across the country will tell you audiences are not all the same. The cliché, "people are people," doesn't check out in practice. There is always the need to investigate local customs, attitudes, beliefs, taboos, and outstanding personalities. In spite of a lack of confirmation from available studies, audiences do seem to possess something that has loosely been called a "group mind." When it is pleased or offended, it lets you know very quickly. Whether it is comprised of Eskimos or Hopi Indians, it requires a feedback from the speaker that shows he knows what is important to them. Since audiences appear less able to change their ways than the people addressing them, it is incumbent upon the speaker to adjust himself and his presentation accordingly. Simple things like speeding up or slowing down one's speech pattern, incorporating some local jargon, deleting unfamiliar references, or demonstrating a high regard for a local source of pride could easily do the trick.

An amusing anecdote comes out of a presidential reelection campaign in the Southwest. It shows what can happen to a speaker when he is ignorant of local jargon. It seems that the candidate's advisors decided it would be a good idea if he addressed a tribe of American Indians on their reservation. During the course of his speech, the Indians frequently interrupted by chanting, "Umpah, umpah, umpah." The speaker interpreted this as a sign of approval. On the way back to his motorcade one of his aides (who happened to be an Indian) suddenly pulled at his arm and said, "Watch out, Mr. President, you almost stepped in the umpah." He soon realized that his audience had not been chanting approval. The moral of this story is that, when you are away from your own home town and obliged to deliver a speech, be extremely careful or you might find yourself "stepping in some umpah."

Education

If there is anything that really gets under an audience's skin it is being talked down to. On the other hand, they don't like talk that goes over their heads. One of the reasons given for Adlai Stevenson's defeat as a presidential candidate was that his intellectual language was too sophisticated for the average citizen. Many were not quite sure of what he was saying. By the same token, an uneducated speaker could also alienate an educated audience through the use of certain unsophisticated language. Every audience, it seems, requires a specific type of communication. For example, referring in a television speech to things that only a small segment of the nation ever heard of could quickly alienate those who hadn't. Thus, it is imperative that you carefully gauge your audience's educational level and gear your speech to it.

Once an audience feels slighted, it can do one of several things: (1) completely tune out the speaker, (2) get up and leave, (3) become antagonistic and hurl epithets, or (4) physically remove the speaker from the platform. In sum, while being educated is certainly commendable, superior knowledge should not be flaunted before an audience.

Health

Most audiences are made up of essentially healthy individuals. There are, unfortunately, exceptions. Certain organizations send entertainers to veterans' hospitals to make the lives of the disabled members of the Armed Forces a little more enjoyable. Other audiences periodically addressed reside at institutions for the deaf and blind. The list goes on to include nursing homes for senior citizens, retarded children, youngsters with cardiac and kidney disease, and so on. In each case, the person communicating from a stage must tailor his presentation according to their particular health problem. For the blind, certain descriptions unnecessary to a sighted audience would be indispensable. Deaf audiences have special needs which must also be met. What would you do in preparation for delivering a speech to one or more of the following special audiences? List your ideas in the spaces provided. Be specific as to what you would or would not say or do.

BLIND AUDIENCE (between the ages of 18–25)

_____

_____

_____

_____

_____

_____

_____

DEAF AND DUMB AUDIENCE (between the ages of 10–18)

_____

_____

_____

_____

_____

_____

_____

SENIOR CITIZEN AUDIENCE (between the ages of 70–105)

_____

_____

_____

_____

_____

_____

_____

After entering your suggestions, discuss the basis for them with your classmates and teacher.

Dress

It is not uncommon to find an audience behaving the way it is dressed. If its attire is informal, comfy, and casual, it will tend to behave informally and casually. If it is dressed formally, it often behaves more formally. From this author's experience, Black Tie audiences with women in evening gowns conduct themselves in a rather staid manner and are somewhat more guarded in conversation. Alcoholic beverages, acting as a personality solvent, have been known to make short work of these affected mannerisms (in those cases where they are affected, of course).

Exceptions to this generalization are those people whose lives involve the wearing of formal attire on a regular basis, such as waiters in elegant restaurants, members of symphonic orchestras, and people in high society.

Speakers addressing uniformed audiences, such as cadets at West Point, Annapolis, or various military academies, often find them to be more respectful, less restless, and not as prone to hostility. If you know of exceptions, so do we all. For some reason, an audience made up of people dressed in the same way is able to rob each member of at least his external distinctiveness. Perhaps this is why, on occasion, feelings of sameness breed frustration. It might not be a bad idea if someone compared the attitudes and behavior of uniformed versus nonuniformed audiences. Related to this question of dress, public schools that heretofore enforced rigid regulations of dress have either markedly modified or rescinded them. Children are now, for the most part, permitted to wear (within limits) whatever they wish. A friend of this writer has a son who recently graduated from high school wearing a traditional cap and gown over an army surplus shirt, jeans, and a pair of torn sandals (or perhaps it was sneakers). When his parents were asked why they allowed him to go to graduation dressed in that way, they replied, "If we didn't let him, he said he wouldn't go at all." What would you have done if he were your son?

Economics

Do audiences differ according to their financial status? Are wealthy people more secure, more confident, more assertive, and less willing to tolerate that which displeases them? A "yes" answer does seem inviting. While wealth cannot buy good health and personal happiness, it does make bad health and misery more tolerable. Financial success generates a self-confidence that is communicated from an audience to a speaker. When a person feels secure, he has less need to pull others down. The one trait that is common to the majority of affluent audiences is "a sense of security"; to low-income audiences, "a sense of insecurity." One evening, wander into a high-class, very expensive night club and sit down. In the midst of this affluent audience, see what kind of vibrations you get. Note the texture of their responses to the performers during the stage show and notice the manner in which they express their approval or disapproval. The next evening, visit a low-class night club—a "joint." Again register some impressions. For the maximum benefit, write an impression paper and bring it to class the next day.

In show business there are performers who, because they know and understand the affluent audience, are booked into high-class night clubs exclusively. Other performers fare better with low-income audiences. It might also be useful to mention that a speaker who relates well to affluent audiences need not be affluent himself; he need only have an insight into their personality and values. The same applies to those who successfully relate to low- and middle-income audiences. The crux in each case seems to be how well and how accurately a speaker analyzes his audience on the basis of economics.

Kinesics

Kinesics, or the science of body language, often provides the observant speaker with clues to his audience's character. From the way they sit, stand, position their arms and legs, and move their bodies in general, he can derive considerable insight into their personality and mind-set. How would you interpret these kinesic cues from an audience?

1. Slumped in their seats.
2. Arms folded across their chests.
3. Feet outstretched or propped up on a chair in front of them.

Would you judge them to be vitally interested, couldn't care less, or planning to give you a hard time? What if their kinesic cues consisted of:

1. Looking directly at you.
2. Leaning forward in their seats.
3. Displaying very little movement in their seats.

What connotation do you read into these behaviors? Needless to say, drawing any firm conclusions on the basis of these kinesic elements without knowing a great many other factors would be irresponsible.

Applause, like the umbilical cord that unites mother and child, serves similarly between speaker and audience. Few devices communicate the mood of an audience as well as applause. "It is an overt gesture of thanks for enjoyment; by giving it, one enriches one's own enjoyment. Applause is, or can be, a mild form of autointoxication; it helps, so to speak, to convince oneself of one's own pleasure. It has muscular value, for after a scene of high drama it relieves the tension within you and clears the way for the next experience. And it welds the audience into a community."[11]

The method by which audiences show their approval or disapproval is not the same throughout the world. Applause as we know it (slapping the hands together) is not universal. In the eighteenth century it was

[11] George R. Marek, "Applause," *Opera News* (December 18, 1971), p. 6.

customary for gentlemen to strike their walking sticks against their seats. Provincial townspeople in France stamp their feet when they are pleased; in some opera houses in Spain the people "hiss" to show approval; audiences of ancient India snapped the fingers on one hand to show mild enthusiasm; the fingers of both hands to produce an ovation.[12]

Some speakers are, or appear to be, totally impervious to the kinesic behavior of their audience. They fail to realize that nonverbal messages, properly decoded, can provide the vital information necessary for oratorical success. Take a situation like this: You notice your audience is becoming restless. Instead of ignoring their movements and rushing to a premature end of your speech, it might be wiser to incorporate your audience's need for a muscular release with some reference to body tension and its management. Ask them to do some deep breathing, stretching, or shoulder shrugging right then and there. In this way, their restlessness becomes part of your speech and not something that distracts from it. Conversely, if you notice several members of your audience half asleep and slumped in their seats, segue smoothly into a few remarks about the relaxing effects of sleep and the therapeutic benefits of hypnosis. This will draw some attention to their kinesic state and help reestablish your communication with them. The important thing to remember is that your audience is generally a rather malleable creature and will respond to your directions. Rather than disregarding an adverse action or reaction by your audience, use it to your advantage by including it in your presentation.

Audiences are constantly transmitting kinesic cues to the speaker and, for the most part, they are remarkably reliable as indicators. Members of an audience also get kinesic cues from each other. A few rabble-rousers could upset an entire audience by their disruptive kinesic activity—clapping their hands inappropriately, getting up and down from their seats, moving about in the aisles, chewing gum noisily, and rustling candy wrappers. In the future, watch the people who are watching and listening to you and adjust your remarks in relation to their behavior.

Affiliation

In this day and age, most of us are "belongers." Have everyone in class empty out on his desk all of the cards in his wallets or handbags signifying membership or affiliation with some formal organization (library cards, credit cards, I.D. cards, and whatever). Each represents a commitment of some sort. In some instances, the possession of a specific card could have certain serious implications and be potentially damaging in the wrong hands, such as membership in the Communist Party or Ku Klux Klan.

12 *Ibid.*, p. 6.

It is seldom possible for a speaker to know the affiliations of members of his audience except for those they admit or publicize, such as membership in the Daughters of the American Revolution, Jehovah Witnesses, Black Panthers, Phi Beta Kappa Society, B'nai Brith, Gay Liberation Movement, and Women's Liberation Movement. Being aware of these affiliations enables a reasonably alert speaker to design his speech accordingly, and thereby avoid any gross errors in judgment. It is the *hidden agendum* of which the speaker must beware. A *hidden agendum* is any axe a member of an audience may have to grind which is deliberately concealed from the speaker. Some people, for example, on the surface profess to be staunchly liberal and anxious to help the world; yet, when this veneer is scraped away, some ugly or vicious bias they have been harboring comes to light. This is but one of the reasons political speechmakers have their researchers carefully check out the composition of the audiences they will be addressing. Such advanced knowledge may help them avoid forfeiting an entire campaign or even a career.

Least Common Denominator

A situation arises in which you must deliver a speech to a completely strange audience. All you know for sure is that they are human beings. Although a dilemma like this is rather unlikely, its hypothetical nature serves a purpose here. Knowing pitifully little about a given group of people, you must speculate as to what they have in common solely on the basis of their humanity. Consider this experiment by Ellingsworth and Clevenger:

> From this imaginary middle-sized American town, a total of 100 randomly selected telephone numbers, one from every fifth page, was made. Each of these people was then called and asked to appear at some predetermined place to listen to a speech. If they all showed up, a nearly random (technically an "accidental") collection of people who are very different from one another would assemble. They will probably range from very old to very young, from well-off to poor, from unschooled to educated. There will be Democrats and Republicans; Catholics, Jews, and several varieties of Protestants; people of various racial and ethnic backgrounds; men and women; the representatives of various professions and occupations, as well as the unemployed. All these people—though widely different—have two things in common: Each is a member of a household that owns at least one listed telephone, and each was willing and able to come to participate in the experiment.
>
> On the basis of these two bits of information we may be able to make other inferences about this audience before it assembles: (1) that it will probably not include very young children or the aged or infirm since parental consent or refusal and physical inability would act as barriers,

(2) that it would not be likely to include the destitute (who could not afford a telephone) or the enormously rich (who generally don't list their telephone numbers in the public directory). However, there is a remote possibility that these inferences may be mistaken and that a four year old will show up with a parent in tow; a palsied octogenarian will be brought in on a stretcher; that the one pauper in town spends whatever money he has on a telephone, and that the town millionaire does not have an unlisted number. In a very loose sense, then, we can say that members of this audience have something in common with each other.[13]

The bonds that all audiences share can be divided into two groups: *physiological* and *psychological*. The former dictate that everyone in an audience needs to eat, sleep, eliminate waste products, satisfy a sexual urge, and find shelter from the elements; the latter are exemplified by such needs as to love and be loved, to engage in social interaction, to find ways of combatting the effects of loneliness, and to exercise whatever creativity beats in one's breast. These are the major forces that move men—the necessities of life. The probability is high that every person in every audience, to varying extents, shares these characteristics. YOUR JOB: to build word bridges that will enable you to communicate with them.

Depending upon your interests and rhetorical strength, you as a speaker must now select one of these physiological or psychological themes, or a blend of both. For argument's sake, assume that you decide upon man's sexual urge. Immediately, every member of your audience, regardless of age, will grasp your meaning. Historically, a well-written love story told in print or on film has one of the best chances of "touching" the greatest number of people. Therefore, if you are going to choose a *least common denominator*, "love" is a very wise choice. Your problem now is to construct your speech so that it presents a minimum of specifics and a maximum of generalities. Everyone reading or hearing your words must be able to translate them into images. See what these words do for you in terms of images:

> Last night, while lying in my bed asleep, I awoke for no reason at all. My pillow was wet from perspiration and I was extremely restless. I looked up at the ceiling through the dark, and then out of the window. I ran my hand across my forehead and down on to my stomach to see if I was alive and still able to feel. My mouth was dry and so was my soul. I was so very, very, lonely—so damned lonely. Have you ever felt like this? God knows we all need someone to love, hold, and care for.

With few exceptions, this kind of communication (at the risk of being very corny) cuts through all language systems and seems to be able to stir

---

[13] Ellingsworth and Clevenger, *Speech and Social Action*, pp. 108–9.

saint and sinner, young and old alike. Absolutely no audience need be labeled "unreachable" if you can invent and then implement just one of its *least common denominators*.

Culture

Today, more than ever before, people of varying races, colors, and creeds have been brought closer together by the mass media. In television, films, and print, culturally different people can be seen relating to one another. Audiences, for the first time, may peek inside the minds and hearts of individuals who are ethnically unlike themselves. People have come to realize that the similarities between members of the human race exceed the differences; that many of their feelings of hostility, distrust, and superiority have little more than an illusory basis in fact. Through the medium of humor, a great many television shows, Broadway plays, books, magazine articles, posters, and buttons have made it possible for us to penetrate, and in many cases explode, those stereotypes that have plagued us for years and kept us strangers. Using communication as the "stuff" from which to build bridges and not walls, a universal consciousness is developing.

Transcultural or intercultural communication is no longer an option, but a necessity. International diplomacy is nothing more than interpersonal communication with its throttle wide open. Hall[14] relates an episode in which an American professor was invited to teach a group of Japanese university professors about American history. Unaware that in Japan all educated men speak English, he insulted them by requesting an interpreter. Like the presidential candidate mentioned earlier, our American professor also stepped in the umpah.

Every culture, directly or indirectly, imprints upon its members a variety of culture-specific communication cues that outsiders must learn to read. He who fails to do this will, as in the past, alienate rather than integrate. Thus, to help improve your ability to cope with a culturally different audience, take the first opportunity you get to include yourself in one and compare its behavior with that of the type of audience to which you are accustomed.

SUMMARY

This chapter proposed that a speaker and his audience be looked upon as a unit. It began with what it took to be the most troublesome aspect of

[14] Edward Hall, *The Silent Language* (New York: Doubleday, 1959), pp. 11–12.

public speaking—stage fright. Not only was it represented as plaguing the speaker but, indirectly, the audience as well. The etiology (causes), symptoms, and treatment of stage fright were discussed, together with some exercises that the stage-frightened individual might try.

Then, consistent with the holistic premise mentioned above, we looked at an audience in depth. If, indeed, a reciprocal relationship exists between speaker and audience, then whatever affects one must in some way affect the other. Based upon this premise, the chapter proceeded to examine the anatomy of an audience, dissecting it into its component parts. Hopefully, having laid before the reader those constituents of an audience that make it tick, it will serve as an anxiety-reducing device—another means of coping with an audience.

CHAPTER 9

SURVIVAL
IN A
SMALL GROUP

INSIGHTS

After reading this chapter you should have a clearer understanding of:

- *what is needed to survive in a small-group situation.*
- *the types of people you are apt to meet in most groups.*
- *how crucial it is to know the values held by other members
  in a group.*
- *the fact that a person may behave one way outside a small
  group and quite differently inside one.*
- *why people join groups in the first place.*
- *why it is important to know where to sit in a group situation.*
- *the vital role LISTENING plays in group life.*

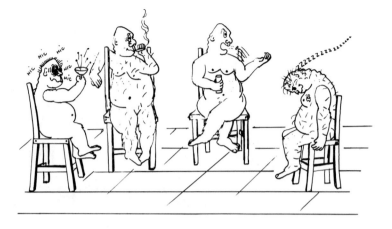

GENERAL REMARKS ABOUT THE SMALL GROUP

Since childhood, most of us have been members of one group or another. Figure 9–1 represents three basic life groups common to us all. Until we begin school at approximately age 6, the major part of our lives is spent in the *family* group. Next, the *school* group contains us until we graduate; then we are taken over by the *social* group. Although we exist in no one group exclusively, each dominates a given phase of our lives and fills those needs indigenous to it. In short, society navigates us through each of these group affiliations, and they in turn make it possible for us to participate in that humanity-sharing enterprise called "living."

Social norms throughout the world generally defer to "group-man" rather than "man alone." Casually thumbing through any conventional textbook in social psychology will disclose the importance of being able to successfully interact with others. Failure to do this usually indicates a need for some serious introspection. If the inability to relate to others is pronounced, professional counseling should be sought. The message is clear: learning to survive in a small group is no longer optional, it is a necessity for man as a social animal. Although some contend that personal survival can best be achieved by "minding one's own business," it is usually accomplished at the expense of, rather than together with, other people.

In this chapter we shall arbitrarily consider a small group to consist of from six to twenty-four people gathered together for the purpose of interacting verbally and/or nonverbally on a face-to-face basis. Only the family, school, and social groups will be discussed, because every reader is familiar with them as areas in which most people need help. For example, some-

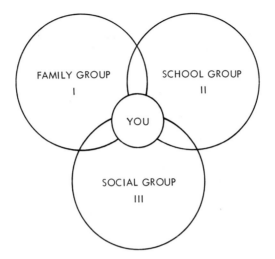

FIGURE 9–1 Basic Life Groups.

one may have had success in school and social groups but failed miserably with a family, or may have succeeded with a family and school group but felt gross dissatisfaction with a social group. Being mature and capable of faring well in one basic life group doesn't automatically guarantee success in the others. As this chapter unfolds, some of the ramifications that make survival under different circumstances possible will become more evident.

Although small groups have flourished throughout history, only recently have they attracted so much attention. The business world now recognizes the value of the T-group and encounter group as excellent tools for improving intraorganizational communication among their employees. Sensitivity training groups likewise (if properly managed) have also made a contribution to the improvement of mental health; discussion groups in high school and college classrooms have served as sound vehicles for helping expand a student's awareness. Even those nonconformists who have rejected the value of small groups have formed nonconformist groups to protest against conformist groups.

The days of the rugged individualist who, single-handedly, altered the course of history have rapidly faded. These days *ein Mensch ist kein Mensch* (a solitary man is no man at all); the battle cry is "organize! unite! affiliate! join!" The lone wolf, once romanticized in literature and films, today is frequently taken to be either a weirdo or "into himself."

Loneliness

Humans are born with a thirst to communicate, to make contact. A failure in this effort often results in some degree of "loneliness." The term, because of its many psychological ramifications, is extremely difficult to define. In fact, it is one of the least satisfactorily conceptualized psychological phenomena; few psychiatric textbooks even mention it. Related states such as solitude, isolation, aloneness, seclusion, and shut-in-ness add further confusion to our meager understanding of it. Loneliness is an unpopular and frowned-upon state of mind in our group-conscious culture. Most people who are alone try to keep their aloneness a secret from others; they even try to hide it from themselves. It's just not something one goes around bragging about.

All members of a family share the need to feel wanted. Father, in private, fancies his role as breadwinner and head of the household as indispensable; mother, likewise, deludes herself that if anything were to happen to her, daddy and the children would have difficulty managing; children, known to fear being deserted by their parents, frequently exaggerate their own importance in the family. Each secretly fantasizes his indispensability to other members of the group.

At school, similar behavior occurs. Faculty members occasionally afford themselves the luxury of feeling indispensable, muttering to themselves, "How would this department get along without me?" Students also harbor feelings of indispensability in certain classes and to certain teachers. Even deans and college presidents are not exempt from this harmless pastime.

Comparable practices crop up also in the business and professional worlds. Whether a member of a large corporation, political party, or church sisterhood, you will inevitably run into people who think they are indispensable. For these individuals, here is an interesting poem:

Indispensable?

Sometime, when you're feeling important,
Sometime, when your ego's in bloom,
Sometime, when you take it for granted
You're the best qualified in the room.
Sometime when you feel that your going
Would leave an unfillable hole,
Just follow this simple instruction
And see how it humbles your soul.
Take a bucket and fill it with water,
Put your hand in it up to the wrist,
Pull it out and the hole that's remaining,
Is the measure of how you'll be missed.
You may splash all you please when you enter,
You can stir up the water galore,
But stop, and you'll find in a minute,
That it looks quite the same as before.
The moral of this quaint example,
Is to do just the best that you can,

Be proud of yourself, but remember,
There is no indispensable man.

Anonymous

Dealing with loneliness, as with any other condition, requires an understanding of its causes and effects. To gain such insight, the author informally questioned several individuals spanning three generations hoping to discover the existence of any common denominator. The first group consisted of children between the ages of 12 and 14; the second, of adults between 28 and 40; the last, of senior citizens over 75.

"What is loneliness?" Some of the responses made by the first group to this question were:

1. Not having friends with the same interests.
2. Not having friends and being on your own.
3. You think nobody loves you and you think you're all alone in the world.
4. When everybody leaves you out of things.
5. When you have problems and can't decide what to do and your friends can't help you and you have to decide for yourself.

Responses from the second group included:

1. An unshared opinion.
2. Unshared happiness or not having anyone to share your problems with.
3. An emptiness—a void when you return to your room.
4. Being alone when the whole world has someone.
5. Going unrecognized in anything.

Responses from the third group were:

1. The need to be needed—the feeling of usefulness.
2. Being without hope or a goal—feeling disillusioned.
3. It is undefinable. You must experience it for yourself.
4. Not being visited.
5. Eating by yourself—all alone.

Someone once said, "Loneliness is a spiritual affliction which knows no age limit." Studies at Johns Hopkins University in Baltimore showed that children who were believed to have growth failure due to hormonal malfunction were actually lonely because of parental rejection. Studies at Duke University have shown that mental and physical deterioration accelerate rapidly in the elderly when they are deprived of companionship and a sense of worth. According to sociologist William Sadler, Jr., director of Interdisciplinary Studies at Bloomfield College in New Jersey, the search for friendship and discussions about loneliness have replaced sex as the number-one topic on college campuses. Sadler cites four types of loneliness: (1) *interpersonal*—widows, prisoners, or hospital patients, (2) *cosmic*—people who feel an absence of some kind of ultimate reality, whether it is Nature or God, (3) *cultural*—often experienced by immigrants who miss the customs of their homeland, (4) *social*—felt by those who have been blackballed or rejected by a group.[1]

Perhaps the most enlightening thing about loneliness is its ability to transcend time. It seems to create essentially the same dilemma in the mind, heart, and gut of a child as it does in the senior citizen. Ways of coping with it all seem to boil down to busying oneself by:

1. Joining various groups (AFFILIATION),
2. Visiting different places (TRAVELING),
3. Getting your head together (INTROSPECTION).

More people are experiencing loneliness today because of too much leisure time. A century ago, the average man and woman worked from sunrise to sunset and flopped into bed exhausted. There was no time left to nurse feelings of loneliness.

This might be a good time to differentiate *loneliness* from *aloneness*. Not everyone who prefers to be alone is lonely. It is common knowledge among creative people that withdrawing oneself from the milling throng is a necessity which few can forego. Aloneness is something we impose upon ourselves, whereas loneliness is imposed upon us. Understanding this distinction reduces the possibility of invading someone's privacy on the assumption that he or she is lonely. Thus, at no time should the person preferring aloneness be presumed lonely.

To illustrate the felt need for combating loneliness, society has come forth with various forms of group-oriented means of surviving it. For the individual seeking to ward off the horrors of loneliness through affiliation, there are countless public service groups. To those preferring an escape from the familiar surroundings which perpetuate feelings of loneliness, there are group activities such as ski trips, cruises, fishing, hiking, orgies, and sightseeing. Finally, there are groups employing the introspective approach. By interacting with others, they believe that a deeper and more meaningful understanding can be had of the self and its relationship to loneliness.

[1] *Long Island Press* (Jamaica, New York), October 21, 1973, Sec. 5, p. 46.

Of particular relevance is finding ways and means of enabling the lonely person to survive in a group. Of all the possible solutions, the following seems most workable: In every group, a concerted effort should be made by each of its members to interest himself in the interests of others. We all have a tendency to talk about that which interests us most. This predisposition also applies to listening habits; we listen best to that which interests us most. Consequently, if the human need for communication is as crucial to dispelling loneliness, as it appears to be, we must learn to share the process of living. The loneliness of one member of any group is the responsibility of *all* of its members.

Survival means different things to different people. To some it means getting through a small-group discussion without attracting any attention, remaining anonymous. Others construe survival to mean an ability to cope with "fighting words" from other members of the group. Regardless of individual interpretations, it all comes down to a lessening of any threatening situation and a heightening of one's sense of security. Together, they hopefully provide a viable means of self-defense—a means of surviving in the company of others.

As the title of this chapter suggests, it contains information geared to help those disenchanted with either how they feel or how they act in small groups. They might feel absolutely petrified and unable to utter a sound, or, conversely, feel alienated because of an outspoken or overbearing personality. Actually, it makes little difference what label we put on such reactions; the important thing is: *what can be done about it?* Is there a remedy? In the most fundamental sense, what we've all experienced in a small group is one or a combination of the following responses:

1. I like you and your ideas.
2. I like you, but I do not like your ideas.
3. I do not like you, but I like your ideas.
4. I do not like you and I do not like your ideas.[2]

Having psychologically registered a response, one has the option of either translating it into motor behavior or simply storing it as a guideline for future behavior.

What responses will one evoke from others? In this regard we might roughly divide the world's people into three categories: (1) those who would like you under any circumstances, (2) those who wouldn't like you under any circumstances, (3) those who couldn't care less about you one

[2] Elwood Murray, Gerald M. Phillips, and J. David Truby, *Speech: Science-Art* (New York: Bobbs-Merrill, 1969), p. 28.

way or the other. It is naive for any of us to believe that he will be liked by everyone.

"The human organism seems capable of enduring anything in the universe except a clear, complete, fully conscious view of himself as he actually is." How much stock would you put in such an opinion? Whom do you think would be better off in a small group, someone who is not too bright, dresses sloppily, has an unattractive physique, and is a lousy athlete but who behaves as if he possessed none of these traits, or a person who possesses all these traits and behaves realistically in relation to them? Although common sense warrants a bias in the direction of the latter, this question should strike up some lively controversy in a group discussion. Every person enters a group with either a private self-image or one conferred upon him by society. His survival may depend upon whether he subscribes to the idea that the more clearly we see ourselves as others see us, the more effectively we are able to interact with others.

In column A, list three major characteristics with which you strongly identify yourself; in column B, list three major characteristics by which you think others identify you.

COLUMN A
(*how you see yourself*)

1. Example: Intelligent
2. *Emotional*
3. *shy*
4. *overweight*
   weak

COLUMN B
(*how you think others see you*)

1. Example: Average intelligence
2. *logical*
3. *aggressive*
4. *average weight*
   strong

To determine the extent to which your self-image corresponds with the view others have of you, it might be worthwhile having several of the items listed above read aloud in class. Communicologists and psychologists alike seem to share the opinion that survival, both personal and public, draws considerable support from one's self-image.

Since personality traits are portable, the "whole you" is available to others at all social functions. Thus, the more insight you have into yourself, the better your chances of survival in the small group. Bear in mind, however, that the chemistry responsible for human behavior is far from pure science. At best, we grasp at straws and, if we are fortunate, we stumble upon an occasional signpost. Here is one such marker: "The more closely an individual conforms to the norms of the group the more liked

liberal   *conservative*
not very religious   *religious*
impatient   *patient*
athletic   *not athletic*

he will be . . . the more he ignores and dislikes the group's standards of behavior the more disliked he will be."[3]

VALUE SYSTEMS AND THE SMALL GROUP

Wherever we go, our search for people with similar attitudes, values, and beliefs continues. Life experience seems to confirm the belief that we are attracted to people who contribute to, rather than detract from, our self-esteem. If someone makes you feel good inside, you are both intellectually and emotionally drawn toward him. If, conversely, the displeasure of his company causes you to feel upset, you will probably avoid him. Therefore, in the last analysis, casting aside man's physiologically shared needs (food, shelter, and so on), it is his values that largely determine the nature of his interpersonal relationships. "Tell me with whom you go and I'll tell you who you are." While this is, indeed, a trite, sweeping generalization, it seems a fairly reliable one. Countless organizations as well as personal relationships are founded on the basis of people's having similar interests.

Whenever people congregate, values are exchanged. The next time you have the opportunity to be part of a strange group, spend the first ten or fifteen minutes "listening hard." It won't be long before someone leads off with a value or two. According to Spranger, people can be divided into six primary types according to the values they hold. Realizing that people hold more than one value simultaneously, Spranger felt that one particular value system, more often than not, characterized an individual. In this connection, he proposed the following primary value types:

> *Theoretical Type*—Values the pursuit of and discovery of truth, the "intellectual" life.
> *Economic Type*—Values that which is useful, practical.
> *Aesthetic Type*—Values form, harmony, and beauty.
> *Social Type*—Values love, sympathy, warmth, and sensitivity in relationships with people.
> *Political Type*—Values competition, influence, and personal power.
> *Religious Type*—Values unity, wholeness, and a sense of purpose above man.[4]

This classification should by no means be taken as gospel. It may, however, serve as an example of how people, through some kind of natural

[3] Gerald M. Phillips and Eugene C. Erickson, *Interpersonal Dynamics in the Small Group* (New York: Random House, 1970), pp. 34–35.
[4] Eduard Spranger, *Types of Man*, trans. P. Prigors from the fifth German edition (Halle: M. Niemeyer, 1928).

selection, group themselves on the basis of their values. Imagine picking at random two dozen individuals representing each of Spranger's types and placing them in a room with sandwiches and drinks. They should have assimilated themselves into groups according to their assigned types within an hour. In two hours, even more homogeneous assimilation should have taken place. People who give cocktail parties count on this process of searching and sorting. If you have ever attended one, you must have noticed that, while circulating around the room, clusters of people with similar interests have found each other; scholar finds scholar, salesman finds salesman, pervert finds pervert, and so on.

Grant, for a moment, that how a person thinks and feels about such things as love, marriage, government, education, and morality could affect his social life. Moving into a small-group setting, imagine yourself an ardent opera buff seated next to a gentleman who, in the course of conversation, has just expressed his dislike for not only classical music but opera as well. Instinctively, you reject not only his clodlike notions about classical music and opera but the individual as well. Few of us are disciplined enough to separate what a person says from what he is. It seems far more expedient to "throw the baby out with the bath water," so to speak; and the more emotionally committed you are to a belief, the less inclined you are to discuss it rationally.

The mainspring of any individual's personality is firmly moored to his values. To be ignorant of them is to deprive yourself of a distinct advantage in any group situation. Anytime you discover yourself sitting among people whose values are entirely unknown to you, your survival in that particular situation has the potential of suffering significant depreciation. Furthermore, the longer you remain ignorant of their values, the more precarious your situation will become. The reason for such a state of affairs derives from the fact that communication within a group, or any group for that matter, rests more upon *why people say what they do* than *what they actually say*. An ethnic slur, for example, can be taken several ways, depending not only upon the values of the person making the remark but upon those of the listener as well. For this reason film makers, and those who import and export films, are very careful in dubbing dialogues. Values crossing cultural lines may be offensive in their new setting, and what seems to be a minor error in judgment can in fact be extremely costly.

The majority of people who engage in small-group discussions are inclined to be more self-centered than group-centered. The tendency is to be more concerned with the survival of the individual than of the group. This raises an important question you should ask yourself right now: "To what extent do I really care about the group as compared with myself?" Most people indicate that it would depend upon the individual circumstances. In some situations they would behave in a self-centered manner, in others on behalf of the group. As acceptable as this response might be, there is an inclination for most people to behave in a less situational fashion and more stereotypically—self-centered types behaving selfishly nine out of ten times, and group-centered types usually serving the group. Most people are more predictable than they are willing to admit, and their value systems are usually responsible for it.

Regardless of whether you are interested in your own survival or that of the group, it is your responsibility to familiarize yourself not only with your own values but also with those of every other member of the group. *Question:* "How do I discover what other people's values are?" One does so in one or more of three ways: (1) by researching the individual in terms of reputation, publication, and affiliation, (2) by asking direct or indirect questions, (3) by listening carefully while he is in communication with others. It should be stressed that these techniques require considerable practice, as do most art forms. Effectively worded probes and prods grow out of a skill not developed overnight, so don't be too disappointed if, at first, you bungle a few. Your objective should be the harvesting of other people's values. It might be a good idea, however, to start with your own.

CHARACTERS FOUND IN A SMALL GROUP

The types of people to be described are not indigenous to certain groups but to all groups—family, school, and social. Since the reader has been introduced (in Chapter 7) to the dangers of stereotyping, he should be able to consider these types without trying to fit people into them too tightly. Little or no effort will be made to explain why the characters mentioned behave as they do. The focus will be on a general philosophy of dealing with these people in terms of your survival.

POLICEMAN

This is the type of individual who, without the benefit of vote or appointment, presumes to act as a sergeant-at-arms. Rarely does he contribute any substantive material to the group; rather, his sole function seems to be the preservation of law and order within it—law and order as seen through his eyes, of course. You might recognize him by a remark like, "All right now, let's keep it down and give Danya a chance to get a word in edgewise." If performed discreetly, which is a rare occurrence, this role can be an asset rather than a liability to the group.

PLAYBOY OR PLAYGIRL

People of this ilk feel that unless they "fool around," they serve no useful purpose. They are often convinced that everyone else is genuinely interested in their shenanigans and seem taken aback when told to "shut up!" Although, at times, their conduct can be said to reduce group tension, more often it produces tension by blocking constructive communications. For whatever psychological reasons the PLAYBOY or PLAYGIRL behaves as he does, it is incumbent upon the group to decide whether such conduct should be tolerated or put down. It is important to remember, however, that these may not be malicious people but simply outsiders trying to survive in the small group as best they can. You will recognize this type by a remark such as: "Hey, that reminds me of the story about the three drunken polar bears floating down the river on a marble slab." (At best, an inane attention-getter.)

GATEKEEPER

This individual, also by his own authority, makes decisions as to what is or is not admissible to the discussion at hand. If a group member should attempt to introduce a subject or another dimension of a subject under discussion which the GATEKEEPER feels is irrelevant or immaterial, he will simply take it upon himself to label such a remark as inadmissible. Depending greatly upon the composition of the group, this person may or may not be tolerated. A great deal depends upon how such a role is enacted. If excessively intrusive, it can quickly become obnoxious. You will recognize this type by a remark such as: "Whoa, wait a second! We're talking about apples and Donald is talking about pears!"

BLOCKER

As the name suggests, this individual interferes with any forward movement in discussion. An expert at *communicatus interruptus*, the blocker is dedicated to the task of preventing people from completing their thoughts or developing their ideas. Like the PLAYBOY, POLICEMAN, and GATEKEEPER, this character also contributes little or nothing to the discussion. The BLOCKER appears to be concerned with only one aspect of the group situation; if his performance in relation to it satisfies his psychological needs, he seems content. Almost without fail, the BLOCKER finds whatever other people say either irrelevant or immaterial.

MARTYR

If you haven't seen a MARTYR in action, you're missing a treat. He is the professional victim who is forever acting out the role of the injured party: "No, please don't interrupt your conversation because of me. I'll be O.K.—I'm fine just sitting here listening to you all having a good time." Naturally, if no one snaps at the bait, this role fails miserably. The MARTYR thrives on other people's "caring" how he feels or what happens to him.

THE CONTRARIES

Certain people, no matter what you say to them, say just the opposite. If you say, "My, it sure is a lovely day," they parry with: "Not really, it was much nicer yesterday." The ritual goes on and on—you say up, they say down, you say terrific, they say lousy. Not only are such people impossible to talk to, they contaminate entire groups with their contrariness.

RECORDER

A RECORDER is someone with a compulsion for jotting things down. At the slightest provocation, he whips out a notebook and a pen and away he goes. Whereas the procedure serves a larger good in most instances, it does at times interfere with a smooth flow of conversation by causing the group to wait for the RECORDER to do his thing. The making of repeated notations can, if overdone, have a disruptive effect.

QUALIFIER

Supplying a group with unsolicited commentaries on what other people have said is the stock in trade of the QUALIFIER. If you had just made some remark about mutiny on the high seas, the QUALIFIER would probably chime in with, "What Sylvia or George really means to say is . . . ." After a while, the person having to bear the brunt of these unwelcome remarks begins to feel like a ventriloquist's dummy having words put into her mouth.

ORACLE

Conventionally defined, the ORACLE is someone believing himself to possess a "direct line" to God. Professing to know everything, he is forever handing down decisions and judgments on matters large and small, invited and uninvited. An ORACLE seldom posits an idea of his own which might be subject to criticism by the group. His role, as he conceives it, is to pontificate like a ruler over affairs of state.

INFORMATION GIVER

Suffering from what is called "logorrhea," the INFORMATION GIVER has a compulsion to disseminate information. "Did you know . . ." are the lead words presaging his performances. Totally uninterested in conversational continuity, he rarely misses an opportunity to sneak in a "Did you know . . ." and its train of unasked-for enlightenment.

HISTORIAN

"I remember when a hot dog was a nickel and a newspaper only 2 cents." Nostalgia like this immediately identifies the HISTORIAN in a group, especially if references to the past are repeated several times. Unwilling to turn loose the past and what used to be, he continually rehearses events that are long since dead and gone. The moment a current event is raised, the HISTORIAN almost invariably counters with an item from yesteryear having little or nothing to do with the conversation at hand.

PROPHET

Occasionally a group will be graced not only with a HISTORIAN but with a PROPHET as well. The PROPHET is preoccupied with things to come. His rhetoric might include such pronouncements as, "Twenty years from now, we'll all be under water," or "In the year 2500 A.D. the institution of marriage will be obsolete." These prognostications are usually based, not on evidence, but on intuition or freewheeling inferences. Like the HISTORIAN, the PROPHET also relates poorly to the "here and now."

"ACCORDING TO" FREAK

Few things are more disconcerting in a small group than having to put up with this type of individual. Every chance he gets, the "ACCORDING TO" FREAK spouts off using borrowed words and ideas from others. To make matters worse, he comes to believe that what he has plagiarized was rightfully his in the first place. Although his contributions to the group are certainly not worthless, they do deny people the first-person immediacy the group thrives on.

SITUATIONIST

It is extremely difficult to have an interesting discussion without generalizing; frankly, those based exclusively upon fact are generally a bore. Precise fact, nonetheless, is what the SITUATIONIST demands. Every time someone makes a general statement, such as "Latin people are hot-blooded and are good lovers," the SITUATIONIST retaliates with "Oh, come on now, that depends upon many other factors—diet, geography, genes, etc." Although *everything* man knows *depends upon something else*, he persists in rejecting any statement not based upon verifiable evidence.

Most of the natural phenomena that surround us defy a completely satisfactory explanation or definition. Consequently, assumptions, inferences, presumptions, and generalizations help implement a free flow of information between members of society. The SITUATIONIST insists that we document everything we say. This, obviously, seriously limits interpersonal communication. Thought sequences are continually blocked; even the most innocent generalization may collide with demands for justification.

OPTIMIST or PESSIMIST

The OPTIMIST sees his world as a bowl of cherries, the PESSIMIST, as a bowl of . . . ! While those around him grunt, groan, and moan, the OPTIMIST whistles a happy tune. The PESSIMIST, regardless of impeccable evidence to the contrary, has mastered the *power of negative thinking*. Granted we all from time to time lean in either the optimistic or pessimistic direction, the leaning becomes serious when it interferes with our judgment.

If you should encounter one of these types in a group, avoid trying to browbeat him into believing whatever it is that you consider to be realistic or rational. Instead, try to get at why he believes as he does. After all, it takes many years to build up such psychological armor and it is folly for you to expect to straighten him out in a matter of ten minutes. It may also be that his attitude is completely justified.

MANNEQUIN

The MANNEQUIN is someone who, while physically present, makes no verbal contribution. On the basis of what you have learned in Chapter 5, you realize that not talking does not preclude the making of nonverbal contributions. Carefully watched, these people will be observed to provide some very definite kinesic feedback in relation to whatever is said in the discussion. It might take the form of a raised eyebrow, a Mona Lisa smile, arms folded across the chest, or a loss of eye-contact. All of these nonverbal messages should be considered bona fide currency in any discussion.

Unfortunately, our culture is still somewhat reluctant to accept non-verbal communication as legitimate exchange. As things now stand, people who do not make verbal contributions to a small group are labeled anti-social, shy, unintelligent, screwed up psychologically, or just plain quiet. By remaining silent, they are able to survive. Would you personally force them to surrender their silence? How sure can you be that getting them to "talk" would be better for them? Talking for some people is a very risky business. In these special cases, perhaps the MANNEQUIN had best be left alone.

DISTRICT ATTORNEY (D.A.)

As the name suggests, this type of person delights in cross-examining other members of the group. At his own discretion, whenever someone makes a remark that fails to meet with his approval, he takes it upon himself to "grill" the person as if he were on a witness stand.

MIDDLEMAN

When friends or lovers have an argument, they occasionally stop talking to one another directly. Instead, they speak through a mutual or impartial friend. "Tell Beverly I never want to see her again." The person relaying this message is called the MIDDLEMAN. In a group, someone may nudge you and say, "Tell that moron he's full of crap," to which you reply. "Tell him yourself, big shot." The MIDDLEMAN is often called upon out of a fear of getting negative or adverse feedback and being unable to handle it.

GIGGLER

Unfortunately, many GIGGLERS are written off by groups as not being terribly bright. Often, however, giggling is a symptom of nervousness. Being difficult to control at times, it may aggravate other members of a group. If it gets too far out of control, the GIGGLER might be asked to leave. Notice that whatever sets a GIGGLER off is usually not funny in the popular sense. Proof of this is that the GIGGLER and perhaps his CO-GIGGLER are the only ones giggling. Everyone else is looking on in quasi-disgust.

CHANGE AGENT

The CHANGE AGENT is usually anxious to get you to do something. It might be to join an organization, vote a particular way, or take a course in scuba diving—and it always involves a change from what you have, want, or are doing to what he has, wants, or is doing.

LEADER

A LEADER is generally in charge of other people or of their instruction. The qualities of a LEADER or of LEADERSHIP are far too complicated to be even hinted at here. In looking at a group we should be able to identify the LEADER by such things as (1) where he is seated, (2) the way he is dressed, (3) the attitude of the group toward him—but not always. An individual, too, might be a LEADER type in one set of circumstances and a follower in another. To test some of your present notions, list below the *physical* and *psychological* characteristics you would assign to a LEADER:

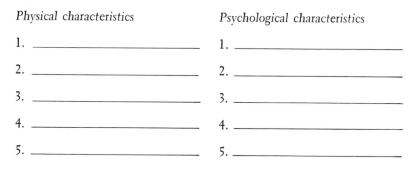

Physical characteristics

1. _____
2. _____
3. _____
4. _____
5. _____

Psychological characteristics

1. _____
2. _____
3. _____
4. _____
5. _____

HOW TO SURVIVE AMONG THEM

In the years to come, most of your life will be spent in the company of others, particularly if the population explosion continues at its present rate. Unless you become most efficient in coping with some of the skirmishes that are certain to occur, look forward to your share of embarrassment, insults, altercations, and an occasional fight. Naturally, a great deal will depend upon your temperament and upbringing.

Many of the people with whom you will have these encounters have just been described as characters found in small groups. Bear in mind that this is not a psychology text, and we will not attempt psychological explanations of their behavior. Nor should the rules for survival in a small group to be presented now be construed as either absolute or infallible. People are too complex to warrant such a presumption. Instead, take whatever you find appealing to your sensibilities, reject that which offends them, and hold in abeyance anything that might potentially be useful. In short, process the forthcoming survival rules through the neurological grid in your brain and arrive at whatever conclusions they precipitate. Then, in time, based upon future experience, modify your conclusions accordingly.

Survival Rule I

If you are of the opinion that "people change," it might be wise to back off a little and relabel such an opinion as *tentative*. Granting that, as a result of experience and psychological shifts in biochemistry, many people do manifest certain superficial changes over the years, rarely do such changes significantly involve the core of the SELF. If you don't believe this, recall meeting someone whom you haven't seen for years. After exchanging the usual clichés and platitudes over a cup of coffee or a gin and tonic, the telling remark is made: "You know something Mary, aside from looking a little older, you haven't changed a bit. You're still the Mary I remember."

Thus, SURVIVAL RULE I recommends you sacrifice the illusion that people, in the deeper sense, change. Be wary of the people you clash with in a small group who, after an apology, promise to behave differently next time. With both reverence and due respect for people's good intentions, they are seldom fulfilled. What you must do under the circumstances is accept people as you find them and figure out the best method of dealing with them. *Relate to others as they are, not as you would like them to be.*

Survival Rule II

If you should be confronted by an obnoxious BLOCKER in a group setting, try to avoid getting into a one-to-one feud with him. What usually happens when two members of a group clash is that the rest of the group merely looks on and does absolutely nothing; "It's not my problem; why should I get involved? Let the two of them fight it out." The superior strategy, if it can be done, is to rally the entire group to your cause. Attempt to get across the idea that when a breakdown in communication occurs between two members of a group, the entire group should share the responsibility. If you're lucky, one or two other people will sense their ethical or moral obligations and align themselves with your cause.

Unlike the street-corner scene in which someone witnessing an innocent person being attacked refrains from intervening for fear of his own personal safety, sitting face-to-face in a group seems to present a somewhat different claim on one's allegiance. If there is a leader in the group, and he is capable, enlisting his help can also strengthen your position in relation to a BLOCKER. Generally speaking, once a BLOCKER comes to realize that his attacks upon you soon graduate into attacks upon the whole group, the probability is high that he will soon cease and desist from such aggressive behavior toward you. REPEAT: In situations like this, *think group, not self.*

Survival Rule III

When feeling insecure in a group, your best ally is a good question. There are times when you find yourself sitting among people engaged in a lively discussion and, for some reason, you are reluctant to "jump in." Perhaps one of the members of the group intimidates you with his tone of voice or the way he looks. Whatever it is, you sit there in conversational range not saying a solitary word. Here's what you might try doing:

Listen carefully to the people whom you consider to be the center of attraction. Concentrate on the subject in which these people excel and, when the next lull in the conversation arises (you must be ready or it will quickly pass you by), ask one of them a direct question (not too wordy). Then, wait patiently for an answer. If the answer is another question back to you, simply indicate that you have wondered about the answer to that very same question for years and have never been able to get a satisfactory answer. If people and group discussions run true to form, someone with a slightly inflated ego will snap at the bait and attempt to supply you with the answer you claim to be seeking. The important thing to remember is that this survival rule, if properly used, will keep you out of jeopardy. To wit, when in doubt—ASK A QUESTION rather than make a statement. A good idea would be to practice various ways of asking questions so that you don't appear too obvious when you do it. Here are some suggestions:

1. Is it really true that . . . ?
2. Why is it that whenever I . . . ?
3. Someone once told me that . . . . Is that really possible?
4. I once read in an encyclopedia that . . . .
5. In one of my classes, the teacher said . . . .
6. Could someone please tell me why . . . .

Questions are less likely than statements to "get people's backs up." Remarks that begin with *I think, I believe,* or *In my opinion* seem to certain individuals to represent a challenge—or are more readily construed to be. If you soften your opinion by couching it in question form, the adrenalin level in the other fellow's bloodstream is not as apt to soar. DANGER: A false sense of security may be had by using the questioning format and betraying the wrong message by your tone of voice or facial expression. Monitor them as well as *what* you say.

Survival Rule IV

All the characters previously cited, if they are to continue in their roles, require a specific kind of feedback. For example, if one of the CONTRARIES fails to get a desired response from a member of the group, his effectiveness depreciates rapidly. If the PLAYBOY is unsuccessful in eliciting laughter and attention from others, he soon becomes rhetorically impotent. The MARTYR is similarly robbed of his effectiveness when nobody feels sorry for him. This survival rule, then, stresses not what you do but what you don't do. By not giving a MARTYR or any other troublesome character in a group the feedback necessary for his psychological purpose, you render him ineffectual. Now go back over the list of characters; see if you can put your finger on exactly what makes each of them tick. Then imagine what would happen if that ingredient were missing in a group situation.

Be observant the next time you are in a group of any kind. Try to determine what each member of the group needs in order to survive. You might even want to try your hand at manipulating that need to see what happens.

Survival Rule V

If you will extend at least partial credence to the adage, "Nothing succeeds like success," this survival rule will appeal to you. Single out a member of your group who, on the basis of performance, is clearly a winner. Then declare yourself in agreement with him. If, during the course of conversation, he ventures an opinion, on any subject—make sure that your view coincides with his. If it should conflict with your personal values, it may be necessary for you to temporarily swallow your opinion for survival's sake.

If you require even more "group insurance," it will be advantageous to align yourself with still other strong members of the group. The main thing when opting this means of survival is to be sure that you are in the right camp. It is not unlike riding the back of a winner at the crap tables in Las Vegas, Nevada. Apply the same psychology here and get on the back of a winner.

By the way, one other alternative exists. If behaving in such an opportunistic manner goes against your sense of ethics, you may just want to pick yourself up and leave. Bear in mind, however, that if you do, you are trading personal survival for survival in the small group—a decision that will have to depend upon which is more important to you.

The Survival Value of Knowing Your Own Place

Look at Figs. 9–2 and 9–3. If you had your choice in each of these seating arrangements, which seat would you choose? Try and make your selections correspond to real life. The words "your place," as you can see, do not refer to a rank or position but to a geographic location you would occupy in relation to others. As already pointed out in Chapter 5, where you sit, stand, or lie could have a significant effect upon any associated interpersonal or intrapersonal communication.

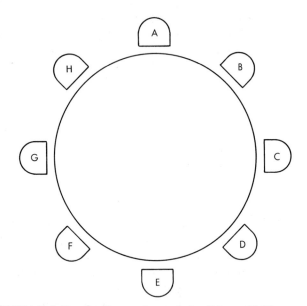

FIGURE 9–2 Family Group Around the Dinner Table.

According to Ball,[5] "Irrespective of any other situational properties, all face-to-face encounters take place within an intimate spatial context—a microecological environment within which interactants are territorially located; spatially defined vis-à-vis one another as their interdepartment outcomes, evaluations, and experiences are geometrically anchored." Knapp[6] believes that where you sit is not generally accidental or random, an opinion strongly supported by this writer. Because the greater part of human behavior is patterned, our territorial preferences appear to follow suit.

Let us chat for a minute about seating behavior in the family group at mealtimes. Would it be safe to assume that you usually sit in the same place day after day? Would it be safe to further assume that if another member of your family were to sit in your chair, it would disturb you? The degree, of course, would depend upon your temperament and relationship with the trespasser. Whereas the seating arrangement around the dinner table is generally arbitrary, and follows no conventional idiom, there are one or two determinants that dictate "your place." For example, the person serving the meal (usually the mother) occupies a chair convenient to the kitchen so that she can move in and out and not disturb

[5] Donald W. Ball, *Microecology: Social Situations and Intimate Space* (New York: Bobbs-Merrill, 1973), p. 3.
[6] Mark Knapp, *Nonverbal Communication in Human Interaction* (New York: Holt, Rinehart and Winston, 1972), p. 46.

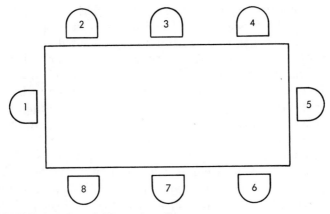

FIGURE 9–3 Social Group in a Restaurant.

the rest of the family. Another determinant pertains to the individual carving the meat (usually the father), who must be in a strategic position so that he can dish out the food and pass the plates without too much difficulty and, parenthetically, avoid being separated from any of his fingers. Beyond these mechanical factors, seating places remain pretty much a matter of psychological whim on the part of the person in charge. Can you think of some reasons other than those already mentioned why certain people sit in particular places at the dinner table?

1. _____

2. _____

3. _____

4. _____

A round table provides everyone with the greatest sense of personal security and survival. The fact that each member can engage every other member in eye-contact neutralizes positions of strength and weakness. To learn more about people's attitudes toward sitting at a round table, Sommer[7] conducted studies which revealed that people whose purpose was to cooperate tended to sit in adjacent chairs, whereas those in competition with one another selected opposite seating. It is reminiscent of the father who wants his favorite son or daughter seated at his immediate right, with the black sheep of the family further removed from his "personal bubble."

[7] Robert Sommer, "Further studies of small group ecology," *Sociometry* 28 (1965), 337–48.

(For those who have forgotten, the personal bubble is an imaginary sphere surrounding each of us and into which only certain people are invited.)

Unlike the rectangular table soon to be discussed, the round table makes escape from threatening eye-contact virtually impossible. No matter where you sit, someone whom you would rather not look at remains constantly in view. Even sitting a seat or two away from such an individual at a round table does not seem as distant as when sitting at a rectangular table. In the round, people just seem to have a greater sense of *psychological oneness*.

Now examine Fig. 9–3, depicting a social group in a restaurant around a rectangular table. Which position do you think a person who likes to talk and who is a leader-type would choose? Hare and Bales[8] observed that a person like this usually chooses positions 1, 3, or 5. In contrast, people who are less dominant and more retiring tend to choose positions 2 and 4. These observations, like so many others of their kind, are not infallible and are subject to a variety of modifying agents, such as moods, medication, alcohol, and overcrowding. Mehrabian's "immediacy principle" provides us with an excellent basis for evaluating the proxemic choices people make in small groups. It states: "People are drawn toward persons and things they like, evaluate highly, and prefer; and they avoid or move away from things they dislike, evaluate negatively, or do not prefer."[9] Operating in every small group, the "immediacy principle" motivates practically all of us in one direction or another. Like the amoeba, we move toward that which serves our survival and away from that which threatens it.

Anyone who has ever had the responsibility of preparing the seating arrangements for a wedding, sweet sixteen party, bar mitzvah, or some other social function knows only too well the hysteria that goes with deciding who should be seated next to whom. The dialogue goes something like this: "Let's see, Bob is rather quiet and Claire never stops talking—we'll put them next to each other; Gertrude is 26 and still looking for a husband and Jack is a bachelor—another natural pair; as for the older folks past 40—we'll put them all together at one table so they can talk about how great things used to be and how terrible they are now."

After a social evening at the movies, theatre, or concert hall, a suggestion is made to go out and get a bite to eat. Entering a restaurant or diner, the problem of seating comes up. If the crowd is too large for one table, a couple of tables must be pulled together. Then, who sits where? Cook[10] collected some data reflected in Figs. 9–4 and 9–5.

8 A. Hare and R. Bales, "Seating position and small group interaction," *Sociometry* 26 (1963), 480–86.
9 Albert Mehrabian, *Silent Messages* (Belmont, Calif.: Wadsworth, 1971), p. 1.
10 M. Cook, "Experiments on orientation and proxemics," *Human Relations* 23 (1970), 61–76.

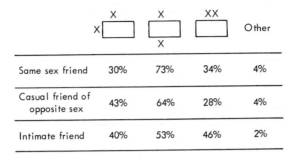

	X	X	XX	
	X [ ]	[ ]	[ ]	Other
		X		
Same sex friend	30%	73%	34%	4%
Casual friend of opposite sex	43%	64%	28%	4%
Intimate friend	40%	53%	46%	2%

FIGURE 9–4 Seating Preferences in a Restaurant.

As you have already deduced from these diagrams, restaurant seating involving couples seems to favor opposite placements regardless of sex. However, more intimate friends tend to prefer side-by-side seating because it seems to lend itself to more effective nonverbal communication at the expense of verbal communication. If further speculation is allowed, where members of a dyad (two people) sit in relation to each other in a restaurant certainly appears to be guided by their intent. If they are hungry and eating is their immediate goal, opposite seating prevents them from poking each other in the ribs while wielding a knife and fork. If romance is what they hunger for, side-by-side seating may be their microecological or proxemic choice. If, however, during the meal they chance to have an argument, an instantaneous change in seating arrangement may be witnessed. No matter how you evaluate the role seating behavior plays in human communication, there is persuasive evidence to indicate that the positions people assume in relation to one another in a group either positively or negatively influence their personal survival.

Figure 9–6 presents a classroom situation. Study the diagram and place an "X" on the spot you usually occupy if you have a choice. Allow, of course, for those seating circumstances over which you have no control. Ask yourself whether you are a *front, back,* or *side* of the roomer. Next,

	X	XX	X	
	[ ]	[ ]	[ ]	
	X		X	
Two males	6%	0%	0%	
Two females	6%	0%	1%	
Male with female	36%	7%	1%	
Total	48%	7%	2%	

FIGURE 9–5 Observations of Seating Behavior in a Restaurant.

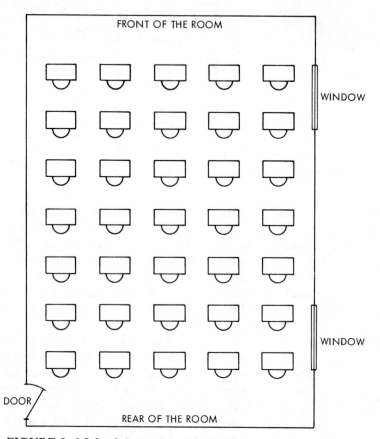

FIGURE 9–6 School Group in a Classroom.

ask yourself why you seem to end up in a particular part or sector of most of the classrooms you have been in since kindergarten.

Before we discuss what one study revealed with regard to classroom seating, here is an opportunity to venture a few guesstimates of your own. Figure 9–7 is a diagram of a classroom. Imagine rows of seats and the instructor at the front of the room. Using percentages, enter the amounts of participation you think would normally come from each sector of the room.

Now compare your judgments with those arrived at by Sommer in Fig. 9–8.[11]

Herbert Kohl,[12] in his studies of student life in ghetto schools, dis-

---

[11] Robert Sommer, *Personal Space* (Englewood Cliffs, N.J.: Prentice-Hall, Inc., 1969), p. 118.
[12] Herbert Kohl, *Children* (New York: New American Library, 1967), p. 13.

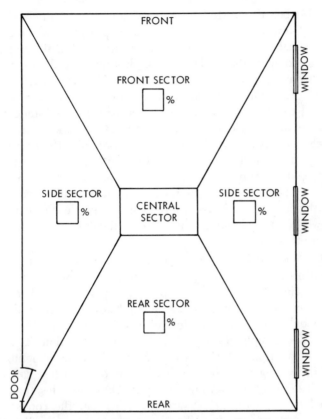

FIGURE 9–7 Ecology of Estimated Classroom Participation.

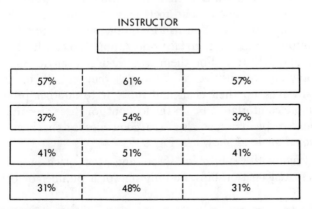

FIGURE 9–8 Ecology of Participation in a Straight-Row Classroom.

covered that permitting students to move about freely in class and change seats at will was not disruptive. Instead, it provided the student with a sense of spatial freedom, allowing him to satisfy internal needs for adjustments and compensations. This author has introduced this concept into his classes on the college level with considerable success, referring to it as "the fluid classroom." At the beginning of each semester, students are encouraged to sit wherever they wish. On days when a student is feeling out of sorts and would rather not participate in class activities, he has the privilege of sitting in whichever seat affords him the greatest sense of psychological comfort and security. On days when he feels great and desires to plunge into the swing of things, he may choose a more active seat right up front. Students confessed that such mobility relieved tension both in themselves and in the entire class as a whole. Perceptive teachers, after a while, can gain insight into their students on the basis of when and where they sit.

Another microecological determinant capable of affecting your relationship with others in a small group is how you are physically oriented to them. Experiments by Mehrabian point out that "the 180-degree side-by-side position consistently produced *less affiliation*, whereas the 90-degree angle was only slightly less conducive to conversation than the face-to-face position. Very emphatically, the 180-degree orientation in conversation seems to be a 'crippler.' "[13] The classical movie scene depicting a teenage boy and girl sitting at opposite ends of a sofa on their first date epitomizes this 180-degree-angle conversation crippler. Only after this angle is reduced or altered by one's turning toward the other can the conversation even begin to shows signs of life. What this means in plain words is that if you want to keep interpersonal relationships from getting off the ground in a small group, arrange the people in it so that as many as possible are sitting at 180-degree angles. If, on the other hand, you want to insure success, seat as many as you can about four feet apart and (as nearly as possible) squarely facing each other. You will find, however, that certain individuals feel uncomfortable in a face-to-face orientation (especially those who are rather shy and retiring). For them, the 90-degree angle might be best. Some people are so sensitive to the angles they find themselves in that they literally pick up their chair and move it to another position where they feel more comfortable. Be on the lookout for these "furniture movers" at your next party. It might also be a good idea to check out your own conversational angle as shown in Fig. 9–9.

Before leaving the subject of space, and your place in it, we should note that spatial relationships are only one of a number of determinants

---

[13] Albert Mehrabian and S. G. Diamond, "Seating arrangement and conversation," *Sociometry* 34 (1971), 281–89.

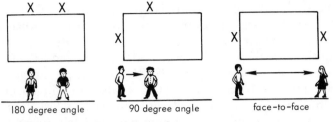

FIGURE 9–9 *What's Your Angle?*

capable of influencing the communicative process. Their importance will depend upon the specific context in which they occur.

TOO MANY, TOO FEW

Group size affects people differently. Some are intimidated by large groups; others find warmth and comfort in them. Aware of this, many leaders adjust the group's size according to the needs, nature, and goals of its members.

A college sophomore found herself unable to participate in large-group discussions. The teacher, intuiting her dilemma, paired her with one other student to discuss the assigned topic of the day. She had no difficulty communicating with just one other person. The teacher then sent a third student to join them. She still engaged in an open and untroubled discussion. However, when another individual joined her group, she reverted back to her silent self. Apparently, the young lady was unable to cope with more than two people at one time. By contrast, there are those who become speechless when obliged to engage in a one-to-one conversation; they require the support of a larger group in order to communicate freely.

One cannot say which is better, a large or a small group. It naturally will depend upon many factors, such as the personalities of the individuals involved, the goal of the group, the location, the time, and so on. Students, for instance, have been known to select their classes on the basis of their projected or reputed size. Mass lectures scare the shoes off some while providing anonymity for others. Small classes, to certain students, means stark vulnerability which they just cannot handle. The majority of us are not chameleons able to adapt to any size group; we must, therefore, exercise a modicum of selectivity.

LISTENING: There's More to it Than Meets the Ear

Have you ever had the feeling while you were talking with someone that he wasn't listening? To test your suspicion, you generally ask him to repeat something you've said and are exasperated when he can do it verbatim. Was he really listening—or simply hearing and repeating what was said like a parrot or mynah bird?

A distinction should be made between HEARING and LISTENING if you are to survive in a small group. HEARING is the physiological process by which sounds are transmitted from your external environment to your brain; LISTENING is the psychological process by which these sounds are assigned meaning and organized into units of intelligible thought.

Large segments of a conversation can take place on a purely physiological (reflex) basis. Such transactions occur in families where words are exchanged and no one actually listens. Mothers have been known to insist that they told a child or husband something which the child or husband denies he ever heard. Teachers likewise have vowed that they covered certain material during the semester which the students all swear was never given.

Is it possible that more communication breakdowns are the result of faulty listening than of faulty talking? The Russells[14] may have been on the right track when they said, "Few people really listen to each other, primarily because they are self-centered or are intensely diverted by what they see."

Studies probing the amounts of time people spend listening, talking, and writing have yielded quite consistent findings. Enter your estimates below and compare them with the researchers' figures:

A. LISTENING _____

B. TALKING _____

C. READING _____

D. WRITING _____

	Rankin[15]	Bird[16]	Breiter[17]
1. LISTENING	45%	45%	48%
2. TALKING	30%	25%	35%
3. READING	16%	15%	10%
4. WRITING	9%	18%	7%

[14] David H. Russell and Elizabeth F. Russell, *Listening Aids through the Grades* (New York: Teacher's College Press, 1959), p. 46.
[15] P. T. Rankin, "The measurement of the ability to understand spoken language," *Dissertation Abstracts* 12 (1926), 847.
[16] Donald E. Bird, "Teaching listening comprehension," *Journal of Communication* 3 (1953), 127.
[17] L. Breiter, "Research in listening and its importance to literature," Unpublished master's thesis, Brooklyn, N.Y., 1957.

Something is wrong here. If these studies indicate (and they do) that people listen more than they talk, why are there so many communication breakdowns? Teachers in kindergarten and on through primary and secondary schools have repeatedly told us that if we paid attention, and listened well, everything would be all right. But everything is not all right with many of us in terms of communication. Perhaps the key lies in the difference between hearing and listening mentioned earlier—that we hear but do not listen. Here are some definitions of listening proposed by several learned scholars in the field. Again compare them with your own:

Place your own definition here:

_____

_____

_____

Their definitions:

A. An analysis of the impressions resulting from concentration where an effort of the will is required.[18]
B. The attachment of meaning to oral symbols.[19]
C. The ability to understand and respond effectively to oral communication.[20]
D. The process of relating the spoken language in terms of past experiences and future courses of study.[21]
E. When a human organism receives data aurally.[22]
F. Listening is a complex and unique function of perception and attention which involves both auditory and visual capacities of a listener.[23]

Superadded to these definitions is the following, which incorporates some of the concepts proposed by this text:

*LISTENING: A conscious or unconscious
process by which internal (intrapersonal)
and external (interpersonal) vocal stimuli
are translated into conscious*

[18] W. Tucker, "Science of listening," *19th Century*, 97 (April, 1925), 548–57.
[19] R. Nichols, "Factors accounting for differences in comprehension of materials presented orally in the classroom," unpublished doctoral dissertation, State University of Iowa, Iowa City, 1948.
[20] K. Johnson, "The effects of classroom teaching upon listening comprehension," *Journal of Communication* 1 (May, 1951), 57–62.
[21] W. Barbe and R. Meyers, "Developing listening ability in children," *Elementary English* 31 (February, 1954), 82–84.
[22] Carl H. Weaver, *Human Listening* (New York: Bobbs-Merrill, 1972), p. 5.
[23] John W. Keltner, *Interpersonal Speech-Communication* (Belmont, Calif.: Wadsworth, 1970), p. 130.

and unconscious verbal and nonverbal
responses ("nonverbal" includes changes in
blood pressure, muscle tension, heart rate,
and so on).

A colleague of this writer[24] once greeted him on his return from a summer vacation with, "Hi Ab, what's new (pause)—that would be of interest to me?" The question was followed by at least 20 seconds of dead silence. The thought of having to come up with something that would be of interest to him really gave me a jolt. Brimming over with succulent bits and pieces of interest to me, I could summon absolutely nothing to mind that would be of interest to him. It confirmed my belief that most of the things we are ready and willing to listen to are of interest to us, not others.

Reasons Why People Listen

1. To get information.
2. Because of an interest in the topic.
3. To increase one's understanding.
4. To be courteous.
5. To be ready to answer questions.
6. For enjoyment.
7. In self-defense.
8. To alleviate boredom.
9. To achieve a sense of belonging.
10. For profit (psychologist, counseling, and the like).
11. To compare opinions.
12. To be nosey (a "listening Tom").

Can you think of any other reasons why people listen?

A. _____

B. _____

C. _____

Few things are able to traumatize your ego as much as having people fail to listen while you talk. You feel like a fool. In that predicament, however, you have these alternatives: (1) stop talking; (2) tell the person to whom you are talking to pay attention; (3) ask, if in a group situation,

---

[24] Professor Marvin Gottlieb, Herbert H. Lehman College of the City University of New York.

the leader to intervene on your behalf; (4) continue talking for the benefit of those who are listening to you; (5) talk louder in the hopes that they will get the message; or (6) talk softly so as to make them strain to hear you (this seldom works). The possibility also exists that none of your efforts will succeed, so be prepared to accept complete rejection.

Research has turned up some rather interesting reasons why people don't listen—that is, *listening barriers*. See if you have ever locked horns with any of these phenomena:

Barriers to listening

1. The mind wanders.
2. Speaker talks too fast or too slow.
3. Disinterest in either the speaker or topic.
4. A closed mind (prejudice, bias, etc.).
5. Too much detail to follow.
6. Distractions (street noises, room temperature, uncomfortable seat, cigarette or cigar smoke, crowdedness, people walking in and out of the room).
7. No eye-contact.
8. Disorganized material.
9. Monotonous voice or gesturing.
10. Not intelligent enough to follow conversation or speech.
11. Emotionally immature.
12. Incoherent speech.

In the final analysis, more important than definitions of listening, why people listen or fail to listen is learning HOW TO LISTEN. Studies indicate that contrary to the belief that listening is an inborn trait that some people have and others lack—*it can be learned!* Many authorities are confident that anyone's listening skill can be improved if he is willing to put in the time and effort it requires. Here are a few of their sober recommendations:

Hints for better listening

1. Try to develop the desire to listen.
2. Become determined that you will find something in what the other fellow says that will interest you.
3. Become actively involved by asking for qualification when you are not perfectly clear on something that was said, or if you need additional explanation of a point.
4. Go into the listening situation physically and psychologically alert (not when you are either tired or emotionally upset).

5. Carefully observe the speaker's nonverbal behavior in relation to what he is saying.
6. Try to empathize with the speaker and his point of view.
7. Don't interrupt. Let him finish before taking issue with what he has said.
8. Listen well for main points being made.
9. Think about the topic beforehand.
10. Make a pronounced effort to conceal any negative nonverbal feedback you might be sending a speaker, such as an angry look, arms folded defiantly across your chest, drumming your fingers on the arm of your chair, dozing off.

Modest hopes of surviving in a small group demands that you bear in mind, "Speech is a joint game between the talker and the listener against the forces of confusion,"[25] and that while the physical barriers to communication have all but disappeared, the psychological barriers remain.[26] It is with the inner self that most of us must grapple. Only after we are able to comfortably listen to ourselves can we ever hope to listen comfortably to others. According to Barker,[27] most of us take the listening process for granted and are less effective listeners than we could be. Also embraced by this text is Barker's view that a failure to listen probably creates more interpersonal [and perhaps international] problems than any other aspect of human behavior.

SUMMARY

This chapter sought to provide the reader with a more candid view of small group life. It first described a serious and often subtle problem found among certain group members—"loneliness." Next, reasons for learning how to survive in the three basic life groups (family, school, social) were spelled out as crucial to contemporary living. Among the items stressed was the importance of discovering the values held by other members of the group. Next, a series of characters one is likely to meet in a small group was briefly described: policeman, playboy or playgirl, gatekeeper, blocker, martyr, the contraries, recorder, qualifier, oracle, information-giver, his-

[25] Norbert Weiner, *The Human Use of Human Beings* (Garden City, N.Y.: Doubleday, 1954).
[26] Daniel Katz, "Psychological barriers to communication," in *Mass Communication*, ed. Wilbur Schramm (Urbana: The University of Illinois Press, 1960), p. 316 (originally published in *Annals of the American Academy of Political and Social Sciences*, March 1947).
[27] Larry Barker, *Listening Behavior* (Englewood Cliffs, N.J.: Prentice-Hall, Inc., 1971), p. xi.

torian, prophet, according-to freak, situationist, optimist-pessimist, mannequin, district attorney (D.A.), middleman, giggler, change agent, and leader.

Five rules for survival were then proposed as means of coping with the more threatening of these characters. The advantages and disadvantages of various seating arrangements were analyzed. The significance of being in a larger or smaller group and the role played by listening brought the chapter to a close.

CHAPTER 10

CLASSROOM EXERCISES
IN LIVING
COMMUNICATION

INSIGHTS

After reading this chapter you should have a clearer understanding of:

- *how sorely theory suffers without some means of practical application.*

- *the various levels of communication you have engaged in all these years.*

- *why it might be a good idea to perform some of these classroom exercises more than once (for example, at the beginning and at the end of the term).*

- *how living communication virtually infiltrates every phase of your life through each of these exercises.*

- *why certain students will come much further out of their shells in an exercise than in routine classroom questioning.*

UNDERSTANDING

RATIONALE

Most students find theory boring unless they can see some immediate application and relevance for it. The question, thus, is reduced to one of "immediacy and relevance."

Observation suggests that while course content accounts for a good measure of a student's opinion of a class, more lasting impressions generally result from what happens in a class rather than what is said in it. "Happens" refers to nonverbal as well as verbal events—the teacher's actions, proxemic arrangement of the class, a subjective feeling that the teacher cares, a relaxed and unthreatening classroom environment, and so on. In short, while there are courses that enjoy great popularity among students because of what is said in them, the basis for their popularity may also be derived from some nonverbal phenomenon.

The majority of schools in this country are speaker-listener oriented. The teacher speaks—the student listens (and takes notes frantically). Learning theorists seem to agree that the greater the number of sense modalities (seeing, hearing, tasting, touching, and smelling) involved in a learning experience, the better the understanding and recall. These exercises have deliberately been designed to cause something "to happen" and, incidentally, spark the student's understanding and interest in living communication.

EXERCISE 1 What's in a Name?[1]

Purpose

To dramatize the ways in which students react to being artificially labeled.

Procedure

STEP 1

Teacher should buy as many small gum-backed labels (about an inch by a half-inch) as there are students in the class.

STEP 2

On each label type one of the following words:[2]

cheapskate	teacher's pet	mamma's boy
communist	ex-convict	hero
antisemite	trouble maker	genius
lover	hypochondriac	gossip
snob	neurotic	fool
masochist	sadist	belly dancer

STEP 3

Students should line up and each have the teacher affix a label (randomly selected) to his forehead.

[1] Abne M. Eisenberg and Ralph R. Smith, Jr., *Nonverbal Communication* (New York: Bobbs-Merrill, 1971), p. 110.
[2] Teachers and students are invited to make up their own labels for this exercise.

STEP 4

Students are then to mill about the room and interact freely and respond to each other on the basis of the label which appears on the forehead of each classmate. Permitted to use any means *other than talking*, they are to try to communicate to one another what is written on their label.

STEP 5

After a 10–15 minute TIME LIMIT, each student should return to his seat and jot down what he believes his own label reads. After removing the labels, the students form a circle to discuss what took place during the exercise.

Discussion

We all wear labels: body movements and gestures, clothes, the kind of books people see us carrying on buses and trains, the buttons and insignias on our jackets and jeans, the kind of friends we associate with. There are also the invisible labels worn on the inside and hidden from view. Taken together, they are responsible for most of our public and private behavior.

One of the questions the class should ask itself is whether any of its members resented the label he found himself wearing. If so, why? Did anyone impulsively remove the label before the proper time? Were any of the participants upset by the exercise and inclined to call it "stupid" and a waste of time? Explore this reaction. An excellent question which should be put to each member is, "If you were forced by law to wear a label on your forehead every day, what would you want it to say?" Explanations should accompany all responses. Would you vote for such a law? Wouldn't society be better off if its antisocial members could be recognized on sight as thieves, gunmen, rapists, con artists, child molesters, perverts, and so on? Justify your point of view. If honestly done, this exercise should expose many seldom-thought-about dimensions of the self.

EXERCISE 2   Reincarnating the Self

Purpose

To provide insight into both the student and the character chosen to be reincarnated.

Procedure

STEP 1

Students are to select a historical character whom they will reincarnate in a class discussion. The figure may be male or female, fictional or nonfictional, or even nonhuman. Male students may assume female characters and vice versa.

STEP 2

The lifestyle and philosophy of the chosen character should be researched —attitudes, values, beliefs, and so on. (Encyclopedias provide some excellent source materials.)

STEP 3

On the day the exercise is to be performed, students should come to class prepared to engage in discussion, the topic of which will be announced by the teacher. Costumes and props are to be encouraged.

STEP 4

Circular seating arrangement.

STEP 5

When all members of the class are seated, settled, and psychologically "tuned in" to the character they have reincarnated, the teacher should announce the discussion topic. Here are a few suggestions:

(a) Mercy killing
(b) Corporal and capital punishment
(c) Welfare assistance
(d) The weaker sex
(e) The proper way to raise children
(f) Cryonics (freezing after death)
(g) Transsexual surgery
(h) Licensing motherhood
(i) Compulsory education
(j) Psychological screening of college teachers
(k) Sterilization of the sociologically unfit

STEP 6

At a signal from the teacher, students are to begin the discussion as *though they were* the persons they have reincarnated.

Time Limit

Half of the period for the discussion, half for an analysis of what happened in the discussion.

Discussion

The most striking thing about this exercise is noticing which characters your classmates chose to reincarnate. Were they similar to or different from themselves? Did someone who was a leader type pick George Washington, Napoleon, Churchill, or Joan of Arc, or did he select a character diametrically opposed to his own personality? The discussants should concentrate on why they chose their characters, how they felt while impersonating them, and whether playing them provided an insight into either themselves or the person being reincarnated.

Another source of interest is the manifestation of nonverbal cues. Did the students whose kinesic personalities were sluggish choose characters who were kinesically hyperactive? An example of this happened in class one day when an extremely shy young woman entered the discussion as the famous actress Sarah Bernhardt. Her behavior literally bowled the entire class over. She was outspoken, vivacious, used flamboyant body movements and gestures, and commanded unquestionable authority. On another occasion, the sweetest and most lovable boy in the group arrogantly strolled in as the infamous Adolph Hitler, exterminator of six million human beings during World War II.

Since this exercise is capable of eliciting genuine class interest, it may be repeated more than once with the selection of an entirely new cluster of reincarnated selves.

EXERCISE 3   Who Are You?

Purpose

Psychotherapy probes the strata and substrata of a person's self-image. This exercise reveals, through his own admissions, various aspects of the participant's core-identity.

Procedure

STEP 1

Students pair off and sit facing each other.

STEP 2

Equipped with pencils and paper, students are to take turns asking each other the question, "Who are you?" ten times. Each time the question is asked, the answer is to be recorded verbatim. An effort should be made to ask the question in exactly the same way each time, leaving a 15-second interval between questions. For example: Who are you?—(pause)—Who are you?—(pause)—Who are you?

STEP 3

After all pairs of students have both asked and answered the question, the whole class should form a circle ready for discussion.

NOTE

The asking of the question "Who are you?" should not be alternated. First one student asks it ten consecutive times and records the answers given, then the other student does likewise.

Discussion

In this exercise the class should be on red alert for the student who moans, "This is stupid!" Such an individual, rather than being an aggravation to the class, will prove to be an asset. There are several reasons why certain students, from time to time, take exception to what the class or teacher says or does. Some have the psychological need to be recognized; others, a need to display their knowledge, right wrongs, help some misguided soul find his way, and so on. In their quest, however, they seldom support their protestations with any concrete evidence, but rather with sweeping generalizations. Note these statements if you will:

"*What's the point of all this psychological crap?*"
"*This is just one more of those stupid games they play in those dumb encounter groups.*"

"If there is anything I can't stand, it's a teacher who uses these silly games instead of teaching what he is supposed to, something worthwhile."

"I'm not paying all this money per credit to sit around asking some pimply-faced kid next to me who he is. I couldn't care less!"

Ironically, it is often the student who resists this exercise who stands to derive the most benefit from performing it.

Now look at the responses you made to the question. Aside from giving your name, did you identify yourself as a man or woman, male or female? If you failed to make such a distinction, ask yourself why. Did you qualify saying you were a man or woman by adding a *good* man or a *kind* woman? Did certain answers represent the individual as property, or extension of someone else (such as: my mother's son or daughter, Phillip's wife, or Cindy's husband)? Did some members of the class get bogged down after the question was asked five or six times and start repeating their answers? Why do you think this happened?

At the beginning of this book, an attempt was made to differentiate between WHO and WHAT a person is. Did such a confusion arise in this exercise? Did you answer the question, "Who are you?" by telling WHAT YOU ARE? Discuss the practical significance of making such a distinction. Also, consider whether answers to this question tend to vary with age. Ask it of your younger brother or sister, then of someone whom you hold in very high esteem (rabbi, priest, doctor, teacher, lawyer, guru). Close the discussion with some recommendations as to how you would change the name and purpose of this exercise.

A FINAL WARNING

This is a classroom exercise and should not masquerade as anything more.

EXERCISE 4   Diagnostic Quiz for Body Bigots

Purpose

To determine people's attitudes toward various parts of the human body in relation to their attitude toward the entire individual.

Procedure

Fill in the following blanks according to the introductory phrase, "IF THERE IS ANYTHING I CAN'T STAND, IT'S . . . ."

EXAMPLE

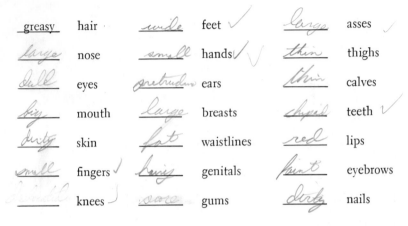

greasy	hair	_wide_	feet ✓	_large_	asses ✓
large	nose	_small_	hands ✓✓	_thin_	thighs
dull	eyes	_protruding_	ears	_thin_	calves
big	mouth	_large_	breasts	_chipped_	teeth ✓
dirty	skin	_fat_	waistlines	_red_	lips
small	fingers ✓	_hairy_	genitals	_faint_	eyebrows
_____	knees ✓	_sore_	gums	_dirty_	nails

Discussion

Attitudes toward the human body vary throughout the world. For instance, here are some of the ways modest women, in their baths, used to behave upon being surprised: the Mohammedan covered her face, the Laotian her breasts, the Chinese her feet, the Samoan her navel, and the Alaskan made haste to replace the ornamental plug she wore in her lip.[3]

Most "body bigots" do not realize that they are body bigots. They sense something wrong when they communicate with others, but they can't for the life of them find out what it is. This exercise may hold out a possible reason: perhaps it is their anatomical prejudices. For some yet unexplained reason, people whom we shall affectionately call "body bigots" reject others on the basis of one objectionable body part. Haven't you ever heard someone say, "I would never marry someone with hairy legs or a big nose." It would be interesting to learn if people who say these things actually carry them out.

After everyone has filled in the blank spaces of this quiz, look around the room for the students who themselves possess some of the traits they complained of. Take some time exploring this seeming contradiction if you discover it; ask why these body parts are considered offensive. Conclude your discussion by venturing some theories as to how attitudes toward our bodies, or its parts, can influence interpersonal communication. Give specific examples of what you mean.

[3] John Langdon-Davies, The Future of Nakedness (sometimes known as Lady Godiva: The Future of Nakedness) (New York: Harper & Row, 1928).

EXERCISE 5   Let's Stereotype!

Purpose

To expose the subliminal prejudices we harbor.

Procedure

Fill in the following blank spaces.

A. If it breaks five minutes after you bought it, it was probably made in

    _____ .

B. Male ballet dancers are usually _____ .

C. Most politicians are _____ .

D. Show me an Irishman and I'll show you a _____ .

E. Textbooks are usually _____ .

F. Jewish men make good _____ .

G. If he carries a knife, he's probably _____ .

H. Frenchmen make good _____ .

I. The sexier the girl, the better developed her _____ .

J. If he is Chinese, he probably owns a _____ .

    Since stereotypes are inclined to change with time, trend, and geographic location, here is an opportunity to construct some of your own. See if you can design them so that each one elicits essentially the same response from your classmates:

A. _____

B. _____

C. _____

D. _____

E. _____

F. _____

Discussion

The responses to this quiz should reveal whether the stereotypes elicited were flattering or derogatory. Compare the answers from various members of the class. How does the student think his parents would have answered them? Why does he think they would have answered that way? Were there any blanks not filled in? Why? Have the students draw up a list of their own and ask a neighboring student to complete it. Discuss what can be learned from knowing how people conceive and perceive others to be different from themselves. Voice some of these stereotypes as they appear in films, books, newspapers, and magazines (and textbooks). Would you vote for a bill making it legal for the mass media to stereotype people? Are you, or have you ever been, a victim of stereotyping? Explain.

EXERCISE 6 The Generation Gaps

Purpose

To detect the philosophical differences in the SELF of a parent, grandparent, and student.

Procedure

STEP 1

Below are three sets of sentences. Each is to be completed by a student, a parent, and a grandparent. If a grandparent is not available, a surrogate may be used.

STEP 2

None of the respondents should be allowed to see the answers given by the others.

STEP 3

All statements are to be completed *spontaneously*.

STUDENT

1. In order to be happy, you must _____ .

2. People who believe in God _____ .

3. A good education _____ .

4. Sex is something that _____ .

5. Good health _____ .

6. To have a really good time you must _____ .

7. People who do bad things _____ .

8. Cleanliness _____ .

9. Women without children _____ .

10. A good wife is one who _____ .

11. A good husband is one who _____ .

12. The best way to relax is to _____ .

PARENT (OR GUARDIAN)

1. In order to be happy you must _____ .

2. People who believe in God _____ .

3. A good education _____ .

4. Sex is something that _____ .

5. Good health _____ .

6. To really have a good time you must _____ .

7. People who do bad things _____ .

8. Cleanliness _____ .

9. Women without children _____ .

10. A good wife is one who _____ .

11. A good husband is one who _____ .

12. The best way to relax is to _____ .

GRANDPARENT

1. In order to be happy you must _____ .

2. People who believe in God _____ .

3. A good education _____ .

4. Sex is something that _____ .

5. Good health _____ .

6. To really have a good time you must _____ .

7. People who do bad things _____ .

8. Cleanliness _____ .

9. Women without children _____ .

10. A good wife is one who _____ .

11. A good husband is one who _____ .

12. The best way to relax is to _____ .

Discussion

The results growing out of this exercise almost invariably surprise the students. While they insist beforehand that they know how their parents and grandparents will complete these sentences, they are frequently fooled. One of the reasons might be that communication between most parents and their children is superficial. If the daily verbal exchanges between them were monitored, one would find the parent doing a great deal of "telling" and precious little "listening." After a while the child, too, ceases to listen. This may, in part, account for the superficiality of *intergenerational communication*.

One of the directions in which this discussion should take the class is toward the analysis of sentence completions by people from different ethnic backgrounds, cultural heritages,[4] and religious experiences. Do similar organisms think and behave similarly? The class should then speculate as to how such variance in sentence completion could be responsible for

---

[4] Reread *The Cultural SELF* in Chapter 2.

the "communication gap" people talk about. Would there be any gap if people completed these sentences in the same way?

Another consideration should be the speed with which the sentences were completed. If there was hesitation, on which sentences did it occur and why did it occur? Do you think you would communicate better with those people who completed the sentences the same way you did? Why? If any of the sentences presented a problem of interpretation, explore this also. Perhaps a particular word or phrase was semantically unclear. Occasionally a parent or grandparent is bilingual and has difficulty grasping the intended meaning. For this reason, these same sentences will now be presented in Spanish, French, and Italian.

To illustrate the consequences which may result from a linguistic misunderstanding, consider this episode. Several years ago at a psychiatric clinic, a Puerto Rican man was admitted for observation. He was examined by a non-Spanish-speaking psychiatrist and declared schizophrenic. A week later he was reexamined by a Spanish-speaking psychiatrist and found perfectly sane. Obviously, moving from language to language is not without serious risk under certain circumstances.

Here now are the same sentences in Spanish:

1. Para ser contento, Usted debe _____ .

2. La gente que cree en Dios _____ .

3. Una buena educación _____ .

4. El sexo es una cosa que _____ .

5. La buena salud _____ .

6. Para divertirse, Usted tiene que _____ .

7. La gente que hace las cosas malas _____ .

8. La limpieza _____ .

9. Las mujeres sin niños _____ .

10. Una buena mujer es una que _____ .

11. Un buen marido es un que _____ .

12. La mejor manera de relajer es _____ .

And in French:

1. Pour être content, vous devez _____ .

2. Ceux qui croient à Dieu _____ .

3. Une bonne éducation _____ .

4. Le sexe est quelque chose qui _____ .

5. La bonne santé _____ .

6. Pour s'amuser, il faut _____ .

7. Ceux qui font de mauvaises choses _____ .

8. La propreté _____ .

9. Les femmes sans enfants _____ .

10. Une bonne femme est celle qui _____ .

11. Un bon mari est celui qui _____ .

12. Le meilleur moyen de se reposer est _____ .

And finally in Italian:

1. Per essere contento, uno deve _____ .

2. Le persone che credono in Dio _____ .

3. Una buona educazione _____ .

4. Il sesso è una cosa che _____ .

5. Buona salute _____ .

6. Per divertisi, uno deve _____ .

7. Le persone che fanno brutte cose _____ .

8. Pulizia _____ .

9. Le donne senza figli _____ .

10. Una buona moglie è una che _____ .

11. Un buon marito è uno che _____ .

12. Il miglior modo per rilasciarsi è _____ .

If at all practical, the teacher should invite some of the students' parents and grandparents to class to discuss their responses to these completions.

Unfortunately, most discussions involving the "generation gaps" take place without the generations in question being present to speak for themselves.

EXERCISE 7   Retrograde Impressions of a Self

Purpose

To generate inferences about a person's past on the basis of current impressions.

Procedure

STEP 1

The teacher should reserve the right to be the first subject. If this right is waived, a student can be asked to volunteer to launch this exercise.

STEP 2

With a subject standing in front of the class, each member of the class should write his responses to the following five questions:

A. Describe the subject as a child.
B. Describe the subject's father and mother.
C. Describe the type of house the subject was born in.
D. Describe the subject's toys as a child.
E. What name do you think the subject should have been given at birth?

Discussion

For some mysterious reason, students frequently relate to their teachers as though they weren't human beings. Rarely do they think of them as having existed before the current semester unless they had them for a previous course. It is almost as if they sprang from nowhere and, voilà— instant teacher! While the student is intellectually aware that these same teachers are fathers, mothers, brothers, and sisters of real people in the outside world, he occasionally behaves as though he were dealing with androids. Naturally, this is an exaggeration, and only the student can testify to the extent of its validity. If nothing more, the exercise provides the teacher with a *past* as well as a *present*.

The discussion in Chapter 2 of the *Evolution of a SELF* suggested that it does not exist in a vacuum. Yesterday's Self must be considered part of today's Self. Some people, however, refuse to turn loose of the childhood Self in spite of their chronological age. You must have had someone approach you at a wedding, pinch you on the cheek, and say, "Aren't you Josie's little boy, or Marsha's little girl? I remember rocking you in your carriage." They behaved as though you were still that little child. This also brings to mind the adage, "No man is a prophet in his own home town." People who knew you when, seem reluctant to surrender that image of you.

The class should now discuss the degree to which public communication draws upon retrograde impressions of the Self. Do people communicate with you as you are, or the way they remember you? Think back on situations in which a conversation went awry because of an unwarranted or misguided inference. A pathetic example comes to mind of a man, accused of child molestation, who was arrested, tried, and found NOT GUILTY. Although he had been completely cleared of all charges, the people in his neighborhood continued to treat him, on a nonverbal basis, as though he were guilty (for example, they pulled in their children when he went past). How sad it must be to be shackled to such a morally degrading retrograde Self. Whether yesterday or today, it seems that people in public and private life must maintain a constant vigil against attempts at resurrecting a retrograde Self.

EXERCISE 8   The Lying Self

Purpose

To illustrate the behavioral consequences of misrepresenting oneself— that is, *lying*. TIME LIMIT: 5 minutes each.

Procedure

STEP 1

Each member of the class is to relate one incident about himself or about someone he knows personally.

STEP 2

In selecting their stories, students have the option of either telling the truth or lying.

STEP 3

Taking turns, each tells a story. When the story is over, the class is to vote on whether it was TRUE or FALSE by a show of hands (thumbs up if TRUE, thumbs down if FALSE).

STEP 4

The storyteller is then obliged to confess whether or not his story was TRUE or FALSE.

STEP 5

The teacher should then question at random some of the students as to why they voted as they did.

Discussion

Is there a way of determining whether a person is lying or telling the truth? Each day, literally tons of information is dumped in our laps by the mass media and it is our job to sort out the fact from the fiction. Millions of people must decide what to believe and what not to believe. On what possible basis can they do this? Most of them are not sophisticated enough to consider such criteria as context, intent, relevance, alternatives, credibility, objective versus subjective evidence, and so on. Therefore, the first order of the day is to have each member of the class state the basis upon which he or she decides whether something is TRUE or FALSE.

One of the most embarrassing experiences an entire class can have is to be completely "taken in" by someone who doesn't look like a liar, sound like a liar, or talk like a liar, but who IS A LIAR. Some people, like the enigmatic smile on Mona Lisa's face, are very deceptive. Was there such an individual in your class? Analyze the basis for his success in pulling off such a hoax. Was it due to good eye-contact, a ring of sincerity in the voice, an air of confidence in kinesic behavior? What was the credibility formula? Or perhaps you would like to examine why those who were caught lying were such easy prey for the rest of the class.

If you were in charge of a "training program for liars," how would you set it up? Do you think a person can learn to be a good liar, or must he be born one? This exercise has the capacity to expose at least one born liar in your class. Try and find him.

EXERCISE 9 The Graffiti-Centered Self

Purpose

To find out why certain members of an institution are singled out to have their names inscribed on the walls and doors of public lavatories.

Procedure

STEP 1

For one week prior to doing this exercise, all members of the class are assigned the task of researching the lavatory walls in their school.

STEP 2

The walls and doors of these wash rooms are to be searched for graffiti which makes specific reference to an individual, not some limerick about Humpty Dumpty or a handsome young man from Kent. It may be a teacher, administrator, office worker, or fellow student. *Example*: Prof. Bundrehofferly is a horse's ass; Mrs. Ainserbwerf strips at stag parties.

STEP 3

The material gathered should be transferred to 3 x 4 filing cards and brought to class.

STEP 4

A *round* should consist of each student's reading three entries. The teacher will determine how many rounds are to be played.

Discussion

How would you react if you found out that your name had been written on a lavatory wall? Would you regard it as an honor or a shame? Further, would you assume that whoever wrote it was weird, moronic, or an average individual? Look around the room and see if anyone present looks like the type who would write on bathroom walls. Now discuss your responses to these questions.

While public opinion is inclined to dismiss graffiti as the work of playful kids caught in the throes of growing up, responsible psychological literature suggests that it might have a far deeper meaning. What do you think? It might be a good idea for the class to try its hand at writing graffiti just to discover what it is like. Everyone tear a sheet of paper from a notebook and write, without identifying yourself, three samples of graffiti about someone you know. Since you are protected by anonymity, you may want to use actual names. Fold the paper and pass it to the front of the room. An articulate student should then, at random, read aloud some of the graffiti you have authored.

At some time, we have all had the burning need to tell someone something. The desire to communicate like this varies in intensity and, in the more pressing cases, has been responsible for such public services as DIAL-A-FRIEND or DIAL-A-SHOULDER. You simply pick up your phone day or night and, like a magic genie, someone is waiting to listen and talk about anything your heart desires. Then, you are billed as if it were any other kind of service. Graffiti, since it is free and anonymous, may serve a real need for people who are either unwilling or unable to avail themselves of such socially acceptable channels of communication. To wit, they must use antisocial channels—graffiti. The obscene call is nothing more than an orally transmitted graffito, right?

EXERCISE 10   You Look Like the Kind of Person Who . . .

Purpose

To give you some idea of how others see you.

Procedure

STEP 1

Circular seating arrangement.

STEP 2

On a large sheet of paper, print your name legibly (Cheryl, Freddy, Cindi, Sue, Robin, or whatever).

STEP 3

The teacher should then write the following words on the board: SENSITIVE   INTELLIGENT   SEXY

SYMPATHETIC   QUIET   AGGRESSIVE.

STEP 4

Each student on a separate sheet of paper should write down these headings, leaving room beneath them to enter names.

STEP 5

Students should now look around the room at their classmates, each holding up in full view the paper on which he has written his first name. Each student then enters on his own list the names which best fit the headings, like this:

Sensitive	Intelligent	Aggressive
Beverly	Donald	John
Lynn	Marianna	Marco
Maria	Bruce	Jim
Pearl	Danya	Beatrice
Rozalind	Robert	Claire
Mickey	Gladys	Marnie
Eric	Arthur	Ted
Stephanie	Kathleen	Shirley

STEP 6

The completed lists should now be handed to the teacher or his assistant, who will transfer some of them to the blackboard.

STEP 7

This done, the teacher should call to the front of the room several of the students whose names appear on the board under the various headings. The class should now study the people up front and try to determine why their names were placed under the respective columns.

Discussion

It could be very upsetting to be taken for the kind of person you know you are not. Girls mistaken for "swingers" are often shocked by their date's behavior the first time out. Conversely, a young man who takes out a girl he judges to be the paragon of virtue is flabbergasted when he discovers that she's the hottest gal on campus. Participants should volunteer experiences in which they have been misjudged on the basis of how they looked. Notice how many members of the class accepted and how many rejected the way they were classified by their classmates, plus the reasons for these reactions.

How much faith do you put in first impressions? In the long run, have you found them to be reliable or misleading? Why? If you were your own press agent, and wanted to give people a false impression of yourself, how would you go about doing it? Exactly what would you do if you wanted to be considered intelligent? Be specific. Consider each of the words on the blackboard and tell how you would persuade others to arrive at that impression of you.

There are certain myths that help perpetuate the phrase, "You look like the kind of the person who . . ." Would you believe:

Thin lips—mean, stingy, quick-tempered.
Full lips—Passionate, hot-blooded.
Shifty eyes—untrustworthy, dishonest.
Weak chin—lack of character, timid.

Can you think of any others? Discuss the advisability of making snap judgments about people on the basis of their name or appearance. Can one's intuition be relied upon at all? To what extent do first impressions influence communication?

EXERCISE 11   The Rumor-Making Self

Purpose

To gain an insight into what people would like others to think about them and their families.

Procedure

STEP 1

All of the remarks made by members of the class are to remain confidential whether written or oral.

STEP 2

Using two sheets of paper, students should make up two rumors: one about themselves and one about some member of their family.

STEP 3

The rumor about the student should be labeled STUDENT, and the one about a member of the family, FAMILY.

STEP 4

All papers are to be handed in to the teacher and randomly redistributed to the class for discussion.

Discussion

As a rule, several thoughts pass through the student's mind: (1) should I say something good or bad in my rumor, (2) should it be the truth, or should I just fool around and make up something silly, (3) which member of my family should I choose to spread a rumor about, (4) will anyone in this class be able to tell that it is my rumor?

In open discussion, the rumors should be screened for common themes and patterns. Participants should speculate as to why certain rumors were selected and others not. Are any students presently aware of a rumor going around about them that they would like stopped, or at least revised? How was the rumor discovered? While the majority of rumors should be placed under rigid scrutiny, they occasionally contain a germ of truth that has been distorted as it passed over the grapevine. Nevertheless, the rumor a student invents to spread about himself or a member of his family could say more about the rumor-spreader than about the person serving as its target.

Are rumors good or bad? Do political parties enlist the use of rumors to worm their candidates into office? Should rumors be outlawed? Why? What is the best way to understand rumor as a bona fide tool of communication in today's society? End the discussion with a tight definition of the word rumor.

EXERCISE 12   Dialogue for an Ethnic Self

Purpose

To see how people, if given the chance, would put words into the mouths of members of certain ethnic groups.

Procedure

Here are four scenes: Each involves either Negro, Puerto Rican, Japanese, or Jewish people.

STEP 1

Pretend that you are a playwright and complete the following dialogues any way you wish.

STEP 2

When you are finished, a discussion will consist of exchanging the various dramatic treatments provided by different members of the class.

Scene One opens in a kitchen where a black family has just finished supper and the father is about to tell his family something.

Father: Well, it's happened! The boss called me in today and said,

_____ .

Mother: But did you tell him that _____

_____ , Daddy?

Father: Yes, darlin, I told him _____

_____ .

Son: Jesus Christ, Pop, if you do that, we'll all _____

_____ .

Daughter: I love you, Daddy, and I'll do anything you say if only you ____

_____ .

Scene Two opens in a bar where two Puerto Rican men are having a drink after work.

1st Man: You know, Miguel, today, for the first time in my life, I ____

_____ .

2nd Man: I don't believe you, Juan. That just couldn't happen in America

unless _____ .

1st Man: Well, I tell you one thing, if that ever happened to me, I would

have _____ .

2nd Man: And, do you know what they would do to you if you tried that?

They would _____ .

Scene Three opens as a Japanese family, consisting of a father, mother, grandmother, and two teenaged sons, enter a moderately priced restaurant in San Francisco.

Father: A table for five, please; and we would appreciate if you would

_____ .

Mother: Toru, I would prefer not to stay in this place because _____

_____ .

Grandmother: Yoko, we are here already and the hour is late. You must not

mind if _____ .

Sons: Father, why must we _____ .

Scene Four opens as a Jewish mother confronts her 35-year-old unmarried son in his bedroom and cross-examines him as to why he doesn't get married.

Mother: Peter, how is it that _____ .

Peter: Mom, you must understand that whenever I _____

_____ .

Mother: Peter, if your father were alive, God rest his soul, he would _____

_____ .

Peter: O.K., Mom, I'll move out; but, remember _____

_____ .

Discussion

Depending upon ethnic distribution and the part of the country in which this exercise is performed, these scenes will take on different meanings. Hearing or having them acted out will disclose a variety of inferences, assumptions, and innuendos. Students should be watchful for similarities, differences, and patterns which tend to crop up in these dialogues. Central to the discussion should be an examination of why the dialogues took their particular forms. What were the values featured in each scene—economics, freedom, ethics, morality, racial superiority, status, nationalism, happiness, politics?

A paramount lesson to be learned from performing this exercise is that crossing culture-bound language lines is not without distortion, and any interethnic communication based upon such inherent distortions must be guarded against. Only through the processes of confrontation, correction, and understanding can we hope to effectuate a commonly respected flow of cross-cultural communication. Therefore, to extract the maximum benefit from this discussion, students should attempt to write a few scenes of their own, using the ethnic group of their choice. When finished, each should give his scene to a classmate to complete the dialogues.

EXERCISE 13   Stereophonic Speaking

Purpose

To find out why members of an audience focus on one speaker rather than another. Exactly what is it that holds the attention of an audience? If there is any truth to the belief that unless a speaker has his audience's attention he might as well go home, then this exercise will be of value to the reader.

Procedure

STEP 1

Have two members of the class come to the front of the room, face the audience, and stand three feet apart from each other.

STEP 2

Each speaker is told, at a signal from the teacher, to begin talking about anything of interest to him; anything that he either likes or dislikes with a passion.

STEP 3

Using any and all rhetorical devices to get and hold his audience's attention, each speaker, TALKING AT THE SAME TIME, is to continue for two to three minutes. Both are forbidden to step outside an imaginary 12-inch circle while talking.

STEP 4

As soon as the first pair of speakers is finished, another pair should be ready to do the same thing. After several pairs of speakers have spoken stereophonically to the audience, the class members are ready to discuss what they saw and heard.

Discussion

At some time, we have all had two people speak to us at one time. Out of politeness, we desperately tried to give each the feeling we were paying attention to him and not the other party. Generally, one of these two people was more interesting than the other and, human nature being what it is, we tended to divide our attention unequally. With each pair of speakers you have just seen and heard, did you find yourself favoring one over the other while they were talking? Perhaps your attention shifted back and forth from one to the other. Was one more believable than the other? Why? Do you think your reaction might have been different had you been unable to see them? Why? How important were such things as gestures, loudness, physical appearance of speaker, sex, topic of speech, pitch of voice, and eye-contact? Based upon what you have learned from this text, was the greatest impact of each speaker's presentation *what he said, how he said it,* or *how he looked when he said it?*[5]

What do you think would happen if, instead of two speakers for this exercise, three or even four were used? Would the end results be the same? If not, why? List below those characteristics you deem necessary for a speaker to hold the attention of his audience. Begin with the most important one first:

1. _____

2. _____

3. _____

4. _____

5. _____

6. _____

7. _____

8. _____

[5] Eisenberg and Smith, *Nonverbal Communication,* pp. 109–10.

EXERCISE 14   The Humorous or Humorless Self in You

Purpose

It has been said that you can judge a person's character by carefully noting what he finds laughable. This exercise tests the reader's sense of humor.[6]

Procedure

STEP 1

Read each of the following jokes and rate them on a five-point scale according to how funny you find them: +1,   +2,   +3,   +4,   +5.

STEP 2

When you have read and rated all four jokes, add your score and multiply the answer by 5. This will give you your *Peer Group Humor Score.*

STEP 3

In discussion, compare your score with those of your classmates and try to determine the basis for your ratings.

Joke One: A Scotsman got on a train and said to the conductor, "How much is the fare, laddie?" The conductor answered, "Thirty-five cents." All at once an argument started with the Scotsman complaining that he was being overcharged. Suddenly, the conductor became furious and threw the Scotsman's suitcase out of the window into the river below. The Scotsman cried, "My god, mon, it's not bad enough you try to overcharge me but now you try and drown me little boy."

Score: +1   +2   +3   +4   +5   (circle one)

Joke Two: A woman's husband died and his wife, in making the funeral arrangements, specifically instructed the mortician to lay her husband out in his blue suit. But, as fate would have it, the mortician made a mistake and laid him out in a brown suit. Well, the wife was fit to be tied. She insisted that the funeral director do something about it immediately. He assured her that he would take care of everything. He wheeled her husband out into another room and, in what seemed like minutes, wheeled him back dressed in a blue suit. Delighted, the wife asked how he man-

---

[6] The jokes used in this exercise have been classroom tested to contain *surprise, ridicule, absurdity, exaggeration, distortion,* and *exploitation.*

aged the change so quickly. He answered, "It was simple, madam, all I did was switch heads."

Score: +1   +2   +3   +4   +5   (circle one)

Joke Three: A drunk was walking down the street with one foot on the curb and one foot in the street. A police car pulled up beside him and the officer said, "Hey, buddy, I'm going to arrest you for drunkenness." "Oh, thank God," uttered the man. "I thought I was a cripple."

Score: +1   +2   +3   +4   +5   (circle one)

Joke Four: A man went to a psychiatrist with a problem. He was seriously troubled by the fact that he was so short. The doctor had him lie on the couch and tell about everything that bothered him. After the hour was up, the psychiatrist reassured him that he was fine and there was absolutely nothing to worry about. Some of the greatest people in the world were short. The man left, whistling, with a whole new lease on life. He walked two blocks and was eaten by a cat!

Score: +1   +2   +3   +4   +5   (circle one)

Discussion

Most of us know what it feels like to tell a joke and not have a soul crack a smile out of common courtesy. A trait indigenous to man alone, humor appears to be attended by a great deal of personal commitment. Politicians have been known to alienate entire audiences with an ill-chosen joke, anecdote, metaphor, or simile. Like the surgical scalpel, it can help or hurt your cause.

The class should begin this discussion by taking an inventory of which jokes were judged most humorous and which were judged most humorless. Explanations should follow as to why they were or weren't funny. After this, a special effort should be made to set down hard criteria for judging something as humorous. Surprise, ridicule, absurdity, exaggeration, distortion, and exploitation are some of the criteria which will probably be suggested.

Organizations in business and industry have recently become interested in humor as a basis for hiring personnel. Prospective employees, in some cases, are given a battery of tests among which is a panel of cartoons. The objective is to rate them according to how funny they are thought to be. There was a time not too long ago when humor and business were said to be unmixable. This same antihumor attitude also prevailed in our schools where there were those who believed that laughter in the classroom meant *no learning was taking place.*

The class might benefit at this juncture by listing all of the places it can think of where laughing is considered *out of order*: funeral parlors, churches, synagogues, courtrooms, and so on. On what basis does society decide what should and what should not be laughed at? This is an extremely important question and should not be swept aside too casually. What has been your personal experience when you laughed when you shouldn't have laughed. Have you ever found yourself laughing your fool head off in a theatre with the rest of the audience just sitting there in silence convinced that you should be carted off to the funny farm? Communicologists agree that laughing communicates—but does *where, how,* and *why* you laugh also enter the picture? How important do you think a sense of humor is to effective communication, and why? Can you think of a situation in which a sense of humor could be a handicap rather than an asset? Explain. Terminate the discussion by arriving at some generally agreed upon definition of the word "humor."

EXERCISE 15   Self-Preservation

Purpose

Most of us possess certain personality and character traits which we prefer to keep to ourselves. This exercise subscribes to the notion that making some of these idiosyncrasies known to new acquaintances insures rather than threatens the survival of an interpersonal relationship. The rationale for this view will be explored in its discussion.

Procedure

STEP 1

Each member of the class is given a blank 3-by-5 index card.

STEP 2

Without using their names, students are asked to list some of their idiosyncrasies—for example, a compulsion to overanalyze everything, being on medication that dampens the power of concentration, a Prima Donna Syndrome, pathological lateness.

STEP 3

When finished, all cards should be returned to the teacher, shuffled, and redistributed to the class.

STEP 4

Taking turns, each member of the class should read a card aloud. The entire group should then arrange itself in a circle and discuss the implications of the exercise.

Discussion

The discussion should be initiated by having each student give a "gut reaction" to the exercise. Does forewarning a new acquaintance of a personal idiosyncrasy actually help or hinder interpersonal communication? Reasons should accompany all opinions expressed. It will be noticed that certain members of the class are unable to come up with anything on their cards—they seem blocked. Explore this reaction. Is it justifiable? Under what circumstances could this practice of self-disclosure be harmful or dangerous?

The usual class response to this exercise is one of interest and excitement. Just being made aware of the fact that other people have the same hang-ups that you do sparks a desire to inquire further. Often, an attitude, value, behavior or belief kept secret for years, coupled with guilt, loses its force once disclosed and made public. The very process of sharing one's thoughts and feelings seems to be a worthwhile pursuit. Here are some of the idiosyncrasies students have expressed in this author's classes. Compare them with your own and see what hypotheses you can develop.

1. "I am inclined to be somewhat irritable and grumpy in the morning until I have my cup of coffee."
2. "I have a kind of 'deadpan' expression on my face, which often gives people the impression that I'm not happy or having a good time. Please, do not judge my inner state by the look on my face."
3. "I giggle and fidget when I'm nervous and under stress."
4. "Because of my retiring nature, I don't say much until I get to know someone. Don't construe this as apathy or disinterest."
5. "I am a 'last-minute' person who is late wherever I go. This idiosyncrasy does not mean I don't care."
6. "Please, don't think that because I'm sloppy, I'm dirty."

EXERCISE 16   Alterations Free

Purpose

Most of us are not completely satisfied with ourselves, either physically and/or psychologically. If it were possible to magically have these characteristics altered, how many people would have it done; what would be the consequences of such changes? This exercise probes how people think about having themselves altered.

Procedure

Answer the following questions by spontaneously filling in the blank spaces. (There is no right or wrong.)

1. If only I had a bigger _____ , I would _____ .

2. If only I had a smaller _____ , I would _____ .

3. If only I could stop _____ , I would _____ .

4. If I had one of those _____ , I would _____ .

5. If my parents were _____ , I would _____ .

6. If I didn't have a _____ , I would _____ .

7. If people would stop talking about my _____ ,

    I would _____ .

8. If only I had a different _____ , I would _____ .

9. If I could alter my personality, I would want to be _____

    and then I could _____ .

10. I wish God had made me _____ so I could _____ .

11. That which holds me back most is my _____ .

Discussion

Maxwell Maltz's excellent book *Psychocybernetics* is a must if you are interested in the psychological effects caused by having your anatomy altered through plastic surgery. You will be amazed by some of the answers given in this exercise. Notice how preoccupied many people are with external appearances and the value they place on them. Special attention should also be paid to the correlations they make between behavior and its social significance.

If successful, this exercise will reveal the ways we distort our inner and outer realities to conform with some arbitrary philosophy or ideology. One more thing. Be prepared to have a few students adamantly refuse to answer these specific questions or reject the entire exercise. Don't press them. They may have perfectly valid psychological reasons for not participating. Some may feel that they are perfect and, therefore, do not need any kind of alterations.

EXERCISE 17 Anyone with a Name like . . .

Purpose

To see whether a person's name could influence the manner in which he or she communicates, and to discover its effect upon others.

Procedure

STEP 1

Teacher is to hand out to each member of the class a sheet of paper with the following material printed on it:

Instructions: Below are a series of first names. According to your personal experience with each, fill in the blank space.

Sample: Anyone with a name like John _____ must be a real man _____ .

1. Anyone with a name like Percy _____ .

2. Anyone with a name like Lulu _____ .

3. Anyone with a name like Hector _____ .

4. Anyone with a name like David _____ .

5. Anyone with a name like Seymour _____ .

6. Anyone with a name like Lolita _____ .

7. Anyone with a name like Mary _____ .

8. Anyone with a name like Harold _____ .

9. Anyone with a name like Duke _____ .

10. Anyone with a name like Mervin _____ .

11. Anyone with a name like Kitty _____ .

12. Anyone with a name like Peter _____ .

13. Anyone with a name like Mimi _____ .

14. Anyone with a name like Alvin _____ .

15. Anyone with a name like Lynn _____ .

16. Anyone with a name like Burgess _____ .

17. Anyone with a name like Roger _____ .

18. Anyone with a name like Dick _____ .

19. Anyone with a name like Corky _____ .

20. Anyone with a name like Mortimer _____ .

STEP 2

When you have filled in the blanks on the paper, pass it to the teacher. He will redistribute the papers to students other than those who originally answered them. Upon receiving the sheet, go through each name and underline in red those characteristics assigned to that name.

STEP 3

The class should now form a large circle, and each student in turn should read from the page he is holding the characteristics which are underlined.

Discussion

Do you like the name your parents gave you? If you do, you are one of the more fortunate ones. Some people are not as lucky. Members of the group should relate stories of people they know who had names they hated and the consequences these names produced in their lives. Banter about a few names personalities of stage, screen, and radio have adopted and speculate why they chose them: Rip Torn, Cary Snodgrass, Englebert Humperdinck, and so on. When you have children, what names will you give them and why? To what extent do you think a person's name actually influences his or her lifestyle, the profession he enters, or the kinds of people he attracts as friends? Would it be better if people were simply numbered?

EXERCISE 18   Build a Parent

Purpose

To determine what characteristics students feel would make a "good" mother or father.[7]

Procedure

STEP 1

Each member of the class should be given a large sheet of paper.

STEP 2

When told to begin, each student is to imagine he is going to build either a mother or father from a kit. The ingredients to be used shall be selected from four groups: *physical, psychological, spiritual,* and *special effects.* They are to be listed under each of these headings and numbered accordingly (see the example below).

Physical	Psychological	Spiritual	Special Effects
5′ 7″ tall	I.Q. 124	Catholic	Shut-off button
180 lbs.	High common sense	Church-going	Money switch
Athletic	Gentle nature	Sunday school	Agreement control

STEP 3

With their papers in hand, students should arrange themselves in groups of five or six and discuss their projects.

Discussion

Before getting the discussion under way, three important questions should be given special attention: (1) Which parent did the student choose to build? (2) Why was this parent chosen and not the other? (3) Does the builder possess any of the traits or characteristics he has built into the parent?

If properly executed, this exercise also has the capacity to reveal more

---

[7] See Eric Berne's discussion of parent-ego state in *What Do You Say after You Say Hello?* (New York: Grove, 1972), pp. 11–20.

about the builder than the android he is building. To illustrate, imagine the builder to be rather short in stature (by conventional standards) and coming from a family of short people. It would not be unnatural for such a builder to invest his man-made parent with a little extra height, would it? The same would apply to a variety of other socially deficient characteristics. The tendency, however, becomes a bit more complex when it involves certain psychological characteristics. For argument's sake, do you think a builder with an I.Q. of 180 would want his mother or father, or both, to also have such an I.Q.? Would such a dilemma cause too great a climate of competition in the home environment? Would a builder who was raised as a strict Roman Catholic automatically design such religiosity into an android parent?

Special effects invariably liven the discussion. One of this author's students designed into his android mother a "self-destruct switch." When asked whether he was joking, he emphatically said, "No!" Another case involved a student who rendered his android father sterile so that he would not bring any other children into the world. When the student was asked why, he refused to answer.

From the standpoint of communication, this exercise makes a significant statement: students, rather than relating to their parents the way they actually are, relate to them, through communication, on the basis of how they would like them to be. Take a college senior who is a philosophy major and who has a mother that never went beyond the eighth grade. Communicating with her could be quite frustrating unless it was on her level. Too often, we communicate with people on the basis of what we would like them to be and not what they really are. This same phenomenon works in reverse. There are parents who entertain some very definite ideas as to what their children are, the reality of which exists only in their imaginations. The parent who insists that his son pull straight "A's" in college and who is blind to the fact that he is not college material, may be doing more harm than good. Endless hours of futile communication between such a parent and son are sure to occur. This exercise, if it hits its mark, will provide the student with an insight into how a communication breakdown can result from misreading another human being on the basis of one's own projection of what he should be and not what he actually is.

EXERCISE 19   Don't I Get a Hat or a Badge or Something?

Purpose

To explore the kinds of intrapersonal experiences people have when they hold or wear a symbol or emblem representing a position or rank in society.

Procedure

STEP 1

Students are instructed to bring into class some object which symbolically represents a particular position, rank, or affiliation in society, such as a badge, skull cap, stethoscope, nurse's cap, army jacket, or gavel.

STEP 2

On a prearranged day, these articles are to be brought to class and students are to assume the roles they denote.

STEP 3

The teacher should then have the class sit in a large circle and announce a topic to serve as the basis for a group discussion. Here are some suggestions:

1. Should every 18-year-old (male and/or female) have to serve in the armed forces?
2. Should compulsory education be abolished?
3. Should all policemen be psychoanalyzed before they are appointed to the police department?
4. Should pay toilets be outlawed?

STEP 4

Students should then engage in a group discussion and assume the roles dictated by their props. *Time Limit:* One half of the period is to be spent in discussion while displaying symbols and emblems. During the remaining half the class should examine their reactions to the experience.

Discussion

To what extent do we advertise our attitudes, values, and beliefs? Do the emblems we wear, the ways we decorate our homes or apartments, and the type of stickers we affix to our automobiles represent a valid form of communication? This exercise should generate awareness not only of the people who wear them, but of how the people themselves feel while wearing them. To dramatize this, picture five men sitting naked in a steam room. All are members of the armed forces. While sweating out body poisons and passing the time of day, they engage one another in casual conversation. Shortly, the informal chat graduates into a somewhat lively difference of opinion between two of the men; each lashes out at the other. After a half hour of argument, they all return to the locker room to dress. As each puts on his uniform, rank becomes apparent: a brigadier general, a colonel, two captains, and one lowly second lieutenant. As fate would have it, guess who was arguing with whom in the steam room? Yes, the general and the lieutenant. Without their brass, they were simply men of equal station.

Situations like this are not uncommon in our society. Have you ever noticed children at play? After squabbling over who will be the doctor, nurse, or policeman in a certain game, they are quick to don the stethoscope, nurse's cap, or badge. Without these props, the role just doesn't seem to come alive for them.

With adults whose profession or occupation involves wearing a uniform or emblem, a curious thing happens. The policeman, off duty, is frequently observed to behave in an authoritative manner as if he were still in uniform. The physician, entering a hospital without his bag or an exposed stethoscope to identify him as a doctor, still moves with a certain air of confidence which immediately communicates his role to the nurse at the desk. Obviously, these markers (symbols) produce an imprint not only on the self-image of their possessors but also upon those who view them.

If successful, participants in this exercise should come away with varying degrees of reaction. One student came into the group wearing a priest's collar. He admitted that he not only felt uncomfortable and restrained in the discussion but also sensed a decided *holding back* on the part of the others. Of course, there are many who will not be moved by these props. But, again, others fall right into the swing of things and dramatically role-play the identity prescribed by the prop. In short, our society seems quick to recognize the symbol rather than the man.

A young man in service thought very little of an officer on his base. Upon meeting him each morning on the way to mess, he neglected to extend him the customary hand salute. Annoyed, the officer put the young man on report. Summoned before his commanding officer, he was asked why he refused to salute the complaining officer. He answered that he disliked the man and had no respect for him. To which, the commanding officer replied, "Son, it is not the man that you are obliged to salute, it is his rank."

Thus, to derive full value from this exercise, each student should express his or her feeling about the relationship between the man and the symbol. Speculation should also be made to the consequences of a symbol-free society—one devoid of flags, badges, uniforms, emblems, and the like.

EXERCISE 20   Your Anatomical Self-Worth, or Let's Make a Deal

Purpose

To find out just how an individual feels about his body in monetary terms. Since everything in life has a value placed on it, this exercise is designed to discover how people actually value specific parts of their anatomy (inside and out).

Procedure

Have each student in the class fill out the following questionnaire.

Questionnaire

Name (optional) _____

Age _____

Sex _____

Self-Image: (example)   Extrovert   Ambivert   Introvert

Instructions: Below, you will see a list of body parts and internal organs. Next to each is a place for you to write a price. If you feel you could not possibly place a price on the part listed, check the NOT FOR SALE line.

	Price	Not For Sale
1. Little toe of left foot	_____	_____
2. Appendix	_____	_____
3. Weaker eye	_____	_____
4. One testicle or ovary	_____	_____
5. Gall bladder	_____	_____
6. Little finger of left hand (right, if left-handed)	_____	_____
7. One ear	_____	_____

Discussion

This exercise has the reputation of producing some shocking moments in class. In some instances, the attitude expressed by certain students toward parts of their bodies is unreal. You cannot imagine the prices they put on them. There are, of course, those who refuse to surrender any part of their bodies regardless of the price. Whereas one boy offered to sell a little toe on his left foot for no less than $1,000,000, another would sell his entire leg for that price.

Since the willingness or unwillingness to sell body parts varies in any group, try to find out the basis for the value placed on them. For example, is it true that students are more inclined to sell parts that are on the inside rather than exposed parts? You will also notice that certain members of the group will bargain over price and when the "price is right," they will sell. Others need a more compelling reason to sell, such as providing a small child with a cornea or skin graft. The psychological implications are deep and well guarded, so much so that some students adamantly refuse to participate in the exercise. However, with those who are willing to play, attempt to find out if their psychological self-worth corresponds with their anatomical self-worth.

Television commercials make assumptions regarding the worth you place on certain parts of your body and their well-being. They also speculate as to what you might be willing to do or pay to keep them in shape. This same principle of communication, though more extreme, is at work in this exercise. By finding out how an individual feels about himself—his self-esteem—you can better communicate with him. Surely you have met people who literally hate their hands, feet, ears, teeth, skin, or hair. In most of these cases they even hate talking about them.

Before going on, ask each member of the group to write his candid impression of this kind of exercise on an unsigned piece of paper, fold it, and pass it to the leader or teacher. Redistribute the papers to the group and anonymously read them aloud. As a final insight, go back and see how these same people handled Exercise 16 (Alterations Free). Compare their reactions.

EXERCISE 21   Read that Face

Purpose

To find out the extent to which people will react similarly or differently to a series of facial expressions, the connotation they will assign them, and the basis underlying each judgment.

Procedure

STEP 1

Look at each facial expression in Fig. 10–1 and allow yourself to register an initial response to it.

STEP 2

Beginning with Face I, write in the space beneath it whatever you think the person is saying to you (use one short sentence). Example: "Are you kidding?"

STEP 3

After you have labeled them all, compare your responses with those of your classmates. This is best done by starting with Face I and having each member of the class in sequence read his captions aloud. Also, in specific terms, explain the physical basis for their judgments—the raised eyebrow, pursed lips, wide-eyed look, or whatever.

Discussion

More important than the caption you wrote beneath each face is the basis for your reaction. Is the meaning you have assigned to it resident in the face itself, or in you? Could your mood at this time influence your reaction to it? Precisely what, in a face, makes you read it a certain way? Do you think there is any truth to the rumor that, after people have lived together for a long time, they begin to look alike? Most students will have some difficulty explaining the impressions they received from each face; others will be able to point to a particular zone of the face and identify it as the cause of the expression or emotion being nonverbally communicated. At best, the reasons given for each label will be predicated upon some extremely fuzzy foundations.

Television and film makers are keenly sensitive to how people will react to a face. When they cast for a commercial or film, the "wrong face" could mean certain failure. Why? How do the casting directors determine whether a face is right or wrong? If you asked one of them, "Exactly what do you look for in a face?" how explicitly do you think he would answer? Discuss your own face in terms of how you feel others read it.

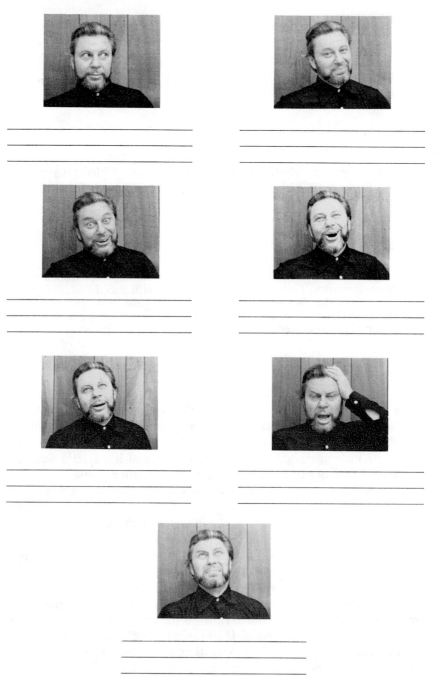

FIGURE 10–1

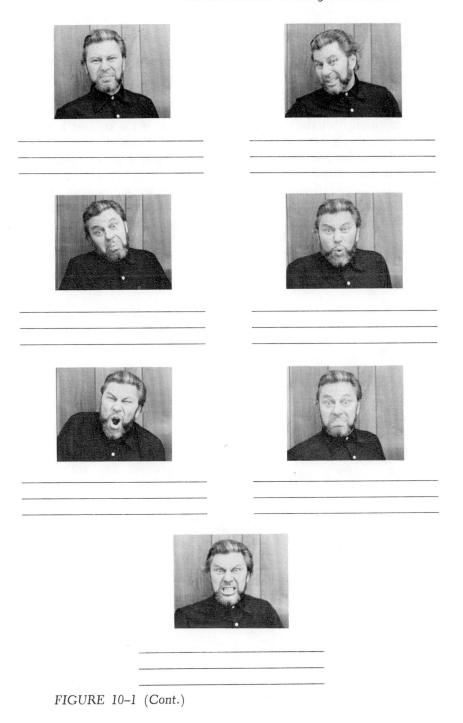

FIGURE 10–1 (Cont.)

SUMMARY

In addition to the numerous opportunities given the reader to interact freely with this text, this chapter goes one step further. It allows the student to test his functional understanding of the communicative process. Each exercise has been invested with one or more of the principles distributed throughout the substances of this book; if the student has done his homework, they should easily be discernible to him.

Another realization that should also have ripened is that theory can carry a communicator only so far. The rest of the way can only be traveled by *practice*. Understanding without doing, or doing without understanding, both come up wanting. Since communication is a very personal experience, you cannot grasp its meaning by simply reading these exercises. You must become actively engaged in them, experience their impact, share the reactions of others. The best of all possible ways to learn how to communicate is TO COMMUNICATE! There is no substitute.

P.S.

Well, you've gotten through this book and it is now ready for retirement to wherever used books go. Actually, it is a fate not terribly different from that of the people you have met throughout your life. Most of them have disappeared from your consciousness; an occasional one or two remain. Although you and I have never met in person, we have so many things in common simply because we share a common humanity. Chances are excellent that you know exactly what I mean when I speak of being hungry, tired, angry, anxious, or bloated after eating too much at a party. The odds also favor our never meeting face-to-face, and yet, we know the other exists.

Writing a book is like writing a letter to a friend. You assume that he or she will be glad to learn that you are alive and well. A book, for me, is like a long letter to you. For a year I grappled with what I should say to you until, finally, it was done. I realize that I shall never know some of the thoughts that passed through your mind while reading it. It is like a one-way telephone conversation in which you can hear me but I cannot hear you. As a result, I tried to imagine what you would be interested in and wondered about, or are wondering about at this very moment.

Do you remember what I said at the beginning of this book? I suggested that the majority of textbooks tended to be boring because they lacked a first-person approach. Seldom, if ever, do textbook readers come away with the feeling that they "know the author." On the few occasions that I have read a textbook in which the humanness of the writer filtered through to me, I found it a thoroughly heart-warming experience. I sure hope that some of Me, and my inner world, seeped through into yours. If it did, I am pleased.

RELATED READINGS

CHAPTER 1

BARKER, LARRY L., AND ROBERT J. KIBLER. *Communication Behavior: Perspectives and Principles* (Englewood Cliffs, N.J.: Prentice-Hall, 1971).

BROSS, IRWIN D. *Design for Decision* (New York: Macmillan, 1953).

BUDD, RICHARD W., AND BRENT D. RUBEN, eds. *Approaches to Human Communication* (New York: Spartan Books, 1972).

DEUTSCH, K. W. "On communication models in the social sciences," *Public Opinion Quarterly* XVI (1952), 356–80.

DE VITO, JOSEPH A. "Other codes, other channels," *Today's Speech* XVI (1968), 29–32.

GERBNER, GEORGE. "Toward a general model of communication," *Audio-Visual Communication Review* IV (1956), 173.

HARRAH, DAVID. *Communication—A Logical Model* (Cambridge: M.I.T. Press, 1963).

MILLER, G. R. "On defining communication: another stab," *Journal of Communication* XIX:2 (1966), 88–98.

NIELSON, THOMAS R. "On defining communication," *The Speech Teacher* VI (1957), 10–17.

PIERCE, J. R. *Symbols, Signals and Noise: The Nature and Process of Communication* (New York: Harper & Row, 1961).

WEINER, NORBERT. *The Human Use of Human Beings: Cybernetics and Society* (Boston: Houghton Mifflin, 1950).

CHAPTER 2

ADORNO, T. W., ELSE FRENKEL-BRUNSWICK, DANIEL J. LEVENSON, AND R. NEVITT SANFORD. *The Authoritarian* (New York: Harper & Row, 1950).

ALLPORT, GORDON W. *Becoming* (New Haven: Yale University Press, 1955).

———, AND L. POSTMAN. *The Psychology of Rumor* (New York: Holt, Rinehart and Winston, 1947).

ARIETI, SILVANO. *The Intrapsychic Self: Feeling, Cognition, and Creativity in Health and Mental Illness* (New York: Basic Books, 1967).

BREAN, H. "Marvin Hewitt Ph(ony)D," *Life*, April 12, 1954.

BUBER, M. *I and Thou* (Edinburgh: T. & T. Clark, 1937).

CORNELISON, F. S., AND J. ARSENIAN. "A study of the response of psychotic patients to photographic self-image experience," *Psychiatric Quarterly* 34 (1960), 1–8.

CORTES, J. B., AND F. M. GATTI. "Physique and self-description of temperament," *Journal of Consulting Psychology* 29 (1965), 432–39.

DEUTSCH, HELENE. "The impostor: contribution to ego psychology of a type of psychopath," *Psychoanalyst Quarterly* 24:4 (1955), 483–505.

ERIKSON, E. H. *Identity:Youth and Crisis* (New York: Norton, 1968).

FLUGEL, J. *The Psychology of Clothes* (London: Hogarth Press, 1930).

FROMM, E. *Man for Himself* (New York: Holt, Rinehart and Winston, 1947).

GOFFMAN, E. *Presentation of Self in Everyday Life* (New York: Doubleday, 1959).

HENRY, J. *Culture against Man* (New York: Random House, 1963).

HERZOG-DÜREK, J. *Menschsein als Wagnis* ("Being Human as a Venture") (Stüttgart: Klett, 1960).

JOURARD, S. M. *Disclosing Man to Himself* (New York: Van Nostrand-Reinhold, 1968).

———. *The Transparent Self* (New York: Van Nostrand-Reinhold, 1964).

LAING, R. D. *The Divided Self* (London: Tavistock, 1960).

LYND, H. M. *On Shame and the Search for Identity* (New York: Science Editions, 1958).

MASLOW, A. H. *Toward a Psychology of Being* (New York: Van Nostrand-Reinhold, 1962).

MAY, ROLLO. *Man's Search for Himself* (New York: Norton, 1953).

McCARTHY, J. "The master impostor," *Life*, April 12, 1952.

MODELL, A. H. "Changes in human figure drawing by patients who recover from regressed states," *American Journal of Orthopsychiatry* 21 (1951), 584–96.

MOUSTAKAS, C., ed. *The Self* (New York: Harper & Row, 1956).

POWELL, J. *Why Am I Afraid To Tell You Who I Am* (Niles, Ill.: Argus Communication, 1969).

ROGERS, C. R. *On Becoming a Person* (Boston: Houghton Mifflin, 1961).

ROSENTHAL, R., AND L. JACOBSON. *Pygmalion in the Classroom* (New York: Holt, Rinehart and Winston, 1968).

SHERWOOD, JOHN J. "Self identity and referent others," *Sociometry* 28 (1965), 66–81.

SISLEY, EMILY L. "The breakdown of the American image: comparison of stereotypes held by college students over four decades," *Psychological Reports* 27 (1970), 779–86.

STRAUSS, A. *Mirrors and Masks: The Search for Identity* (New York: Free Press, 1959).

TRACEY, W. S. "Advice from a speech teacher: put humor in your speeches," *Today's Speech* XV (1967).

WASHBURN, DONALD. "Intrapersonal communication in a Jungian perspective," *Journal of Communication* 14 (1964), 131–35.

WHEELIS, A. *The Quest for Identity* (New York: Norton, 1958).

WHITE, R. W. *The Abnormal Personality*, 3d ed. (New York: Ronald, 1964).

CHAPTER 3

BARKER, LARRY L., AND GORDON WISEMAN. "A model of intrapersonal communication," *Journal of Communication* XVI (1966), 174.

DANCE, FRANK E. X., ed. *Human Communication* (New York: Holt, Rinehart and Winston, 1967).

EISENBERG, ABNE M., AND RALPH SMITH, JR. *Nonverbal Communication* (New York: Bobbs-Merrill, 1971).

MACLEAN, PAUL. "Psychosomatic disease and the visceral brain," *Psychosomatic Medicine* XI (1949), 347.

MEERLOO, JOOST A. M. "Contributions of psychiatry to the study of communication," in *Human Communication Theory*, ed. Frank E. X. Dance (New York: Holt, Rinehart and Winston, 1967).

PAVLOV, IVAN PETROVITCH. *Conditioned Reflexes and Psychiatry* II, trans. and ed. W. Horsley Gantt (New York: International Publishers, 1941), pp. 162–63.

PINES, MAYA. "We are left brained or right brained," *New York Times Magazine*, September 9, 1973, pp. 32–37.

REIK, THEODORE. *Voices from the Inaudible: The Patients Speak* (New York: Farrar, Straus & Giroux, 1964).

REUSCH, JURGEN, AND GREGORY BATESON. *Communication: The Social Matrix of Psychiatry* (New York: Norton, 1968).

VON BUDDENBROCK, WOLFGANG. *The Senses* (Ann Arbor: University of Michigan Press, 1958).

WISEMAN, GORDON, AND LARRY BARKER. *Speech—Interpersonal Communication* (San Francisco: Chandler, 1967).

WOOLRIDGE, DEAN E. *The Machinery of the Brain* (New York: McGraw-Hill, 1963).

ZUBEK, JOHN. *Sensory Deprivation: Fifteen Years of Research* (New York: Appleton-Century-Crofts, 1969).

CHAPTER 4

BAKER, JERRY. *Plants Are like People* (New York: Pocket Books, 1971).

BASTIAN, JARVIS. "Primate signalling systems and human language," in I. DeVore, ed., *Primate Behavior: Field Studies of Monkeys and Apes* (New York: Holt, Rinehart and Winston, 1965).

BERMAN, CLAIRE. "A Member of the Family," New York Times Magazine, October 7, 1973, p. 15.

BOURNE, GEOFFREY H. The Ape People (New York: Putnam, 1971).

GARDNER, ALLEN, AND BEATRICE GARDNER. "Teaching sign language to a chimpanzee," Science 165 (1969), 668–69.

LILLY, JOHN C. The Mind of the Dolphin (New York: Doubleday and Harold Matson Company, 1967).

"Startling new research from the man who 'talks' to plants," National Wildlife, October–November, 1971, pp. 21–22.

TOMPKINS, PETER, AND CHRISTOPHER BIRD. The Secret Life of Plants (New York: Harper & Row, 1973).

CHAPTER 5

ARGYLE, MICHAEL. Social Interaction (New York: Atherton Press, 1969).

———, AND JANET DEAN. "Eye-contact, distance and affiliation," Sociometry XXVIII (1965), 289–304.

BIRDWHISTELL, RAY L. Kinesics and Context (Philadelphia: University of Pennsylvania Press, 1970).

DAVIS, MARTHA. Understanding Body Movement: An Annotated Bibliography (New York: Arno Press, 1972).

DAVITZ, JOEL R., ed. The Communication of Emotional Meaning (New York: McGraw-Hill, 1964).

DEUTSCH, FELIX. "Analysis of postural behavior," Psychoanalytic Quarterly XVI (1947), 195–213.

EFRON, D. Gesture and Environment (New York: Kings Crown, 1941).

EISENBERG, ABNE M., AND RALPH R. SMITH, JR. Nonverbal Communication (New York: Bobbs-Merrill, 1971).

EKMAN, PAUL, WALLACE V. FRIESEN, AND PHOEBE ELLSWORTH. Emotion in the Human Face: Guidelines for Research and an Integration of Findings (New York: Pergamon, 1972).

———. "Communication through nonverbal behavior: A source of information about an interpersonal relationship," in Affect, Cognition, and Personality, ed. Silvan Tompkins (New York: Springer, 1965), pp. 390–442.

———. "A methodological discussion of nonverbal behavior," Journal of Psychology XXXXIII (1957), 141–49.

FELDMAN, SANDOR. Mannerisms of Speech and Gestures in Everyday Life (New York: International Universities Press, 1969).

FISHER, SEYMOUR, AND SIDNEY E. CLEVELAND. Body Image and Personality (New York: Dover, 1968).

FRANK, LAWRENCE K. "Tactile communication," in Communication and Culture, ed. Alfred Smith (New York: Holt, Rinehart and Winston, 1966), pp. 199–209.

HALL, EDWARD T. The Silent Language (New York: Doubleday, 1959).

———. The Hidden Dimension (New York: Doubleday, 1966).

HARRISON, RANDALL P., et al. "The nonverbal communication literature," Journal of Communication XXII (December, 1972), 460–76.

IZARD, C. E. The Face of Emotion (New York: Appleton-Century-Crofts, 1971).

KNAPP, MARK. *Nonverbal Communication in Human Interaction* (New York: Holt, Rinehart and Winston, 1972).

LA BARRE, WESTON. "The cultural basis of emotions and gestures," *Journal of Personality* XVI (1947), 49–68.

MEHRABIAN, ALBERT. *Nonverbal Communication* (Chicago: Aldine-Atherton, 1972).

———. *Silent Messages* (Belmont, Calif.: Wadsworth, 1971).

MONTAGU, ASHLEY. *Touching: The Human Significance of Skin* (New York: Columbia University Press, 1971).

RUESCH, JURGEN, AND WELDON KEES. *Nonverbal Communication: Notes on the Visual Perception of Human Relations*, 2d ed. (Berkeley: University of California Press, 1971).

SCHEFLEN, ALBERT E. *Body Language and the Social Order* (Englewood Cliffs, N.J.: Prentice-Hall, 1972).

SEBEOK, THOMAS A., ALFRED S. HAYES, AND MARY BATESON, eds. *Approaches to Semiotics: Transactions of the Indiana University Conference on Paralinguistics and Kinesics* (The Hague: Mouton, 1964).

CHAPTER 6

BARASCH, FRANCES K. *The Grotesque: A Study in Meanings* (New York: The Humanities Press, 1971).

BROWN, ROGER W. *Words and Things* (New York: The Free Press, 1958).

CARROLL, JOHN B. *Language and Thought* (Englewood Cliffs, N.J.: Prentice-Hall, 1964).

CONDON, JOHN C. *Semantics and Communication* (New York: Macmillan, 1966).

HAYAKAWA, S. I. *Language in Thought and Action*, 2d ed. (New York: Harcourt Brace Jovanovich, 1964).

HOCKETT, CHARLES F. "The origin of speech," *Scientific American* CCIII (1960), 89–96.

JOHNSON, WENDELL. "The spoken word and the great unsaid," *Quarterly Journal of Speech* XXXVII (1951), 419–29.

KORZYBSKI, A. *Science and Sanity* (Lancaster, Pa.: Science Press, 1941).

MCLUHAN, MARSHALL. *Understanding Media: The Extensions of Man* (New York: McGraw, 1964).

MCNEILL, DAVID. "The creation of language," *Discovery* XXVII (1966), 34–38.

OGDEN, C. K., AND I. A. RICHARDS. *The Meaning of Meaning*, 8th ed. (New York: Harcourt Brace Jovanovich and London: Routledge & Kegan Paul, 1946).

PARTRIDGE, ERIC. *You Have a Point There* (London: Hamish Hamilton, Ltd., 1953).

SINGH, J., AND A. L. ZING. *Wolf Children and Feral Men* (New York: Harper & Row, 1942).

SKINNER, B. F. *Verbal Behavior* (New York: Appleton-Century-Crofts, 1957).

SZASZ, THOMAS. *The Myth of Mental Illness* (New York: Harper & Row, 1963).

ULLMAN, L. P., L. KRASNER, AND BEVERLY COLLINS. "Modification of behavior through verbal conditioning: effects in group therapy," *Journal of Abnormal Social Psychology* 62 (1961), 128–32.

VALERY, PAUL. "Style," in J. V. Cunningham, ed., *The Problem of Style* (Greenwich, Conn.: Fawcett, 1966).

WHORF, B. L. "Language, thought and reality," in J. B. Carroll, ed., *Selected Writings of B. L. Whorf* (New York: Wiley, 1956).

CHAPTER 7

ANDERSON, JERRY M., AND PAUL J. DOVRE, eds. *Readings in Argumentation* (Boston: Allyn & Bacon, 1968).

BROCKRIEDE, WAYNE, AND DOUGLAS EHNINGER. "Toulmin on argument: An interpretation and application," *Quarterly Journal of Speech* XLVI (1960), 44–53.

CAPP, GLENN R., AND THELMA R. CAPP. *The Principles of Argumentation and Debate* (Englewood Cliffs, N.J.: Prentice-Hall, 1965).

EISENBERG, ABNE M., AND JOSEPH A. ILARDO. *Argument: An Alternative to Violence* (Englewood Cliffs, N.J.: Prentice-Hall, 1972).

FLESCH, RUDOLPH. *The Art of Clear Thinking* (New York: Harper & Row, 1951).

FREELY, AUSTIN. *Argumentation and Debate: Rational Decision Making* (Belmont, Calif.: Wadsworth, 1961).

HUBER, ROBERT B. *Influencing through Argument* (New York: David McKay, 1963).

KRUGER, ARTHUR. *Modern Debate: Its Logic and Strategy* (New York: McGraw, 1960).

MILLS, GLEN E. *Reason in Controversy*, 2d ed. (Boston: Allyn & Bacon, 1968).

———. *Putting a Message Together* (Indianapolis: Bobbs-Merrill, 1972).

SMITH, CRAIG R., AND DAVID M. HUNSAKER. *The Bases of Argument: Ideas in Conflict* (Indianapolis: Bobbs-Merrill, 1972).

THOMPSON, WAYNE N. *Modern Argumentation and Debate* (New York: Harper & Row, 1971).

TOULMIN, STEPHEN E. *The Uses of Argument* (New York: Cambridge University Press, 1958).

WINDES, RUSSEL, AND ARTHUR HASTINGS. *Argumentation and Advocacy* (New York: Random House, 1965).

CHAPTER 8

ANDERSON, MARTIN P., LEWIS WESLEY, AND JAMES MURRAY. *The Speaker and His Audience* (New York: Harper & Row, 1964).

CLEVENGER, THEODORE, JR. *Audience Analysis* (Indianapolis: Bobbs-Merrill, 1966).

FRIEDRICH, GUSTAV W. "An empirical explication of a concept of self-reported speech anxiety," *Speech Monographs* XXVII (March, 1970), 67–72.

HOLLINGWORTH, H. L. *The Psychology of the Audience* (New York: American Book Co., 1935).

HOLTZMAN, PAUL D. *The Psychology of Speaker's Audiences* (Glenview, Ill.: Scott, Foresman, 1970).

McCROSKEY, JAMES C. "Measures of communication-bound anxiety," *Speech Monographs* XXVII (November, 1970), 260–77.

————. "The effect of systematic desensitization on speech anxiety," *The Speech Teacher* XIX (January, 1970), 32–36.

PEASE, RAYMOND B. "The audience as the jury," *Journal of Public Speaking* III (1917), 218–33.

SMELSER, NEIL J. *Theory of Collective Behavior* (New York: The Free Press, 1963).

TIPTON, ALBERT. "Is stage fright all that bad?," *The School Musician, Director and Teacher* XXXXII (January, 1971), 4, 6.

WILSON, JOHN F., AND CARROLL C. ARNOLD. *Public Speaking as a Liberal Art*, 3d ed. (Boston: Allyn & Bacon, 1974).

CHAPTER 9

BARKER, LARRY. *Listening Behavior* (Englewood Cliffs, N.J.: Prentice-Hall, 1971).

BARLUND, DEAN C., AND FRANKLYN S. HAIMAN. *The Dynamics of Discussion* (Boston: Houghton Mifflin, 1960).

BINDRIM, P. A. "A report on a nude marathon: The effect of physical nudity upon the practice of interaction in the marathon group," *Psychotherapeutic Theory, Research and Practice* V (1968), 180–88.

CATHCART, ROBERT S., AND LARRY A. SAMOVAR, eds. *Small Group Communication: A Reader* (Dubuque: Wm. C. Brown, 1970).

EGAN, GERARD. *Encounter: Group Processes for Interpersonal Growth* (Belmont, Calif.: Brooks-Cole, 1970).

FROMM-REICHMANN, FRIEDA. "Loneliness," *Psychiatry* XXII (February, 1959), 1–15.

JACOBSON, E. *Progressive Relaxation*. 2d ed. (Chicago: University of Chicago Press, 1938).

MASLOW, A. H. "Fusion of facts and values," *American Journal of Psychoanalysis* XXIII (1963), 117–31.

MORENO, J. L. *Who Shall Survive* (New York: Beacon House, 1953).

PHILLIPS, GERALD M., AND EUGENE C. ERICKSON. *Interpersonal Dynamics in the Small Group* (New York: Random, 1970).

REISMAN, D. *The Lonely Crowd: A Study of the Changing American Character* (New Haven: Yale University Press, 1950).

SALTER, ANDREW. *Conditioned Reflex Therapy*, 2d ed. (New York: Putnam, 1961).

SCHMUCK, RICHARD, AND PATRICIA SCHMUCK. *Group Processes in the Classroom* (Dubuque: Wm. C. Brown, 1971).

SCHUTZ, W. C. *Joy* (New York: Grove, 1967).

THOMAS, EDWIN J., AND CLINTON F. FINK. "Effects of group size," *Psychological Bulletin* 60 (1963), 371–84.

Name
Index

Subject
Index

NOTES

NOTES